JOURNAL OF A SOUL

In the garden at Castel Gandolfo. 'More than half a century of living pen in hand'

POPE JOHN XXIII

JOURNAL OF A SOUL

TRANSLATED BY DOROTHY WHITE

IMAGE BOOKS

DOUBLEDAY

New York   London   Toronto   Sydney   Auckland

Nihil obstat Joannes M. T. Barton, S.T.D., L.S.S.
Imprimatur Patricius Casey, Vic. Gen.
Westmonasterii, die 29 Augusti, 1964

AN IMAGE BOOK
PUBLISHED BY DOUBLEDAY
a division of Random House, Inc.
1540 Broadway, New York, New York 10036

IMAGE, DOUBLEDAY, and the portrayal of a deer drinking from a stream
are trademarks of Doubleday, a division of Random House, Inc.

First Image Books edition of *Journal of a Soul* published in 1980 by arrangement with
Geoffrey Chapman, a division of Cassell Ltd. This edition published November 1999.

First published in Italian under the title *Giovanni XXIII Il Giornale dell'Anima*.
Copyright © 1964 Edizioni di Storia e Letteratura.

Library of Congress Catalog Card Number: 79-7786

ISBN: 0-385-49754-7

3   5   7   9   10   8   6   4   2

Contents

I—JOURNAL OF A SOUL
1895–1962

1895–1900: *In the Seminary at Bergamo*

1901–1903: *In the Seminary in Rome*

1904: The Year of My Ordination as Priest

1905–1914: Secretary to Mgr Radini Tedeschi, Bishop of Bergamo

1915–1918: The War

1918–1920: Spiritual Director of the Seminary at Bergamo

1921–1924: Rome, in the Service at Propaganda Fide

1925: Episcopal Consecration

1925–1934: Papal Representative in Bulgaria

1935–1944: Papal Representative in Turkey and Greece

1958–1963: Pope

II—FOUR LETTERS
1901–1961

III—SPIRITUAL TESTAMENT

IV—THE HOLY ROSARY

V—SOME PRAYERS

VI—APPENDICES

List of Illustrations

xi

Translator's Note

A translator's duty is to present his author to his readers and then efface himself completely. His task is to present and not misrepresent, *tradurre e non tradire* as the Italians say, and this is all the more necessary and desirable when the author of the book is as well known, beloved and revered as Pope John.

So I have aimed at the closest possible translation consistent with acceptable English. Nothing has been heightened, toned down, or omitted.

The quotations from holy Scripture are from the Revised Standard Version of the Bible, except where the context, particularly in the Psalms, required a closer resemblance to the version used by Pope John, in which case the Douai version is used.

I am very grateful to all who have so generously helped me with suggestions and research, and particularly to Father I. G. Capaldi, S.J., for his patient and scholarly advice.

DOROTHY M. WHITE.

Introduction

I

This volume needs no preface: a few words will suffice to introduce it and give some explanation of how it has been put together. The reader will form his own opinion and, after reading it, will draw the conclusions and perhaps make the new resolves that have already been suggested to him by the sense of trustful affection which the author's name at once inspires.

These pages have been put together by the patient willing labour of secretaries, with the loving anxiety of sons. Although we have known the original text for a long time, this compilation has been for us like a new discovery.[1] This book, in the very nature of its prayers and its spontaneous outpourings, reveals the intimate feelings and true character of a man and priest whose transparent goodness enabled us to catch a glimpse of an inner life rich in the beauty of holiness, and we are sure that it will console the hearts of men and keep them better company than many accounts of his life which may unintentionally dwindle into rhetoric and become the stuff of legend.

Whoever sets out to write about Pope John and his work must perforce take into account his writings, especially the most personal of these: some are already published[2] and others, particularly his letters, will

[1] Jacques Maritain, speaking of the *Journal* of Raïssa, his beloved companion, wrote: 'Although I had loved Raïssa's poems so much and had been privileged to see them born, as it were, although I had been the witness of her life and sufferings, nevertheless the reading of the notes gathered into this collection has been like a revelation of what I already knew, and knew very well, but only through that veil of futilities which clouds all human understanding. Now I find myself a little bewildered by it.' (*Journal de Raïssa*, edited by J. Maritain, Paris, Desclée de Brouwer, 1963, pp. 6–7.)

[2] (1) Sac. Dott. Angelo Roncalli, *La 'Misericordia Maggiore' di Bergamo e le altre istituzioni di beneficenza amministrate dalla Congregazione di Carità*, Bergamo, S. Alessandro Press, 1912, 133 pp., 2 maps, 1 full-page plate; (2) (Angelo Roncalli), *In memoria di Mons. Giacomo Maria Radini Tedeschi, Vescovo di Bergamo*, Bergamo, S. Alessandro Press, 1916, 488 pp.; 2nd ed., 1922; 3rd ed., Rome, Edizioni di Storia e Letteratura, 1963, 320 pp., 50 illustr.; (3) Angelo Giuseppe Roncalli, *Gli inizi del Seminario di Bergamo e S. Carlo*

gradually see the light. Meanwhile, eight months after his most holy death, we present these intimate and transparent records.

II

The present fairly substantial volume is a rare, if not indeed a unique, document, for we know of no other collection of this kind which records, through an almost uninterrupted series of spiritual notes, the whole life of a priest who became Pope, and reveals what he kept a jealously guarded secret behind his smiling and innocent gaiety: his prayer, his soul. In fact it contains notes, resolutions, meditations written on the occasion of various retreats and Spiritual Exercises from 1895, when the author was barely fourteen, until 1962, a few months before his death at the age of eighty-one. It therefore embraces a span of almost seventy years—one might say his whole life. In the first period (1895–1904) there are simple, detailed records; then comes the more complete vision of the whole, and the immediate programme. There are some chronological gaps; in fact the almost complete absence of any notes between 1916–1923 suggests that some pages are missing.[1]

Pope John called these diaries of his *Journal of a Soul* (*Il Giornale dell' Anima*), a title suggested to him in his youth, and which he used as a heading for his notes for 1902. These unpremeditated notes, written at night, by the flickering light of an oil lamp, consist of reminiscences of ascetic effort reconsidered in tranquillity. In the freshness and spontaneity of style

---

Borromeo. Note storiche, con una introduzione sul Concilio di Trento e la fondazione dei primi Seminari, Bergamo, S. Alessandro Press, 1939, 90 pp., 7 full-page plates; (4) Fontes Ambrosiani in lucem editi cura et studio Bibliothecae Ambrosianae moderante Johanne Galbiati. XIII–XVII: *Gli Atti della Visita Apostolica di S. Carlo Borromeo a Bergamo* (1575), edited by Angelo Giuseppe Roncalli, with the collaboration of Don Pietro Forno, 2 volumes in 5 parts, Florence, Leo S. Olschki, 1936–57; (5) *La vita diocesana*. Official periodical of the Bishop and Curia of Bergamo, 1909–14. 'The historical notes contained herein, biographical references, chronicle, and reviews of books, are almost all by Prof. Don Angelo Roncalli' (from a note by Pope John); (6) Angelo Giuseppe Card. Roncalli, *Scritti e discorsi*, 4 volumes, 1953–8, Rome, Ed. Paoline, 1959–62; (7) *Discorsi, messaggi, colloqui del Santo Padre Giovanni XXIII*, 5 volumes, 1958–63, Vatican Polyglot Press; (8) Angelo Roncalli, *Il Cardinale Cesare Baronio*, Rome, Edizioni di Storia e Letteratura, 1961, 64 pp., 10 plates; (9) Angelo Giuseppe Roncalli, *Souvenirs d'un Nonce: Cahiers de France (1944–1953)*, Rome, Edizioni di Storia e Letteratura, 1963, 280 pp., 82 illustr.; (10) Seven letters written by Card. Roncalli to Don Giuseppe De Luca are published in *Giovanni XXIII in alcuni scritti di Don Giuseppe De Luca*, Brescia, Morcelliana, 1936, pp. 69–81.

[1] There are also nine notebooks containing records of Masses, beginning with 10 August, 1904. The notebook containing the days from 11 July, 1915, to 31 December, 1920, is missing.

they well deserve the title, which applies equally to all the other notes which follow: bundles of dog-eared papers, rumpled copy-books—he kept them always by his side, often re-reading long passages in which he recognized his old self. These records were known only to his spiritual directors and to a few other intimate and trusted friends.

In the spring of 1961 the Pope handed over to me these notebooks and papers. At the time I was busy finishing the first collection of his writings and speeches, and planning other volumes for which he suggested the generic titles: *Bergomensia* (1899–1920), *Romana* (1921–4), *Orientalia* (1925–44), *Gallica* (1945–52), and *Veneta* (1953–8).

On this occasion I asked him whether I might publish these notes as well and he replied: 'You may do so. At first I felt some reluctance about publishing and letting others re-publish my private papers. . . . I am well aware that people want to know everything about a Pope, and every-thing may be useful to historians. But they are a more intimate part of me than anything else I have written; my soul is in these pages.' He paused to read over again the first pages of 1895–9, and with his mild eyes suffused with tears he went on: 'I was a good boy, innocent, some-what timid. I wanted to love God at all costs and my one idea was to become a priest, in the service of simple souls who needed patient and attentive care. Meanwhile I had to fight an enemy within me, self-love, and in the end I was able to get the better of it. But I was mortified to feel it constantly returning. I was troubled about my distractions during prayer and I imposed severe sacrifices on myself to get rid of them. I took everything very seriously and my examinations of conscience were detailed and severe. . . . Now, at a distance of more than sixty years, I can look upon these first spiritual writings of mine as if they had been written by someone else, and I bless the Lord for them. . . . You may publish them after my death. They will do some good to souls who feel drawn towards the priesthood and the more intimate union with God.'[1]

[1] We quote here three thoughts recorded by Pope John:

'*Sunday, 9 July, 1961.* A peaceful Sunday. Mgr Loris showed me my old notebooks, which he has kept and is now carefully arranging. We passed the time pleasantly among these notes I wrote half a century ago, and those which refer to my later spiritual and priestly service. He would like to publish them all; I feel a certain reluctance, however; they are papers that might perhaps do some good—but they should be published after my death.'

'*Monday, 10 July, 1961.* [. . .] Meanwhile Mgr Loris is full of enthusiasm about the collec-tion of my old manuscripts, which I too am glad to go through again. Spare me, O Lord.'

'*Tuesday, 11 July, 1961.* [. . .] In the garden this evening I met Cardinal Valeri and I made him stay with me under the pagoda, re-reading my old notebooks with Mgr Loris, in an edifying exchange of memories we have in common.'

III

To the *Journal of a Soul* we have added those papers (prayers, letters and successive drafts of his will) which best illustrate the characteristics of the whole series.

Everything here speaks of the piety of John XXIII, who talked constantly with God and was always at God's disposal, not for a life of contemplation (although he had the qualities this life demands, as is clearly shown in these pages) but for a life of priestly service to souls, and in circumstances which were radically changed eight times during his life: he was a seminarist, then secretary to a Bishop, spiritual director of the seminary at Bergamo, President of the Central Council for Italy of the *Pontificie Opere Missionarie*, Visitor and Apostolic Delegate in the Near East, Nuncio in France, Patriarch of Venice, and Pope.

This profound piety is at the roots of his simplicity as a man and his dignity as a priest, his unalterable serenity and his courage.

Something he said in 1959 illustrates his imperturbable inner calm and certitude. As we read the words today they seem to explain his ecclesiastical career, and serve as a fitting introduction to this volume: 'Above all I am grateful to the Lord for the temperament he has given me, which preserves me from anxieties and tiresome perplexities. I feel I am under obedience in all things, and I have noticed that this disposition, in great things and in small, gives me, unworthy as I am, a strength of daring simplicity, so wholly evangelical in its nature that it demands and obtains universal respect and edifies many.'[1]

This piety made him accessible to other men. People called him the good Pope, everyone's Pope, the parish priest of the world: he persuaded men to pray, to ponder the Gospels, to reform the morals of the world by reforming themselves. And at the end he drew everyone to be present not at a spectacle of splendid liturgical pomp but at a death bed as solemn as a Papal Mass. He ennobled death. He made people say it was a beautiful thing to die like that. The crowds who gathered in St Peter's Square, many of them for the first time and feeling astonished at such an unexpected occurrence, looked each other in the eyes and suddenly, mysteriously, felt they were all of one family. They wondered how this had come about.

The voice of the people at once proclaimed their judgment: he was a great priest! In this generally voiced opinion, the people were praising this man's service to souls, a service which no alteration of time or circumstance could diminish or restrict in its range.

[1] Cf. p. 299.

When Pope John died, some astonishing things happened, from which mankind may still draw comfort and renewal of faith. Peace returned to many homes, sick men who had despaired accepted their fate; disobedient children became biddable; young married couples, mindful of his words, 'Caress your children from me',[1] said to each other: 'We must love each other in the right way.' His poverty impressed public opinion, was a consolation to the poor; many prodigal sons tried to alleviate his terrible sufferings by repeating prayers remembered from their childhood, almost as if they were standing around his bed; some decided to return to the sacraments.

This book offers the key to the mystery, if indeed there be a mystery, of his priestly soul, which succeeded in making contact with the soul of his age, thus arousing such deep, sincere, I would almost say thoughtful, feelings that even now it is hard to explain them.

IV

Journal of a Soul reveals much to those who wish to know its author better.

First of all, there is the influence of his upbringing in his own family, an education made up of few words but good examples and ingrained habits.

Almost more vivid than the memory of his father and mother is that of his bachelor uncle, great-uncle Zaverio, the *barba*, the real head of the family. A man who had never got beyond the first grades of the elementary school but had learnt the law of God from the order he saw in nature and from the simple, profound teaching of his humble parish priest and who, in his dealings with his neighbour, was guided by his readings in Sacred Scripture. He was a Christian wholly absorbed in the love of God, in his devotions to the Sacred Heart of Jesus and the Most Precious Blood, and in the constant practice of Christian discipline and piety.

Then there is the memory of the priests whom Providence had placed in his path, and who had a profound influence on his training; in particular, Father Francesco Rebuzzini, the parish priest who baptized him and watched over his youth; Father Francesco Pitocchi, a Redemptorist, the spiritual director of the Roman Seminary at the Apollinare; Mgr Vincenzo Bugarini, the Rector of this seminary; and above all and by far the most important, the Bishop, Mgr Radini Tedeschi. After his family,

---

[1] *Discorsi, messaggi, colloqui, cit.*, vol. IV, pp. 592-3.

it was these priests who imparted to this predestined youth that respect for God's law, that fear of God, upon which a noble destiny may be founded, the pure whole-hearted love of the Gospel, with its supreme lesson of the Beatitudes; the sense of service in the Church and for the Church, who is the guardian of truth, mistress of charity, source of our most daring hopes, and finally that fidelity to practices of piety which bred in him the noblest and most hard-won Christian virtues. The proof of this lies in the text of the exercises drawn up by Mgr Radini Tedeschi, which the young secretary copied in his own hand and then, as it were, made his own, keeping it always by his side among the other notebooks of *Journal of a Soul*. Thus it was that this man, who when raised to such a great position amazed his contemporaries with his extraordinary accessibility to everything and everyone, was rooted in the strongest, purest and most ancient tradition of Christian piety. This is what kept his faith invincible, making him receptive to the mysterious revelations of God; this is what gave him a tranquil, firm hope because of which, in all circumstances, his heart enjoyed perfect peace in union with his Lord. Because of this piety, no obstacle could prevent him from undertaking great enterprises and announcing them even at the advanced age of seventy-seven. Because of this piety the practice of the hardest virtues, humility, conformity to God's will, self-denial and patience, became second nature to him and led even to the willing acceptance of everything: physical suffering, misunderstanding, scorn.

Here was a boy of fourteen who, on entering the seminary, at once wrote in his unformed hand in his penny copy-book the august words addressed by the Council of Trent to all priests: '. . . Let them also avoid minor faults, which in them would be very great' and made of these a rule for his whole life. As a young seminarist, seized with the holy horror of sin—not only of grave sin but even of those small failings which are called venial sins—he made a solemn vow to keep himself free from voluntarily committing the slightest venial sin; and, as a grown man and a Bishop, after twenty-five years of priesthood (and many times again in later life) he could thank the Lord for having preserved him from grave sin, and even from venial sin, deliberately intended.

There are entries like these: 'All around me in this great house is solitude, absolute and magnificent solitude, amid the profusions of nature in flower; before my eyes the Danube; beyond the great river the rich Rumanian plain, which sometimes at night glows red with burning waste gas';[1] or again: 'Every evening from the windows of my room, here in

[1] Cf. p. 215.

the residence of the Jesuit Fathers, I see an assemblage of boats on the Bosporus; they come round from the Golden Horn in tens and hundreds; they gather at a given rendezvous and then they light up, some more brilliantly than others, offering a most impressive spectacle of colours and lights. I thought it was a festival on the sea for Bairam which occurs just about now. But it is the organized fleet fishing for bonito, large fish which are said to come from far away in the Black Sea. These lights glow all night, and one can hear the cheerful voices of the fishermen. I find the sight very moving. The other night, towards one o'clock, it was pouring with rain, but the fishermen were still there, undeterred from their heavy toil.'[1] The precise details reveal a keen observer and a clear, simple style of writing which has its own charm.

There are notes like the following: 'It really looks as if God has lavished upon me his most tender and motherly care; he has led me out of so many difficulties and, through countless acts of kindness he has brought me here to Rome. It must be for some particular purpose of his: there can be no other reason for my Master's infinite generosity.'[2] (This is written by a young man of twenty who has been selected to complete his studies in Rome.) 'I do not seek, I do not desire, the glory of this world; I look forward to greater glory in heaven.'[3] 'So long as charity may triumph, at all costs, I would choose to be considered as of little worth. I will be patient and good to a heroic degree, even if I am to be crushed.'[4] 'Above all I wish to continue always to render good for evil, and in all things to endeavour to prefer the Gospel truth to the wiles of human politics.'[5] 'I insert in my coat of arms the words *Obœdientia et Pax* (Obedience and Peace), which Cesare Baronius used to say every day when he kissed the Apostle's foot in St Peter's. In a way these words are my own history and my life. O may they be the glorification of my humble name throughout the centuries!'[6] These words reveal both his habitual humility before God and his clear consciousness of his own worth before men . . . so clear as to be disconcerting.

But it is impossible to describe all that may be found in this book, whether clear and explicit, or barely perceived through the veil of intimate records, or reflected in a mind which examines itself with regard to things, places and men, and refers everything to God. A whole life is here, and what a life!

[1] Cf. p. 234.   [2] Cf. p. 87.   [3] Cf. p. 206.
[4] Cf. p. 218.   [5] Cf. p. 228.   [6] Cf. p. 206.

V

Some things are more easily understood if one has some idea of the geography of Sotto il Monte.

The bells of the Franciscan Friars Minor of Baccanello, near Calusco d'Adda, two kilometres from the Roncalli homestead, could be heard calling the Brothers to choir; for the country-folk they chimed the hours of prayer, work and rest. Beyond the river Adda lies Somasca, where the Venetian nobleman St Jerome Emiliani (1486–1537) founded his Congregation for orphans and for the education of the children of the poor. Also beyond the Adda, in Milanese territory, is the sanctuary of the Madonna del Bosco. As a child little Angelo Roncalli used to go with his mother to the Madonna del Bosco; they went on foot, or in a little cart drawn by a donkey. On the hills of the *Comune* of Sotto il Monte the ruins of austere monuments and even the very place names still speak of the great age of the Benedictines.[1] Not far away is the restored monastery of Pontida. Memories such as these of a poor and innocent childhood are not easily forgotten.

Then came the years spent in the seminary of his native diocese. The seminary of Bergamo was founded by St Charles Borromeo and reformed by St Gregory Barbarigo; in recent times, during the period of the suppression of their Order,[2] it benefited from the labours of the Society of Jesus.

So it is that we find in Angelo Roncalli, through the merits of his kith and kin and his contacts with the great institutions of the Church, a devotion to the Sacred Heart, to the Most Precious Blood, and to the Mother of Jesus; a Franciscan kind of poverty, cheerful and contented; the care of the poor and the destitute; an application to humanistic studies; and a desire, of Ignatian inspiration, for the reform of morals and methods, in order to preserve undiminished the powerful appeal of Christian doctrine which sanctifies men and sets them free.[3]

[1] Cf. *Monumenta Bergomensia*, II, N. Tagliabue—L. Chiodi, *Il priorato di Sant'Egidio dei Benedettini Cluniacensi in Fontanella del Monte* (1080–1473), with a dedication to Pope John XXIII, Bergamo, 1960.

[2] Cf. introductory note to the '*Little Rules*', p. 413 below.

[3] Throughout his life John XXIII listened most anxiously and carefully to all pronouncements, particularly those of the Popes, which aimed at the encouragement of the missionary and pastoral spirit among the clergy. For example, we quote this passage from 'Notes of an Audience', written after a meeting with Pius XII, on 16 September, 1949: 'I went on to thank him in the name of France for the welcome which His Holiness gives to the French people of all ranks of society who go to see him and are so much edified by him. It was a great joy to hear him say: "But it is my great preoccupation and consola-

VI

The last time Pope John spoke to the faithful gathered in St Peter's Square was on 22 May, 1963, the eve of the Ascension. The air seemed to throb with expectation, anxiety and hope. He came to the balcony, very pale but unfaltering, greeted the crowds with a wide gesture of his hands, then recited the Marian antiphon: 'O Queen of Heaven, rejoice, alleluia.' Then he spoke a few words, pleasantly and cheerfully. His voice was strong and melodious. 'I wish you all a happy Feast of the Ascension! Let us hasten after our ascending Lord; as we cannot follow him yet but must remain on earth, in his Holy Church, let us imitate the apostles who gathered in the room of the Last Supper, praying for the Holy Spirit. Just now you have heard and every day you hear: everything in the name of the Father, Son and Holy Spirit.'[1]

After he had given his blessing the Pope lingered a little, smiling, and ended with a greeting: '*Saluti, saluti . . .*'

The next day he again recited the prayer and blessed the crowd but did not speak to them. His Way of the Cross was now ascending, mounting towards the summit of his sacrifice; henceforth nothing was to distract him from preparing for the great passing.

The sunset of his long life saw his piety as clear and pure as it had been in the morning hours: trust in God, imitation of Christ, readiness to set out for the realms of eternity, without regrets, without fears; charity towards all, most tender and generous, and, for all, forgiveness: 'Having loved his own who were in the world, he loved them to the end',[2] and all returned his love.

VII

Pope John often mentioned a letter he intended to write to all the clergy (*Epistola ad clerum universum*) for the close of the Council, after the example of St Pius X who, on the fiftieth anniversary of his ordination as a priest (1908), issued his *Haerent animo*, an apostolic exhortation to holiness of life, addressed to all the Catholic clergy in the world.

He intended to put this together from his personal papers, from the notes he was preparing, and from his collections of jottings, in which

---

tion, Monsignor, to welcome these men of the world, even if they are of another way of thinking. Is this not the true business of the shepherd? Am I not here for those who have sinned and gone astray, who are all equally my children?" '

[1] *Discorsi, messaggi, colloqui, cit.*, vol. V, pp. 489–90.
[2] John 13: 1.

almost every day he used diligently to copy thoughts and comments from the Fathers of the Church and other spiritual writings.

The letter got no further than his heart; but its substance, indeed its very soul, is in this volume. Today, with lovable simplicity and tenderness, he would offer it to young and old, in order that, meditating upon it together, they might find in it the everlasting truth of the Gospel.

It is our humble and confident prayer that this truth may be expressed in new religious devotion, such as he showed in life and death, and may attract, confirm or inspire with fervour the souls of all who read it.

VIII

My grateful and heartfelt thanks go to:

The Sisters of the Istituto delle Poverelle for their aid in the transcription from the original texts;

The Edizioni di Storia e Letteratura for checking the transcribed texts and the editing of this volume in its first, Italian, edition;

Luigi Felici, the papal photographer, to whose kindness and courtesy I owe many of the excellent photographs here reproduced;

Giacomo Manzù, the sculptor, who has enriched this volume with two photographs of his Door of Death (in St Peter's in Rome), Plates 23 and 26.

Padre Giulio Bevilacqua, of the Oratory at Brescia, for the 'Meditation' which in a few short pages expresses all his love for the Pope whom he had known since they were young together.

DON LORIS CAPOVILLA.

Vatican City, 25 January, 1964.

Fifth anniversary of the announcement of the
  Second Vatican Ecumenical Council.

Meditation

As we ponder on Pope John's *Journal of a Soul* we understand the complexity of the Church today, as she sets forth bravely and determinedly 'towards new ways of feeling, wishing and behaving',[1] her mind and heart absorbed in the study of all those modes of life in which men are hastening and struggling in their search for security. If Pope John were to send one more message to the Church he would surely begin with Paul's words to the Church of Corinth: 'You yourselves are our letter of recommendation, written on your hearts, to be known and read by all men; and you show that you are a letter from Christ delivered by us, written not with ink but with the spirit of the living God, not on tablets of stone but on tablets of human hearts.'[2]

To understand St John the Baptist, the forerunner of Christ, we must understand the solitude in which he grew to maturity and of which he became the loud, authentic voice; so, if we are to understand the bold direction given to the Church by Pope John, we must enter into his interior solitude: it was this daily examination of his spiritual life which turned him into the man of mission, the Good Samaritan of our time, the man who makes straight the highways 'to make ready a perfect people for the Lord'.[3]

In *Journal of a Soul* we perceive and are allowed to enter the flowering solitude of his intimate relations with God. And yet a superficial perusal might leave a doubtful, even a disappointing, impression. It might be thought that we are confronted here with a literal and formalistic piety,

[1] Cf. speech of Pope Paul VI, inaugurating the second session of the Ecumenical Council (*L'Osservatore Romano*, 30 September, 1963).

[2] 2 Cor. 3: 2–3.

[3] 'God grant that both Johns may make their voices heard in the universal Church through our very humble pastoral ministry . . . and that there may be proclaimed to the clergy and all people this work of ours by which we would make ready a perfect people for the Lord, to make straight his paths, so that the crooked may be made straight, and the rough ways may be made smooth, and all flesh may see the salvation of God' (cf. *Discorsi, messaggi, colloqui, cit.*, vol. I, p. 4).

such as we find in thousands of pious books which have abounded in post-Tridentine times: a piety centred more on human contrivance than on the word of God, one that puts its trust in an exasperating profusion of wire entanglements, instead of in that wide free air we breathe when we are familiar with Sacred Scripture, the liturgy and the writings of the Fathers. This spirituality might seem to be reduced to interminable examinations of conscience, which arouse in the minds of our contemporaries distrust or even revolt; it is a method which apparently sees God not as love and fatherhood, from whom all fatherhood derives, but only as the Judge who pronounces eternal judgments on the frailty of the creature, a breath of wind that passes and comes no more. Does the question that haunted Job not rise to our lips too: 'Who can bring a clean thing out of an unclean?'[1]

Yet this kind of spirituality produced Pope John: the tree is to be judged by its fruit. This rigorously constructed spirituality is technique, the letter of the law; yes, but it is not only technique and the letter of the law, for within it lives and from it soars a great conception. Every technique degenerates if it remains purely mechanical, that is, isolated from all noble inspiration. On the other hand no great conception can be realized without a rule, without a discipline. Now there is evident in Pope John's *Journal* a powerful and exalted evangelical impulse which dominates his whole existence, and preserves this constant examination of his own life from any puritanical or pharisaical contamination. His confessions are too precise, too detailed, too intent on calling everything by its right name, ever to become a stale habit or, worse still, a mask or a pose. Today, too many rebels publish their confessions, shameless exhibitions before a public greedy for scandal, and destined merely to disguise their shame. Here, instead, all is real: the simplicity, the awareness of being a creature, scrupulous moderation and reserve, extreme human sensibility, above all, the will to aspire to the fulness of Christ.

The *Journal* records constant, one might almost say, obstinate growth, in step with the very slow rhythm of nature and grace. It is a growth in understanding and knowledge of God's purpose, and an increasing embodiment of this purpose in his personal life and ecclesiastical office. God's design for us, being eternal, keeps pace with us; it grows with us and we grow with it.

'What is the result of this spiritual concentration of mine? Nothing remarkable or exciting but, as it seems to me, a consolidation of my principles and positions in the eyes of the Lord and in all that regards my

[1] Cf. Job 14: 4.

own humble life and my sacred ministry in the service of Holy Church. Even without exaggerating the importance of my entering upon this last, possibly rapid and brief, period of my life, I feel something more mature and authoritative in me, in relation to all that interests and surrounds me . . .' (p. 237).

Thus the formal framework becomes less rigid, the letter yields more and more to the spirit, all effort is unified and directed towards a few very clear purposes: 'After having skimmed through the doctrine of various ascetical authors, I am now quite content with the Missal, the Breviary, the Bible, *The Imitation* and Bossuet . . .' (p. 267). 'My spiritual life must be intensified. No overloading with devotions of a novel and secondary character, but fidelity to those which are fundamental, with passionate fervour . . . gather[ing] speed as I near the end' (p. 280).

The great faith of his childhood is gradually transformed into charity: 'I desire and think of nothing else, but to live and die for the souls entrusted to me' (p. 282).

Two great aspects of his pastoral mission have now taken possession of him: 'To preach the good news to the poor and to comfort the brokenhearted' (p. 290).[1]

He was born with an ecumenical mind: he understood everyone and was accessible to everyone; he made every effort to speak with all. 'I want to study Turkish with more care and perseverance. I am fond of the Turks . . . I know that my way of dealing with them is right; above all it is Catholic and apostolic' (p. 228).

In 1959, when he was Pope, he could sum up his life in these words: 'Since the Lord chose me, unworthy as I am, for this great service, I feel I have no longer any special ties in this life. . . . The whole world is my family. This sense of belonging to everyone must give character and vigour to my mind, my heart and my actions' (pp. 298–9).

The *Journal* shows an ever more concentrated and profound understanding of the Paschal mystery, which teaches us that only by dying can we conquer death. He is now calmly and steadfastly endeavouring to 'empty' himself.[2] He is beginning to see nought but Christ, and Christ crucified, 'the solution of all difficulties' (p. 146).

His life was peaceful, because Pope John knew how to turn the very stones into gestures of love, and so into joy. But towards the solemn sunset of his life he was aware of the impending mystery of pain. 'I think the Lord Jesus has in store for me . . . for my complete mortification . . . some great suffering and affliction of body and spirit' (p. 292).

[1] Cf. Luke 4: 18.   [2] Phil. 2: 7.

'. . . The rather sombre prospect for the future convinces me that the Lord wants me all for himself along the royal road of the holy Cross' (p. 217).

But he set out along this road not as we, poor bundles of aching atoms, would have done, resigned to what we cannot avoid, but as a giant who runs his race: he asks for suffering, seeks the hard road, prepares his soul for the sacrifice. What he asks for (he who had always asked for so little) is 'to be always and evermore a vicitm, a sacrificial offering, an apostle . . .' (p. 218).

So when he wrote these solemn and significant words about the opening of the Council: 'After three years of preparation, certainly laborious but also joyful and serene, we are now on the slopes of the sacred mountain' (p. 325), perhaps in his heart he already knew that the mountain was not the Council but the hill of Calvary. We may deduce this from some words, spoken confidentially, which show his usual sublime faith and charity: 'Now I understand what contribution to the Council the Lord requires from me: my suffering.'[1] So the Cross took possession of him and set its dread mark on every one of his senses, on his speech, on the mystery of his silences, on all the inmost recesses of his soul.

During his unforgettable agony, the angel who watches by the altar of the holy sacrifice explained to him his sublime purposes. 'I make the sign of the Cross on your eyes, that you may see the splendour of God; on your ears, that you may hear the Lord's voice; on your nostrils, that you may breathe the sweetness of Christ; on your lips, that you may utter words of life; I make the holy sign upon your shoulders, that you may bear the yoke of Christ's service.'

His wounds have become the wounds of the Church in Council, a Church determined to abandon all triumphal ways, and to follow the Via Dolorosa, the only road upon which the Son of Man can meet the tragic man of our own times. This is the Church handed on by John XXIII to Paul VI.

The new Pope, in order to make more apparent this unbroken continuity between the bed on which Pope John suffered his agony and the throne upon which Paul had begun to drink from his own chalice, decided, twenty centuries after Peter's departure thence, to return to the land where the Cross had been erected, where the sepulchre was left

[1] 'Oh je sais quelle sera ma part personelle de collaboration au Concile. . . . Ce sera la souffrance.' (From the Commemoration of Pope John, preached in the Vatican Basilica by Cardinal Suenens, 28 October, 1963. Cf. L'Osservatore Romano, 28–29 October, 1963.)

empty, where the primacy was established, not as a primacy of power but only as a primacy of love.

The immeasurable emotion and enthusiasm of the whole world have shown that this gesture has been understood as a gesture of return to Christ crucified, as a gesture of continuity with this brief pontificate which conquered the world,[1] as a gesture of communion and peace with Christian churches and with the community of all peoples. Hearing the message from Bethlehem,[2] Pope John must have rejoiced like Abraham, who desired to see the day of the Lord: he saw it and was glad.

GIULIO BEVILACQUA, CONG. ORAT.

Brescia, 18 January, 1964.

[1] 'But what had he done to arouse such world-wide expressions of love and gratitude? In one of the most arresting books of recent years a Jewish child asks the Elder what the Just Man must do. The Elder, without hesitation, replies: "Do you ask the sun to do anything? It rises, it sets, it rejoices your soul" (Cf. André Schwarz-Bart, Le dernier des justes, Paris, du Seuil, 1959, p. 157). This is what Pope John did: he was born, he died, he rejoiced our souls. Perhaps someone will feel tempted to repeat about the Pope what has recently been written about Christ, the "gracious messenger of impossible love". The Pope of Pentecostal mind has indeed inspired irresistible impulses of love. Elijah has gone and only an Elisha can wear his cloak. Pope John, I kiss your hand that can never cease to bless, I would kiss your heart that no heavy tombstone can stifle.' (From Giulio Bevilacqua, 'Il Morte di Giovanni XXIII', in Humanitas, XVIII, June, 1963, pp. 559-60.)

[2] Pilgrimage of Pope Paul to Palestine, 4-6 January, 1964. 'We all promise you to live as Christians, trying constantly to respond to your grace and to reform our morals. We shall endeavour to spread throughout the world your message of salvation and love.' (From Messaggio di Betlemme, 6 January, 1964. Cf. L'Osservatore Romano, 7-8 January, 1964.)

It is instructive to reflect for a moment on the task which Pope John's pontificate, with the far-reaching changes that it has wrought not only in the actual working of the Church but also in the expectations with which from now on people, Christian and non-Christian, Catholic and non-Catholic, look to the Church, presents to those who follow him in the papacy.

This has been summed up by Cardinal Bea, in his essay 'On the Image of Paul VI':

'Seldom was the familiar phrase "difficult succession" to a pontificate rich in prestige and in works so true as after the death of Pope John XXIII. "Good Pope John" had acquired a widespread popularity even outside the Catholic Church; he had decided upon, prepared and begun the vastest and the best-prepared Council of all time; he had set the Church in motion towards a rediscovery of the traces of her more fervent youth, towards the revelation of her conquering power to the men of today; by his encyclicals and especially by the Council, he had attracted the interest and admiration of world opinion. Now he was dead, his work just begun, and there was universal grief and consternation.

'The vacancy of the Apostolic See, with the inevitable and numerous conjectures as to his probable successor, was far from creating a halo of prestige for whoever should succeed Pope John and receive his heritage. Conjectures, while partly assisting the more

XXX   MEDITATION

perspicacious minds to a discernment of persons and of their qualities, are always largely equalizing, at least as regards the various likely candidates, because conjectures—even when calmly voiced, which is not generally the case—tend to exalt one's own candidate by criticizing those of others. For all these reasons, it was certainly no empty word when Paul VI himself, the day after his election, spoke of his "spirit trembling before the vastness of the task" imposed upon him, and of the weighty legacy received from his predecessor.' (From *The Mind of Paul VI*, London, 1964, p. ix.) *Translator's note.*

Bibliographical Note

This book consists chiefly of previously unpublished writings. These are as follows:

Journal of a Soul. Exercises and Spiritual Notes, 1895–1962 (pp. 4–325)
Three letters, one to Angelo Roncalli's parents and two to the rector of the Roman Seminary (pp. 329–34)
The rejected part of the *Spiritual Testament* (pp. 345–54)
The '*Little Rules*' *of Ascetic Life* (pp. 417–26)
Maxims Heard or Gleaned from Various Sources (pp. 427–30)

The main core of the volume is *Journal of a Soul*, the text of which is arranged in chronological order, together with pertinent letters and prayers. All the individual sections of the text, whether previously published or not, have been numbered consecutively in arabic numerals in square brackets, placed in the margin in order to facilitate reference.

The text is taken from a series of notebooks and loose sheets kept in folders. The notebooks are worn with use and the ink is often faded. The folders contain sheets of different types of paper in different sizes; some are hand-written and others are typed, the latter in the small characters found on some portable machines. In the sheets the individual sections do not always follow in the chronological order observed in this book.

As has been stated in our Introduction, John XXIII, having agreed to publication of the manuscripts after his death, re-examined the material in 1960–2. He restricted himself to minimal revisions, for the most part stylistic, adding a few indications of date and place. These revisions are easily identifiable, apart from the handwriting, by the blue ink and by the uniform thickness of line indicating constant use of the same fountain pen. Inasmuch as a critical text is not offered here, the revisions are not specifically indicated as such. Note that occasionally italic type has been used for some passages underlined in red in the manuscript.

We give here a summary description of the notebooks and groups of sheets, indicated by roman numerals, as well as of the individual sections of the text, indicated by arabic numerals, as has been mentioned. Not included in this summary are certain previously published materials whose source is stated in footnotes accompanying the text.

I. [1, 112]; 1895. Notebook with black cover containing square-ruled sheets; 6 × 12·5 cm.; 64 pp., 5 blank. On the inside of the cover is a Latin motto, 'Fuge quae . . . in ore saecularium nugae sunt, in ore sacerdotum blasphemiae' (Faults which are trifles in the mouths of lay people are blasphemies in the mouths of priests). Boyish handwriting. In addition to text [1] and [112], there is a copy of [111] with minor variations. See below, No. XXXVIII.

II. [2, 4¹, 6]; 1896, 1898. Notebook with black cover containing square-ruled sheets 6 × 11 cm.; 40 pp. Does not follow chronological order. Boyish handwriting.

III. [3]; 1897. One square-ruled sheet, yellowed; 13·5 × 21·5 cm. Written on both sides in a small, compact hand.

IV. [4]; 1898. Notebook with black cover containing square-ruled sheets; 9 × 12·5 cm.; 58 pp. Boyish handwriting.

V. [5, 7, 10, 11]; 1898–1901. Notebook with black cover containing square-ruled sheets; 10 × 13·5 cm.; 52 pp., of which the last 18 are blank. On the inside of the cover is an author's note from 1961–2: '4 October, 1898. Spiritual notes from the monthly retreat after the death of my parish priest, Father Rebuzzini, the saintly guardian of my childhood and my vocation.' The first sheet containing writing was removed by the author. Boyish handwriting.

VI. [8, 9]; 1900. Four square-ruled sheets, 22 × 27·5 cm., folded in half, plus a half sheet; in all 18 pp., of which 6 are blank. On the first page below the title of [8] the author added in 1961–2: 'February, Seminary of Bergamo,' and below the title of [9]: '27 February, 1900.' Minute handwriting.

VII. [12]; 1902. Four sheets, 21 × 31 cm., folded in half, forming 16 pp., densely covered. In 1961–2 the author added below the title: 'With Father Francesco Pitocchi', underlining in red these words, together with the date and the passage printed in italics on p. 91.

VIII. [13, 14]; 1902, 1903. Fifteen sheets, 21 × 31 cm., folded in half, forming 60 pp., of which the first serves as a title page; the verso of this sheet and the last 5 are blank. On the title page is written 'Soli Deo honor

---

¹ Text [4] is divided between notebooks II and IV. The first group of 'Spiritual Notes' goes from 27 February to 26 May, 1898, the second from 3 June to 1 October, 1898.

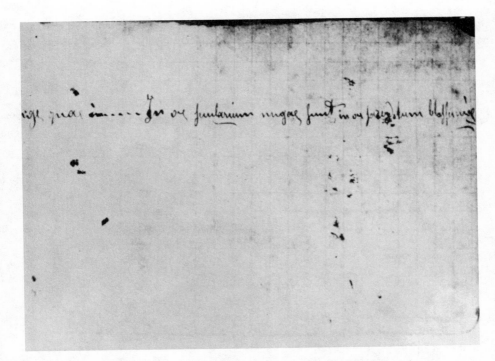

1. Facsimile, inside front cover, first notebooks used

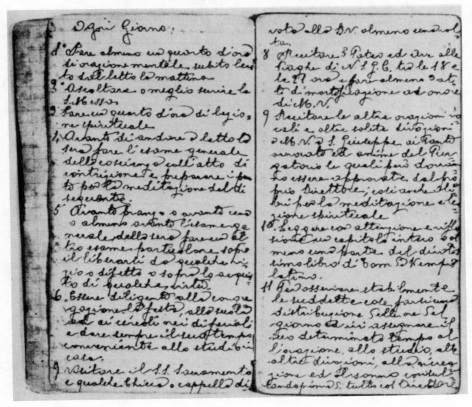

2. Facsimile, first two pages of first notebook

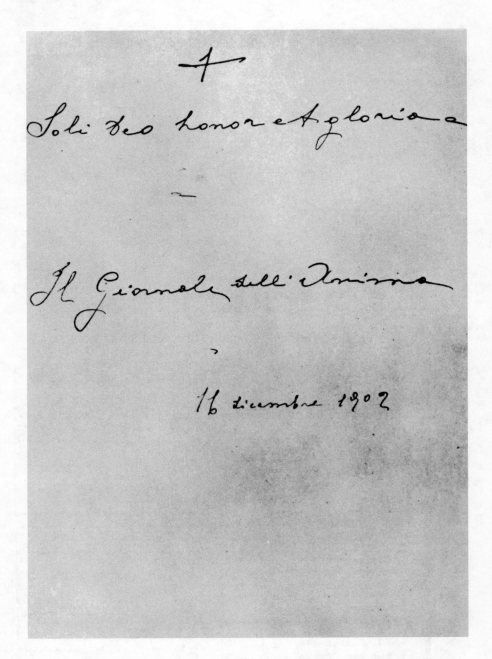

3. Facsimile, the first use of the title 'Il Giornale dell'Anima'

et gloria—Journal of a Soul—16 December, 1902'. In 1961-2 the author added beneath the heading of [13] '1902', and made a few very slight changes in the text.

IX. [15–17]; 1903. Six sheets, 21 × 31 cm., folded in half, forming 24 pp., of which one is blank.

X. [18–20]; 1903, 1904. Six sheets, 21 × 31 cm., folded in half, forming 24 pp., of which three are blank. In 1961-2 the author added two words to [18] and the date to [20].

XI. [21–8]; 1904, 1907-11. Ten sheets, 21 × 31 cm., folded in half, forming 40 pp.; on the first is a table of contents for the group, except for [22] and [23] inserted later. The verso of the first sheet and eight others are blank. In 1961-2 the author made a few slight corrections. [22] is written on a lined sheet, 13·5 × 21 cm., inserted in the fascicle. [21] and [23] are incomplete. There is a change in the handwriting between 1904 and 1907, and a note of 1912 affixed at the end of [21].

XII. [29–35]; 1912-15, 1919, 1924. Nine sheets, 21 × 29 cm.,[1] folded in half, forming 36 pp.; on the first is a list of writings contained in the fascicle, except for [33]. The list ends with the words 'Thoughts and spiritual resolutions' and the signature 'd.a.r.'. The verso of the first sheet and two others are blank. In the middle are two little fascicles related to [31] and [32]. The first consists of 8 square-ruled sheets, 15 × 19 cm., torn from a pad and written on one side only. The second consists of three sheets of paper headed 'Bishop of Bergamo—Private Office', 21 × 27·5 cm., folded in half, forming 12 pp., of which one serves as a title page. The verso of this is blank. There are some underlinings from 1961-2. The handwriting has reached a maturity which was to be preserved with little change until 1960-1.

XIII. [36]; 1925. Two sheets of watermarked paper, 16 × 23 cm., folded in half, forming 8 pp. The sheets are in a folder, 17·5 × 25 cm., upon which is written: 'Retreat in preparation for episcopal consecration. Rome—Villa Carpegna—13-17 March, 1925.'

XIV. [37, 38]; 1926-7. Two sheets, 20·5 × 28·5 cm., folded in half, forming 8 pp.

XV. [39–43]; 1928, 1930, 1931, 1933-4. Five sheets of watermarked paper, 20 × 26·5 cm., folded in half, forming 20 pp. In the middle are two fascicles relating to [40] and [41]; the first comprises 2 sheets, 17 × 29 cm., folded in half, forming 8 pp., of which 7 are typewritten and the

---

[1] The second part of [35], 'Particular Reflections', comprises 5 pp., 11 × 16·5 cm., taken from a diary of 1924.

last blank; at the end of the text, a handwritten signature and date.[1] The second comprises two sheets, 22 × 29 cm., folded in half, forming 8 pp. Some corrections from 1961–2.

XVI. [44]; 1935. One sheet of watermarked paper, 19·5 × 26·5 cm., folded in half, forming 4 pp. At the beginning the words 'Spiritual Exercises' are typewritten.

XVII. [45]; 1936. Two sheets, 20 × 22 cm., folded in half, forming 8 pp.

XVIII. [46]; 1937. Two sheets, 22 × 27 cm., folded in half, forming 8 pp., of which the last is blank.

XIX. [47–53]; 1939–40, 1942–5, 1947–8. Fourteen sheets, 20 × 29 cm., folded in half, forming 56 pp., of which the last four are blank; pencilled numbers on the upper right of the rectos, from 1 to 31, covering [47] and [48]. In the middle is an additional small fascicle containing [49], of 5 sheets, 22 × 29 cm., folded in half, forming 20 pp., of which one is blank, numbered in ink on the upper right of the rectos, from 1 to 10. [50] is written in ink on the last page of [49]. [49, 52, 53] are typewritten. Some corrections from 1961–2.

XX. [54]; 1950. Six sheets, 21 × 27 cm., written on both sides and numbered on the upper right of the rectos, from 1 to 6. In 1961–2 they were enclosed in a white sheet upon which is written 'Spiritual retreat at Oran in Africa. 6–9 April, 1950'.

XXI. [55]; 1952. Four sheets, 21 × 27 cm., folded in half, forming 16 pp., of which one serves as a title page, numbered on the upper right of the rectos from 1 to 7. The verso of the title page is blank. At the end the prayer to the Sacred Heart is underlined in red.

XXII.[2] [56, 57]; 1953–4. Four sheets, 21 × 27 cm., folded in half, of which 2 are blank. Corrections and additions from 1961–2.

XXIII. [58]; 1955. Four sheets, 21 × 28 cm., folded in half, forming 16 pp., of which the last 4 are blank.

[1] On p. 7, which contains the 'Offering of a Crucified Life' by Father Lintelo, is stapled an undated clipping from an unidentified newspaper with the following prayer of Cardinal Tosi: 'O sweet Jesus, grant me true love, the love of the Cross, not of those heroic crosses whose splendour nourishes self-love, but of those ordinary crosses which we bear with such repugnance, of those crosses which appear every day in our lives and which are found at every hour along our path—opposition, failure, abandonment, obstacles, adversities, coldness, impatience, rejection, scorn, bodily infirmity, mental depression, silence and aridity of the heart. Only then shall I know that I love you; though I may not feel or know this, it will be enough.—O sweet Jesus, may your will always and without exception be fulfilled in me!'

[2] [56–60] are preceded by a small sheet, 12 × 15 cm., probably from 1961–2, listing them under the general heading 'Exercises with the episcopate'.

XXIV. [59]; 1956. Four sheets of paper headed 'The Cardinal Patriarch', 21 × 28 cm., folded in half, forming 16 pp., numbered on the upper right of sheets 1 to 3; only the fourth sheet is written on both sides. The last 8 pp. are blank.

XXV. [60–1]; 1957–8. Three sheets of paper headed 'The Cardinal Patriarch', 21 × 29 cm., folded in half, forming 12 pp., of which the last is blank. On the first was added in 1961–2 the date '1958' and the name of the preacher.

XXVI. [62]; 1958. Three sheets, 15 × 20·5 cm., torn from a pad and written on one side only.

XXVII. [63, 64]; 1959, 1960. Four sheets, 22 × 31 cm., folded in half, forming 16 pp., of which the last 3 are blank.

XXVIII. [65, 67]; 1961, 1962. Sixty-three pp., 13·5 × 20·5 cm., written on an unused diary for 1959. Numbering from 1 to 54 in the upper left and right for [65]. Some corrections.

XXIX. [66]; 1961. Three sheets, 13·5 × 20 cm., with the papal emblem at the top, written on both sides. The text breaks off at the end.

XXX. [68]; 1962. Nine pp., 13·5 × 20·5 cm., written on the same 1959 diary.

XXXI. [69]; 1962. Six pp., 15·5 × 20·5 cm., written on a diary for 1962; the fifth page is blank.

XXXII. [70]; 1962. Two pp., 20·5 × 30 cm., written in a large notebook with a dark red cover, which bears the title 'Second Vatican Council. Various Notes'.

XXXIII. [71]; 1901. A letter on one sheet, 21 × 29·5 cm., folded in half.

XXXIV. [72, 73]; 1901. Two letters, each on a single sheet, 21 × 26·5 cm., folded in half.

XXXV. [76]; 1954. Six typewritten sheets, 22 × 30 cm., numbered from 3 to 8 in the upper right. All the sheets, except no. 6, are signed at the bottom in ink 'Ang. Gius. card. Roncalli Patriarca'. On the last the final invocations, the signature and the date are written in ink. Some corrections. These six sheets contain the second part of the typewritten will prepared in September, 1954. The first 2 sheets contain [75], previously published by *L'Osservatore Romano*.

XXXVI. [77]; 1939–44. Two typewritten sheets, 22 × 30 cm., of which one is written lengthwise; corrections, various additions, and handwritten signature.

XXXVII. [110]; 1959. Thirty-six sheets written on the recto only, of which 25 are 14·5 × 22·5 cm. and 11 20·5 × 28 cm. On the first

two sheets are pasted 2 half pages of printer's proofs[1] with various corrections and additions. The lower part of sheet 3 has been cut away.
Numbering in the upper right with red ink from 1 to 25 and from 27 to
37.

XXXVIII. [111]; 1895. Five small square-ruled sheets, torn from a
notebook, 7·5 × 10 cm. Worn pages, faded ink, tiny handwriting.
These sheets are in a letter envelope on which the Pope, perhaps in
1961–2, has written 'The Little Rules. Special direction reserved for
certain seminarists. Bergamo Seminary, 1895.'

The executor of Pope John XXIII's will has placed all the manuscript
material of this volume in the secret archives of the Vatican. The *Fondo
Giovanni XXIII* of the archives, established in 1960, contains other
documents and letters of the Pope.

---

[1] See note 1, p. 403.

Chronology 1881–1963[1]

This chronology will help the reader to understand the spiritual pilgrimage of John XXIII, whose life was truly spent in unceasing contemplation, meditation and prayer. These are the salient events of his life as seminarist, priest, Bishop and Pope, with special reference to his religious activities.

1881–1900

1881	25 November. Angelo Giuseppe, son of Battista Roncalli and Marianna Mazzola, was born at Sotto il Monte (Bergamo) in the Brusico district. He was baptized the same day by the parish priest, Father Francesco Rebuzzini, in the church of Santa Maria. His godfather was his great-uncle Zaverio Roncalli, head of the family, the brother of his grandfather Angelo.[2]
1888	First communion at Sotto il Monte. The admission to communion of a boy of seven was unusual at that time.
1889	13 February. Confirmed at Carvico by the Bishop of the diocese, Mgr Gaetano Camillo Guindani.
1892–1895	A pupil at the minor seminary of Bergamo.

[1] For a more detailed chronology of His Holiness John XXIII cf. Loris Capovilla, *Giovanni XXIII, Sette Letture*, 2nd ed., Libr. Ed. Vaticana, 1963, pp. 226–71; and for the time he spent in France, 1944–53, cf. *Souvenirs d'un Nonce, Cahiers de France* (1944–53), Rome, Edizioni di Storia e Letteratura, 1963, pp. 233–72.

[2] His grandfather was Angelo, 1826–1914; his great-uncle, patriarch of the family, Zaverio, 1824–1912; his father Battista, 1854–1935; his mother Marianna Mazzola, 1854–1939. His brothers and sisters were: Maria Caterina, 1877–83; Teresa, 1879–1954 (married Michele Ghisleni in 1899); Ancilla, 1880–1953; Zaverio, 1883 (married Maria Carrara in 1907); Maria Elisa, 1884–1955; Assunta Casilda, 1886 (married Giovanni Battista Marchesi in 1907); Alfredo, 1889; Giovanni Francesco, 1891–1956 (married Caterina Formenti in 1919); Enrica, 1893–1918; Giuseppe Luigi, 1894 (married Ida Biffi in 1922); Luigi 1896–98.

1895–1900	A student at the major seminary of Bergamo, until his second year of theology.
1895	24 June. Received the clerical habit and the first tonsure.
1896	Beginning of *Journal of a Soul*.
1897	First written resolutions about 'Holy Purity'.
1898	3 July. Received the minor orders of porter and lector.
	28 August. At the closing ceremony of the celebrations for the sixteenth centenary of St Alexander, patron saint of Bergamo, he was present in the church of Sant'Alessandro in Colonna for the Pontifical Mass and heard the sermon preached by Cardinal Giuseppe Sarto, Patriarch of Venice (the future Pius X).
	25 September. Death of Father Francesco Rebuzzini, parish priest of Sotto il Monte.
1899	25 June. Received the minor orders of exorcist and acolyte.
	September. At Ghiaie di Bonate Sopra, in the house of Father Alessandro Locatelli, he met for the first time Mgr Giacomo Maria Radini Tedeschi.
1900	February. Retreat at the seminary of Bergamo.
	27 February. Consecration to the Sacred Heart of Jesus.
	September. Pilgrimage to Rome for Holy Year. On 20 September he went to Loreto and then to Assisi.

1901

January 4	At half past six in the morning he arrived in Rome, as a student of the major Roman Seminary, the Apollinare. He held a scholarship from the foundation of Canon Flaminio Cerasola.[1] Because of his youth, he began his theological studies again from the begin-

---

[1] The diocese of Bergamo, besides its major seminary in the city, has its own college in Rome, founded as early as 1640 by Canon Flaminio Cerasola, inaugurated in 1729, and now for the last hundred years absorbed into the Pontifical Roman Seminary. Here are lodged for their theological studies from ten to fifteen diocesan students recommended by the Bishop and chosen, after a competitive examination, by the Guardians of the *Confraternita dei Bergamaschi* in Rome, which administers the charitable foundation.

ning. With him were two clerical students from Bergamo, Achille Ballini from Boltiere and Guglielmo Carozzi from Curnasco.

10   Attended the multilingual congress in honour of Christ the Redeemer at the Collegio Urbano di Propaganda Fide, in the Piazza di Spagna.

31   Attended the performance of Lorenzo Perosi's Christmas Oratorio at the church of the Santi XII Apostoli.

April 28   First spiritual retreat at the Roman Seminary of the Apollinare.

June 25   Degree in theology. Prize for Hebrew.

November 30   Began his military service in the 73rd Infantry, Lombardy Brigade, at Bergamo, in the Umberto I Barracks.

1902

May 31   Promoted Corporal.

November 15   Indefinite leave while awaiting discharge.

30   Promoted Sergeant.

Rome. Returned to his studies at the Roman Seminary.

Prefect of young students of theology.

December 10–20   Retreat at the Roman Seminary, after military service.

1903

January 2   Father Domenico Spolverini was appointed Vice-rector of the Roman Seminary.

17   Present at the funeral of Cardinal Lucido Maria Parocchi at the church of San Lorenzo in Damaso.

April 1–10   Retreat in preparation for the subdiaconate.

11   Ordained subdeacon at the church of St John Lateran by Cardinal Respighi, Vicar General to the Pope.

29   Watched the procession of Edward VII, King of England and Emperor of India, to the Vatican.

May 2   Watched the procession of the Emperor of Germany, William II, to the Vatican.

July 20   Death of Pope Leo XIII.

August 4–10   Election and coronation of Pope Pius X.

December 9–18	Retreat, in preparation for the diaconate.
18	Ordained deacon at St John Lateran by Cardinal Respighi.

1904

July 13	Received doctorate in sacred theology. Professor Eugenio Pacelli was Invigilator at the written examination.
August 1–10	Retreat under the Passionists at the Church of SS. Giovanni e Paolo, Rome.
10	Ordained priest at the church of Santa Maria in Monte Santo in the Piazza del Popolo by Mgr Giuseppe Ceppetelli, Titular Patriarch of Constantinople, Vicegerent.

His first Masses were said as follows:

11	At St Peter's, in the Crypt. The same day he was received in special audience by Pope Pius X.
12	At Roccantica, the country villa of the Roman Seminary. He visited the Cathedral of Orvieto.
13	In Florence, at the church of the Santissima Annunziata.
14	In Milan, at the Cathedral, at the altar of St Charles.
15	At Sotto il Monte, for the feast of the Assumption, the titular feast of his native parish.
November	Resumed his studies in the higher classes of the Roman Seminary at the Apollinare.
December 1–4	Rome. He took part in the Marian Congress for the fifteenth anniversary of the proclamation of the Immaculate Conception of Mary. The promoter of the Congress was Mgr Giacomo M. Radini Tedeschi.

1905

January 8	Beatification of Jean-Marie Vianney, the Curé d'Ars. In the afternoon, after the papal choir music in St Peter's, the appointment of the Vatican Canon, Mgr Giacomo Maria Radini Tedeschi, as Bishop of Bergamo, was announced.
9	Mgr Bugarini presented Father Angelo Roncalli to Mgr Radini.

January 29	In the Sistine Chapel Pius X consecrated Mgr Giacomo M. Radini Tedeschi as Bishop; Father Angelo Roncalli, appointed secretary to the new Bishop, acted as his ordinary chaplain and held the book of the Gospels on the shoulders of Mgr Radini.
March 23	Visited the Abbey of Grottaferrata.
30	Visited the original Benedictine monastery of Subiaco.
April 2	Mgr Radini left Rome.
9	Arrival of Mgr Radini at Bergamo.
19–21	Retreat in the monastery of the Camaldolesi of Frascati.
30— May 17	First pilgrimage to Lourdes. Also visited Lyons, Paray-le-Monial, Ars and Montpellier.
December 8	Mgr Radini began his pastoral visitation. Father Roncalli accompanied him as his secretary. First friendly contacts with Cardinal Andrea Ferrari, Archbishop of Milan.

1906

September 19— October 22	Pilgrimage to Palestine.
October	Began teaching Church history in the diocesan seminary; later on he was also to hold the chair of apologetics and then that of patrology.

1907

September 1–7	Retreat at Martinengo (Bergamo) with the Religious of the Holy Family.
December 4	Lecture on Cardinal Cesare Baronius on the third centenary of his death.

1908

Began his historical account of *Gli Atti della Visita Apostolica di san Carlo Borromeo a Bergamo, 1575* (*Records of the Apostolic Visit of St Charles Borromeo to Bergamo*).

First meetings with the Prefect of the Ambrosian Library of Milan, Mgr Achille Ratti.

September 10–19   Pilgrimage to Lourdes. Visited Marseilles, Toulouse and Nîmes.

October 25–31   Retreat at Martinengo.

1909

January   Publication of the first number of *La Vita Diocesana*, the official periodical of the Bishop and Diocesan Curia. Printed at the Tipografia Vescovile Seccomandi, Via Pignolo 103, Bergamo. Editor: Rev. Dr Guglielmo Carozzi. Father Angelo Roncalli was on the editorial staff.

September 19–25 Retreat at Martinengo.

November 3   Mgr Radini instituted the Diocesan Congregation of the Priests of the Sacred Heart.

1910

April 26–28   The 33rd Synod of the diocese of Bergamo, of which Father Angelo Roncalli was secretary.

October 2–8   Retreat at Martinengo.

20   After the approval of the new diocesan statutes of Catholic Action he was appointed president of its fifth division. Niccolò Rezzara was general president.

1911

June 11   At Padua with Mgr Radini he took part in the celebrations for the 150th anniversary of the beatification of Gregory Barbarigo.

July 30—   Stayed at Einsiedeln in Switzerland, and made visits
August 12   to Geneva, Fribourg and Annecy.

October 1–9   Retreat at Martinengo.

November 6   Was inscribed as a Member (external) of the Diocesan Congregation of the Priests of the Sacred Heart.

1912

September 11   Pilgrimage to Mariazell in Austria.

12–16   Vienna for the 23rd International Eucharistic Congress. Celebrated Mass in the Capuchin Fathers' church of St Augustine (Augustinerkirche).

September 17	Cracow. Celebrated Mass in the Cathedral. Visited the salt mines of Wieliczka.
19	Budapest. Celebrated Mass in St Peter's Church.
21	Publication of the collective letter of the Lombard episcopate: *Il XVI centenario dell' editto di Milano e la libertà della religione nelle scuole* (The 16th centenary of the Edict of Milan and religious liberty in schools). Father Roncalli edited the text, at the request of his Bishop, with permission from Cardinal Ferrari.
October 13–19	Retreat at Martinengo.

1913

August 8	Celebrated Mass at the shrine of Oropa, Piedmont.
October 19–25	Retreat at Martinengo.

1914

August 20	Death of Pope Pius X.
22	Death of Mgr Radini.
September 27—October 3	Retreat with the Priests of the Sacred Heart at Bergamo.

1915

May 24	Recalled to military service. Organized the 'Soldier's Mass' in Bergamo, and was co-ordinator of religious assistance to the troops.

1916

March 28	Military Chaplain to the reserve hospital at Bergamo, called the 'new hospital' (*ricovero nuovo*), and of others in various places.
August 22	Publication of his volume: *In memoria di Mons. Giacomo Radini Tedeschi, vescovo di Bergamo*, Società Editrice S. Alessandro, Bergamo.
September 24	Presented this volume to Pope Benedict XV.

1918

November	Opened the Students' Hostel (*Casa dello Studente*)

in Bergamo in the Palazzo Marenzi, via San Salvatore, 8.

December 10   Finished his military service. Was appointed spiritual director of the seminary at Bergamo.

1919

April 28—May 3   Retreat with the Priests of the Sacred Heart in Bergamo.

1920

September 9   Addressed the Sixth National Italian Eucharistic Congress held in Bergamo on the theme 'The Eucharist and Our Lady as objects of the Christian's love'.

December 10   Received the first notice of his appointment to Rome in the service of Propaganda Fide.

1921

January 18   Rome. At the Sacred Congregation of Propaganda Fide. Began his work as president of the central Council for Italy of the Pontificie Opere Missionarie (Papal Missions).

February 2   The Cardinal Archbishop of Milan, Andrea Carlo Ferrari, died in Milan. Father Angelo Roncalli, deeply moved, was present at his funeral on 7 February.

April 1   He started a tour of the Italian dioceses in order to spread the missionary ideal and to organize the Pontificie Opere della Propagazione della Fede.

October 29   Celebrated Mass in the Marian shrine of Bonaria in Sardinia.

December 5–7   Retreat at Montecassino.

17–30   Travelled in France, Belgium, Holland and Germany. Celebrated Mass in the following places:

17   Chambéry Cathedral.

18–19   Fourvière, Lyons.

20   Paris, Redemptorist Fathers.

21   Paris, Montmartre.

22   Paris, Redemptorist Fathers.

23	Brussels, Redemptorist Fathers.
24	Aachen Cathedral.
25–28	Witten, in Holland, Redemptorist Fathers.
27	Cologne Cathedral.
28–29	Munich Cathedral.

1922

June 13	Death in Rome of Francesco Pitocchi, Redemptorist, formerly spiritual director of the Roman Seminary.

1924

January 13–19	Retreat at Villa Carpegna, Rome.
February 14	Mgr Vincenzo Bugarini, formerly Rector of the Roman Seminary, died in the home of Mgr Roncalli at Santa Maria in Via Lata.
November	Appointed Professor of patrology at the *Pontificio Ateneo Lateranense* (the Lateran University).

1925

March 3	Appointed Apostolic Visitor in Bulgaria and raised to the episcopate with the title, *pro hac vice*, of Archbishop of Areopolis.
13–17	Retreat at Villa Carpegna (Rome).
19	Consecrated Bishop by Cardinal Giovanni Tacci, Secretary of the Sacred Congregation for the Eastern Church, at San Carlo al Corso (Rome); assistant consecrating Bishops were Mgr Francesco Marchetti Selvaggiani and Mgr Giuseppe Palica.
April 25	Began his residence in Sofia, Ulitza Lioulin, 3.
August 26	Courtesy visit to the Holy Bulgarian Synod in Sofia, and meeting with the Metropolitan Stefan Gheorghiev.

1926

November 27—December 2	Retreat in Rome at the monastery of St Paul, accompanied by Father Kurteff. Retreat given by the Abbot Ildefonso Schuster.

December 5   Present at the church of San Clemente in Rome at the episcopal consecration of Mgr Stefan Cyril Kurteff, Titular Bishop of Briula, Apostolic Exarch for the Bulgarian Catholics of the Byzantine rite in Bulgaria.

1927

August 20   Meeting with the Armenian Archbishop of Nicomedia, Primate of Bulgaria, Stépanosse Hovagnimian.[1]

November 1–4   Guest of the seminary at Bressanone.

9–13   Retreat at Ljubljana in Slovenia, Jesuit House.

1928

December 20–24 Retreat at Babek on the Bosporus, Istanbul, villa of the Lazarist Fathers. Immediately afterwards he began his Apostolic Visit to the Georgian Catholics of Turkey, which ended on 5 February, 1929.

1929

August 17   Czestochowa. Celebrated Mass in the national Marian shrine of Poland.

September 21   Sotto il Monte. Consecrated the parish church.

1930

April 28—May 4 Retreat at Rustchuk in Bulgaria, with the Passionist Fathers.

1931

June 18–21   Retreat at Bujukada (Istanbul) with the Conventual Franciscans.

September 26   Appointed first Apostolic Delegate to Bulgaria.

1933

September 4–8   Retreat at Sofia with the Capuchin Fathers.

---

[1] During the Audience granted to the Observers at the Second Vatican Council, on 13 October, 1962, John XXIII spoke of this priest (cf. *L'Osservatore Romano*, 14–15 October, 1962).

1934

August 27–31	Retreat at Rustchuk in Bulgaria with the Passionist Fathers.
September	Sofia. President of the Congress of Byzantine studies.
November 24	Transferred to the Apostolic Delegation to Turkey and Greece and appointed Apostolic Administrator of the Apostolic Vicariate of Istanbul.
30	His title *pro hac vice* Archbishop of Areopolis was changed to that of Archbishop of Mesembria.

1935

January 4	Took leave of the Bulgarians.
5	Arrived at the Apostolic Delegation in Istanbul.
May 3–12	First apostolic tour of Greece and the islands.
June 13	In Turkey the government decrees prescribing lay attire for the clergy in public were announced.
July 28	Death of his father, Battista Roncalli, at Sotto il Monte.
December 15–22	Retreat in Istanbul.

1936

January 12	Initiated Sunday catechetical instruction at the Cathedral and the recital of the Divine Praises in Turkish.
April 18— May 29	Greece. He visited Corinth, Nauplia, Mycenae, Epidaurus, Delphi and Thebes in Boeotia. From 17–20 May on Mount Athos.
	Publication of the first volume of *Gli Atti della Visita Apostolica di San Carlo Borromeo a Bergamo* (see note p. xvi)
October 13–16	Retreat at Ranica (Bergamo), villa of the Daughters of the Sacred Heart.

1937

May 4–8	Visited the monasteries of Yalova, Gemlik and Bursa in Asia Minor. Also to Nicaea and to Mudanya.
July 25	Consecrated Mgr Antonio Gregorio Vuccino, Bishop of Syra, Greece.

August 7–30	Greece. Visited the islands of Tinos, Delos, Syra and Corfu. Then Patras, Aghis Laura, Olympia, Sparta, Messene and Tripolis. On board the ship *Kephallinia*, near Patras, he met the Greek Archbishop John Chrysostom Papadopoulos.
December 12–18	Retreat in Istanbul.

1938

January 30	Celebrations for the fifteenth centenary of the translation from Cappadocia to Istanbul of the remains of St John Chrysostom.
February 20	Consecrated Mgr Giuseppe Descuffi Archbishop of Smyrna (Izmir).
March 6	Began the pastoral Visitation of the Apostolic Vicariate of Istanbul.
November 1–10	In Greece; visited Volos, the Meteora monasteries, Thebes and Chalcis.

1939

February 20	Death of his mother, Marianna Mazzola, at Sotto il Monte.
May 27	At the Phanar he paid an official visit to the Patriarch Benjamin, to thank him, in the name of the Holy See, for his participation in the mourning of the Catholic Church for the death of Pope Pius XI, and in the universal rejoicings for the election of Pius XII.
June 1–6	Beirut. Cardinal Eugène Tisserant presided over the Eucharistic Congress.
7–10	Palestine: Jerusalem, Jaffa, Palmyra, Homs and Aleppo.
July	He published the volume, *Gli inizi del seminario di Bergamo e san Carlo Borromeo. Note storiche con una introduzione sul Concilio di Trento e la fondazione dei primi seminari*, Società Anonima Editrice S. Alessandro, Bergamo.
November 12–18	Retreat at Istanbul with the Jesuit Fathers of Ayas Pasa.

1940

November 25—
December 1

Retreat at Terapia (Istanbul) with the sisters of Our Lady of Sion.

1941

June 26—July 8

At Sofia. Meeting with the Orthodox Metropolitan Stefan.

July 8—October 7

Visited war-devastated Greece. On 10 September met the Archbishop of Athens, Damaskinos.

1942

October 25–31

Retreat at the Delegation in Istanbul.

1944

December 6

Received confidential information of his appointment as Apostolic Nuncio to Paris.

22   Nominated Apostolic Nuncio in France.

23   Departure from Istanbul.

24–27   Christmas at Ankara.

27–28   Travelling by air via Cairo, Benghazi, Naples to Rome.

29   Audience with Pius XII.

30   Arrived at Orly airport, Paris.

1945

January 1

Presented his credentials. In the name of the Diplomatic Corps he offered New Year greetings to General Charles de Gaulle, President of the provisional government of the Republic.

March 26–April 2

Retreat in the Benedictine Abbey of Solesmes.

June 22–27

Lyons, for the seventh centenary of the First Ecumenical Council of Lyons. Visited Ars and the Abbey of Cluny.

September 18

Visited German prisoners of war at Chartres, paying special attention to the many seminarists among them. He supported the efforts of the heroic Abbé Franz Stock, and with the help of the Holy See and the collaboration of generous priest instructors from Germany, he was able to start regular courses of theological studies and ecclesiastical training in that concentration camp.

1946

June 11	Consecrated Mgr Alfredo Pacini, Titular Archbishop of Germia.
August 15	Celebrated Pontifical Mass in the Marian shrine of Our Lady of La Salette (France).

1947

December 8–13	At Clamart in 'Manresa', the country house of the Jesuit Fathers, for the annual retreat.

1948

November 23–27	At En Calcat (Dourgne), a Benedictine monastery, for annual retreat.

1949

June 29	Ordained forty-nine priests at Notre-Dame in Paris, during the vacancy caused by the death of Cardinal Emanuel Suhard.

1950

February 15–23	In Belgium and Holland, staying at the Apostolic Nunciatures of Brussels and the Hague. Visited Namur, Louvain, Malines, Antwerp, Ghent, Bruges, Schoten, Amsterdam and Rotterdam.
March 18–April 15	Visit to North Africa. Arrived at Algiers in the m.v. *La Ville d'Oran* on 19 March, twenty-fifth anniversary of his consecration as Bishop.
April 6–9	Retreat at Oran, in the Bishop's palace.
16–20	Visited various places and shrines in Spain.
November 1	Rome. Present at the proclamation of the dogma of the Assumption of Mary.

1952

April 10–12	Retreat at Montmartre in Paris, at the Convent of the Carmelite Nuns.
August 30— September 1	Visited Savoy for the 350th anniversary of St Francis de Sales' consecration as Bishop.
November 10	Because of the grave illness of the Patriarch of Venice, Pius XII asked Mgr Roncalli to accept promotion to that See, when it should fall vacant.
29	Announcement of his promotion to the Cardinalate.
December 28	Death of Mgr Carlo Agostini, Patriarch of Venice.

1953

January 12	Created a Cardinal.
15	Received his Cardinal's *biretta* from Vincent Auriol, President of the French Republic. On the same day Pius XII announced in Consistory the promotion of the new Cardinal to the Patriarchate of Venice.
March 15	On *Laetare* Sunday (the fourth Sunday in Lent) celebrated Mass at the altar of the Blessed Gregory Barbarigo in the Cathedral of Padua. In the afternoon made his solemn entrance into Venice.
May 15–21	Retreat at Fietta del Grappa with the Episcopate of the Three Venetias.
August 26	Bergamo. Consecrated as Bishop Mgr Giacomo Testa, Apostolic Delegate in Turkey and Greece, Titular Archbishop of European Heraclea.
September 11–13	Turin. Took part in the National Eucharistic Congress. In the evening of 11 September, at the Alfieri Theatre, gave a talk on the subject 'The Eucharist as the foundation of social solidarity and peace'.
20	Venice. In the Carmelite church consecrated his auxiliary, Mgr Augusto Gianfranceschi, Titular Bishop of Emeria.
26	Somasco (Bergamo). Consecrated the altar of the chapel dedicated to 'Mary, Mother of Orphans'.
27	Piacenza. Consecrated Bishop Silvio Oddi, Apostolic Delegate to Jerusalem and Palestine, Titular Archbishop of Mesembria.
October 29	Castel Gandolfo. Received his Cardinal's hat.

1954

February 28	Began his pastoral visitation of the diocese of Venice.
May 28–June 1	Rome. Present at the canonization of St Pius X.
June 6–12	Retreat at Torreglia (Padua) with the Bishops of the Three Venetias.
29	Set his spiritual testament in order and made various arrangements, which were further revised at different times, until the final note of 12 September, 1961.
July 8–15	Lourdes. Took part in the pilgrimage from the Three Venetias.
16–28	Pilgrimage in Spain.
29	Stopped at the Abbey of Saint-Michel de Cuxa (Perpignan, France) to venerate the relics of the Venetian Doge, St Peter Orseolo.
August 29	Crowned the Madonna del Bosco (at Imbersago, Como).
October 20–31	The Lebanon. Papal Legate at the National Marian Congress at Beirut.

1955

May 20–25	Retreat at Torreglia (Padua) with the episcopate of the Three Venetias.
September 5	Inaugurated the celebrations for the fifth centenary of the death of St Lawrence Giustiniani.

1956

May 4	Lecce, Fifteenth National Eucharistic Congress. Spoke on the theme 'The Holy Eucharist and Social Life'.
9–15	Fatima. Present at the national celebrations of the twenty-fifth anniversary of the consecration of Portugal to the Immaculate Heart of Mary. In Lisbon, visited the Italian colony and the Patriarchal Seminary.
June 11–15	Retreat with his clergy in the seminary in Venice.
September 5	Close of the celebrations for the fifth centenary of St Lawrence Giustiniani, which were honoured

during the year by the presence and addresses of the Cardinals Lercaro, Archbishop of Bologna; Piazza, Secretary of the Sacred Consistory; Siri, Archbishop of Genoa; Feltin, Archbishop of Paris, and Mgr Montini, Archbishop of Milan.

1957

February 17   At the Teatro Regio of Parma he commemorated, twenty-five years after his death, Mgr Guido Maria Conforti, the revered Bishop of that illustrious See and the founder of the Xaverian Institute for Foreign Missions.

June 2–7   Retreat at Torreglia (Padua) with the Bishops of the Three Venetias.

September 18   Palermo. Speech at the Seventh week of Prayer and Study of the Association for the Christian East.

November 24   Venice. Reconsecrated the High Altar at St Mark's and opened the Thirty-first Diocesan Synod, which was held from 25–27 November.

1958

March 2–3   Went to Milan for the translation from Venice of the body of Mgr Angelo Ramazzotti, formerly Patriarch of Venice, and associate founder of the Institute of Foreign Missions.

24–25   Consecrated the underground church of St Pius X at Lourdes.

September 1   Castelfranco (Treviso). Present at the Tri-Venetian celebration for the centenary of the ordination of St Pius X to the priesthood.

22–26   At Col Draga di Possagno. Joined the retreat of the Venetian clergy.

October 9   Death of Pius XII.

12   Left Venice for the Conclave.

25   Entered the Conclave.

28   Afternoon. Elected Pope. Took the name of John XXIII.

November 4   Solemn Coronation.

November 23	Took possession of the Lateran Arch-Basilica.
30	Celebrated Mass at the Collegio Urbano di Propaganda Fide, on the Janiculum.
30— December 6	Retreat in the Vatican, Matilda Chapel.

1959

January 25	At the Benedictine monastery of St Paul he announced the holding of a Synod for the Roman Diocese and a Council for the Universal Church.
April 16	At the Lateran he celebrated the 750th anniversary of the Franciscan Rule.
May 11	Venerated the sacred remains of St Pius X and St John Bosco in St Peter's Square.
June 29	First Encyclical *Ad Petri Cathedram*.
August 1	Encyclical *Sacerdotii Nostri primordia* for the centenary of the death of the saintly Curé d'Ars.
25	Visited the shrine of the Mother of Good Counsel (*Mater Boni Consilii*) at Genazzano, and the hermitage of St Francis at Bellegra on the Alban Hills.
September 26	Encyclical *Grata recordatio* on devotion to the Holy Rosary.
October 11	Presented the crucifix to 510 missionaries in St Peter's.
November 28	Encyclical *Princeps Pastorum* for the fortieth anniversary of the *Maximum illud* of Benedict XV.
29— December 5	Retreat in the Vatican, Matilda Chapel

1960

May 26	At the Lateran. Canonization of St Gregory Barbarigo.
June 30	Apostolic Letter *Inde a primis* on the devotion to the Precious Blood.
September 12	Went to Roccantica in the Sabine Hills, thence to launch, with the students of the Papal Roman Seminary, the world-wide appeal to seminarists for prayer for the Ecumenical Council.
23	Visited the original monastery of Subiaco.
29	Apostolic Letter *Il religioso convegno* on the recital of

the rosary, and as an appendix, *Piccolo saggio di devoti pensieri distribuiti per ogni decina del rosario con riferimento alla triplice accentuazione: mistero, riflessione e intenzione* (Some devout thoughts for each decade of the rosary, with three-fold emphasis on mystery, reflection, intention).

November 13 Celebrated Mass in the 'divine liturgy' of the Byzantine rite at St Peter's.

27— Retreat in the Vatican, Matilda Chapel.
December 3

1961

May 15 Encyclical *Mater et Magistra* for the seventieth anniversary of Leo XIII's encyclical *Rerum Novarum*.

August 10–15 Retreat at Castel Gandolfo.

September 19 Visited the catacombs of San Callisto.

November 11 Encyclical *Aeterna Dei,* for the fifteenth centenary of the death of St Leo the Great.

26— Retreat in the Vatican, Matilda Chapel.
December 2

3 Letter-testament to the Roncalli family.

25 Promulgation of the Apostolic Letter *Humanae salutis,* with which he announced that the Second Ecumenical Vatican Council was to be called in 1962.

1962

January 6 Apostolic Exhortation *Sacrae Laudis,* on the saying of the Divine Office for the intention of the Council.

February 2 *Motu proprio: Consilium,* to announce that the opening date of the Council was to be 11 October.

May 3 Papal Letter *Amantissimo Patris consilio* to Cardinal Agagianian, for the fortieth anniversary of the *motu proprio: Romanum Pontificum.*

July 1 Encyclical *Poenitentiam agere,* for fervent prayer and penance for the success of the Council.

2 Letter *Il Tempio Massimo* to nuns, asking for their special prayers for the Council.

September 6 The *motu proprio: Appropinquante Concilio* to announce the regulations for the Ecumenical Council.

September 8–16	Retreat in the Vatican, in the tower of San Giovanni.
23	First signs of the disease which attacked his strong constitution.
October 4	Pilgrimage to Loreto and Assisi.
11	With magnificent ceremonial and an inspired discourse from the Pope, the Second Ecumenical Vatican Council began. In the evening he spoke to the people joyfully gathered in St Peter's Square for a torchlight procession.
12	Received in the Sistine Chapel the special Missions which had been present at the opening of the Council.
13	Received in the Sistine Chapel the journalists who had come to Rome from all parts of the world. In the afternoon, in the Consistory Hall, received the observers representing non-Catholic communities who were attending the Council, and the guests of the Secretariat for Christian Unity.
14	In the church of Sant'Agostino, venerated the Madonna there invoked under the title of her Divine Maternity.
25	Addressed to the rulers of all peoples a message imploring the exercise of wisdom and prudence for the peace of the world.
November 4	St Peter's. A papal choir sang the Mass in the Ambrosian rite, for the anniversary of his coronation. Cardinal Montini, Archbishop of Milan, celebrated the Mass. Discourse in praise of the pastoral spirit of St Charles. In the afternoon in the church of San Carlo al Corso he venerated the relic of the heart of St Charles.
13	At Sant'Andrea al Quirinale with the Polish Bishops he venerated St Stanislaus Kostka on his feast day.
December 8	Preached a sermon in St Peter's to close the first Session of the Second Vatican Council.

1963

February 10	In the Clementine Hall signed the decree introducing the beatification cause of Cardinal Andrea Carlo Ferrari, Archbishop of Milan, and blessed the found-

ation stone of the new Lombard Seminary on the Esquiline.

March 1	Was awarded the International Peace Prize of the Eugenio Balzan Foundation.
18	In the Clementine Hall blessed the foundation stone of the new Missionary College of John XXIII, to be erected at Sotto il Monte.
19	Beatification of Luigi Maria Palazzolo, a Bergamasque priest, Founder of the Istituto delle Poverelle.
31	Sent a telegram to the Cardinal Vicar announcing his imminent encyclical *Pacem in terris*.
April 9-10	Publication and distribution of the encyclical *Pacem in terris*, which bears the date 11 April, Holy Thursday.
May 10	Received the Eugenio Balzan Peace Prize.
17	Celebrated holy Mass for the last time.
20	Last day of Audiences.
31	With a joyful heart he prepared to return to God. He asked to receive the Last Sacraments, and said a few grave and solemn words.
June 3	At the end of the Mass celebrated by Cardinal Luigi Traglia in St Peter's Square, he died a serene and holy death at 7.49 p.m. The window of his apartment was illuminated. 'And his lamp is the lamb' (cf. Rev. 21:23).

4. View of Sotto il Monte

5. The house in which Pope John was born, from the street

I

Journal of a Soul

Exercises and Spiritual Notes
1895—1962

6. The courtyard of the house

1895—1900

In the Seminary at Bergamo

1895

[1]   *Rules of life to be observed by young men who wish to make progress in the life of piety and study*[1]

'Sic decet omnino clericos in sortem Domini vocatos vitam moresque suos omnes componere, ut habitu, gestu, incessu, sermone, aliisque omnibus rebus, nil nisi grave, moderatum ac religione plenum prae se ferant; levia etiam delicta, quae in ipsis maxima essent, effugiant, ut eorum actiones cunctis afferant venerationem' (*Ex. act. S. Concilii Tridentini*, Session XXII, Decretum de reformatione, c. 1).[2]

'Bonum est viro cum portaverit iugum ab adolescentia sua' (*Lamentations* 3: 27).[3]

First and main principle: choose a spiritual director from among the most exemplary, prudent and learned, in whom you may have full trust, and on whom you may depend entirely, accepting his advice and direction with complete confidence.

[1] The 'Rules of Life' seem to be a personal re-elaboration of the confidential 'Little Rules' which the young cleric received from his spiritual director in 1895, and which are printed in full in Appendix 2. The 'Little Rules' (*regoline*) constituted a method of more perfect ascetic life than the ordinary rules of the *Istituto*. The spiritual directors communicated them discreetly to some of the best students, who formed the Sodality of the Annunciation of Mary Immaculate. The fourteen-year-old Angelo Roncalli, who received the tonsure in 1895, was at once admitted to the knowledge and practice of the 'Little Rules'. He copied them out by hand, in minute writing, kept them always by him and constantly observed them, even when he was Pope. In the spiritual notes of the following years there are frequent references to the Rules, which in all probability are these, found in his first notebook.
The solemn Latin words which precede the text of this first notebook, and so form a preface to the whole of *Journal of a Soul*, give a detailed picture of the character of a 'cleric'. These are words which, as Bishop and Pope, he never ceased to repeat and comment upon.
[2] 'Thus it is in every way fitting that clergy who have been called to the service of the Lord should so order their lives and habits that in their dress, gestures, gait, conversation and all other matters they show nothing that is not grave, controlled and full of religious feeling; and let them also avoid minor faults which in them would be very great, so that their actions may receive the respect of all.'
[3] 'It is good for a man that he bear the yoke in his youth' (Lamentations 3: 27).

Every day

(1) Devote at least a quarter of an hour to mental prayer as soon as you get out of bed in the morning.

(2) Hear, or better, serve Holy Mass.

(3) Devote a quarter of an hour to spiritual reading.

(4) In the evening, before going to bed, make a general examination of conscience, followed by an act of contrition, and prepare the points for the next day's meditation.

(5) Before dinner or before supper, or at least before the general evening examination, make a particular examination concerning the best way to rid yourself of certain vices or failings and concerning the acquiring of certain virtues.

(6) Be diligent in attending the meetings of the Sodality on feast days, in school and in study circles on week days, and always allow sufficient time for study when you are at home.

(7) Visit the Blessed Sacrament and some church or chapel where there is a special devotion to the Blessed Virgin, at least once a day.

(8) Recite five Our Fathers and five Hail Marys in honour of the wounds of Our Lord Jesus Christ, between six and nine o'clock in the evening, and make at least three acts of self-mortification in honour of the Virgin Mary.

(9) Recite the other vocal prayers and practise the other usual devotions to the Virgin Mary, to St Joseph, to the patron saints and the Holy Souls. These devotions must however meet with the approval of your own director, as must also the books for meditation and spiritual reading.

(10) Read carefully and thoughtfully a whole chapter, or at least a part of one, of the very devote Latin book of Thomas à Kempis.

(11) So as to be constant in your observation of these points, arrange the hours of your day, and set apart the special time for prayer, study and other devotions, for recreation and sleep, after consulting with your Spiritual Father.

(12) Make a habit of frequently raising your mind to God, with brief but fervent invocations.

Every week

(1) Make your confession and communion.

(2) Fast on Friday and Saturday.

(3) On these days perform some penance, on the advice of your Spiritual Father.

(4) On these days devote also an extra quarter of an hour to prayer or

spiritual reading and this, if possible, in the quiet of some church. Instead of this you may give or attend some lectures on a spiritual subject, or perform any other act of piety substituted by your director at his choice.

(5) When sitting or walking with one or more companions, discuss good and spiritual things. The subject for the discussion might be taken from the morning meditation, or from the spiritual reading, or from some of the Rules, sharing with others in friendly conversation the pious feelings these have aroused in you, or other feelings the Lord has inspired.

(6) Every Saturday relate, or listen to someone else relating, an example or miracle from the life of Mary most holy and let this inspire in you some moral or devout reflections.

(7) Always ask pardon sincerely of your director if you have failed in any of these above-mentioned matters; tell him if you are to blame for every other infraction of the Rule, and ask him to set you a penance.

Every month

(1) Choose one day for more profound recollection, in order to examine yourself more closely concerning the remedying of faults, progress in virtue, and observance of the Rule.

(2) Choose one of the most exemplary and zealous youths and beg him attentively to observe your behaviour; let him tell you with candour and charity about any faults he may see in you, warning you about these on that day, or as soon as possible.

(3) When this has been done, go to your spiritual director and confer with him about this matter and any other special points that may arise; accept his counsels and be most careful to follow them.

(4) Make sure that the director is told about any failings on your part.

(5) Choose a saintly advocate in heaven every month, besides the usual saints.

Every year

(1) Make the Spiritual Exercises[1] here in the seminary during Carnival time, or in any other time or place, even if there is no special necessity because of ordinations; if there is any legitimate impediment, consult your own director.

(2) On the occasion, or at another more opportune time, make your general or annual confession.

---

[1] A systematic series of meditations on the fundamental truths of religion and the spiritual life, deriving from St Ignatius Loyola. When making the Spiritual Exercises, one goes into retreat.

(3) Consult your director before going away for the holidays, and ask him to suggest rules for your behaviour during these.

(4) Before these holidays give some souvenir to your companions and accept one from them, to help you all to pass the time profitably in the Lord.

At all times

(1) Above all other evils beware of bad or unworthy companions, those whose speech contains impure suggestions, filthy or cynical words, or dialect expressions. Avoid those who cultivate the company of the other sex and talk about love-making; those who hang around in inns, or are intemperate, particularly in drinking; those who wish to be admired as revengeful, quarrelsome men, swift to draw a weapon; those who walk up and down or loiter in the squares and before the shops; those who go to gaming houses, or gamble even in private, with cards or dice, and in general those who are known to be youths rebellious to good discipline, averse to study and given over to frivolous pastimes.

(2) Never converse familiarly or play or jest or in any other manner show too much confidence with women, whatever may be their state in life, their age or relationship; never confide in them the slightest thing which might in any way be dangerous or suspect.

(3) Never play at forbidden games or even at games which are permitted, such as those with cards or dice, and least of all in public or where all sorts of people gather, and never linger to look on at these games.

(4) On no account or pretext must you use the intimate 'thou' in talking together or lay your hands on each other, or run after, push or strike each other, even in jest, nor should you indulge in other careless actions, words or gestures which might provoke scorn or be the cause of even greater danger.

(5) Take the greatest care to guard the stainless lily of purity, and to this end keep a close watch on your feelings; guard your eyes especially, never fixing your gaze on a woman's face, or on any other source of danger; and beware of eating or drinking too much or between meals, and of being idle.

(6) Make a special profession of humility, and for this purpose frequently reflect that of our own nature we are but filth, as far as our bodies are concerned, and ignorance and sin as regards our souls; and that, if there is anything good in us in nature, fortune or grace, it is a free gift from God. Beware therefore of praising yourself and of wishing to be esteemed more than, or even as much as, others.

(7) These two virtues must always be accompanied by the queen of all virtues, charity; the best way to exercise this virtue is to bear injuries with patience and be ready and willing to forgive them from your heart; show affection to the poor; above all, beware of material interests or desires, or too much attachment to money.

(8) Pray to the Lord for the conversion of sinners, all and sundry, and especially for those in the Sodality of the seminary, if any such there be. Try all possible and opportune means, if necessary seeking the advice of discreet and prudent persons and that of your own director, to remedy what is wrong with the greatest possible gentleness and secrecy, thus putting an end to the evil and the scandal, without giving the evil-doer a bad name.

(9) Before leaving the seminary, at the end of your studies, seek your director's advice about your employment and about the rules you should observe for the rest of your life.

Special rules for young clerics in ecclesiastical dress

(1) Whoever wears the ecclesiastical habit must make even greater endeavours to improve himself, and to work for his neighbour's welfare and salvation. This is an indispensable obligation of his state.

(2) He will always wear the cassock in town and in centres of population. When he is staying in the country or travelling, his clerical suit must always be decent and such as the Church prescribes; even at home he must always behave decorously and wear clerical dress.

(3) He will be cleanly, but without vanity in his clothing or in his person. He will cultivate modesty, dignity and decorum during liturgical functions, in churches and sacristies; with this in mind he will seek to become proficient in the sacred rites; he will observe the Church's regulations proper to his state, and will profess particular obedience to his Bishop.

(4) He will be more assiduous in study, and will not leave the seminary before he has completed his courses, so as to make himself as useful as possible in the service of God and for the salvation of others, in preaching, hearing confessions, and other such holy occupations, according to his capabilities.

(5) He will never desire or lay claim to any positions or benefices that are more honourable, easier or more profitable, but in matters of such import and danger he will always maintain indifference, resigned to the will of God, the judgment of his superiors and the advice of his own director. He must therefore never pursue his studies or do good works with a worldly end and intention in view, because by so doing he would forfeit

all merit, nor would he ever acquire solid virtue or that tranquillity and peace of mind 'which passes all understanding.'[1]

'Peace and mercy be upon all who walk by this rule.'[2]

Recommendations

All ecclesiastical students, especially those in holy orders (*in sacris*), are recommended to wear the girdle (*cinta*); they are advised that this is a great help towards perseverance and setting others a good example; it is part of a priest's prescribed attire; in the past it was regularly worn, and even now it is worn by the most strict and exemplary clerics, such as all ought to be. 'To know nothing contrary to the Rule is to know all things.'[3]

Additions

(1) If one of the . . .[4] is in special need, all must pray for him and offer a communion.

(2) Everyone must also every day, when offering his devotions to the Blessed Virgin, or at other times, recite for all the others . . . three Hail Marys to the Immaculate Conception, in order to obtain and preserve the most important gift of holy and lovable purity: chastity.

(3) Even those who are not priests must offer communion every month for all the others, that they may persevere steadily in the observance of the holy Rules, true personal devotion and ardent, untiring zeal for the spiritual good of others. Every year on a prescribed day the priests will offer a Mass with that same intention, especially for the preservation and good progress of . . . , as satisfaction for the sins of all, and to obtain for all true contrition for their own sins and eternal salvation.

(4) In the event of the death of any one of the . . . , those who are not priests will recite an Office for the Dead, hear a Mass, recite five decades of the rosary, fast on a Saturday or on another day, and offer a communion with the intention of applying a Mass as soon as he can, and gaining an indulgence.

Triduum to St Francis Xavier. 30 November

(1) We are to imitate him in his most profound humility and in our endeavours to know ourselves and our wretchedness of soul and body, in all our studies and good works desiring not the esteem, honour and

---

[1] Phil. 4: 7.   [2] Gal. 6: 16.

[3] Tertullian, *De praescriptionibus adversus haereticos*, chap. 14 (P.L., II, 27).

[4] Here, and further on, the blank spaces were left by the author.

good report of men but God alone, his glory, our own spiritual welfare and that of other souls.

(2) We are to imitate him in his mortification of self, subduing wherever possible our own will and our own desires, and mortifying ourselves a little even by external means, by not trying to find the most comfortable position to sit or kneel but contenting ourselves with the way we are, and controlling undisciplined desires to look, know, speak, etc.

(3) In imitation of his zeal, for the glory of God and the salvation of souls, we must attend Holy Mass with particular and extraordinary under-standing and faith, offering it for the health, prosperity and safety of the Pope, for the triumph of the Church and the conversion of infidels, desir-ing to acquire for ourselves that spirit of zeal, piety, humility and self-sacrifice, of scorn for all that is of this world, of which our fathers have given us such great and shining examples.

Four days of prayer in honour of St Francis de Sales. 25 January

Let us honour this great saint:

(1) By imitating him in his gentleness and by showing cheerfulness, good-nature and gaiety in all our dealings with others, yet always with dignity and modesty, especially with those who have been unkind to us, with people we do not like, with those who are tried and tempted or in difficulties, etc., doing our best to draw them to God.

(2) By imitating him in the severity with which he always treated him-self and by trampling upon, breaking down and mastering, so far as lies in our power, our own will and our own private judgment.

(3) By imitating him in his love of God, frequently offering ourselves to God with acts of self-immolation, and by holding ourselves ready and willing to do whatever he will deign to tell us that he wants us to do in these holy Exercises, meanwhile praying with fervour that we and our companions may live righteously.

(4) Finally, let us imitate him in his charity towards his neighbours, praying for sinners, for the success of the Catholic missions, for the Supreme Pontiff and the triumph of the Church.

A prayer that the will of God may be fulfilled

O most merciful Jesus, grant to me your grace, 'that it may be with me, and labour with me'[1] and persevere with me even to the end. Grant that I may always desire and will that which is to you most acceptable and most dear.

[1] Wisdom 9: 10.

Let your will be mine, and let my will ever respond to yours, in perfect accordance. Let me desire what you desire and hate what you hate, and let me desire and hate nothing but what you desire and hate. Let me die to all that is of this world and for your sake rejoice to be despised and ignored in this generation. Grant me, above all other desires, the desire to rest in you, that my heart may find its peace in you. You are the true peace of the heart, you are its only resting place; apart from you all things are harsh and restless. In this peace, in this very peace which is yourself, the one supreme, eternal Good, I will sleep and rest. Amen (Thomas à Kempis,[1] III, c. xv).

Prayer to Jesus Christ

O Lord Jesus Christ, who have deigned to call me, Angelo Giuseppe, your poor unworthy servant, to the life of a priest, not through any merits of my own but out of your charity alone, grant me I beseech you, through the intercession of my most holy and beloved Mother, Mary Immaculate, and of all my holy patron saints, to whose care I commend myself, that I, like your beloved John, burning with the fire of your charity and adorned with all virtues, especially humility, may be able to consecrate my soul and body and all my doings to the greater glory of your name, and that of your spouse the Catholic Church, and to inflame the hearts of all men with your love so that they may choose you alone and serve you alone. May there be restored on earth your kingdom, of which you are the eternal King, full of the blessings of charity and peace, you who with God the Father in the unity of the Holy Spirit live and reign, world without end. Amen.

---

[1] *The Imitation of Christ.*

1896

Resolutions made during the Spiritual Exercises of 1896 and confirmed in 1897 and 1898

Ad majorem Dei gloriam.[1]

(1) I resolve and promise never to approach the holy sacraments out of mere habit or with indifference, and never to spend less than a quarter of an hour in my preparation.

(2) I resolve moreover to persevere every day, and especially in the holidays, in my meditation, in general and particular examinations of conscience, in saying the rosary, in spiritual reading and in visits to the Blessed Sacrament, and in saying the other prayers usually recited in the seminary, and to do all this with great devotion and according to my time-table, which I promise to keep as faithfully as possible, both in the seminary and during the holidays.

(3) When I am told to do so I will also recite in honour of Mary most holy the Psalter[2] and the five Psalms, and also three Hail Marys for holy purity every day.

(4) I will watch myself most carefully, trying not to succumb to distractions during prayers, and especially during meditation, during the five Our Fathers after dinner, during Vespers and the recitation of the rosary. To this end, both when I am praying and at all other times, I will imagine myself in the presence of Jesus and with him on some occasion of his life, at the Last Supper, or on Calvary, etc.

(5) Above all, I will watch myself carefully, lest the tree of pride should grow in me; I will beware of this, keeping myself humble-minded and the lowliest of all, both in pious practices and in study.

(6) As regards my studies, I will apply myself to them with love and

---

[1] 'To the greater glory of God': St Gregory the Great, *Dialogues*, I, II (P.L., LXXVII, 160). Cf. also *Exercitia spiritualia Sancti Ignatii de Loyala et eorum Directoria* (*Monumenta Ignatiana, series secunda*), Matriti, 1919, p. 897.

[2] The Psalter (*Salterio*) referred to here would seem to be either the small book containing various psalms, which Italian children were given as a reading book, or Our Lady's Psalter.

enthusiasm to the best of my powers, taking care to give due attention to all subjects without any distinction, never proffering the excuse that I do not like any of them.

My sole object in studying will be to work for the greater glory of God, the honour of the Church, the salvation of souls, and not for my own honour, not in order to be cleverer than all the others—and I will always remind myself that God will ask me to render an account of that talent also which I have wasted in merely acquiring glory for myself.

(7) I will make a special effort to mortify myself, above all and at all times chastising my self-love, my besetting sin, avoiding all occasions which might foster it. Therefore I will not try to display my learning in conversation, I will never find excuses for any of my actions; indeed, I will consider the behaviour of others as always better than my own. I will not use phrases or words which give me an air of superiority, I will shun all praise, and will be most careful to curb my desire to show off, to hold people's attention or to attach any importance to myself.

(8) I will give myself no rest until I have acquired a great love and devotion to the Blessed Sacrament, which will always be the dearest object of my affections and my thoughts, indeed of my whole life as a seminarist and, if God so chooses, as a priest.

(9) I promise and I vow to Our Lady, who will always be my dearest Mother, to guard myself most scrupulously as far as lies in my power from any thought or act to which I might give consent, which might cast so much as a shadow over the heavenly virtue of holy purity. With this end in view I now and always invoke this Queen of Virgins, in order that she may help me to keep far from me the temptations which the devil will prepare to weaken my resolve.

(10) The devotion to the Sacred Heart in the Blessed Sacrament, which I must first of all show in my own behaviour, I will try to impart to others, especially to children, taking pleasure in speaking of this devotion, and I will do the same concerning devotion to Our Lady.

(11) I will never be unmindful of St Joseph, and will say some prayers to him every day for myself, for the dying and for the Church.

(12) During the Novenas[1] in the months of March, May, June and October, and at all times, I will try to mortify my own feelings, denying my appetites what they desire, and in the holidays, especially where there are people present, I will pay special attention to modesty, not so much in order to be an example to others as to avoid those occasions that might perhaps be harmful to me.

[1] Nine days' prayer in preparation for the great feasts of the Church's year.

(13) I myself will pray and will encourage others to pray to the Blessed Sacrament, to the Virgin and the saints, for the conversion of the East and, above all, for the return of the dissident Churches. I will never forget to pray for the Supreme Pontiff, for the triumph of the Church, for my own beloved Bishop, for my relations and benefactors, and especially for those to whom I owe most.

(14) To sum up, I will so behave that all my doings may be in accordance with the oft-repeated maxim of St Ignatius Loyola: 'To the greater glory of God.'

1897

3

Of holy purity

Through the grace of God and the intercession of my Mother, Mary most holy, I am convinced of the inestimable worth of holy purity and of my own very great need of it, called as I am to the angelic ministry of the priesthood. In order to preserve this shining mirror free from all stain, I have in these holy Exercises, with the approval of my Spiritual Father, written down the following resolutions, which I desire to keep most scrupulously. I offer them to the Virgin of Virgins by the hands of those three angelic youths, Aloysius Gonzaga, Stanislaus Kostka and John Berchmans, my special protectors,[1] so that she, through the merits of these three lilies of chastity, so precious in her sight, may deign to bless these resolves and grant me the grace to put them into practice.

(1) First of all, I am profoundly convinced that holy purity comes as a grace from God, and that without this grace I am incapable of it, and so in this matter I will start on the sure foundation of humility, distrusting myself and placing all my confidence in God and most holy Mary. Therefore every day I will pray to the Lord for the virtue of holy purity, and I will pray to him with particular fervour at holy communion, since it is in the Eucharist that he offers me the 'grain that shall make the young men flourish, and new wine the maidens'.[2] I will have a tender love for the Queen of Virgins. I will always offer the Hour of Prime of the Little

---

[1] In this Journal there frequently occur the names of the saints Aloysius, Stanislaus, and John Berchmans, who were all born within a few years of each other, followed each other into the Society of Jesus and resembled each other in their edifying deaths. All three were canonized. By their example of ready obedience to the divine call they showed the young people of their own and later generations how to follow a 'Little Way' in the heroic exercise of virtue, of purity and holiness of life. *Aloysius Gonzaga*, born at Castiglione delle Stiviere in 1568, died in Rome in 1591. He entered the Society of Jesus in 1585. He was beatified in 1605 and canonized in 1726. He was proclaimed patron saint of youth in 1729. *Stanislaus Kostka*, born at Rostkoff, Prasnysz, Poland, in 1550, died in Rome in 1568. He entered the Society of Jesus in 1567, was beatified in 1660 and canonized in 1726. *John Berchmans*, born at Diest, Brabant, in 1599, died in Rome in 1621. He entered the Society of Jesus in 1616; he was beatified in 1865 and canonized in 1888.

[2] Zech. 9: 17.

Office,[1] the first Hail Mary of the Angelus and the first decade of the rosary for the acquiring and preserving of holy purity. I will also ask Joseph, Mary's most chaste spouse, to help me, addressing to him twice a day the prayer 'O Guardian of Virgins',[2] and I will cultivate a devotion to the three saintly youths I have mentioned, whose purity I will try to copy in my own life.

(2) I will take pains to mortify my own feelings severely, keeping them within the bounds of Christian modesty; to this end I will set a special guard on my eyes, which St Ambrose called 'deceitful snares'[3] and St Anthony of Padua 'thieves of the soul',[4] avoiding, as far as possible, large gatherings of people for feasts, etc., and when I am obliged to be present on these occasions I will make quite sure that nothing that even suggests the sin against holy purity may offend my eyes: on such occasions they shall remain downcast.

(3) I will also take care to behave with the greatest decorum when I am passing through towns or other places full of people, never looking at posters or illustrations, or shops which might contain indecent objects, bearing in mind the words of Ecclesiasticus: 'Do not look around in the streets of a city; nor wander about in its deserted sections.'[5]

And even in the churches, besides behaving with edifying decorum during the sacred functions, I will never gaze at beautiful things of any sort, such as pictures, carvings, statues or other objects of art which, however slightly, offend against propriety, and particularly where paintings are concerned.

(4) With women of whatever station in life, even if they are related to me or are holy women, I will be particularly cautious, avoiding their familiarity, company or conversation, especially if they are young women. Nor will I ever fix my eyes on their faces, mindful of what the Holy Spirit teaches us: 'Do not look intently at a virgin, lest you stumble and incur penalties for her.'[6] So I will never confide in them in any way, but when I have to speak with them I will see that my speech is 'dry, brief, prudent and correct'.

(5) I will never hold in my hands or look at books containing frivolities or immodest pictures, and if I find any of these dangerous objects, even in my companions' hands, I will tear them up or burn them, unless by so doing a graver scandal should ensue.

[1] The Little Office of Our Lady.
[2] Prayer to St Joseph, 'O virginum custos' (Pope Pius IX), 4 February, 1877.
[3] Cf. De Poenitentia, I, 14, 73 (CSEL, LXXIII, VII, 153).
[4] Cf. Sermo II in Dominica II Quadragesimae.
[5] Ecclus. 9: 7.   [6] Ecclus. 9: 5.

(6) Besides giving an example of perfect modesty in my own speech, I must also, when with my family, try to keep the conversation free from subjects ill-befitting holy purity, never allowing anyone, especially in my presence, to speak of love-making or use any coarse or indecent words or sing love songs. I will always gently rebuke any immodesty on the part of others, and if they should persist I will go right away from them, showing my deep displeasure. In the seminary I will be most careful in this respect and on my guard to prevent any demonstrativeness or particular friendships among my companions, and all those acts and words which, though acceptable in the world, are unbecoming for clerics.

(7) At table, whether speaking or eating, I will never be greedy or immoderate; I will always find an opportunity for a little mortification; as regards the drinking of wine I will be more than moderate, because in wine lies the same danger as in women: 'Wine and women lead intelligent men astray.'[1]

(8) I will likewise observe the greatest modesty with regard to my own body at all times and in every movement of my eyes, hands and mind, etc., both in public and in private. To this end, then, and to remove any occasion for these movements, however innocent, at night before falling asleep I will place the rosary of the Blessed Virgin around my neck, fold my arms crosswise on my breast, and see that I find myself still lying in this position in the morning.

(9) In everything I will always remember that I must be as pure as an angel, and I will so bear myself that in everything about me, in my eyes, words and actions, may be seen that holy modesty shown in the highest degree by Saints Aloysius, Stanislaus and John Berchmans, a modesty that is pleasing, that commands reverence and is the expression of a chaste heart and soul, beloved of God.

(10) I will not forget that I am never alone, even when I am by myself: God, Mary and my Guardian Angel see me; and I am always a seminarist. When I am in danger of sinning against holy purity, then more urgently than ever will I appeal to God, to my Guardian Angel and to Mary, with my familiar invocation: 'Mary Immaculate, help me.' Then I will think of the scourging of Jesus Christ and of the Four Last Things, mindful of the Holy Spirit's words: 'In all you do remember the end of your life, and then you will never sin.'[2]

---

[1] Ecclus. 19: 2.   [2] Ecclus. 7: 40.

1898

27 February, 1898

Considering that it is only a week since I finished the Spiritual Exercises, I must admit that I have spent the time very badly, because of my continual distractions during prayers. Although I think I did my best to be attentive I cannot deny that sometimes these distractions were my own fault, because I was not sufficiently recollected in anything I did. In any case it has been a wretched week.

The worst of it is that, instead of making an act of humility when I became aware of these wandering thoughts, I grieved over them and became anxious. Enough of this, and may God forgive me! Evidently he wanted to disillusion me; he has put me to the test and shown me how worthless I am. Blessings on his name!

Now I am resolved to be more recollected, and may the most holy Virgin come to my aid, and my Guardian Angel and my own St John Berchmans! God knows that even in the midst of my miseries I love him and want everyone to love him. May he bless me and not despise me, although I am a sinner. 'Lord, you know that I love you.'[1]

6 March, Sunday

I have been less distracted at prayer, but still not always and entirely recollected. In these last days I have had little recourse to invocations, with the result that I have been less united with Jesus than hitherto.

The more I try to go forward the more I realize how backward I am. From now onwards I will try to be particularly recollected in the morning and at night, in the dormitory. I will utter innumerable invocations during the day and especially during recreation and study. I will be less of a chatterbox during recreation and will not let myself become too merry. I will so behave that Jesus may say to me as he said to St Teresa: 'I am called Jesus of Teresa.' First, however, as my name is Angelo, I

[1] Cf. John 21: 17.

must be an angel of Jesus. So be it. May St Joseph help me and give me his spirit of recollection. My Jesus, mercy.

13 March, Sunday

So many failings this week too! In school I have allowed myself to say frivolous or foolish things. I have made my examination of conscience in great haste and I have not maintained the necessary spirit of recollection on rising in the morning, which has meant that I have not got much good out of my meditation.

I have not even made very frequent invocations, as I had determined to do. This week I shall have to be very careful about these three points. I will not let myself be cast down when I think of my family's present situation. When this thought enters my mind I will implore the good Jesus to help them all, to grant them the spirit of resignation, and that he may forgive those who wrong them, so that no one will do anything which may be an offence to God.[1]

I shall refer this matter to Mary and St Joseph in order that truth and innocence may prevail. This is a very great trial for me. In any case, whatever the outcome, God be praised and his most holy will be done.

20 March, Sunday, during retreat

A month has already gone by since I came out from the holy Exercises. Where have I got to now in the way of virtue? Oh poor me!

Having made a general examination of my behaviour during these recent days, I have found good reason to blush and feel humble. I have found that all my actions are far from perfect; I have not meditated satisfactorily, I have not heard Holy Mass in the way I should, because I have allowed myself to be distracted as soon as I got up, while I was washing myself; I have not paid my visit to the Blessed Sacrament with all the fervour I used to feel; I have made my general self-examination with very little, if any, profit; I have let my thoughts wander, especially during Vespers; I have given way to the languor that the hot weather brings. In a word, I find that I am still at the very beginning of the journey which I have undertaken, and this makes me feel ashamed. I thought I could have been a saint by this time, and instead I am still as miserable as before.

---

[1] Financial difficulties. The Roncallis then worked as *mezzadri*, tenants who farm their land on the crop-sharing system, and the very large family group found it difficult to make ends meet.

All this must humiliate me profoundly and make me realize what a good-for-nothing I am. Humility, humility, still more humility! However, in all my distress I can still thank the Lord for not having abandoned me as I deserved. Thanks be to God, I still have the will to be good, and with this I must go on. Go on, do I say? I must start again from the beginning. Well, I will do so. What am I waiting for? 'In the name of the Father and of the Son and of the Holy Ghost, under the protection of the Virgin Mary and blessed Joseph' let us go forward.

These points, about which I must be more watchful, will help me to avoid the faults I have already mentioned. Enough! In the next retreat we shall see what stage we have got to! Meanwhile, God bless me.

28 March, Monday

What good indeed has come out of all these promises? Alas! I had already forgotten them. If I go on like this I shall end in trouble. I am still in the same plight. When I try to find out why, I see it is because I have not always been sufficiently recollected.

For this reason my exercises of piety always leave something to be desired. In fact, during meditation, in my visit to the Blessed Sacrament, and during Vespers—ah! those Vespers!—in my examination of conscience, in every single thing—there is always something missing. The worst of it is that I am always out of breath with recommending others to practise recollection. How shameful!

I, who ought to be the example, have let others excel me in goodness! It is I who must first practise this recollection, and in everything. This morning I made my meditation on the means which the Lord has given me for my salvation, and I found a good deal to make me feel ashamed.

This must now stop, once and for all. Until now I have always trifled with God, and God is not to be trifled with. From now onwards I will really be good. I will carefully practise recollection throughout the day, not letting myself be distracted by the thought of the half-yearly examinations. Above all, I will beware of disobeying our common Rules, especially that of silence.

In the Blessed Sacrament I will be united with Jesus, my friend and comforter, and all will be well. My Jesus, mercy.

4 April, Monday

This week I think I have done a little better, but not altogether well: some things have been neglected in the general flurry of the examination period.

I still have very much to do, particularly as regards recollection during prayers. I must deny myself and despise myself. Jesus in his Passion implores me to make this sacrifice during Holy Week. Can I refuse him? No, my Jesus, never!

22 April, Friday

Holy Week has gone by, the vacation also is over, and instead of moving forward I have continued to slip back. How can this be, after so many good resolutions? Yet the fact is that this is just the situation in which I find myself. The worst of it is that for the last eighteen days I have made no notes, as I had been doing every week after the holy Exercises. My Jesus, mercy.

I do not know how to explain this. I do seem to feel some love for Jesus, I wish to do well, and yet I carry out my pious practices very badly, my thoughts are always wandering, and I rarely make any invocations. Who knows if the Lord will be satisfied with these holidays? I am not altogether displeased with them, but I was expecting rather better results, because of the greater care I have taken with my religious exercises and my greater diligence in everything. There is one matter in which I have been most at fault, because this is a natural failing with me: wanting to be a Solomon, to sit in judgment, to lay down the law left and right! Alas! what presumption, what pride! it is my old self-love making itself felt again. This will make me more careful during the next vacation. Well, it's over now. I do not think I disgraced myself during these holidays, thanks to Jesus Christ. Tomorrow I begin another term. What a joy!

The Lord is preparing so many graces in the months of May and June. Family worries torment me, but courage! All in Jesus and for Jesus, and let come what will!

1 May, Sunday

What a lovely day! What a heavenly day after a week of scant fervour, indeed of distractions, almost of indifference! The good Jesus has again this year granted me the grace to take part in the devotions of the month of May: he has given me another most precious chance of loving him more by honouring most holy Mary. In this month I hope for much from my Mother Mary: with her help I am sure of taking some steps forward. I shall ask the Blessed Virgin particularly for two virtues this month: firstly, great humility, which means knowledge and distrust of myself and, secondly, a great love of Jesus in the Blessed Sacrament; it is this second grace which I will most often ask her to give to my companions also. I shall ask Jesus for a great and constant devotion to his Mother and mine, Mary. In this way the objects of my affections, my desires and my prayers will be offered to Jesus through Mary and to Mary through Jesus! St John Berchmans will help me this month and pray for me, I am sure: he was so devoted to Our Lady. I will endeavour above all to keep my thoughts from wandering, so that I may watch over myself and little by little master my passions, especially my self-love. I will be scrupulous in the exact observance of the Rules, subduing my own will. I will try particularly hard to keep silent in school, never letting the slightest word escape my lips. My invocations shall be without end, and I will do my best to teach others this truth, that the most direct way to Jesus is through Mary. In a word, I will be all for Mary so as to be all for Jesus. I will be most faithful to all those pious practices for the month of May which I have in writing. Thus I will really be what, during the holy Exercises, I resolved to be. My Guardian Angel will sound the alarm when I forget. Meanwhile, may Jesus and Mary bless me, help me, give me what I need—give me a good will, and I will yet be holy.

15 May, 1898, Sunday, in retreat

This month, even I myself have been able to see how full I am of self-esteem, and when I went to see my director he made me see it even more clearly.

Who knows why this should be so? The good Jesus sees that I have no other desire than to serve him, and that I try to stifle the impulses of my self-love. And yet I still fall, and so frequently! Perhaps Mary required something more of me, and indeed I think this may well be true, because until now my devotion has consisted merely of superficial observances, and I have been very remiss many times, and often absent-minded during prayers. Oh, if only I could succeed at least in being really recollected!

I must go on hoping; there are still fifteen days left and I hope to achieve something. Meanwhile I will continually pray to Jesus and Mary to make me humble, and my best invocation shall be this: 'O most humble Mary, make me like yourself.' I will ask Jesus in the Blessed Sacrament for humility and I will endeavour to be humble, especially when things go wrong, humble with others, humble in my thoughts. It is in my thoughts, above all, that I am proud, and by this sin fell the angels. 'Jesus and Mary, you know that I love you.' My Jesus, mercy.

26 May, Thursday

To my great shame I must confess that I have not made this Pentecostal Novena well. If I go on like this I shall undo the little good I think I did before. I can only humble myself and trust. There are still three days left before the solemn Feast of Pentecost: well, I will make a Triduum of reparation, making every effort to be perfect in my religious exercises and always recollected in God and Mary, and make very frequent invocations. I will pray particularly for the ordinands, for the conversion of sinners and for the return of the dissident Churches. This will be the finest way to conclude the month of May and will be the fitting prelude to next month, which is very dear to me, the month of the Sacred Heart of Jesus. In confirmation of all this I will pay the greatest attention to my lectures and keep absolute silence in school.

O Mary, in whom alone I trust, accept my resolutions, send me the Holy Spirit who will make me realize my own nothingness and teach me to love Jesus.

3 June, Trinity Sunday

'To the greater glory of God.'

May Jesus Christ be praised! During the month of May and the Novena to the Holy Spirit I begged Jesus and Mary for the virtue of humility, and I seem to have had excellent opportunities for exercising it. My Superiors received an account, I think exaggerated, of my having behaved arrogantly during the vacation, and I have been duly rebuked.[1] So I have had to humble myself against my will. But as a matter of fact, there is a grain of truth in this. Ah well, if I am now to be out of favour with my Superiors, what am I to do about it?

I shall let the matter rest, leave it alone; time will show how much was true and how much false in these accusations against me. In any case it has been a nasty blow, and has given me food for thought and for tears. Perhaps I have thought too much about it. And the reason for all this is that although, thanks be to God, I was never guilty of those excesses

---

[1] It appears that a Religious of the small Franciscan Friary of Baccanello, not far from Sotto il Monte, was in the confidence of the Roncalli family. It is common knowledge that in large families, and in this case there were ten brothers and sisters on the one hand and ten more brothers and sisters on the other, all children of two cousins, there is bound to be a certain amount of unkind gossip. Angelino's excellent mother paid some special attention, particularly in the matter of food, to the young son who came home for his holidays from the seminary. This led to a little grumbling, almost as if the young seminarist had laid claim to such preferential treatment. All this was recounted to the Superiors of the seminary.

imputed to me, nonetheless pride is always present, and it is this pride which gave rise to the accusations. Now at last my eyes have been opened and I have begun to learn. Well, that's over, I have had my lesson. For the present let us suppose that it was all true and have done with it. I must not think of whoever it was who reported the matter, but I must pray for one who was perhaps an instrument in God's hands, used to set me on the right path.

Humility then, more and more humility, and above all special attention to those points in which I am said—and I must admit there is a little truth in this—to have erred. To this end I must often remind myself of my resolutions, which might have been made with this particular purpose in view. A closer union with Jesus will help me to improve; to tell the truth, I have been very remiss recently. I must be more careful in my examinations of conscience and visits to the Blessed Sacrament.

This is the month of the Sacred Heart, and my own month, and so I must make some progress in humility, which means also in love, and in this way I shall prepare myself better for those tiresome holidays and give certain people no further excuse for making up stories about me.

For the present I thank Jesus Christ who grants me at least the will to become humble. For the rest, Jesus sees my heart; he knows how much I wish to love him. More fervour now then, for we are in the month of love.

12 June, Sunday

I think this week has not been too bad. However, I must still reproach myself for not having been sufficiently attentive in class in certain periods, the literature lessons, and also for having sometimes yielded to the desire to play the wit, letting some foolish or frivolous expressions escape me. I have let my thoughts wander in the rosary, been full of distractions during my general examination of conscience, and rather inattentive also in my meditation. Alas! I have slipped back to where I was before. So I must try once more, with more enthusiasm, more attention, more humility. One of my failings is that I am never orderly, not even in spiritual matters, and yet I am always recommending orderliness to others.

I really must make sure that I never tell others to do what I do not try to practise myself, because until now I have been doing just the contrary. For example, those to whom I speak of love for Jesus in the Blessed Sacrament may perhaps get a very good impression of me in this respect, because I think I speak of this with the greatest fervour. But the truth is that I know I am still a thousand miles behind, certainly a long way behind all my companions. I must put myself in order. Therefore, when I examine my conscience I will concentrate on one particular fault and pay the greatest attention to it. Now, this week I will be particularly attentive in the literature lessons and especially recollected in my meditation, rosary and general examination of conscience. For the rest, humility always and in all things, especially with others, never speaking of myself in the study circles, nor will I expose the faults of others or encourage others to expose them, instead of covering them up.

19 June, monthly day of recollection

This week I have been a little more closely united with Jesus; through his grace I have received some good inspirations and good thoughts; in a word, I have rejoiced in the Sacred Heart and especially at communion during Friday's solemn celebration. Yet, in spite of all this, I cannot say that the Sacred Heart of Jesus is pleased with me, for once again I have fallen into almost all those weaknesses with which I reproached myself last time.

For example: I have been too talkative during school hours, not as recollected as I ought to be when saying the rosary, drawing little profit from my meditation and none at all from my general examination. Alas! all these thorns in the heart of Jesus! What does this mean? It means that I do not love him as I say I do; I love him in word only and not in deed. Above all, I must blame myself for not having kept my continuing resolutions, especially with regard to that about never speaking of myself, even in disapproval, and never speaking of others except to praise them, etc.

21 June, feast of St Aloysius Gonzaga

When the little bell rang on Sunday to mark the end of the retreat I cut short my notes; I have taken them up again today, a most beautiful day because it is consecrated to St Aloysius Gonzaga. I was saying, then, last time, that I had often failed in humility. It is absolutely necessary for me to concentrate on this because I am so interlarded with pride that I fall again, even unawares, when I think I am doing well and being charitable. It is a good thing that I have plenty of opportunities for self-humiliation.

This very day, for instance, I carried the thurible for the first time at Solemn Vespers and I cut the figure I deserved, I who am always picking holes in the others. Everybody laughed behind my back, and it serves me right. So another time I will be more humble, and do things better, all the more because, being a prefect, I was a source of scandal to others also. However, may this humiliation be to the greater honour and glory of St Aloysius! It shall never occur again, because I am resolved to study these ceremonies also during the holidays.

Besides this close attention I intend to pay to my words, I must have a greater spirit of recollection in everything, especially in my practices of piety, and make more use of frequent invocations, etc. St Aloysius is the witness of my promise to observe all these rules: he will help me to keep it.

10 July, Sunday

At last, after so much time wasted in distractions, I have come to myself again. What dreadful days I have been through! How little I have shown my love for the Lord! I have received another grace, that is of the two minor orders: I am a porter and a lector, and yet I am still the same. In the very middle of the year I have taken my final examinations. I have allowed myself to give way to weariness during my practices of piety, especially during my visits to the Blessed Sacrament and in my examinations of conscience. Now I have not so many worries in my head and I want to set myself once more on the right road, especially as the holidays are so near. Enough of this! I have offended my good Jesus too much. May he help me now, and I am his for ever.

19 July, Tuesday

'Save us, Lord, we are perishing.'[1]

I have had three days of my vacation and already I am tired of it. At the sight of such poverty, in the midst of such suspicions, weighed down by so many anxieties, I often sigh and sometimes I am driven to tears. So many humiliations for me! I only try to do what is right, to love sincerely even those who do not seem to have much affection for me, and perhaps think me a worthless fellow. At times I think that even those who have taken an interest in me, those to whom I confided all, now look at me askance and are afraid to touch certain chords, certain subjects. Ah, how sad this makes me feel! Perhaps I am only imagining this. I hope so, I would like to be sure this was so, but meanwhile I must suffer; I am suffering when I thought I would be rejoicing.

[1] Matthew 8: 25.

Oh how the world forsakes me, just when I try to please it! No one sees my sufferings, save Jesus alone. He alone knows them because I have told them to him alone, asking him only to do something about them, not so much in order that I may no longer have to endure them but so that there may be an end to all those stories which were the beginning of it all—they serve no good purpose.

May he at least, my good Jesus, give me the consolation of being able to love him as much as I desire, of being able to humble myself as much as I need, and of finding joy only in my humiliations. It is my duty to glory in the Cross of Our Lord Jesus Christ.[1]

Humility and love, these are the two virtues I will strive to make my own during this vacation. Humility above all in my thoughts because there is no doubt that, if there had been more humility on my part or, to be more precise, less pride, perhaps what has happened would never have occurred. The further I advance the more convinced I am of the need for humility. It is humility alone that will lighten my suffering which, grievous as it is, is not so grievous as the sufferings of Jesus Christ, Mary and innumerable saints. And I need love, to shine forth and burn, especially when I am in church, occupied with my practices of piety.

In the vacation there are no more classes in science or literature, but in the Blessed Sacrament a heavenly school is open to me, with the best Teacher one can possibly imagine, Jesus Christ himself. And the two chief subjects taught in this school are: humility and love.

So I will go to the school of Jesus; there I will learn to be always humble and loving. May God and the most holy Virgin help me and make me worthy to listen to these divine lessons and to learn from them. The former students, my models, are the saints, my fellow students are those just souls who live only to serve the honour of God and to extend the boundaries of the kingdom of Jesus Christ.

Since I have a greater need of humility than of love, because humility is the surest road to love, I will take more pains to acquire it. To this end, as I resolved in the Spiritual Exercises, every evening I will make a note of my faults, especially as regards this virtue, so that I can mend them the following day.

Enough! humility and love, and all the rest as God wills. If Jesus wants my sufferings to continue, his will be done; as for me, may he make me worthy of such a grace, that is, worthy to be allowed to suffer with him and for him.

Moreover, I must be strong in tribulation, because this is but a trifling

[1] Cf. Gal. 6: 14.

prelude to what I shall suffer when I am a priest, when I am a priest and belong wholly to Jesus Christ. May the Blessed Virgin come to my aid, may my Guardian Angel keep me on the alert, may my St John Berchmans accompany me and preserve in me that peace and calm, that diligence in all things, of which he was such a rare example.

Let this always be the reward I seek from Jesus Christ, for any good I may do, the reward desired by St Camillus de Lellis: 'to suffer and be despised for thee.'[1] Amen.

19 July, Tuesday evening

In general I need to be more attentive while I am saying the Office of the Blessed Virgin and the rosary at home. Also, although I feel united to Jesus in the Eucharist, sometimes I am not over-generous with my invocations.

In all this I will try to be more diligent tomorrow.

Moreover I will not waste time in useless chatter in the kitchen.

As for my familiar friend,[2] I must confess that this morning he made his presence felt a little while I was coming back from Baccanello,[3] where I had called on that excellent person who, I thought, received me coldly. He made himself felt when I thought of what had happened at Pentecost, and the part played, as I think, by that person in that affair.

But enough of this—these occasions must serve to humble me more and more, and the next time anything of this sort happens I shall at once try to stifle my self-esteem, saying: it serves you right! If this has happened, you deserve it; everything, even the most unfriendly treatment you may receive, must be an honour for you, who are nothing else but filth and vermin, ignorance and sin.

20 July, Wednesday evening

I still need:

(1) greater concentration when saying my prayers;
(2) a little less drowsiness during meditation;
(3) many more invocations.

I have failed in these three things today. Otherwise, as for the familiar friend, today he has behaved well; he has given little trouble. Well, we shall see tomorrow. 'Lord, you know that I love you!'[4]

---

[1] These words, which so many saints have made their own, are from St John of the Cross.

[2] Pride, self-esteem. [3] Cf. note 1, p. 23. [4] Cf. John 21: 17.

21 July, Thursday

Today again I let my thoughts wander a great deal during the rosary. At this rate I shall certainly not please Mary, and what then?

Several days have now passed since I came home for the vacation; I must begin to study seriously, so I will start tomorrow. Also from tomorrow onwards I will pay an extra visit to the most holy Sacrament at midday, for today, when I read about the visits St Alphonsus paid, Jesus gave me to understand most clearly that he delights in the sons of men.[1] At that time of day my poor church is empty, no one goes in to see him. He and I see each other two or three times in all; so it is right that I, who am able to do so, should go more often to visit him, at least to greet him. How pleased he will be! How he will reward me!

22 July, Friday

Is it really quite impossible for me to keep my thoughts from wandering during the rosary? We shall see again tomorrow.

I must find some way of warding off the drowsiness that comes over me when I am studying. I must also beware of joining over much in conversations, as I had begun to do today, because although at the time I may feel sure of myself, it is none the less true that 'when words abound, sin is found'.[2]

Even thoughts good in themselves, which sometimes surprise and delight me, must be controlled, lest they lead to further distractions; for this purpose I need invocations and ever more invocations.

23 July, Saturday

Well, there it is, today I have fallen again: chattering here and there, like the greatest speechifier in the world.

No sooner have I erred in this way than I notice it and am sorry, but I must think before I speak. I do not think I spoke ill of anyone, but vigilance is always needed. It is all self-love making itself heard; it is the desire to cut a good figure.

My good fellow, know yourself as you really are and you will chatter less, and instead you will be more recollected in your prayers and more assiduous in your invocations. 'Jesus, have mercy on me!'

[1] St Alphonsus de Liguori, *Visite al Ss. Sacramento ed a Maria Santissima*, Rome, Ed. Padri Redentoristi, 1954, p. 31.
[2] Cf. Proverbs 10: 19.

24 July, Sunday

Generally speaking, it is true that I have yet to do even one thing really well, for example, a devout recitation of the holy rosary, etc. Indeed, today even the visit to the Blessed Sacrament suffered a little.

I have good reason to feel ashamed! The way I am going on now, I deserve no grace at all.

Tomorrow I will try hard to do everything properly, especially my exercises of piety: meditation, Office, rosary and visit to the Blessed Sacrament. For the rest, humility at all times, because when we are humble God comes to our aid. So I will beware of uttering the slightest word of reproach to my family, however they may hurt me. O Jesus, do see to this!

25 July, Monday

This evening also I have wept, in the presbytery and when I was with Jesus. O Jesus, accept my suffering and my tears. Use them to wash away my sins, and grant humility to me and to my family too. Mary, help me!

26 July, monthly day of recollection

Looking back over the past month I see I have been lacking in recollection and in humility: recollection during the days spent in the seminary, humility during the holidays. And now, since I find myself a little more successful in recollection, although I am still far from perfect in this, I will pay more attention to humility and try to practise it on all the occasions, and there are very many, which require it. In this I shall find immense help in a close union of thoughts and affections with Jesus, my friend, in the Blessed Sacrament, because then there will be real love between him and me, and love for Jesus brings humility along with it. There then will I unburden myself to him, letting him see all my distress and anxiety, and he will give me the patience I need in the difficulties in which I continually find myself. He will help me to fulfil that mission of peace among the members of my too deeply troubled family. He will teach me to love my neighbour and forgive him, and to sympathize with his failings. So, also, if I am disconsolate, injured or forsaken I will console myself, thinking that I am like Jesus himself who also is injured and forsaken, more than I, and yet never ceases to love. In this way the more bitter my tears are the more meritorious and precious will they be, and I will not lose heart, but will hold myself honoured to suffer something for

Jesus who died on the Cross for me, and for my sake lets himself be confined in a tabernacle.

In this way I shall come to realize more and more the nobility of the
priesthood, a service of love, and the many [here some words are missing]
and because of this, how can I fail to be humble? How can I fail always
to keep silence?

O my God, my God, make me love you and I shall be humble, make
me love you more and I shall be humbler still.

26 July, Tuesday

I must not let myself be overcome by drowsiness before midday, as
happened to me this morning. So tomorrow, also, in homage to Our
Lady, I will try to recite the rosary less carelessly than I did today. Why
should I not succeed in this? To discipline myself I will try to carry out
that resolve I made during the Spiritual Exercises, that is, to see that my
words are filed and polished before they are uttered, and that I beware of
discussing certain questions or airing my own opinion about certain
unimportant matters, which nearly happened today. For the rest, union
with Jesus and invocations.

O God, you see what a sinner I am, but have mercy on me: I love you.

27 July, Wednesday

Oh dear!—will I never get it into my head that I must keep silence
with that blessed curate[1] when matters of no concern to me crop up in
conversation? Even if I say nothing wrong, it is obvious that I have a
natural inclination to pronounce judgment like a Solomon. In any case,
when I stop talking, even when I think I have been caution itself, I am
always aware I have talked too much. And this is pride.

Moreover, I waste too much time in the kitchen, in idle chatter. I must
also learn to control my curiosity about things which are nothing to do
with me. I shall also take care not to doze during meditation, as I did this
morning. Apart from this, I have had recourse to very few invocations,
and as for the rosary, what I said last night is still true: I have never yet
said it as a Christian should.

O God, all these sins! Humble yourself once and for all. See what all
your cleverness amounts to! My Jesus, mercy.

---

[1] Ignazio Valsecchi, curate at Sotto il Monte from 1895–1907.

28 July, Thursday

I need greater recollection when saying my prayers, especially in the Office of the Blessed Virgin.

And never again, even absent-mindedly, must I go out of the village and as far as Carvico[1] without wearing a hat, as I did today.

Generally speaking, I do in fact lack that close union with Jesus which sanctifies the whole day, and to remedy this I will use more frequent invocations.

29 July, Friday

Alas! Alas! My love for the Lord gets a little colder all the time. The same is true of the visit—I fit it in barely half an hour before the rosary. And during the day I seldom think of Jesus. Even during the Office I am as bad as ever. How disgraceful for me to be going backwards instead of forwards!

O good Jesus, enkindle in my heart your own burning love.

30 July, Saturday

I really must humble myself at the thought of my own worthlessness. If only I could do at least this! I think of myself as a seraph and instead I am only a little Lucifer in my pride, and worse. For example, today I made my visit badly, carelessly, and when the visit is badly made nothing else will go right. The rosary also I say with my head in the clouds; as for the Office, the less said the better. And all this time Jesus is calling to me from the ciborium and I run away. I run away like all the other worldly Christians.

Oh how heartless I am; how heartless!

If only I could keep more closely united with Jesus with more frequent invocations! I have promised this a thousand times and I have never done it. Well, it must be done, and with God's help I will do it. 'Lord if you will, you can make me clean.'[2]

31 July, Sunday

I am still at the same point as before, in fact I am even worse, for today I made only the merest attempt at a particular examination of conscience. I left out altogether the three Our Fathers and the Angelus at noon. I must put a stop to all this, while the Lord still has patience with me.

---

[1] About two kilometres from Sotto il Monte.   [2] Luke 5: 12.

Tonight the month of July ends and another month begins.

I also come to the end of the month, begging Jesus to forgive my infidelities; and tomorrow I begin a new life.

Tomorrow in fact begins the great Pardon of Assisi.[1] So I must thoroughly cleanse and purify myself, and beg the good Jesus to give me, afterwards, the purity, the love and the profound humility of the seraphic Francis.

O Jesus, do not forsake me!

1 August, Monday

I need more recollection, more invocations and more attentiveness, especially when saying the rosary. I must avoid certain enthusiastic ideas which, however excellent in themselves, are yet harmful at certain times because they distract the mind too much. O God!

2 August, Tuesday

On the whole, I have not pleased Jesus today. I have been far from him; I paid him a visit, or rather it would be truer to say that I did not pay him a visit. O God, humiliate me still more, show me my real nothingness, keep me closely united in heart and mind with you—for if I go on as I have been doing these last few days I shall be in a bad way. Do not let this happen, O God. I protest here and now that I want to love you always.

O Jesus, charity and forgiveness!

3 August, Wednesday

Well really! It is high time to stop playing the fool with the Lord. Jesus calls me by day, he calls me every evening, he implores me, he beseeches me, and I leave him alone. Until now I have been soft with myself but now I must be severe.

How does this come about? Every evening I implore my Jesus for mercy, and every day I sin again. Is this the way for a seminarist to behave? This very day, besides all the other failings, distractions and futilities of which I must accuse myself during these days, I have omitted my spiritual reading. It is true that I have not been idle, but religious duties must always have the preference.

So, let us be quite clear about it. We will begin by getting rid of the

[1] This pardon, or indulgence, may be gained from midday of 1 August until midnight of 2 August in all Franciscan churches and oratories.

most frequent and obvious failings; then, one at a time, we will tackle the others.

My kind Guardian Angel and my own St John Berchmans bear witness to this promise, which I make at this moment.

Tomorrow, either I make my visit and recite the holy rosary as I should, in which case all will be well, or I go on doing as I have done just recently, in which case on Friday I will eat nothing until midday, and I will make two hours' meditation. By this method I mean to gain something either way.

O Jesus, you must look after me a little too.

4 August, Thursday

I have done a little better in this way but for all that I still have not done everything I should. For example, the visit was not one of the most loving I have made; during the rosary my thoughts still wandered a little. Still, let us be content with today; the rest can wait till tomorrow.

In the meantime I have not removed the penalty I set myself in case of transgression: on the contrary, to the rosary and the visit I will add the recitation of the Office of the Virgin Mary.

I must still be careful not to argue with the curate, as sometimes I have done rather too much, in order to defend certain persons or actions which are really blameworthy, or others which seem to me not to be so. Although everyone may know that I speak like this just for fun, or turn the matter into a jest even when I take it seriously, nevertheless it is always wrong to go too far in certain things and even the smallest trifle may be used to build a whole fabrication on. But enough of this, we have understood. We must be humble and then we shall do no harm to anyone. O Jesus!

5 August, Friday

Today, first of all, I neglected one of my most important duties, that of hearing my little brothers say their prayers.

I promise, in homage to Mary in the Novena about to begin, that this shall not happen again; I will be most diligent in this too.

I have also got into the bad habit of sleeping a little too long in the afternoon, so I will set my alarm clock to awaken me after three-quarters of an hour, which ought to be enough.

Tomorrow begins the Novena of the Assumption: more fervour in everything then and union with Jesus and Mary by means of invocations, of which I have a great need.

O Jesus and Mary, let all my love be for you alone, for ever.

8 August, Monday

Last night and the night before I could not write a thing, because of violent toothache. Although this gave me the chance to suffer something for Jesus, it also took up too much of my thoughts.

If I had a little peace of mind, tomorrow I should have to submit to those penalties which I laid down for myself, since I have not satisfactorily carried out those two most important practices of piety: the visit and the rosary.

And then, to tell the truth, I might just as well not be taking part in this Novena, I am doing it so badly.

So, more devotion is needed; not great and extraordinary achievements but great perfection in everyday matters and above all union with Jesus, and Mary ever in my thoughts, as I suggested this morning in the letter I wrote to Carminati.[1] O Mary!

9 August, Tuesday

Before I begin my practices of piety I must remind myself of that great saying: 'Before making a vow prepare yourself.'[2]

I must find a way of becoming like the saints, that is of being able to pass from study or other occupations to prayer with the greatest ease and without being burdened with distractions as I am. For the rest I can only repeat what I wrote last night. I am almost disheartened, finding myself no further forward.

O Jesus and Mary, give me a little more fervour or I shall become dry and sapless.

12 August, Friday

The other evening I had no candle, last night I had no ink, and so for two evenings running I have written nothing.

When I look back over the last few days I must admit that even if I cannot find any serious faults to deplore, I cannot find any virtues either. I am still stuck in the same place, without moving a step forward. I think

---

[1] Giuseppe Carminati of San Gervasio (Bergamo), ordained priest in 1902; Rector of Stezzano; died in 1941.

[2] Ecclus. 18: 23.

all this is due to my not thinking about it enough, not comparing one day with another and noting the difference, as my particular examination of conscience requires, which examination, by the way, I ought to make much more carefully. In a word, there are some trifles which never seem to come right or, to put it better, are never done really well: the rosary, to some extent the visit also and, much worse, the use of invocations.

And yet I am not lacking in good intentions; for this I can only thank the Lord, for it is all by his grace alone. But I must remind myself that hell is full of good intentions. Oh if I only knew how necessary it is for me to be good and holy! Well, no more of this! Tomorrow I am going to confession, and then I will begin a life of greater application and fervour in honour of the Blessed Virgin, who so greatly deserves my love. I will make a start by never speaking with anyone, even in confidence, of small failings in others, which perhaps I alone can see. O Mary!

13 August, Saturday

On the whole, today things have gone better with me than on other days. But I still lack that close union that I should have with Jesus and Mary through invocations, and the rosary and Office are somewhat neglected. I must also be careful with certain people not to touch on certain subjects which irritate them, because by so doing one only provokes irritability over matters which after all have nothing to do with virtue.

O Mary, my Mother, if you do not help me now when I need help so much, what sort of seminarist, what sort of priest shall I become?

15 August, Monday

Today everything has gone by the board: meditation, spiritual reading, particular examination of conscience, visit, etc., everything. But really it was almost impossible for it to be otherwise. Mary will forgive me, because after all I did nothing but take part as far as I was able in the beloved feast of the Assumption, which is celebrated every year with pomp here in my own poor village.

16 August, Tuesday evening

Today through my own fault I have done wrong, or at least I was in grave danger of wrong-doing, through that fault of which I was more or less accused last Pentecost, that is of wanting to talk about things which are no concern of seminarists.

Certainly it is true that for my own part I think I was extremely circumspect, and merely spoke of that simplicity, obedience, devotion to Superiors and desire for true virtue which are required of a priest. It is also true that I was only talking to the curate, and then only when he broached the subject, although I had previously resolved to keep silent. But I am not my own judge; these things are against the wish of the Superiors and that is enough. I must therefore try as far as possible to keep aloof from these questions and pray only that the actions of priests may be to the glory of God.

It is true, it is always the dinner given by the parish priest and the gathering of the priests for the Assumption that kindles this fire in me: but the real cause is pride. Let us have done with it then!

The worst of it is that these occurrences disturb my practices of piety, as happened today, when some were omitted entirely (spiritual reading) and some (meditation, visit, rosary) done but poorly.

O Jesus, when shall I begin to be a real source of satisfaction to you?

17 August, Wednesday

Thank goodness at last I seem to have spent a fairly tranquil day. Thanks be to God!

The toothache which seized me suddenly before noon made it an even more well-spent day. But I am not yet entirely without fault. For example I was sleepy during meditation, I recited Vespers rather hastily and carelessly, and the invocations were still too few and far between.

This evening, when I heard of the death of that fellow parishioner of mine, an inspiration came to me. At the moment of death shall I be content or discontent with my life? If I were as I am now I should find little to comfort me. Oh indeed 'let me die the death of the just',[1] but first 'let me live the life of the just'!

18 August, Thursday

I must remember that it is my duty not only to shun evil but also to do good. However, I cannot say today has been spent free from evil because I still let my thoughts wander during the visit and the rosary; moreover, I always leave the visit to the last. But you cannot behave like that with Jesus, you cannot do that—leave him always to the last.

O my Jesus, when shall I have a little more fervour?

[1] Numbers 23: 10.

19 August, Friday

During the day there must be less idle chatter, such as I indulged in this morning down there in the kitchen, and there must be greater care over my practices of piety and study, above all when I say the Office of the Blessed Virgin and the rosary. Poor Mother! I have yet to please her even once in this. Let this be my homage to her tomorrow, Saturday, her own day.

O God, what a disgrace! To think that with all the graces the Lord has given me I ought to be a saint, and instead of that I am a great sinner!

20 August, Saturday

Another ill-spent day. Before noon I spent nearly all the time with the curate, and afterwards with the doctor, so I have done little or nothing worthwhile. I must make a note of two things:

(1) I need greater fervour and greater attentiveness when I am preparing myself for the holy sacraments, especially the Eucharist.

(2) I must keep myself in the background very much, as much as I possibly can, and never mention, even accidentally, certain topics that are no business of mine, as I have said before; still less should I scatter my words of wisdom about with every Tom, Dick and Harry, telling them how to behave in certain circumstances.

Let us make this little sacrifice, which my good Jesus so much desires.

O Jesus, put an end to my lukewarmness.

21 August, Sunday

'Lord, Lord, have mercy on me, greatest of sinners.' What more can I say? I never carry out my resolutions. My God, so many sins, and so much love from Jesus! And so many broken promises!

St Alexander, tomorrow I am coming on a pilgrimage to visit you: give me the strength not to fall short of my duties as a cleric.[1]

23 August, Tuesday

When I think of all my negligences in the service of God I am so

[1] The celebrations of the sixteenth centenary of the martyrdom of St Alexander (14–28 August, 1898) were honoured by the presence of Cardinals Antonio Agliardi, a native of Bergamo, Vice-Chancellor of the Sacred Congregation of Rites, Andrea C. Ferrari, Archbishop of Milan, and Giuseppe Sarto, Patriarch of Venice. On 28 August, at the church of Sant'Alessandro in Colonna, Angelo Roncalli for the first time saw Cardinal Sarto (later Pius X), whose pastoral and pontifical offices he was to inherit, in 1953 in Venice and in 1958 in Rome.

ashamed in his presence that I can no longer say anything but 'My Jesus, mercy'.

24 August, Wednesday

Not quite so badly as yesterday, but still badly, especially in the saying of my prayers. I let myself be carried away too much by the thought of the festivities for St Alexander; I need to curb my enthusiasm which may at times lead to indiscretion.

31 August, Wednesday, in retreat

The preparations, the Novena, the extraordinary celebrations for St Alexander's feast made it difficult for me to perform all my practices of piety or rather, to tell the truth, they swept me off my feet. Now that I have come back from all the festivities I can settle down and make my retreat. I will not waste time by repeating how badly I have spent the month; the few brief notes I have made till now are sufficient evidence of that.

What alarms me most of all is my inconstancy in God's service. I say a thousand times with St Augustine that I will rise again, but unlike him I always fall back.

Worst of all, recently, partly through my own negligence, partly for other reasons, I have been many days without going to confession. And to think that St Charles Borromeo went to confession twice a day.[1]

Enough! No words can describe how wretched I am: my pride still clouds my intellect. Since the Lord welcomes me once more and clasps me to his bosom, I will rise again. The particular fruit of this retreat, apart from all its other results, shall be:

(1) I will always make my visit to the Blessed Sacrament before going to see the parish priest, that is at about three o'clock.

(2) I will never, never meddle in matters concerning newspapers, Bishops, topics of the day, nor take up the cudgels in defence of anything which I think is being unjustly attacked and which I think fit to champion, but if I were urged by others to do so I would do all I could to champion it with success, while showing charity at all times.

(3) I will make full use of invocations, especially to Mary, to whom I began the Novena[2] yesterday.

[1] Cf. Gio. Pietro Giussano, *Vita di S. Carlo Borromeo*, Rome, 1610, p. 618.
[2] For the feast of her nativity, 8 September.

31 August, Wednesday

Very few invocations; more fervour needed in the visit and the rosary. This very day I barely escaped committing, if I did not actually commit, that fault concerning which I made my second special resolve during my retreat.

I must keep my wits about me then and be prudent, for the devil is more cunning than I.

O my good Jesus!

1 September, Thursday

Not so badly but not so very well either. I am rather lukewarm and need more fervour in my visit and in my rosary, especially as we are making the Novena to Our Lady.

Oh poor Mary, how little I love her! Every now and then I forget her completely. Well, tomorrow I will for the hundredth time renew my promise to Mary to be attentive and very loving in my visit and in saying the rosary. Surely, if I keep to this, all the rest will come right too.

Let us hope and trust that it will be so. 'O my Mother!'

2 September, Friday

I am getting on a bit; but I still need more care and attention in reciting the Office of the Blessed Virgin, and always when I am in church. For the rest, very frequent invocations, for they can help a great deal. Blessings on the name of Jesus!

3 September, Saturday

I am very calm, perhaps too easy in my mind. I should not like to fall into complacency. The rosary and Vespers still leave something to be desired. What an effort for so simple a matter! This is all the result of my ... sanctity! Eh, my good fellow, it is humility you need, more and more humility.

O Mary, amidst all the honours Turin is offering you during these days of the Marian Congress,[1] do not forget my own poor heart which, the humblest of all, is united with the hearts of so many of your faithful, imploring your favours for the Church and for all sinners.

4 September, Sunday

What I need is this: greater recollection in church during the celebration of public functions; to remember Mary more often; never to give

[1] Third Italian National Marian Congress, 1898.

up making a good visit to the Blessed Sacrament and, most of all, more invocations, particularly those in which I can at the same time make an act of humility. O Mary!

5 September, Monday

I need more resolution in resisting the drowsiness which unfortunately overpowers me at times, especially in the morning, and even at holy communion. Moreover, I am still full of distractions in that blessed rosary. Enough of this! When shall I really try to please Our Lady? In these days of joy and triumph for her I wish to join, however unworthily, in the feelings of so many prelates, so many Catholics who in Turin are acclaiming the great Queen of Heaven. I join them in my invocations, and especially when I pay her the loveliest homage of all, the rosary. O Mary!

6 September, Tuesday

It seems quite impossible. The more I make resolves, the less I keep them. This is all I am good for: gossiping away, promising the earth, and then? Nothing! If only I knew how to be humble!

Sometimes I spend far too much time talking with the curate, and it might be said of me 'when words abound, sin is found'. Then there is another thing—I am really very greedy about fruit. I must beware, I must watch myself. Recollection and mortification, above all in the enjoyment of what the palate desires. This is the best physic for the soul and the loveliest gift to offer Mary in these last days of the Novena for her Nativity. O Mary!

7 September, Wednesday

I need still more invocations, especially while I am studying. They will help me out in the difficulties I often come up against because of my lack of brains—and they will give me more energy. I must take note also that I tend to linger too long in the kitchen after supper, talking things over with my family. They always talk about their worries and this depresses me. Indeed it would not be surprising if at times they led me to forget the great law of charity. So, as soon as the rosary is over, I will say a few words and then go to my room.

They certainly have their worries, and many of them! But my own worries are of a different kind. Theirs are about their bodies and material things; mine are about souls. This is what is hardest for me to bear, to think that in the case of my dear ones suffering seems to serve no good purpose, but rather to do them harm.

O God, you who have lived through all this, you know how heart-rending it is!

O Mary, give my dear ones true charity through which they may forgive with all their hearts and bear with resignation the crosses laid upon them by those they believe to be their enemies.

Enough—let us pray.

8 September, Thursday

What a beautiful and yet what a bad day this has been! Beautiful, to think of Mary as a baby girl, bad because I have not sanctified it as I should. It is always like this! When I most need to do well I do my worst, as for example today. Everything goes by the board: my particular examination, my invocations, the visit—everything; all is neglected.

So, I must settle down calmly once more, be more recollected and make many short appeals for help: 'Lord, have mercy upon me, greatest of sinners.'

9 September, Friday

Today has not gone so badly; it certainly might have gone better. As for the visit, I might almost say I did not make it. I made my meditation too late and not very well. Very little study and few invocations. As for the rest—I satisfied my greedy appetite to the best of my ability. So there is very little to feel pleased about. Tomorrow, in honour of Mary, I will do my best to improve and to make amends, even by means of some bodily mortifications, such as going without fruit.

O Mary, see that I really do this.

10 September, Saturday

Today I have been to confession, and already I have broken the resolutions I had made, which were:

(1) To be more attentive when saying the rosary.

(2) Not to waste time in idle talk.

I must hope that tomorrow's communion will wash me clean and make me really live the life of Jesus Christ, as he so fervently desires.

'Lord, heal my soul.'[1]

[1] Cf. Psalm 40(41): 5.

11 September, Sunday

I am almost afraid of finding myself in the same state as that poor Bishop to whom the Lord sent word, by St John, that he would begin to vomit him out of his mouth because he was neither cold nor hot.[1] This would be a dreadful thing to happen. Could it possibly have happened to me? But there would be nothing to be surprised at if it did. I make good resolutions, and I still fall into the same sins. Must I then be vomited from the mouth, from the heart of Jesus? Can I believe this without shuddering? Can I believe it without feeling impelled to escape from this situation?

O my God, deliver me from this. O Mary!

12 September, Monday

Today I have been to San Gervasio to meet that companion of mine, and so I missed my meditation and my Mass, and the other things I did were done as I usually do them in such circumstances.

Meanwhile Mary is suffering, and perhaps the swords that pierce her are sharper because of me. O God, how ashamed I feel!

One thing I have noticed particularly today, and that is that in certain circumstances I have a very ready tongue and perhaps I talk too much; without in the least meaning to, I become a ranter. I must set myself another mortification: prudence and sobriety in speech.

13 September, Tuesday

Today I have done everything wrong. I have done no studying, but let that pass; I have omitted the particular examination of conscience, I have done little spiritual reading. In short, it is always like this with me. At a superficial glance, one might say that on the whole I do not do so badly, but if I consider myself in relation to what I ought to be doing and the graces the Lord has given me for this purpose, I am ashamed of myself and must confess I am a great sinner.

To think that every evening I make these reflections and every evening I am just the same! This is where I fail so badly. Even in these seven days in honour of Our Lady of Sorrows I am making very little use of mortifications and invocations.

O Mary, in the midst of your sorrows weep also for me, not so much because I am ungrateful but so that your tears may soften my heart, which is so hard and so cruel to Jesus. Amen, amen.

[1] Cf. Rev. 3: 15-16

14 September, Wednesday

I can only repeat what I said last night. The chief reason why no improvement is to be seen in me lies above all in the scant profit I derive from the particular examination.

Tomorrow, then, in honour of Our Lady of Sorrows, I will strive to put into practice those rules I have in writing concerning the particular examination. And may God help me.

15 September, Thursday

Perhaps in these days it is I who add to Mary's griefs with my failings. It is true to say that I mortify myself very little or not at all. There is always something wrong with that blessed rosary; my visit today was most unsatisfactory. And to think these are the seven days of penance in honour of Our Lady of Sorrows!

Then there is another thing which I must watch myself about, and that is the longing to read newspapers, which is forbidden in the seminary. As long as it is the parish priest who tells me to read them, to please him —all right, but I must not go in search of them: that would be quite wrong!

Therefore I will arrange all these things better in the future. From now onwards my particular examination will concentrate on the acquiring of humility, according to the resolutions I made during this year's Spiritual Exercises, which I have in writing, and according to the sound principles which Rodriguez lays down on this subject.[1] 'Lord, have mercy upon me!'

16 September, Friday

Recollection—that is what I need. O Mary, help me to acquire it!

17 September, Saturday

Although I generally manage to keep him at arm's length, the 'natural man' still makes himself felt at times in certain hellish dreams in which I find myself entangled unawares. In short, I am still the same, a great, proud sinner. What a humbling thought!

And to think that God still bears with me and seems not to notice my sins. How can I disappoint him? Why am I not carried away by the desire to love him and make him loved? The most holy Virgin of Sor-

---

[1] Alphonsus Rodriguez, *Ejercicio de perfección y virtudes cristianas*, Seville, 1609, vol. II, treatise III, 'On the virtue of humility'.

rows weeps because Jesus is not loved but sinned against: perhaps I too make her weep. Oh console yourself, Mary, preserve ever alive in me the most burning desire to love your Son and enable me, as far as lies within my power, to soothe your bitter sorrows by drawing souls to Jesus and to you. To obtain your help I dedicate to you all my actions tomorrow. Purify them, give them that perfection they so much need, and let the rosary be said at least once as I have never said it yet.

20 September, Tuesday

I have a great need of recollection and concentration, and of reminding myself very often of the resolutions I make from time to time. Also, in everything I do, I must behave like a boy, the boy I really am, and not try to pass myself off as a serious philosopher and a man of importance. It is my natural inclination to do that—this is what I am made of: pride! For the rest, I must in all things resign myself to the will of God, bearing with patience and without irritability the misfortune God sends me in my own family, such as the serious illness of my little brother Giovanni.[1]

Let us pray, let us pray always about everything, and may all be done according to the will of God, to his honour and glory.

Yes, 'to the greater glory of God!' Amen.

21 September, Wednesday

I must beware of deferring the performance of my practices of piety, putting them off till a later hour in order to please myself and my palate.

This would be an insult to God and a sign that I do not love him; it would be like preferring Barabbas to Jesus. And God is not pleased with things done by halves, or grudgingly. Jesus and Mary, be my salvation!

22 September, Thursday

What a heap of trouble! My little brother Giovanni has given me grave anxiety about his health, so I am praying hard. I hope the Lord will hear my prayer. This evening, when I thought about it seriously, the tears came to my eyes. I imagined myself on that sick bed and I wondered how it would go with me if I were to be judged in this very moment. I should deserve to go to hell, but I hope I shall not be sent there. In any case I am sure I ought to be sent to purgatory. Yet the mere thought of purgatory makes me shudder.

What then will become of me? Oh poor me, how wretched I am!

[1] Giovanni was then seven years old.

I have been thinking I might make quite a good death, for I do have some love for God. But there I am again—even while I am thinking of this, I am indulging in thoughts of pride. 'Look,' people would say, 'he has died like an angel!'

This is where the rottenness in me comes out, and cannot be hidden. First of all I must die to myself entirely, so as to be free to fly to the love of God, and avoid, as far as this is possible, the pains of purgatory.

O good Jesus, look upon this wretched creature, because at least I want to love you and to make others love you, as much as you deserve, with a love worthy of you and as great as I can offer.

O Mary, make my little Giovanni better.

23 September, Friday

Every time I think of purgatory I tremble, and yet I never will get it into my head that I must perform all my practices of piety much better, and all my duties. I must curb a certain restlessness I feel when I visit sick people and show more charity when I speak with others. This is all old stuff. In these days the Lord has sent me a heavier cross to bear. May his name be praised; may this make me more like him, and cancel the punishment due for my sins. Praise be to God.

24 September, Saturday

This morning everything was a bit disordered; afterwards, this evening to be more precise, I was perhaps a little ill-mannered with those present, when we were talking about the best way to cure my beloved brother. I ought to have been more calm.

I see that if at times I keep silent even for the best of reasons, I must suffer for it, and I have to bottle everything up and feel stifled, but I will offer up all this to Jesus and Mary for the greater good of my soul and that of my little Giovanni.

When I feel so troubled I seem to cast myself with more confidence into the arms of God, and I rejoice at this. Oh how eblssed, a thousand times blessed, are those religious who live in God alone, far removed from the cares of this world. I long too much to be as they are.

But no, Jesus wants me in this state; he sends me the cross for me to bear it. May he be blessed ten thousand times!

25 September, 4th Sunday in September, evening

What a dreadful thing has happened to me today! O God, I shudder even to think of it.

My good Father, who did so much for me, who gave me my first training and set me on the road to the priesthood, my parish priest Father Francesco Rebuzzini[1] has died, and oh, the poor man! he died suddenly.

O Jesus, you alone can see how heartbroken I am. This morning I could hardly stand on my legs, a sword had pierced my heart; I had no tears, or hardly any.

I did not weep—but inside I turned to stone. To see him there on the ground, in that state, with his mouth open and red with blood, with his eyes closed, I thought he looked to me—oh, I shall always remember that sight—he looked to me like a statue of the dead Jesus, taken down from the Cross. And he spoke no more, looked at me no more.

Last night he said to me 'Arrivederci!' O Father, when will that be? When shall we see each other again? In paradise. Yes, I turn my gaze to paradise and there he is, I see him, he smiles at me from there, he looks at me and blesses me.

Oh how fortunate I am to have been taught by so great a master! Death took him unawares, but he had been preparing for it for the last seventy-three years. He died when he was trying to pull himself together, to master the malady that had seized him—and he was doing this to try to get to the celebration of Holy Mass. So it was, after all, a noble and enviable way to die.

If only my own death could be like that! As I said, the position in which I found him showed that he had knelt down and fallen backwards, unable to rise again.

Twenty-six years ago the Sacred Heart of Jesus granted him the joy of coming among us, his children, for the first time; last year the Sacred Heart permitted him to celebrate his silver jubilee as our parish priest; this year the Sacred Heart had prepared for him a more solemn feast, an eternal feast, and all this on the fourth Sunday of September, which here we dedicate to the Sacred Heart.

Now, after this grave trial that Jesus has sent me, after the greatest sorrow I have ever suffered in my whole life, what am I to do?

We must cease from mourning; we have already given nature more than her due. Where is my Father now? He is there, close to the Heart of Jesus, which he so well resembled. Let us then look above and try to make ourselves just like him. May the prayers which I know my good parish priest always said for me, for I believe I was his Benjamin, and the prayers I now say for him, and his life which I shall always remember, make me

---

[1] Francesco Rebuzzini (1825-1898) was parish priest at Sotto il Monte from 1872 to 1898. He baptized and educated John XXIII.

truly like him. That will make sense of last night's '*arrivederci*' and mean that we shall embrace again in paradise, when I have fulfilled that mission which the good God has entrusted to me.

Above all, may the example he set of humility, simplicity and uprightness impress itself on my mind, so that I may stifle my pride and so make myself more worthy in the eyes of God, that I may stand before God not in my pride but as a 'blameless and upright man, who fears God',[1] like my parish priest. 'He himself will be praised.'

O Jesus, have mercy on me and open my eyes to see such shining examples.

26 September, Monday

Today I have been distracted and prevented from doing my pious exercises, partly by grief and partly by duties and preparations for the funeral. In a word, 'where my thoughts most often turn there is what I love'. But this love, now shown in my grief, certainly does not detract from my love of God, because the object of my love is holy, and holy is its purpose. I have succeeded in obtaining, as a precious token of remembrance of my priest, his *Imitation of Christ*, the same volume he had used every evening since his seminarist days.[2] To think he became holy, poring over this little book!

This will always be my dearest book, and one of my most precious jewels!

27 September, Tuesday

Today saw the funeral of my much mourned Father. Now he is no longer with us in the body but he remains with us in spirit. He is still with us in the impression he has left on us of the finest virtues and he is with us in his fatherly affection.

But I am left an orphan, to my immense loss. How painful it was for me today to have continually to try to hide those tears which nonetheless at times burst from my eyes. This is my greatest sorrow, the greatest I have ever felt! I am bewildered. I do not know how to behave, how to do any good, how to do any good to others also; I no longer know how to live in a world which has become strange to me.

[1] Job 2: 3.
[2] *De Imitatione Christi*, libri quatuor, auctore Thoma a Kempis canonico regulari ordinis D. Augustini; ad autographum emendati, opere ac studio Henrici Sommalii e Societate Jesu. Venetiis, apud Nicolaum Pezzana, MDCCXLV.

But we must take heart. If my Father has gone, Jesus is still here and opens his arms to me, inviting me to go to him for consolation. Yes, I will go to him, and every day I am free to do so I will unite myself with him in holy communion, with this intention. He will give peace to the holy soul of my priest and above all he will help me to imitate him, especially in humility. For the time being I will put myself in God's hands and try to calm my all too troubled mind; indeed, for the sake of that holy soul I will once more resume all my pious observances and offer them with extra fervour. O my beloved Father!

O Jesus, make me like him! 'Look and make it according to the pattern.'[1]

29 September, Thursday

Today I have been a little more orderly than I was yesterday, but still not quite as I should be. For example, I really cannot tell whether I made my visit or not.

During these days I have always before me the saintly figure of my parish priest and so, seeing how very different I am from him, I cannot be satisfied with myself. Perhaps, besides all the other benefits I have already received, this shining example will also inspire me to greater virtue, greater love of my neighbour.

Oh, I hope this may be so; my parish priest loved me so much. If I see a chance to make some act of self-denial I must not let it slip, but offer it to God for the peace of that blessed soul. This sacrifice is nothing compared with those which the good priest made for me.

O God, do not leave us orphans.[2]

1 October, Saturday

Today hardly any invocations. As for the visit, I might as well not have made it—and this is the reason: Jesus seems almost a stranger to me. My great failings, as I have said before, are thoughtlessness and lack of presence of mind. If I were to think over more carefully the resolutions I am continually making, if I made my general and particular examinations according to the principles I have in writing, and about which I have read so much in Rodriguez, I should certainly get on a little faster and be aware of this; instead I am just like a snail, and cannot feel myself moving.

So, I need a fresh effort. I will begin again tomorrow, first of all by trying to achieve perfection in my practices of piety, especially the visit and the rosary, and taking great care never to say anything disparaging about anyone, even if the error is apparent to all.

[1] Exodus 25: 40.   [2] Cf. John 14: 18.

For the rest, let all be done through Mary, and Mary of the rosary will help me to obtain everything, for she is 'powerful and terrible as an army set in array'.

O Mary, save me!

[5]   *Spiritual notes from the monthly retreat after the death of my parish priest, Father Rebuzzini, the saintly guardian of my childhood and my vocation*[1]

21 October

There are still thirteen days left of my vacation. Oh may I behave like the seminarist I have always wanted to be, and have never been! May I be strengthened by the example of my beloved and deeply mourned parish priest, for whom I implore eternal peace and glory. May I have the grace to do two things well: the visit and the rosary. All the rest will follow.

O Jesus in the Blessed Sacrament, I would like to be filled with love for you; keep me closely united with you, may my heart be near to yours. I want to be to you like the apostle John. O Mary of the rosary, keep me recollected when I say these prayers of yours; bind me for ever, with your rosary, to Jesus of the Blessed Sacrament. Blessed be Jesus, my love, blessed be the Immaculate Virgin Mary.

24 October, Monday

Today, on the whole, has not been too bad; however, a few more invocations would not come amiss. In the rosary and the visit, I think I did what I could although there were some distractions. I think it is a great help towards the success of practices of piety if we prepare ourselves first. 'Before making a vow prepare yourself' says the Holy Spirit.[2] O Jesus, O Mary, watch over me always.

25 October, Tuesday

Today too has not gone so badly, thanks be to Jesus. Oh what a joy it would be always to live like this! But I must beware of being cock-a-hoop. I have nothing good in me; I am made up of sin.

Today is the feast of the Blessed Margaret Alacoque. Oh if only I

---

[1] Title added by the author in 1962.   [2] Ecclus. 18: 23.

too could have that devotion, that love she had for the Sacred Heart of Jesus!

Thirty days have now gone by since the holy soul of my dear parish priest entered his paradise. God receive him into his peace and reward him with the glory of the saints.

26 October, Wednesday

Goodwill has not been lacking and yet today has not been quite successful. Nothing extraordinary. May God prevent me from slackening my efforts. With this in mind I must try to be more recollected, especially when I am dressing in the morning. I will be stricter about not wasting time, and above all I will keep a close watch on what I say, whatever it may be. O good St Joseph, you too must do something about this, you who have so much influence with God and Mary.

27 October, Thursday

This will be my safeguard: recollection at all times and in all things. Sometimes I am too much preoccupied with other matters and slow to recollect myself in my religious exercises. If I could find something to do, in order to pass the time better, it would be all to the good and I should run less risk of giving way to distractions. I must watch my words all the time and not let them out till they have been strictly censored; until, to put it frankly, they have been scrupulously censored when they concern others or when they are tinged with impatience. In a word, I need humility, profound humility, or I shall be building upon sand.[1]

My Jesus, have pity on me.

28 October, Friday

I really need a good box on the ears. These last two evenings it could almost be said that I have not made my visit, at least not one of a decent length. I am not to blame for this, because obedience obliged me to go elsewhere, but if I had followed the impulse, which I occasionally feel, to make this visit a little earlier in the day, then there would have been nothing to be sorry about.

And then there is another thing which tomorrow and always I must do with more care, and that is saying the Office of the Virgin Mary, which today I said very absent-mindedly. Well, let us hope that Mary too will do something about this.

[1] Cf. Matthew 7: 26.

For the rest, I must watch my words and make many invocations. O Jesus, have pity!

29 October, Saturday

In truth, it may be that the memory of that saintly parish priest perhaps takes up too much of my thoughts, as it did today when I made my visit and said the rosary. This is not the way to imitate him. There must be moderation in everything and 'for everything there is a season'.[1] Also, I must make a clean sweep of so many idle words and so much chatter with which I waste the evening with my brothers and sisters. And I must endeavour to raise my mind to God still more frequently than I do at present.

Poor me! I go a little further forward, and yet I am still where I was before. Humility, therefore, and distrust of myself, for by myself I can do nothing. O Jesus, in tomorrow's communion, set my heart on fire, that I may ever love you, but with the love of the saints themselves.

30 October, Sunday

I had a grave lapse today, which made me lose the most precious moments of communion and perhaps spoilt my other pious practices—and the cause of it all was the distraction I fell into as soon as I rose from my bed, and the fact that I did not immediately achieve recollection as soon as I got to church. This incident should be recorded. Another thing that alarms me is being treated with that seriousness of conversation and manners usually shown to a priest.

Oh poor fellow! Do I not realize that all this is a snare of the devil? If I could only get into my head that this comes of my behaving with all the airs of a priest, instead of with the simplicity and modesty of a seminarist.

If I could only see that all this comes from my self-esteem. 'O Lord, lighten my eyes, lest I sleep the sleep of death!'[2]

31 October, Monday

The truth is that since last Monday there has been a noticeable change. In short, when I am out and about I am never able to keep in close union with God. I shun evil but I do not do good.[3]

This generally means that I do something that I am sorry for afterwards. Today for example the invocations were no more than could have

---

[1] Cf. Eccles. 3: 2ff.   [2] Psalm 12(13): 3.   [3] Cf. Psalm 36(37): 27.

been counted on my fingers. The particular examination was nowhere. The Office of the Virgin Mary was said carelessly, and the same was more or less true of the rosary. Then this evening what I have regretted before has happened again: I stayed too long chatting and indulging in idle gossip instead of going to my room. Do I not know that I shall have to give an account of all this to God? Let us hope that tomorrow will be like last Monday and not like today, for tomorrow is All Saints Day, and I will begin by making a good communion.

May all God's saints intercede for me and keep me humble. Prepare me for the new year of seminary joys.

1 November, Tuesday

Today did not go too well as regards practices of piety, but I think there was sufficient excuse for this as it was proper for me to go to the curate's to keep company with the priests who were gathered there. In the midst of this distraction, however, the day has not gone too badly and I feel pleased, since I do not think I have fallen into those faults of pride and arrogance which I have shown at other times in similar circumstances. For the present let us be humble, bless God and pray. May this not be the first and last day in which I castigate to good effect my old friend, self-love, the desire to cut a fine figure and to assume the airs of a Solomon.

Evidently this morning's communion had a good effect. Thanks be to God. It is the eve of All Souls Day and I am seized with sadness. The day of the dead brings back to my mind the beloved figure of my parish priest. It is impossible to express all my thoughts. May tomorrow be a day of special prayers for that blessed soul. I feel his continual protection when I see my most beloved landlord and now here on earth my chief benefactor, Canon Morlani.[1] May my prayers bring to that holy soul whatever help he may need! Even in the other life he watches over me and shows his kindness as if he were still alive. These prayers for my dead priest will serve to increase in me the devotion to the Blessed Sacrament, which is admirably linked with prayers for the dead.

Tomorrow I will offer the new extraordinary plenary indulgence, granted by the Pope on the occasion of the ninth centenary of the commemoration[2] of all the faithful departed (998–1898), for the soul of my parish priest, that he may rest in peace.

[1] Canon Giovanni Morlani, Prior of S. Maria Maggiore (Bergamo), was joint owner with his brothers of the land cultivated by the Roncallis. He died at the age of sixty-nine, in 1939.

[2] In the Canon of the Mass.

2 November, Wednesday

I must reproach myself with having wasted time, and with not having had recourse to frequent invocations. I must also take care not to give way to sleep during meditation as I did this morning. O Jesus, have mercy on me and grant peace to the dead.

3 November, Thursday

Today was spent travelling, and so it was as usual. Worst of all, sometimes I showed a little resentment in my words when I thought I was not being treated with sufficient consideration . . . and all this is pride, pride of the first water. And there were hardly any invocations. O God, pity me, for I do want to love you.

Tomorrow is the first Friday of the month and so a day of reparation to the Sacred Heart. Ah, if my own were a real reparation for my offences! O Jesus, why should it not be so, if you come to my help?

4 November, Friday

A little better than yesterday, although my thoughts still wandered very much during communion, and a little during the rosary, which proves I need to acquire the spirit of recollection, especially in the morning. I will use recollection also to obtain, as far as lies in my power, that mildness of manner which I sometimes lack and which is nevertheless most necessary if I am to increase in virtue and do much good to souls. O Jesus, O Mary, O St Charles.

5 November, Saturday

The further I get the more I realize the love Jesus has for us as compared with the ingratitude of men, and especially my own. So many faults, so many failings, so little recollection, so few Saturday mortifications! I am good at thinking up virtues, not at practising them: I merely lay claim to them. 'Have mercy on me, the greatest of sinners; O do not thou utterly forsake me.'[1]

Tomorrow is the last day of the holidays and, with God's help, I mean at all costs to do well. The rosary then, oh the rosary! O Virgin Mary, help me to say it as St John Berchmans did.

20 November, Sunday, in retreat

These last days in the seminary I have been rather too merry and so my mind has fluttered about like a butterfly, neglecting the most impor-

---

[1] Cf. Psalm 50(51): 1 and 118(119): 8.

tant things. Hence distractions, especially during Vespers; hence my not keeping silence in class, as I should. In short, although the rules for seminarists have been obeyed in their substance, my obedience always lacks that salt, that perfection, which would make it finer, dearer to God and more meritorious. I am like a picture which, although cleansed of those stains which made it unrecognizable, is still covered with a layer of specks of dust which, as it were, casts a shade over the whole painting and makes it displeasing to the eye. I am in exactly the same state as these neglected old pictures. So why should I be surprised if I do not feel within me the constant workings of grace and the fire of love, when these little negligences of mine stand in the way?

So I must do as we do with these pictures, when we want to restore them and make them look as beautiful as when they left the painter's hand. A good cleansing with oil is what they need, to make them recognizable. Yes, I must make a clean sweep of all these imperfections. I will do this by being recollected from when I first wake up in the morning onwards, and by not indulging in too much merriment, which makes people silly. Beware of talking about other people and above all of sitting in judgment on Tom, Dick and Harry! It is just in these things that my old friend shows himself.[1]

Apart from this, infinite invocations, loving visits, and severe examination of conscience. And since the good Jesus has sent me another misfortune in the death of my kind director,[2] I shall make it my duty frequently to commend his good soul to God, together with the soul of my parish priest, so that these two persons who knew my conscience only too well, and all my imperfections, may also in their turn commend me to Jesus and Mary and implore for me humility, with a burning love for Jesus and for all the souls redeemed by his most holy blood.

'Jesus, Mary, Joseph, my most sweet loves, may I live, suffer and die for you.'

28 November, Monday

As regards the first failing which I bewailed last Sunday, excessive mirth, I think I have put this right, though not altogether. But, after all, it is always better to be merry than to be melancholy. And remember: 'Be glad in the Lord.'[3]

---

[1] Self-love.
[2] Canon Luigi Isacchi (1839–1898) was spiritual director of the seminary at Bergamo from 1883 to 1898.
[3] Psalm 31(32): 11.

On the whole the visit did not go too badly either, praise be to God. However there are many things still to set right, and others, alas! to get rid of: small distractions during prayers, inattention and carelessness about little things, a few idle words during school, and insufficient attention to those of my fellows who are entrusted to me, now a prefect. I mean I ought to talk more to them and not, as now, almost always to the other prefects. How much still remains for me to do! But the [sentence unfinished].

8 December, Thursday evening

Hail Mary Immaculate! The incomparable, the most beautiful, the most holy, the most dear to God of all his creatures! O Mary, to me you seem so beautiful that if I did not know that the highest honours must be paid to God alone, I would adore you. We speak of your beauty, but who can speak of your goodness? A year has now gone by since you granted me that grace[1] which you well know I was unworthy to receive, and this very day you remind me of this most insistently, recalling to my mind the pleasant duties which were to accompany this grace, duties which are even too delightful and which it was an honour for me to assume. But alas! I have not always returned your love, I have not always behaved with you as you have behaved with me. Looking at myself I see very clearly what I ought to be, after a whole year, and what I am. I have always been a bit crazy, a bit of a numskull, and more than ever so in recent days. This is all my virtue amounts to!

Jesus seems to have moved a little further away from me, because I have moved further from him. I need a firm spirit of recollection, with frequent invocations. It is always the same story. I must also be more careful about little things, little words, little thoughts, etc., and beware of taking things too lightly, which would be very bad for me.

O Mary, since I have not been as I ought to be, since you remind me more insistently than ever of my special duties, keep me always in this frame of mind, that is with the greatest fervour in my endeavour to be good. Again I consecrate myself to you, my Mother; give me some of that good sense, that discrimination in doing good which is so lacking in me, and which would give so much perfection to my good works. Let my thoughts return constantly to you, may my lips speak of you, and my heart long for you! Above all I beg you to see to that matter you know all about. You understand me, make me humble and I shall be

---

[1] Purity. See 1897, p. 15.

holy, make me very humble and I shall be very holy. I offer to you those little mortifications which, with your help, I am resolved to endure. But be always with me in my pious practices and in my studies; teach me the truth about you and your Son. And last of all, O great Mother Immaculate, bring me to Jesus, the final goal of my affections; bind me wholly to Jesus, help me to love him passionately. Amen.

18 December, Sunday, in retreat

Until the feast of the Immaculate Conception I was doing badly; after the feast better, thanks to Mary. What I most need in these days is recollection, with many invocations and great care in meditation, at Mass, in my visits, and above all in my examinations of conscience. For the rest, humility, great humility, in little things. My heart and mind must be full of love, love for the child Jesus. O Jesus, make me a child like yourself; you know how much I desire this.

[6]   *Maxims derived from meditations during the retreat, 1898*

(1) God is my great Master, who with unheard-of condescension has brought me out of nothing that I may praise him, love him, serve him and increase his honour among men. Therefore I belong wholly to God and can and must do only what God wills, what serves his glory. To this end only must my every action, every thought and every breath be directed—to the greater glory of God. Therefore, when I try only to honour myself, to satisfy only my own self-love, I betray God's plans, I go astray, I become a useless fellow, a rebel against my good Lord, and I reject the reward he has prepared for me. What more atrocious insult to the Sacred Heart can there be than thus to forsake him, and use so ill all those capacities he has given me to love him and to make him loved?

The birds of the air, the fishes in the sea, the beasts of the forests, all the animals on earth serve the Lord better than I do. How shameful for me, conceited as I am, to let the beasts surpass me in praising our creator!

(2) When I am about to think myself superior, or satisfy my pride, here is the sovereign remedy which will cure me and humble me: to think what a great sinner I am, I who am not worthy to appear before my Jesus, I who should thank the Lord and think it an honour to be treated as the least, not only of my companions, but of all men.

(3) I am a seminarist, and therefore I must always remember that any fault in me, however slight, is always grave and must be avoided as if it were a mortal sin, the very name of which I ought not to know. Above all, I must remember that great saying of St Bernard: 'Jokes are only jokes among laymen; in the mouth of a priest they are blasphemies.'[1]

And to think that none of my actions has ever been free from these imperfections! What has become of that good seminarist I believed myself to be? What a blow this is to my pride!

(4) I aspire to holy orders; therefore I ought to be like an angel in the sight of God. What a happy coincidence! Divine Providence wanted to show me that this was my duty, and so had me baptized under the name of Angelo. But what a disgrace for me, always to be called Angelo, with the obligation of behaving like an angel, when on the contrary I am no angel at all. So, the name Angelo must inspire me to be indeed an angel seminarist.

Moreover, when I hear my name spoken, I must see that it arouses in me the desire for the perfection which I must achieve, and leads me to make an act of humility, thinking of what my name is and what I am in fact, anything but an angel.

(5) O God! What is this body I care for so tenderly? Or better, as St Bernard said: 'What have you done? What are you? What will you be?'[2] And I will reply with him: 'My body is clay, my good fame a vapour, my end is ashes!' And I care so much for this body, this bag of filth, this breeding place of worms, and to defend it I offend God. What foolishness! What stupidity! And what of my soul? Poor soul! It is just as well that I pride myself on being such a wise and prudent man! My good fellow, you must bow that head of yours, so full of hot air; you must think humbly of yourself, otherwise you will go on groping your way until you fall.

(6) What a lovely thought! An angel of paradise, no less, is always beside me, rapt in an everlasting loving ecstasy with his God! What joy even to think of this! So I am ever under the gaze of an angel who protects me and prays for me, who watches by my bedside while I sleep. What a thought! But how ashamed it makes me feel! How can I entertain certain proud thoughts, say certain words, commit certain actions, under the eyes of my Guardian Angel? And yet I have done this. O my spirit companion, pray to God for me, that I may never do, say or think anything that could offend your most pure eyes.

---

[1] *De consideratione*, bk. II, chap. XIII (P.L., CLXXXII, 756).
[2] Cf. *Var. et brev. docum.* 2 (P.L., CLXXXIV, 1174).

(7) If in this life I feel myself blushing with shame and hardly dare to go into the presence of a Superior who is dissatisfied with me and my actions, what terror shall I not feel when I think of entering into the presence of my angry God, my creator, my Father, my Jesus, who will then no longer be my loving friend but my wrathful foe? And my Guardian Angel? And my Mother Mary? What will she say when God condemns me? Poor angel! Poor Mother!

I believe all this, and when I behave badly I know I have to accept the rebukes of my Superiors and, much more, the dreadful reproaches of God. What stupidity! I must indeed say with St Paul: 'If we judged ourselves truly, we should not be judged.'[1]

(8) I must always be convinced of this great truth: Jesus wants from me, the seminarist Angelo Roncalli, not just a mediocre but supreme virtue; he will not be satisfied with me until I have made myself, or at least have done my utmost to make myself, holy. The graces he has given me to this end are so many, and so great.

[1] I Cor. 2: 31.

1899

15 January, 1899, monthly day of recollection

The death of my beloved director Isacchi,[1] and my acquiring a new director,[2] have brought about some small changes, even if they have not greatly altered my life. For example, I am certainly not so well known to the new director as I was to Isacchi, and so I do not yet feel that sense of familiarity which I had before; but I must just be patient and things will adjust themselves. As for my habit of making these jottings, as I had done from last year until this last month, the new director does not seem to think so highly of this as the other did. In short, one thinks in one way, one in another. That is why there is such a gap between the last entry and today's. But this is by the way. Let us get down to business.

The thought of death, intensified by the recent mourning in the seminary for our director Isacchi, and now renewed by the death of my late beloved Rector, Father Giacinto Dentella,[3] has affected me profoundly. May God grant his peace to them both, and to my parish priest for whom I still mourn.

19 March, monthly day of recollection

It is the day of my own dear St Joseph. I feel I must return to the habit of writing down my thoughts, a custom interrupted, I do not know whether through my own fault or not, since January. How can I fail to think of St Joseph when this year [text interrupted].

16 April, monthly day of recollection

How often I have looked over these few pages and felt ashamed to think how badly I have kept the resolve I made in the Spiritual Exercises

[1] Canon Luigi Isacchi (1839–1898) was spiritual director of the seminary at Bergamo from 1883 to 1898.

[2] Canon Quirino Spampatti, who died in 1919.

[3] Giacinto Dentella di Alzano Lombardo, ordained priest in 1857, was appointed Rector of the seminary at Bergamo in 1876. He died in 1899.

7. Santa Maria at Brusico, the Church where he was baptized

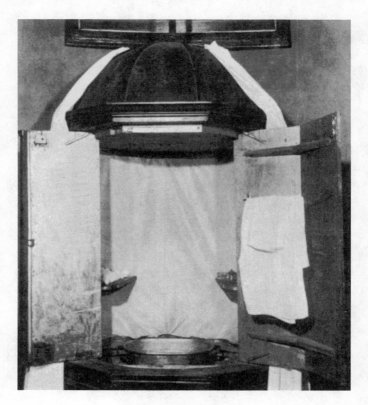

8. The baptismal font

10. Maria Roncalli, née Mazolla, his mother

9. Giovanni Battista Roncalli, his father

last year, 1898, to put down on paper some reflections on the state of my conscience! As can be seen from the entry above, as soon as I began to write the bell rang for the end of the retreat, and so I broke off and did not give it another thought.

Now that I have come back from the Easter vacation I have decided, during today's retreat, to resume this useful custom which, with God's help, I hope never to interrupt again.

Today I have been fairly recollected. Oh! what am I saying? Recollected? Here all my troubles begin. I ought to have been recollected but I never managed to be so, except in a poor way. I am good at suggesting to others how they should behave, but when it comes to doing it myself —never! Therefore, from now onwards, especially with regard to recollection, I will never recommend anything unless I can serve as an example to others in this matter, as I should. I will pay special attention to saying the Office of the Virgin Mary, and take the greatest care over saying the rosary, for in this I have recently left much to be desired. Another thing I need, which could be of great help to me, is the constant use of frequent invocations. Through these my thoughts would always be with God and therefore always under control, and so I would not be in danger of gossiping about others, as has perhaps already happened, when it is impossible to speak without referring to their faults, or without due composure. Here then are three things on which I must concentrate, as the consequence and fruit of the present retreat: the rosary, invocations, and prudence in speech, with due reserve in conversation and no idle gossip.

For the rest, as for appearing too much of a fool and being too easily taken in about matters of no importance, so giving others the chance to laugh behind my back, I can only rejoice at this, seeing my self-love humiliated in this way and considering myself, in the lowest possible degree, similar to the good Jesus, who was treated as a madman. If he would only let me too be mad, for love of him! Nothing else would matter after that.

Lastly, as regards my family troubles, particularly worrying during this vacation, I have offered them all to the Sacred Heart of Jesus my beloved. He knows that what I want for my dear ones is not wealth and worldly pleasures but only patience and charity. He knows that if I grieve over them, it is only because they are lacking in these virtues. May he grant me the grace to see them all one day in paradise, and then let come what will: I will bear all for the greater glory of God and as penance for my sins. O Jesus, let me die of love for you!

24 April, Monday

This month has not gone so badly, especially as regards recollection during my pious practices, for which I must be very grateful to the Lord. I must remember however that I am so feeble and slack that this may not last. The most important thing for me is to acquire that inner piety, whose outward appearance is but a garment, a piety rooted in true humility, of which I have immense need. Therefore I will try harder to mortify myself, especially my thoughts, and to stay more closely united with God, through numberless invocations, so as to be able to prepare myself better for the coming month of May. Amen.

7 May, Sunday

We are already well into the month of May, and I still need more recollection, especially in meditation, in the rosary, etc. In my pious practices I am perhaps a little too much of a poet. However, on the whole, things are not going too badly, and for this I am grateful to God and to Mary.

Last year in May I asked Mary for two things: humility and love. By the end of the month my prayer had been granted, for I had had occasion to practise both. This year I am back at the same point again and I hope Our Lady will hear me again. She is so kind! To tell the truth, I find it hard to humble myself, but I hope this is an effort for which I shall be rewarded. It all depends on making a good start. Jesus, Mary, you know that I want to please you and to love you.

22 May, Monday after Pentecost, in retreat

O Lord, forgive me, for I am the greatest sinner. What more can I say? I am bound to confess it, whether I will or no. This is the thought that can cure all my failings. These last days, even if, thanks be to God, I have not fallen into idle or careless ways, yet my imagination has been too hard at work, to the detriment of my understanding which, although it does not entirely give way to my imagination, but even tries to check it, must nevertheless have been to some extent influenced by it. The festivities for my new parish priest, the little poem I wrote for this occasion,[1] and

[1] He alludes to a poem of eleven verses, composed in the seminary on 22 May, 1899, for the new parish priest and entitled: '*Al novello parroco di Sotto il Monte—M.R.D. Luigi Battaglia—che in questo giorno—Auspice l'Angelico S. Luigi—solennemente inaugura—il suo pastorale ministero*' (To the new parish priest of Sotto il Monte—M.R.D. Luigi Battaglia —who on this day—under the auspices of the angelic St Aloysius—solemnly inaugurates his pastoral ministry). Fr Luigi Battaglia (1852–1917) was parish priest of Sotto il Monte from 1899 to 1917.

then the ordinands, and the secret ambitions of my self-esteem, oh! there was plenty of scope for my pride! I must beware of letting my imagination run riot. Thank God, I do not think my mind was really taken in by these fancies but still it would not do it any harm to be humbled a little. Every now and then somebody humiliates me and, thinking that I do not resent this, they draw blood. These are the moments for rejoicing in silence. They say and believe that I am a fool. Perhaps I am, but my pride will not allow me to think so. This is the funny side to it all. This is why I must practise patience and mortification and try to please Mary, my beloved Immaculate.

In short, I do not know what more to say. O Holy Spirit, O my Jesus in the Blessed Sacrament, O Mary Immaculate, you know my needs, my faults, my longing to cut a fine figure, and my need to remain in the background, to humble myself, to be despised; and with all these faults you know also my desire to love and to make myself holy. So you must humiliate me, you must watch over me, you must sanctify me. Humility and love!

28 May, Sunday

Not so bad; but there is still need for greater recollection, especially in these last days of the month of May. For the rest, O God, set me on fire with love! It is the week of Corpus Christi, of my Jesus in the Blessed Sacrament.

1900

Impressions and reflections during the holy retreat of the Year of Grace 1900, February, seminary of Bergamo

(1) Who am I? Where do I come from? Where am I going? I am nothing. Everything I possess, my being, life, understanding, will and memory—all were given me by God, so all belong to him. Twenty short years ago all that I see around me was already here; the same sun, moon and stars, the same mountains, seas, deserts, beasts, plants and men; everything was proceeding in its appointed way under the watchful eyes of Divine Providence. And I? I was not here. Everything was being done without me, nobody was thinking of me, nobody could imagine me, even in dreams, because I did not exist.

And you, O God, with a wonderful gesture of love, you who are from the beginning and before all time, you drew me forth from my nothingness, you gave me being, life, a soul, in fact all the faculties of my body and spirit; you opened my eyes to this light which sheds its radiance around me, you created me. So you are my Master and I am your creature. I am nothing without you, and through you I am all that I am. I can do nothing without you; indeed, if at every moment you did not support me I should slip back whence I came, into nothingness. This is what I am. And yet I am boastful and display with pride before the eyes of God all the blessings he has showered on me, as if they were my own. Oh what a fool I am! 'For what have you that you did not receive? If then you received it, why do you boast as if it were not a gift?'[1]

God created me. Yet he did not need me; the whole scheme of the universe, the world which surrounds me, everything, in fact, would exist without any help from me.

Why then do I think myself so necessary to this world? What am I but an ant or a grain of sand? Why do I puff myself up so proudly? Arrogance, pride, self-esteem! What am I set in this world to do? To

---

[1] Cf. 1 Cor. 4: 7.

serve God. He is my supreme Master because he has created me, because he preserves my life, and so I am his servant. Therefore my whole life must be consecrated to him, to carry out his wishes, in all things and at all times. So, when I do not think of God, when I attend to my own comforts, my own self-love, my good esteem among men, I neglect my most compelling duty, I become a disobedient servant. And what will God do with me then? O Lord, do not strike me with the thunderbolts of your justice, and do not dismiss me from your service, as I would only too well deserve.

Servant of God! What a proud title and what a wonderful service this is! Did you not say, O Lord, that your yoke is easy and your burden is light? Is it not written in your Scriptures that to serve you is to reign?[1] Is it not the greatest honour for a holy man if people say of him that he is the servant of God? Surely your Pontiff, your Vicar on earth, is proud to be called by this name: the servant of the servants of God?[2] What glory then to serve you, O my God! And yet I so easily forget my duty! What a shameful thing it is not to serve such a Master, so just, so good and holy!

Serve God, and then? What is the prize? My homeland, heaven, paradise the beautiful. Yes, paradise, that is my goal, there is my peace and my joy. Paradise, where I shall see and contemplate my God, 'face to face, as he is'.[3]

O Lord, I thank you for this reward which you have prepared for me after such paltry service, and for the high honour to which you have called me. I am a pilgrim here on earth. I look to heaven as my goal, my homeland, my dwelling place. O heaven, you are so beautiful, and you are for me! In all difficulties, bitterness and discouragements this shall be my consolation: to open my heart to this blessed hope, look to heaven and think of paradise. This is what all the saints did, St Philip Neri, my St Francis de Sales, and the Venerable Cottolengo, who was ever exclaiming: 'Paradise, paradise!'

These are the true and beautiful things that you, O God, have been teaching me. Alas! I know them but do not understand them. I am nothing and I think I am a great man. I come from nothing and I am proud of myself because of those gifts which come from God. I ought to serve my creator and instead, at times, I forget him. I do not think of him, I serve my own ambitions and my self-love. I am invited to paradise and

[1] Cf. Mass for peace, postcommunion prayer, and Mass on the feast of St Irenaeus, collect.
[2] *Servus servorum Dei.* St Gregory the Great, *Epistularum* XIII, 1 (P.L., LXXVII, 1254).
[3] Cf. 1 Cor. 13: 12 and 1 John 3: 2.

yet I think only of the glory of this world. What a paradox! O Lord, help me to understand you, as your Augustine prayed: 'May I know you and know myself, that I may love you and despise myself.'[1]

O Lord, listen to this blind man who calls out to you as you pass by, and implores you to help him, you who are indeed the light of my eyes! Give me light that I may see: 'Lord, that I may see!'[2]

(2) I have a soul! What greatness lies in this! I am not a stone, a plant, or any kind of beast; I am a man, and a man because of my soul which gives me life. Through my soul a ray of light from the divine countenance shines upon me. Through my memory I am made like the Father, through my understanding I am like the Son and through my will I am like the Holy Spirit. But this is not all: the human soul is of infinite worth, because it cost the blood of God. Hence the soul of a savage is more precious than all this world's wealth. How precious the soul is! It is destined to that bliss wherewith God himself is blessed. How then can I have the courage to offend this soul which partakes of the beauty of God himself? How can I allow it to be reduced by sin to the state of a beast of burden, made a slave of the body—the soul that should command the body? Yet this is just what I have done. What a humbling thought for me!

It was for the soul that the divine perfections were revealed: in the creation and still more in the Incarnation, the omnipotence, wisdom and love of God shone forth in their brightest radiance. For the soul God endured all suffering, even death itself. Why should I not mortify myself, and suffer in my turn so as to co-operate in the saving of this soul which is, after all, my own and no one else's?

(3) All men on earth bear in themselves the image of God. They cost him immense pain. And yet so many do not love God, do not serve him; instead they spurn him, and very many do not even know him.

This thought must inspire me with compassion for their souls, and must fill my heart with the burning desire to save them too and, if I can do nothing more, at least pray for them, above all when I remember that the blood of Christ was shed in vain for them—indeed for them it becomes a reason for condemnation.

If all men are in the likeness of God, why should I not love them all, why should I despise them? Should I not rather revere them? This is the reflection which must hold me back from in any way offending against my brothers, for I must remember that they are all made in the image of

---

[1] *Soliloquia*, bk. 2, chap. I, 1 (P.L., XXXII, 885).
[2] Cf. Mark 10: 51.

God and that perhaps their souls are more beautiful and dearer to God than my own.

(4) I boast of myself, I seem almost to lay claim to God's graces, and if I do anything good I come into his presence like the Pharisee. . . . And yet I am a sinner. This must be in my mind whenever I enter a church or any other place. I am a sinner. Therefore no arrogant words, no haughty bearing, but lowered eyes, humility of mind and heart, and friendliness to all my fellows. And before God my behaviour must be that of the publican who, far back from the altar, beat his breast saying: 'God be merciful to me, a sinner!'[1] And when I receive graces and consolations I must look on all these gifts as alms bestowed by God, so that with this in mind I shall not boast about them but admit my own unworthiness.

(5) All the fine honours that may come to me one day through my learning, what use will they be to me on the point of death? When these thoughts upset me and swell my pride, there is one stern and effective way to dismiss them: to think of myself at the moment of death, of the desires I shall have at that moment, and to ask myself: 'What has this to do with eternity?'

(6) All my vanities, all my distractions during my devotions, in meditation, examinations of conscience, the Office of the Blessed Virgin and the rosary, all the words, the witticisms prompted only by a secret desire directly or indirectly to show off how much I have studied, all my castles in the air, my castles of straw and castles in Spain, all the words spoken during the time of silence, all the good inspirations rejected: all these will be judged. My God, what terror I feel! What a mounting heap of sins! How shameful for me, sensitive as I am about my good name and my pride!

But you must think hard about all this, my soul: either you put your thoughts in order now or you will have to endure this humiliation, with all that follows from it. Think well of this truth and before repeating all or any of these faults, draw up your accounts well, so as not to have to repent later and in vain. 'If we judged ourselves truly we should not be judged.'[2]

The thought of hell terrifies me; I cannot bear it. It seems almost impossible to me, I cannot imagine my God being so angry with me as to drive me away, after loving me so much. Yet this is a most certain truth. If I do not fight against my pride, my arrogance and self-esteem, hell awaits me. Oh what a dreadful thought! Is it then true, O beloved Jesus, that I could no longer love you? no longer see your face? that I should be driven from you? I must hope this will never happen, but it

[1] Cf. Luke 18: 13.   [2] I Cor. 11: 31.

might. So I must always with fear and trembling work out my own salvation.[1] Meanwhile it will be well constantly to remind myself of hell, either by the contemplation of external objects or by mortifications. If I see fire I must think it is but a painted flame compared with the fire of hell. If I have toothache or a burning thirst, if I tremble with cold or am racked with fever, I must mortify myself: hell is the place of all tortures, *locus tormentorum*: in hell we shall burn and glow like coal in the furnace; in hell there will be 'weeping and gnashing of teeth'.[2] In hell I shall not be able to move a finger, and yet I cannot recite a prayer or say the rosary or Vespers without fidgeting! In hell we shall be deafened by piercing shrieks, and yet here I cannot bear any disturbing noise! In hell we shall suffer ravenous hunger, yet here I cannot forego a delicate morsel! In hell the damned and the devils will keep me company, and here I cannot endure with patience the presence of a person I dislike. Have I not deserved hell a thousand times? Am I not likely to deserve it again?

O my most sweet Jesus, listen to this prayer of mine. Send me, I beg you, every sort of illness in this life: confine me to my bed; reduce me to the state of a leper in the woods; load my body with all the most atrocious pains here below, and I will accept all these as penance for my sins, and I will thank you for them, but of your charity do not send me to hell, do not deprive me of your love and of the contemplation of you for all eternity. O Jesus, I say from my heart: 'Here let me burn, here let me be tormented, here do not spare me; but spare me in eternity.'

(8) O God, your judgments are terrible, the very thought of them makes me tremble with fear. But who can ever plumb the depths of your mercy? Let whoever so desires exalt your other divine attributes, magnify your wisdom and praise your power, but for my part I will never cease to sing of your mercies.[3] Is the earth, most sweet Jesus, not full of your mercy?[4] And is your mercy not found in heaven too, and above all your other works?[5] And are you not the Father of mercies and the God of all consolations?[6] Was it not you who said you desired not sacrifice but mercy?[7] And I, I myself, miserable sinner that I am, am I not a portent, a miracle of your mercy? I am the lost sheep and you are the good shepherd, who hastened lovingly in search of me, found me at last and after a thousand caresses lifted me onto your shoulders and joyfully carried me back to the fold. I am that unhappy wretch who on the road to Jericho was set upon by thieves, beaten, wounded, stripped naked

---

[1] Cf. Phil. 2: 12.   [2] Cf. Matthew 8: 12.   [3] Psalm 88(89): 1.
[4] Psalm 32(33): 5.   [5] Psalm 35(36): 5; 144(145): 9.   [6] 2 Cor. 1: 3.
                          [7] Matthew 9: 13.

and almost put to death, and you were the compassionate Samaritan who healed me, poured out wine for me (that is, made me understand those dread truths which shook me out of my torpor). You anointed me with the balm of your consolations, you opened wide to me your generous heart. I am, alas! the prodigal son who wasted your substance, your natural and supernatural gifts, and reduced myself to the most miserable state because I had fled far from you, you who are the Word by whom all things were made, and without whom all things turn to evil because they are nothing in themselves. And you are that most loving Father who welcomed me with a great feast when, repenting of my transgressions, I came back to your house and found shelter under your roof, in your embrace. You took me in again as your son, you set me once more at your table, made me share in your joys; you called me once more to take part in your inheritance. What more can I say? I am the treacherous disciple who betrayed you, the presumptuous man who disowned you, the coward who mocked and derided you, the cruel wretch who crowned you with thorns. I scourged you, I laid the Cross upon you, I mocked you in your agony, I buffeted you, I gave you gall and vinegar to drink, and it was I, alas! who pierced your heart with the cruel lance. All this and even more I have done with my sins! What a thought to make me humble! A thought that must perforce wring from my eyes the bitterest tears of repentance. And you, you are my kind Jesus, the gentle lamb who called me your friend, who looked with love upon me, a sinner, who blessed me when I cursed you, who prayed for me on the Cross, and from your pierced heart let flow a stream of divine Blood that washed away my impurities and cleansed my soul of its sins; you snatched me from death by dying for me, and by conquering death you gave me life. You opened to me the gates of paradise.

O the love of Jesus! And yet at last this love has conquered and I am with you, my Master, my Friend, my Spouse, my Father. Here I am in your heart! What then would you have me do? I was in the paths of wickedness and I was blinded by your divine splendour, as was St Paul on the way to Damascus: 'Lord, what shall I do?'[1] Teach me your truth, the way I must go.[2] I will cling closely to you, and I will love you, O my Jesus, I will love you with the love of Paul and of your beloved John, with the love of all your saints, the love that leads to action, the love that endures till death. Nothing can ever separate me from your love, not hunger or poverty or cold or pain, neither suffering nor death.[3] I trust so much in the help of your grace, O Jesus! And now, since you loved me

[1] Acts 22: 10.   [2] Psalm 142(143): 8.   [3] Cf. Romans 8: 39.

till the end, you have overlooked my sins and called me closer to you and chosen me to be your minister, your intimate friend, the dispenser of your mysteries. And so you continually inspire me with the sweet and secret messages of your love, with infinite aspirations, with the honey and heavenly nectar of your consolations. Oh may my heart burn and be consumed in sacrifice for you on the altar of your most Sacred Heart, may I always long for you, seek you, find you; may I clothe myself with your spirit, the spirit of wisdom and understanding, and persuade all sinners to repent and return to you! May we all, gathering under the shadow of your adored Cross, praise your mercy for ever!

(9) I am a Christian; more, I am a cleric. Therefore I must always and in all my actions represent Jesus Christ since, as St Gregory Nazianzen says, priests are clothed in Christ. Here then is my model: Jesus Christ.

Think of him as a child in his cradle. Christ the creator, the Lord of the world, redeemer of mankind, found no one to welcome him when he came on this earth. On the contrary, he could find no lodging; no one would give him shelter, everyone said there was no room for him, so he was obliged to take refuge in an abandoned stable and there he first appeared to men.

What humility is there! And I, who am less than nothing, become angry if I am received coldly or if people show little respect for me or my learning, or if, when I am compared with others, I have to take a back seat. Do I not feel terribly hurt if those whom I try to help show no gratitude or even insult me? Or if my Superiors do not think very highly of me or misinterpret my actions? If others speak ill of me and give unfair accounts of my conduct? O pride, abase yourself before the humility of Jesus! Jesus has clothed the earth with flowers, has given the little birds their soft feathers and the sun its majestic raiment of light, has buried in the heart of the mountains and in the sands of river beds the most precious stones, gold and gems, and yet he was born in dire poverty and without even the clothing he needed to cover him. What poverty! And I, wretch that I am and unworthy of any good thing, dare to grumble because I was born poor, of poor parents, and live and am clothed only by the generosity of others? Should I not rather console myself and rejoice, and thank Jesus from my heart, because at least in this it is very easy for me to imitate him? Ought I to have the slightest desire to be less poor? Can I, without blushing for shame, wish I were better dressed? Can I forget the words of Jesus himself: 'Blessed are the poor in spirit, for theirs is the kingdom of heaven'?[1]

[1] Matthew 5: 3.

Jesus, splendour of the substance of the Father, is born on the spiky straw of the manger, is stiff with cold, is exposed to all weathers. Even from his first hour he submits to all kinds of suffering for the salvation of men. What self-denial was his! And I who for my many sins should be given the hardest penance, shall I not feel ashamed to complain about every little inconvenience, or take any notice of a draught of air, an annoying fly or a change in the weather?

Ought I to choose the most comfortable way of walking, sitting down, etc.? I am compelled to mortify myself in order to avoid occasion for sin and keep on the straight path, but Jesus never sinned, he was free from all sin.

(10) How did Jesus live at Nazareth? He lived the life of a good cleric, the life I ought to lead.

He lived in seclusion. No one knew anything about him. To all appearances he was just the son of Mary, the carpenter's son. No sign as yet of his future greatness, his divine origin. What a fine lesson of reserve for me, always so full of myself, my pride ever driving me to display my few natural gifts, which are accompanied by so many failings. I too must live in seclusion so that, far from the turmoil of the world, I may hear the voice of my Jesus speaking to my heart.

My greatest care must be to hide what little good I am able, with the grace of God, to achieve, lest vanity should debase it and the devil rob me of it. But what is this impulse which impels me to make a public display of everything? What are these castles in the air that my imagination builds to satisfy my self-love? Pride, nothing but pride. It seems to me that the best way to cure myself, at least partially, would be to be confined in a wilderness where nobody would find me, without any communication with my fellows, so that no one would have occasion to speak about me. And if this is not to be my vocation because God has arranged otherwise, then I must always be mindful of my obligation to keep in the background, here in the seminary, wishing not to be known or taken any notice of, and in the holidays remaining in seclusion, alone in my room. St Thomas admonishes me: 'You must often choose to retire into your cell, if you wish to be admitted to the wine cellar (that is, the cellar of love).'[1] One of the finest resolutions of my patron saint, St John Berchmans, was this: 'I will love my cell!' At Nazareth Jesus worked as a carpenter from morning to night. If only I could have seen him there, seen those hands which had created all worlds and launched the stars in

[1] Thomas Aquinas, *Epistola de modo studendi*; ed. Th. Esser, *D. Thomae Aquinatis . . . Monita et preces*, Paderborn, 1890, pp. 16–17.

their swift courses grow callused with the plane, the saw and the other tools of his trade! And to think that Jesus was God! And that he pursued that laborious life for so many years, without respite! And that he was to draw to himself so many million souls! Seclusion was the seminary of that great priest, who was later to fulfil the greatest of all missions, sealed by the greatest sacrifice. Work and pray! In thirty years he himself could have converted and sanctified so many other souls and God alone knows how many wonderful miracles he might have worked. But the heavenly Father had disposed otherwise: thirty years of labour and seclusion. His will must be done and Jesus did just this.

So a divine hand has traced for me the path that leads to the altar. Seclusion, prayer and work. To pray, working and to work, praying. To work hard at my studies, always: that is my duty. To study and not boast of my learning, to study untiringly and draw closer to Jesus who is the giver of light, the reflection of eternal light,[1] and to pray in such a way that study itself may become prayer. In this world there is no getting away from it: we must bend our shoulders to the task. Let us then make a good start and work for love, for this is what the Lord wills. And working with Jesus in Nazareth in prayerful seclusion, I will prepare myself to accomplish more perfectly the mission which awaits me, a mission of wisdom and love, and I shall deserve to be crowned by Jesus with the starry crown of the apostolate.

(11) Here is a thought that might help me. When Jesus was drawing near to the village of Bethany some people ran to tell Mary of his coming, saying: 'The Teacher is here and is calling for you!'[2] What beautiful words! Imagine the loving haste with which Mary ran to greet her divine guest. Well, at the beginning of every one of my actions I will suppose that the bell says: 'The Teacher is here and is calling for you.' When I reflect that Jesus the Master is here, calling me to study, to pray, to rest, to walk—how can I fail to be at once inspired to do my duties as they should be done, with Jesus instructing me as I do them?

(12) Mortal sin! What infamy! I shudder even to think of it. Nevertheless, for its seriousness and for the harm it does, venial sin is no less to be shunned, because although it is not of such a nature as to deserve hell and the loss of grace, nevertheless it gives great displeasure to God. Well then, if I wish to love my God always and entirely I must avoid even the slightest action which may give him displeasure, for love is very sensitive.

My God, is it possible that I could offend you mortally? No, no! Away then with venial sins too, or rather with the attachment to them. Rather

[1] Wisdom 7: 26.   [2] John 11: 28.

death than a venial sin on my soul! Help me then, O Lord, to keep my soul pure, stainless and pleasing to your most pure eyes; may I cast myself on your loving breast and may no one drag me from you. You know what I am made of and the evil things which have struck root in me; give me then your kind hand, lest I stumble in the way; lighten my mind, that I may know those faults which disfigure my soul, and fill me more and more with the burning desire to please you only, you who are infinitely worthy to be loved.

(13) These four qualities sum up for me my duties, the virtues of a cleric: piety, studiousness, self-denial and strength of character. Angelic piety, unwearying study, continual mortifications, especially of self-love and of the eyes, a really priestly character which shall be seen, in the words of the Council of Trent, in my 'gestures, gait, dress and speech'.[1]

[9]   *A solemn promise to the Sacred Heart of*
Jesus, made under the patronage of
St Aloysius Gonzaga

27 February, 1900

Through the grace of God, I am profoundly persuaded and convinced that it is my compelling duty, as a Christian and a seminarist, to dedicate myself wholly and always to his divine service and his holy love.

As I proceed further along the way of perfection and perfect charity, I am inspired by the consideration of how infinitely Jesus deserves to be loved by me, his poor creature, both for his divine perfections and for the immense love of his most Sacred Heart.

Finally, I reflect on the grave danger of failing in this most holy obligation, not only through mortal but also through venial sins which, although less serious, are still a grave offence against Jesus and so estrange me from this perfect love.

Therefore, during the holy Spiritual Exercises of this Year of Grace 1900, the nineteenth year of my age, and on this last day of the holy retreat (27 February), while I am sacramentally united to the most Sacred Heart of Jesus through holy communion, in the presence of my most holy Mother, Mary Immaculate, St Joseph her most chaste spouse and my chief protector, and all the other saints, my special intercessors, my Guardian Angel and all the court of heaven, I, the seminarist Angelo

---

[1] See page 4.

Giuseppe, a sinner, promise the most Sacred Heart, with all the solemnity and power this act of mine may have, always, today and at all times, by the grace of God to keep myself free from the slightest attachment to any voluntary venial sin. And since because of my weakness I cannot guarantee in the future to keep this promise by my own unaided effort, I place it in the hands of the angelic youth St Aloysius Gonzaga, so pre-eminently free from all stain of sin, so pure in heart and mind. Choosing him for this purpose as my special intercessor and patron, I beg and implore him— he is so kind and loving—to deign to accept it, guard it, and by his prayers help me to keep it.

O most sweet Jesus, accept this little token of my love for you or at least of the burning desire I have to love you with all my heart, to be consumed with love for you, my Friend, my Father, my most loving Spouse! I beg you, deign to accept it and to add to it the sustaining power of your grace, without which, as you told your disciples before you left them, and as I myself know only too well, I can do nothing.

'Heart of Jesus, burning with love for us, set our hearts aflame with love for you.'

[10]   *Holy Year, 1900–Jesus, Mary, Joseph!*

22 August, Wednesday, monthly day of recollection

This morning during my period of recollection I was inspired once more to put down on paper my reflections and what I like to think of as my achievements, and this time I have not been able to resist. What conclusions have I drawn from today's retreat? I have realized once more that if I am to be a good seminarist, a seminarist after Jesus' own heart, I still have much to do. As regards humility, I have barely the semblance of it; inside me there is still a great deal of pride which is always trying to make me listen to its claims. As regards charity, well, there is some fervour or at least I think there is, there are good desires; but I am still a long way from the real charity of the saints, the charity that endures all, the strong generous love for God and for the Sacred Heart. However, let us hope we are drawing nearer to it. As regards purity, it is true that, thanks to my Immaculate Lady, I do not feel any strong temptations contrary to this virtue—yet I must confess that I have two eyes in my head which want to look at more than they should, and sometimes, I think unconsciously, they get the better of my soul. As regards meekness, tranquillity, gentleness, in short all that shines so brightly in the gentle St Francis de Sales, my special protector and particular model, although there are no grave faults to deplore, there is still not all that I would like to have and that with divine grace I could acquire. Sometimes I get a little too excited in conversation; at other times I am not very pleasant with my family, or lack courtesy in my behaviour—and there are so many other faults. It is better not to speak of my practices of piety, some of which, especially the holy rosary, are far from satisfactory. And now the retreat is over. Let us get down to business.

I renew my resolution to make myself really holy, and I protest once more before you, O most loving Heart of Jesus, my Teacher, that I wish to love you as you desire, and to be filled with your spirit. Meanwhile, there are four resolutions which I am determined to carry out here, now and always, so as to be able to take a few steps forward. First of all I must have the spirit of union with Jesus, the spirit of recollection in his Heart from my first awakening in the morning until I close my eyes at night and, if possible, also during my dreams at night. 'I slept but my heart was awake.'[1] My best efforts must go into saying the rosary. Secondly, I must never forget the dictum: *Age quod agis!*[2] and always and in all my actions preserve presence of mind. Thirdly, I must observe the most scrupulous modesty in my glances, words, etc. We know what we mean by this. Finally, tranquillity, calm, cheerfulness, good manners, never a cross word with anyone, no excited speech, but simplicity, cordiality, sincerity without cowardice—no flabbiness. And I must add: never to speak of anyone, or of my intimate friends, if their failures should set my own conduct in a better light. If I speak at all I must speak with reserve, saying what good I can of them and covering up their failings when to reveal them would do no good and would only arouse my own vanity which lurks beneath the surface and more often than not quietly slips out. These are the fruits of this retreat.

O Jesus, you see the deep desire of my heart to love you, to become a real minister of yours; grant me the grace really to do a little good. Shall I be able to carry out these modest resolutions? O Jesus, I hope so much from your grace.

22 August, Wednesday evening

From now on I will see to it that I never allow my visit to Jesus Christ in the Blessed Sacrament to come after the visit I usually pay to the parish

---

[1] Song of Solomon 5: 2.

[2] This tag is one used frequently by Pope John. It appears to be a misquotation of Plautus, *Persa*, IV, 4, 107, and may best be translated as 'Pay attention to what you are doing'.

priest in the evening, unless there are grave reasons for this. Moreover, I confirm all that I said this morning, for I have already seen that it is one thing light-heartedly to make resolutions, and quite another to carry them out.

23 August, Thursday evening

On the whole, not too badly. However I must still take great care to watch my words when I am talking with seminarists and about matters in relation to which my vanity may creep out of hiding and try to cut a dash. For the rest, as regards my panegyric on the Sacred Heart, I must not be over anxious, for that would lead to confused thinking, with poor results: in short, I should make a mess of it.

O Jesus, deign to accept my praises.

24 August, Friday evening

It is really true, as we read in *The Imitation of Christ*, that at certain times the less noble part of man, whether he will or not, gets on top of his better nature and crushes it. This is what happened to me this afternoon. Although I racked my brains to try to study with some profit, I could not get anything done. I felt out of sorts with everything, bored stiff with sermons and reading, with everything in fact. What was l to do? Praise be to God all the same. We are always in his hands, come what may. It gave me a good chance to mortify my excessive desire to study, to get on well, etc. However, the good Jesus helped me over this too. Even though, as soon as I opened one book I closed it at once to take up another, at least I was not idle and was able to flout the devil. Thanks be to God. But that blessed rosary went rather badly again this evening. And yet, I am sure I do not do this on purpose; every now and then, as soon as I notice my thoughts are straying, I do try to concentrate.

O my Mother, O my Lady, do something about this yourself, for you see that I am helpless on my own.

25 August, Saturday evening

My visit was a silent one: my thoughts were elsewhere. The same might be said about the rosary. I am determined to imitate the greatest saints and yet I am still incapable of doing the ordinary duties of a Christian as they should be done. O Jesus, you are my hope and my refuge.[1]

[1] Cf. Psalm 30(31): 4.

26 August, Sunday evening

Sunday is the Lord's day; so an even greater spirit of recollection is required. Instead, alas! the contrary was the case. Alas! will Wednesday's resolution about exercising control over my thoughts be cast away so soon? O kind Jesus, give me strength so that this may not happen again. O St Alexander, to whom this day is dedicated, give me your virtue, your energy, your heroism in well doing.

28 August, Tuesday

Last night I did not even remember to write down the findings of my examination of conscience. As for today, there are many things to notice. For example, putting off with idle excuses my visit to the Blessed Sacrament, thus running the risk of making it in haste and not too well, although this is a thing which offends Jesus and reflects little honour on me. Then, my good fellow, you must keep a closer watch over your tongue, because it is in what you say that your self-love creeps out, especially when you are talking with other seminarists. Whether what I say is nonsense or whether it is the truth, self-love is always lurking there. When the conversation is over, I am dissatisfied with myself, and my kind Teacher, Jesus, speaking in my heart, tells me that he too is not pleased. In short, many more invocations are needed; these are the arrows of love which will pierce the Sacred Heart and release a flood of Christian charity. Alas! how far I am from any remotest resemblance to my model, St Francis de Sales! And yet, O Jesus, you know well that I grieve over this estrangement. As often as I become aware of it I repent and am disgusted with myself. Every time I draw near to you I seem to feel growing in my heart a most fervent desire to imitate your humility and meekness. O most kind Jesus, you must come to my assistance. Let me ever hear your voice, which is always gentle, even in reproach. 'Let me hear your voice.'[1] For my heart yearns for you, O Jesus, and I am sure I can say that I bear no grudge against anyone. If you will look after me all the rest will follow. Jesus, Mary, Joseph!

29 August, Wednesday evening

Not so badly on the whole. But one thing is certain: days without holy communion show that something is missing. During this Novena of the Nativity of Mary I will be especially careful not to pander to my palate

---

[1] Song of Solomon 2: 14.

since, as this is the season for fruit, I find many opportunities for indulging this weakness.

This evening, to disturb my peace of mind, there was an incident which, though insignificant in itself, has made a profound and painful impression on me. My mother was rather hurt by something I said (which, I confess, might have been put more gently) rebuking her curiosity about a certain matter. She was deeply offended and said things to me which I would never have expected to hear from my mother, for whom, after God, Mary and the saints, I bear the greatest love of which my heart is capable. To hear her tell me that I am always uncivil with her, without gentleness or good manners, when I feel that I can say with all sincerity that this is not true, has hurt me too deeply; she was distressed because of me, but I was very much more distressed to see her grieving and, to put it frankly, giving way like this. After so much tender love to be told by my mother that I dislike her, and other things that I have not the heart to remember any longer—oh this was too much for the heart of a son, and of a son who feels the most profound natural affections. This gave me the most bitter sorrow, wounded the most intimate and sensitive fibres of my heart. How could I help giving way to tears? O mother, if you only knew how much I love you, and how I long to see you happy, you would not be able to contain your joy!

Will you, my Jesus, accept this sacrifice which I place in your heart, offering it to you that you may grant me more meekness and gentleness, while preserving a proper dignity, and grant my poor, kind mother greater fortitude. O Mary of Sorrows, never cease to help us.

1 September, Saturday evening

On Wednesday evening I was at Bergamo. Last night I was tired and worn out after the exhausting effort of coming back on foot from Bergamo to Sotto il Monte. I was tired too, after the ceremony of the blessing of the bells at Carvico, besides everything else: this is why there are two gaps in my diary. Now, coming back to my notes about my behaviour during these days, I will mention two characteristic occurrences, the former of which concerns particularly the thirtieth and thirty-first of last month. There was of course also a certain irregularity in my pious practices, due to a change of time-table and to the break in the monotony of my life at home. However, I must note that sometimes with the reverend priests I allow myself to hold forth as an authority about politics, airing my opinions about this and that, one question after another—in short, flinging myself into the discussion in a way unsuitable for a seminarist of my condition. It is true that every time I find myself doing this I am truly sorry, but why do I not think of that first? The fact is that especially in these somewhat delicate matters one must set aside one's zeal, which serves no good purpose here, and remember that 'for everything there is a season.'[1] Some things must wait till I am a priest! For the time being I must read all I can and so absorb information in accordance with firm and healthy principles. For the rest, I must be content to listen, even feigning ignorance about these matters, especially when the conversation turns on more important questions than are usually discussed in my homely talks with the parish priest and the curate. How would St Francis de Sales behave in this case?

2 September, Sunday evening

The other thing I meant to make a note of last night was my failure to mortify the desire to gratify my greedy palate. This is really shameful. Therefore I must not neglect these God-sent opportunities to honour Mary, especially during the Novena for her Nativity. I must eat what I require, no more. Finally, I must note that there is still a great scarcity of invocations and this is, I believe, hindering my spiritual progress.

Jesus, Mary, watch over me, that I may never stray from your protection.

3 September, Monday evening

Recollection and mortification. O Jesus, you see that I do wish to love you more truly, with all my heart, with my whole being.

4 September, Tuesday evening

Better, thanks be to God! Today is the Feast of St Gregory the Great, one of the glories of the Church, one of the most brilliant jewels of the Roman pontificate. Before his majestic figure I feel renewed affection and enthusiasm for the Pope, the great Leo XIII, against whom the most grievous, wicked and diabolical insults are being hurled in these days. The times are very grave.[2] Let us pray. Let us pray for our Pope Leo.

[1] Eccles. 3: 1.
[2] The reference is possibly to the national celebrations for the thirtieth anniversary of the 'breach of Porta Pia'. These celebrations did in fact assume an anti-Catholic and anti-papal character.

6 September, Thursday evening.

Today was a day sent from God, during which I have been obliged to do all that my good Lord wished. He sent me a bad headache and so, in spite of some rebellion on the part of that other self, I have had to give up studying and put aside my poor panegyric on the Sacred Heart, which will be finished when Jesus wishes.

This is really a punishment for my impatience to reach some final conclusions. As for feeling resigned, I do not think I failed in this. Thanks be to God. Through his grace I am willing to suffer everything for my Jesus, for the Heart that loves me so much.

What claims my attention just now, however, and cannot lightly be dismissed during a Novena to Our Lady, is the disorderly and at times careless manner in which I am saying my prayers.

O my Jesus, what patience you must have, when you hear me asking for your graces in such a fashion! My good fellow, what kind of manners are these? What will the angels say, who see everything? What would your fellow men say if you spoke to them in such a way?

So, here again more calm. Prayers may be few in number but they must be said composedly, at least as well as if I were talking to my fellows. To make this easier, I will make a special effort to be completely recollected. It is always the same: 'Pay attention to what you are doing.'[1] Tomorrow, the last day of the Novena, reparation for all that is past. In honour of Mary, no fruit shall touch my lips. O Mary, help me.

7 September, Friday evening

Not so badly on the whole. Even the mortification of my greed has been scrupulously observed in Mary's honour. However, I always feel discouraged when I consider myself as I am, in comparison with what I might be, and with what the saints, St John Berchmans and St Francis de Sales, were at my age.

O Lord, you see my heart with its desires. Tomorrow is the day dedicated to thoughts of Our Lady as a new-born child: therefore recollection, prayer—and for the rest, holy joy.[2]

---

[1] *Age quod agis.* Cf. note 2 on page 75.
[2] The 1900 notes end here. The notes beginning 28 April, 1901, are found in the same exercise book.

1901—1903

In the Seminary in Rome

1901

Spiritual retreat, 28 April, 1901. Rome. Third
Sunday after Easter

This is the first retreat I have made since I came to Rome. How am I? Certainly I cannot complain about the graces Jesus has sent me, the indescribable joys, the moments of sheer delight which shed their radiance over all the rest. As for myself, however, I must confess that I have not changed at all from what I was before. Ardent desires to do really well, and to love my Lord as he deserves; longings, perhaps even excessive, and not always free from considerations of vanity, to study, to learn a great deal, to acquire a wealth of knowledge so as to be able to use this means, which has now become one of the most important, of winning souls for Christ. In reality, however, I still fail in many things: above all in a real effort to see that my meditation and recitation of the holy rosary are done as they should be done and that I profit by my general and particular examinations of conscience, in order that I may improve every day in detachment from self, union with God and the practice of true virtue.

Here in Rome, I can say I have all I need. Indeed there are also opportunities for the acceptance of certain rebuffs to my pride, and for the practice of certain mortifications. So I must take courage once more and set my affairs in order. Above all, I will always try to make my holy meditation with the greatest diligence and to good purpose, letting it inspire me with practical resolutions for the day, and I will make this a principal point for examination of conscience. During the day, very many invocations, especially during lessons and while studying. I will say the holy rosary in homage to Our Lady during the coming month of May. I must never think of my studies immediately before or still less during the time I spend in religious duties. I will make my visit to the Blessed Sacrament with special fervour and modesty. Most of all, a careful watch over my eyes during our walks, especially in certain districts. After the walk and before my evening study I must never omit my particular examination, which will have for its object my conversation and my self-esteem. Finally, a great serenity of mind and heart, a profound spirit of recollection and a great orderliness in everything.

O my good St Joseph, whose powerful patronage the Church celebrates today, I dedicate myself wholly once more to you, and commend to you these resolutions of mine. May your intercessions enable me to keep them, especially when I ask of you the grace of a recollected mind during my prayers and the practice of the interior life, such as I admire in you. Grant me this, I pray, and I will always love you and teach others to love you, so that all may share in the great kindnesses of so glorious a patron. So be it. 'Blessed Joseph, obtain for us grace to lead an innocent life; and may our life ever be shielded by thy patronage.'[1]

---

[1] From the gradual of the Mass for the Solemnity of St Joseph.

1902

[12]   *† Jesus, Mary, Joseph!*

Notes made during the Spiritual Exercises after the
Babylonian Captivity,[1] 10–20 December, 1902
under Father Francesco Pitocchi[2]

(1) Who am I? Nothing. What is my name? What are my titles of nobility? I have none. I am a servant and nothing more. I have nothing of my own, not even my life. God is my Master, absolute Master over life and death. No parents, no relations, no masters in this world. My real and only Master is God.

So, I live only to obey God's slightest commands. I cannot move a hand, a finger or an eye, I cannot look before me or behind, unless God wills it. In his presence I stand upright and motionless, like the meanest soldier standing to attention before his officer, ready to do all, even to cast myself into the flames. This must be my task my whole life long, because I was born for this: I am a servant.

I must always look on myself as a servant. Therefore I shall have not one single moment free for serving my own interests, my pleasures, my vanity, etc. If I were to do this I should be no better than a thief because I should be stealing time which is not my own, I should be an unfaithful servant, a wicked servant, unworthy of my hire.[3] Alas! This is exactly what I have done. What confusion and shame I feel! So much pride, arrogance and presumption, and I do not even know how to be a servant.

---

[1] His military service. See letters, pp. 331–4 below.

[2] Father Francesco Pitocchi was born at Vico del Lazio (Frosinone) on 22 September, 1852 and died in Rome on 13 June, 1922. He was ordained in 1875 and, when already a parish priest, entered the Redemptorist novitiate, and was professed in 1885. Leo XIII appointed him confessor of the Roman Seminary in 1899. For many years, inspired by the teaching of St Alphonsus Liguori, he guided his students towards sound piety and generous obedience. Young Angelo Roncalli had him for spiritual director from 1902 to 1905. Subsequently he went to him every time he came back to Rome, and finally also when he was called to Propaganda Fide in 1921. Roncalli tells us that Pitocchi used to say to him: 'Always obey, with simplicity and good nature, and leave everything else to the Lord.' See 'A tribute to the memory of Fr Francesco Pitocchi', Appendix 4 below.

[3] Matthew 18: 32; cf. St Augustine, *Serm.* CXXXVII, 4 (P.L., XXXVIII, 756).

11. The earliest portrait. The caption, in John XXIII's handwriting, reads: 'First
retreat of the cleric Angelo Roncalli, at 20 years.
Student at the Roman Seminary. Rome, January, 1901.'

12. Roman Seminary, 1902–3: final year theology students. Angelo Roncalli is second from the right in the second row

O Lord, my God, I acknowledge the rights you have over me. Forgive my infidelities. Evil inclinations often distract me from attending to your divine service. But now no more of this! I bind myself to your service and stand before you like St Francis Xavier. Look at me, O Lord. 'I am your servant, O Lord: give me understanding that I may learn your commandments.'[1]

(2) And the Lord, my Master, has given me his orders. I am to know him, love him and serve him all my life. What blessed servitude, what glory, what supreme honour! I am the King's page, to go with him everywhere; I am admitted to his secrets. Then, after a miserably short service, I who should have obeyed him without any reward am made a sharer in his own glory in heaven. He has put all the creatures of this earth, all the gifts of nature, all these things at my disposal, so that I may use them only to raise myself towards him and love him. This is the reason for their existence. Therefore, when I use creatures for my own pleasure, I upset the order of Providence, I break the wonderful harmony of the universe, setting myself against God. What a wicked servant!

I must make use of all creatures in so far as they lead me closer to God; I must shun them in so far as they estrange me from him. This is the golden rule, the great fundamental principle to be applied in all practical cases. When they are used according to the will of God no harm .can come of them.

I like to enjoy good health, and God sends me sickness. Well, blessed be this sickness! Here starts the practice of that holy indifference that made the saints what they were. Oh if I could only acquire that tranquillity of soul, that peace of mind in favourable and unfavourable conditions, which would make my life sweeter and happier, even in the midst of troubles! Poor or rich, honoured or despised, poor priest of a mountain parish or Bishop of a vast diocese, it must be all the same to me, as long as in this way I do the will of my Master, fulfil my duty as a faithful servant and save my soul. Indeed if I were allowed a choice, I would have to prefer poverty to wealth, men's scorn to their rewards, the most obscure tasks to important positions. Suppose I should wish to take up some special course of study: my Superiors will not allow it. Very well, then no special study, but cheerfulness always. I would like to be ordained subdeacon at Easter: my Superiors will not hear of it. Then let us wait, in the same cheerful spirit. I would like to be left as I am. Instead my Superiors wish to give me a task which I find humiliating, and which offends my pride.[2] It costs me an enormous sacrifice to obey.

[1] Cf. Psalm 118(119): 73, 125.   [2] As sick-room attendant.

Well then, let us obey; let us pluck up our courage and be cheerful in the Lord.

This is the physic that calms all impatience, sweetens privation and makes us rejoice even in the midst of the troubles of this life.

(3) Not one drop of the blood of Jesus can avail the rebel angels, yet theirs was merely a sin of thought, and their first at that. For me, who sin so frequently, all the fruits of the Passion are available, not once but time and time again. And still I keep my God waiting for me! What a miracle of mercy! and how shameful for me! But enough, Lord—let us make an end of all this. From now onwards, with your help, I will seek you out always, at every moment, and I will take the place of the fallen angels in praising and blessing you for ever and ever. The angels fell like thunderbolts into hell, because of a single thought of pride.[1] And I, with my head so full of it? How easy it would be for my God to take away all my intellectual gifts, my memory and my reason? Or confine me to my bed with sickness? So, softly: less presumption; more distrust of myself and more humility.

(4) Where are my riches, my properties, my assets? Disobedience, acts of pride, negligence in my duties, insufficient control of my feelings, infinite distractions, vanity in my thoughts, words and deeds and sins galore: all these belong to me—they are my very own.

And with all this to boast of I think of lording it over others, making a name for myself, exalting myself, displaying my powers. I consider myself a fine young fellow, a good seminarist, and this is far from the truth. This is the height of imprudence, of unreasonableness, for anyone who thinks himself a reasonable being.

(5) O my good Lord, shall I too be sent to hell? The poor ignorant man to paradise, with the infidel and the savage; and I, called with the first light of dawn, nursed in your bosom, shall I be sent to hell with the devils? I know what life in a barracks is like—I shudder at the very thought of it.

What blasphemies there were in that place, and what filth! And would hell be any better? If I were to end up there, while my fellow soldiers, the poor wretches, who grew up surrounded by evil, were sent to paradise—no wonder I tremble at the thought! I must pity all sinners and never cease to thank my God for the kindnesses he has shown to me; I must make the most of them but take nothing for granted. I am what I am, a sinner, and unstable in the extreme.

[1] Cf. St Athanasius, De virginitate: 208, 5 (P.G., XXVIII, 257): 'Superbia illum inde praecipitavit ad inferiores abyssi partes.'

But what if the justice of God were to take precedence over his mercy? O Lord, let me suffer everything else, but not hell. Rather let me burn continually with the fire of your holy love.

(6) Death comes to all, and yet I never think of it. Every step I take, every fleeting moment brings me nearer to death. I am full of noble dreams, of ideals of study, of work, of a life spent for Christ's glory, for the good of the Church and society. This is all very fine, but often there is pride there too. What if I were to die before I am ordained? Tomorrow, on the threshold of my priestly life?

This thought seems to make no sense. It really looks as if God has lavished upon me his most tender and motherly care; he has led me out of so many difficulties, and through countless acts of kindness he has brought me here to Rome. It must be for some particular purpose of his: there can be no other reason for my Master's infinite generosity. It is hard for me to think that even after all this he might still take my life away. And yet, for him, nothing could be easier! Does he need my help? Has he ever promised me a certain length of life? And who am I to claim to know his plans? After all, did he not treat St Aloysius, St Stanislaus and St John Berchmans in this way?

O Lord, do with me whatever you will; I accept even death with satisfaction and contentment, if that is your wish. After all, you are the centre, the synthesis, the final goal of all my ideals. But at least let me die in your holy love. The strength you have given me to praise you and to make you loved on earth I will use to love you and to praise you more ardently in heaven.

On the other hand let the thought of death, which may be near at hand, serve to give me graver thoughts. Down with pride, ambition and vanity! With death so near, have I any time to give to these miseries?

(7) 'It is appointed for men once to die, and after that comes judgment!'[1] Even if I were to be Pope, even if my name were to be invoked and revered by all and inscribed on marble monuments, I should still have to stand before the divine judge, and what should I be worth then? Not much. I can hardly believe that my Jesus, who today treats me so tenderly and kindly, may one day appear before me, his face suffused with divine wrath, to judge me. And yet this is an article of faith and I believe it. And what a judgment that will be! The stray words during the time of silence, the rather mischievous expression, the affected gesture, the furtive glance, that strutting about like a professor, that carefully studied composure of manner, with the well-fitting cassock, the fashionable shoes, the

[1] Hebrews 9: 27.

dainty morsel of bread—and then the shade of envy always in my thoughts, the castles in the air, the wandering thoughts during my practices of piety, however short these may be—all will be told against me. And what of my graver sins?

O God, how ashamed my soul will feel! Any honours I may have, any reputation for learning, or even the fame of being zealous and holy, what will these be worth in that hour? Degrees, fine theses, vain erudition, and so on, how will they be regarded? O God, grant me today a little of your divine light, so that I may discern my weaknesses and find some remedy for them. Open my eyes that nothing, however minute, may escape them, for one day all will be revealed in your light. 'Lord, lighten my eyes lest I sleep the sleep of death.'[1]

A globe of purest crystal, lit by the sun's radiance, that is how I see the purity of the priest's heart. My soul must be like a mirror to reflect the images of the angels, of Mary most holy, of Jesus Christ. If the mirror should cloud over, however slightly, then I deserve to be broken in pieces and flung onto the rubbish heap. What sort of a mirror am I? O the world is so ugly, filthy and loathsome! In my year of military service I have learnt all about it. The army is a running fountain of pollution, enough to submerge whole cities. Who can hope to escape from this flood of slime, unless God comes to his aid?

I thank you, my God, for having preserved me from so much corruption. This has really been one of your noblest gifts, for which I shall be grateful to you my whole life long.

I did not think that a reasonable man could fall so low. Yet it is a fact. Today, after my brief experience, I think it is true to say that more than half of all mankind, at some time in their lives, become animals, without shame. And the priests? O God, I tremble when I think that not a few, even among these, betray their sacred calling.

Now nothing surprises me any more: certain stories make no impression on me. Everything is explained. What cannot be explained is how it is that you, O most pure Jesus, of whom it was said 'he pastures his flock among the lilies',[2] can put up with such infamous conduct, even from your own ministers, and yet deign to come down into their hands and dwell in their hearts, without inflicting on them instant punishment.

Lord Jesus, I tremble for myself too. If 'the stars of the sky fell to the earth',[3] what hope have I who am made out of dust?

From now on I intend to be even more scrupulous about this matter, even if I become the laughing stock of the whole world. In order not to

---

[1] Psalm 12(13): 4.   [2] Song of Solomon 2: 16.   [3] Cf. Rev. 6: 13.

touch upon impure subjects, I think it is better to say very little, or hardly anything at all, about purity. 'We have this treasure in earthen vessels.'[1] I have reason to tremble. 'Is my flesh bronze?'[2]

I call to mind all the resolutions made about this during past retreats, which I have in writing, and protest to holy Mary, my most chaste Mother, that I will at all costs observe them.

(9) Hail, Christ the King! You summon me to fight your battles and, without a moment's delay, with all the enthusiasm of my twenty years and the grace you have given me, I boldly enlist in the ranks of your volunteers. I dedicate myself to your service, for life or death. You offer me your Cross for a standard and a weapon. I place my right hand on this invincible weapon and give you my solemn word, swearing with all the fervour of my youthful heart absolute fidelity until death. So I, whom you created your servant, have become your soldier, I put on your uniform, I gird on your sword, I am proud to call myself a knight of Christ. Give me a soldier's heart, a knight's valour, O Jesus, and I will always be by your side in the rough moments of life, in sacrifices, in ordeals, in battles —and still with you in the hour of victory. And since the signal for the fight has not yet sounded for me, while I remain in my tent, waiting for my hour to strike, you must teach me by your shining example how to try out my valour against my own interior enemies, so as to get rid of these first. They are so many, O Jesus, and they are without mercy! There is one especially who is up to every trick; he is proud and cunning, he clings to me, he pretends to want to make peace and then he makes fun of me, he offers terms, he even follows me into my good deeds.

Lord Jesus, you know who that is: my self-love, the spirit of pride, presumption and vanity. Help me to get rid of him once and for all or, if that is not possible, at least to hold him in subjection so that, unhampered in my movements, I may run to the breach, stand among the warriors who defend your holy cause and sing with you the hymn of salvation.

(10) When I think of the humiliations endured by the divine Word, of the greatness of Mary, the reward of her humility, of the life Jesus led during his first thirty years, and then of my own situation, I am ashamed and speechless. This evening, remembering how Scripture tells us that 'he was obedient to them',[3] in my talk with the boy Jesus in Joseph's workshop, I felt my eyes fill with tears; and I wept like a child.

O my Lord Jesus, shall I never be able to show you, not only in words but in deeds, that with your grace I can imitate your shining example?

[1] 2 Cor. 4: 7.   [2] Job 6: 12.   [3] Luke 2: 51.

You humble yourself infinitely, you 'empty' yourself.[1] I have no need to do this: I am already nothing. I have only to open my eyes and look at myself. You came to this earth poor, and who is poorer than I, for whom you have had to find every mouthful of food until this hour? Since I became a seminarist I have never worn a garment that was not given me out of charity by some kind person. You toiled from your childhood on, and you know that 'I have been poor and hard-working from my youth'.[2]

You did not dispense yourself from any law, although you were not subject to it, and I have had to submit to military service, which is an unjust and barbarous imposition on your ministers.

In silence, in the quiet seclusion of the house at Nazareth, you passed the first thirty years of your life, and already more than ten years have passed since I withdrew from the world to live in the shelter of your sanctuary. Who more than I has benefited by your kindnesses? Who has been in a position to imitate you with fewer sacrifices and greater facility? Then how is it I am so unlike you? I have already passed the twentieth year of my life, and what have I done that is really good? St Aloysius, St Stanislaus and St John Berchmans by this time had already made themselves holy.

And I must remember that their progress towards holiness must have been far, far harder than mine, as their circumstances were less fortunate. Oh how often have I had to bewail this, and how often have I gone back over the same road! But now I intend to put an end to this trifling with my God. At the age when these saints had finished, I begin! 'And I said: now have I begun.'[3] I come in at the eleventh hour, but not for this will you reject me.[4] Lord, in my confusion, deign at least to tell me what I must do to carry out your will.

(11) I love to think of how Jesus founded his Church! Instead of summoning the wise and the learned from the academies, the synagogues and the schools, he cast his loving eyes on twelve poor fishermen, rough, ignorant men. He admitted them to his school, shared with them his most secret thoughts, made them the object of his most loving care and entrusted to them the great mission of transforming mankind.

In the fulness of time Jesus has been pleased to call me also to extend his kingdom and to have some share in the work of the apostles. He took me, a country lad, from my home, and with the affection of a loving mother he has given me all I needed. I had nothing to eat and he provided food

---

[1] Cf. Phil. 2: 7.
[2] Cf. Psalm 87(88): 16.
[3] Psalm 76(77): 11.
[4] Cf. Matthew 20: 9.

for me, I had nothing to wear and he clothed me, I had no books to study and he provided those also. At times I forgot him and he always gently recalled me. If my affection for him cooled, he warmed me in his breast, at the flame with which his Heart is always burning. His enemies and the enemies of his Church surrounded me, set snares for me, dragged me out into the midst of the world, into the mire and filth, and yet he has preserved me from all ill, he has not allowed the sea to swallow me up. To inspire my soul with stronger impulses of faith and charity he has led me to this place, which is so full of his blessings, where *I may live under the protection of his Vicar, beside the fountain of Catholic truth and the tomb of his apostles, where the very sods are stained with the blood of his martyrs and the air is balmy with the odour of sanctity of his confessors,*[1] and he still cares for me without respite, day and night, more than a mother cares for her child. Yet after all this, in return for so much tenderness, he asks me anxiously one thing only: My son, do you love me?[2] Lord, Lord, how can I answer you? See my tears, my throbbing heart, my trembling lips, and the pen that slips from my fingers. . . .What can I say? 'Lord, you know that I love you.'[3]

Oh if I could love you as Peter loved you, with the fervour of Paul and all the martyrs! My love must be joined to humility, a low opinion of myself and scorn for the things of this world—and then make of me what you will: an apostle, a martyr, O Lord.

Meanwhile, what matters is that I should never be ashamed of my poverty, indeed I should be proud of it, just as the lords of this world are proud of their noble lineage, their titles of nobility, their liveries. I am of the same family as Christ—what more can I want? Do I need anything? Providence will abundantly provide, as always hitherto. I must always remember that what little good I have, which my vanity, to make me boastful, attributes to my own merits, has nothing to do with me, nothing at all. I must convince myself that without the special love that Jesus has shown me I should be nothing more today than a poor peasant, the roughest, the most ignorant and perhaps the most wicked of all.

I am not at all what I believe myself to be or what my pride wishes me to be taken for. My father is a peasant who spends his days hoeing and digging, among other things, and I, far from being better than my father, am worth much less, for my father at least is simple and good, while in me there is nothing but malice.When my self-love is silent for a moment and I think of my obligation to give myself wholly to God and to show in

[1] The words in italics were underlined in red by John XXIII in 1961.
[2] Cf. John 21: 15–17.   [3] Cf. John 21: 15.

deeds that I am really, entirely and unreservedly consecrated to him, and that I want to become holy, I become alarmed and despondent—but I must take heart, reflecting that Jesus, who has done such great things for me, has done them all for some special purpose worthy of himself, and that, as until now it is he who has done everything, so he is all the more willing to shower further graces on me in order to complete his work, as long as he finds plenty of good will on my part.

Finally, I must never forget that among the first twelve disciples of Jesus there was Judas also who, because he did not respond to the tender love of his divine Master, slowly and imperceptibly became a traitor, an execrable monster of infamy. If it is true that love drives out fear, it is no less true that fear makes love more sensitive and more cautious.

(12) At the sight of my most gentle Jesus humbling himself and, like a meek lamb, submitting to persecution, torture, treachery and death, my soul is bewildered, ashamed, prostrated; I can find no words—even my pride hangs its head in shame. 'O most sweet Jesus, comfort of the pilgrim soul, with you I am voiceless, but my very silence speaks to you!'[1]

Jesus stooped to wash the feet of the twelve poor fishermen. This is true democracy, of which we ecclesiastics should be most eloquent examples for all to see. Oh how often my blessed Saviour has washed not only my feet but my hands and my head! Shall I be ashamed to do the same for poor and humble folk?

'Take and eat; this is my body.'[2] He has exhausted all the resources of his love; he has given all, even his life, for me.

Lord, just as you placed yourself in our hands, at our disposal, so once more I consecrate to you my body, my soul, my blood, my whole self, that you may do with me what you please.

'My soul is sorrowful, even to death; watch with me.'[3] So Jesus too had his hour of despondency; he felt our human weaknesses. This is comfort for us who get discouraged over so little and is a divine example for us to follow. When our souls are filled with melancholy and our hearts are bleeding, let us draw near to Jesus, to his altar; let us confide our sorrows in him and we shall find strength and peace.

'Simon, are you asleep?'[4] How sad and wistful are these words of Jesus! I shall imagine him saying them to me whenever I am overcome with fatigue or feel unwilling to work or pray. Have I the heart to sleep while Jesus is praying, working and weeping?

[1] Cf. *The Imitation of Christ*, III, XXI, 4.　　　[2] Matthew 26: 26.
[3] Matthew 26: 38.　　　[4] Mark 14: 37.

'And he kissed him.'[1] Oh the hellish sound of that kiss on the divine brow of Jesus! And yet, how many priests repeat this treachery every day! This is a horrifying thought.

O Jesus, receive in your heart my loving kisses, the kisses of a son who loves you, asks your forgiveness for his sins and promises never to offend you again.

'But Jesus was silent!'[2] Am I accused? Am I slandered? Am I rebuked, rightly or wrongly? Do people speak ill of me? Does my vanity urge me to show off my learning or my virtue? 'But Jesus was silent.' I must always bear this in mind. Silence is golden.

'Then they spat in his face, and struck him; and some slapped him.'[3] How often has Jesus spent the night in the house of Caiaphas when his disciples have abandoned him or disowned him out of cowardice? The reward of God's faithful priests in this world is this: 'That they are counted worthy to suffer dishonour for his name.'[4]

Lord, grant that I may have a share in this glory for love of you, or at least let me go so far as to wish to be scorned for your sake.

'Surely this was the son of God.'[5] As I cannot feel the same anguish as Mary, John and the pious women beneath the Cross of Jesus, at least let me share the emotion of the centurion who came down the hill of Calvary, beating his breast and confessing the divinity of the crucified Nazarene. As I am a sinner, O Lord, I have not deserved the gift of tears. But I have every right to be purified in your blood, which was shed for my sins.

Hail, most Sacred Heart of Jesus!

The Spiritual Exercises are over, let us furl the sails. Again most plentiful grace has been showered upon me. Perhaps I have never before felt, as I feel today, truly and firmly convinced of the absolute necessity of giving myself wholly and for ever to my Lord, who wishes to make use of my poor self to do some good in his Church, and draw souls to his loving Heart.

Best of all, to my mind, is his having sent me, to enlighten my understanding and direct my steps, a good Spiritual Father,[6] whom I needed greatly; and he has enabled me to confide in him everything about my soul, sincerely and frankly, so that now I feel surer and stronger and more hopeful of real spiritual progress.

[1] Mark 14:45 and Matthew 26: 49.   [2] Matthew 26: 63.
[3] Matthew 26: 67.   [4] Acts 5: 41.   [5] Matthew 27: 54.
[6] Fr Francesco Pitocchi, see note 2 on page 84.

As the fruit of the work of divine grace in me during these days, and acting on suggestions from my new director, I now set down these brief reflections or proposals, which I must always keep in mind. I promise, with the help of the Sacred Heart, to carry them out scrupulously, for the true good of my soul.

(1) *In me God is everything and I am nothing.* I am a sinner, and far worse than I can imagine. If I have done any good in my life, it has all been by God's grace, which would have obtained better results if I had not hampered and impeded it.

(2) From signs received, and from the wonderful graces which God has poured into my soul, from my childhood until now, it is quite obvious that, for his own adorable purposes, he wants to make me entirely holy. I must always remain convinced of this. *So I must be holy at all costs.* The little, and very little it is, that I have done up to this point has been but child's play. Time is running out. Today at twenty-one I must start at the beginning again: *nunc coepi.*[1]

I must achieve such a state of union and total abandonment in God's hands as to be ready to give up everything, *even my studies,* in obedience to his divine will. All my actions and attachments to the things of this world must always conform to this principle. I must annihilate myself in the Sacred Heart.

(3) The way I must take, the right way for me, is that of humility. I must go straight along this path and never turn back. From today I take up arms against my pride, whatever shape it may assume. This enemy I always carry about with me must never be given a moment's respite. The particular examination must be used with this end in view and I promise to make it strictly every day.

(4) The youthful, burning, irresistible enthusiasms which seem to fill my heart for the cause of Christ and his glorious triumph and for new ways of developing the Christian life for the good of society are in themselves most holy inspirations, but too vague, and therefore somewhat dangerous. They might make me waste a lot of time, with scanty results. Today what my God wants of me is that, without losing sight of these sacred ideals, all my fervour, my energy and the living fire in me should be directed and used in all that will help to make me a true cleric, an excellent seminarist. This is what I am to be today, nothing more.

The Rule of the seminary must be the object of my persevering efforts, not only the Rule in general but all the detailed regulations. 'To know

---

[1] Psalm 76(77): 11.

nothing contrary to the Rule is to know all things.'[1] And this is the essential and most important result of my Spiritual Exercises.

I must desire, not to be what I am not, but to be very truly what I really am. That is what my St Francis de Sales tells me.[2]

(5) To keep me from sin and to prevent me from straying from him, God has used the devotion to the Sacred Heart of Jesus in the Blessed Sacrament. This devotion must always be the most powerful factor in my spiritual progress.

I shall try hard to foster this devotion so that my affectionate and tender feelings for Jesus in the Blessed Sacrament may inspire my whole being, my thoughts, words and works, and show in all my actions. To do this I need the closest possible union with Jesus, as if I were spending my whole life before his tabernacle, innumerable invocations to the Blessed Sacrament, great devotion and affection in my visits, communions, etc. I must think of myself as living solely for the Sacred Heart of Jesus.

(6) For practical purposes the Spiritual Father whom God has so providentially sent me is everything I need. I will never allow myself the slightest thing without his advice and his approval. All my small problems, even if they seem childish, must be set before him just as they arise in my own conscience; I must be as frank with him as I am with myself. Even in matters that are not strictly spiritual, in fact in the most natural things, I will scrupulously follow his suggestions and advice. His words to me will be as if dictated by my own conscience.

(7) As much mortification as possible, especially of the tongue. I must always be ready to humble myself, especially when things go badly. Bodily mortifications are to be few but constant, and without excessive obligation. I will give up salt altogether; I will never eat fruit in the evening, and never drink more than one glass of wine. As a general rule, I will always leave untouched a mouthful of whatever food is set before me: wine, meat dishes, fruit, pastry, etc. I will never take a morsel of bread over and above the usual amount I find on the table when I begin my meal, nor will I ever mention it to anyone if something is lacking. In general I will pay more attention to the spirit than to the letter of the mortification, deciding each case on its own merits.

(8) Few special devotions, but they must be well observed. Every day I must recite the Office of the Virgin Mary, making use of odd scraps of time during the day, while going up and down stairs, or going to and

---

[1] Cf. Tertullian, *De praescriptionibus adversus haereticos*; chap. 14. (P.L., II, 27).

[2] *Correspondance épistolaire: lettre 842* (cf. *Oeuvres complètes* . . . Migne; vol. V, c. 1569).

from classes, to chapel, for a walk, etc. The practice I will be most careful about is my daily visit to the Blessed Sacrament.

(9) Cheerfulness at all times, tranquillity, a mind free from care. When I see that I have kept my resolutions carefully I will praise God from my heart for all he has done; when I have failed I will be careful not to lose heart and I will think that sometimes God permits this to happen so that I may become more humble and entrust myself more wholly to his loving care. After any fault I will make an act of profound humility and then begin again, as cheerfully as ever, smiling as if God had just caressed me, kissed me, and raised me up with his own hands—and I will set out once more, confident, joyful 'in the name of the Lord'. O good Jesus, you do know how much I desire to love you!

[13]   *The Year of Grace, 1902—spiritual diary in the*
            name of the Lord. Heart of Jesus, burning with love
            for us, inflame our hearts with love for you

16 December

God is all: I am nothing. Let this do for today.

17 December

There is still too much of the dust of battle about me. Youthful enthusiasms, radiant ideals, splendid visions; these dreams are very beautiful but must for the present be handled with care. They could lead to a waste of time, however excellent and holy they may be in themselves. So—I must beware of them, or at least be very cautious.

My own way, which I must pursue for the triumph of God's cause, the surest way to prepare myself for a great future of useful and holy labour in the kingdom of Jesus, is humility. All the rest will follow, and will have this as its firm foundation. This is the advice given me by my spiritual director. The Holy Spirit speaks to me through his voice.

18 December

It is said that very often the Lord attaches his graces to our own good deeds, our little mortifications, etc. So why should we be surprised if in our prayers, meditations and struggles against self-love we do not feel that heavenly comfort, that fulness of spiritual joy which we expected? Perhaps the reason is that we have done something badly or avoided a mortification to which the grace we required was attached. So—the conclusion is clear. Attention in everything and the greatest possible perfection in little things.

19 December

Lord, I need only one thing in this world: to know myself and to love you. 'Give me thy love and thy grace, with these I am rich enough and desire nothing more.'[1]

20 December, Saturday

Every moment seems to bring its own opportunity for me to humble myself. This morning I came out from the holy Exercises full of all the enthusiasm which is natural when one has just received so much grace from God, determined to do everything well, particularly as regards the observance of the Rule.

And yet, in today's particular examination, and in my general examination this evening, I have clearly seen so many little failures and so many things unsatisfactorily done that I am perturbed. What can this mean? Yet it is all my doing. And to think that I am capable of preening myself, as if I were the type of the perfect man!

How my thoughts wandered during the recital of the Divine Office, with my newly ordained companions, and in the Little Office of Our Lady!

And talking to my companion outside the dormitory, and the other words said during the time of silence, and the long conversation about personal matters, of no great importance—are these virtuous acts? Is this the way I start to keep my promises?

As a rule, my general behaviour lacks that holy enthusiasm which would give it character and charm. A certain forthrightness and cheerfulness are necessary even in religious exercises, lest prayers and protestations be presented to Our Lord in a drowsy manner. Remember it is always possible to wear out his patience.

So, courage once more; and humility. Our faults offer us yet another motive to persuade us to draw closer to God, who alone can heal our infirmities.

Today I have done badly. What else could I have expected? Tomorrow, more attention, and more trust in God. '*Lord, you see my unworthiness; help me, you are my hope.*'[2]

---

[1] One of the prayers recommended to be said privately by the priest after Mass.

[2] These words were underlined by the author.

22 December

Lord Jesus, I humble myself in the dust before you. You see how helpless I am; you bring this home to me so clearly day after day, whenever I think of myself. I repent and then begin all over again, with distractions, lack of resolution and self-control, and so many imperfections, especially in my conversation. And yet I have a firm and resolute will. When I see the scanty practical results of the recent Exercises I get worried and anxious. O Lord Jesus, may your graces not be given in vain! I no longer have the heart to come before you. Only two days now remain before the festival of your birth, and you are already expecting my gifts. Lord, I have only my contrition and my grief at not being able to content you, although I feel a great love and a strong desire to show this love in a practical way. Help me in these last two days to make amends for the past and prepare my soul for your coming, so that on Christmas Day my joy may be more intense, knowing that you are more pleased with me, that you caress me and fill me with your holy love.

Mary, St Joseph, spare one look and one prayer for me. 'Jesus, Mary and Joseph, may I live for you, suffer for you, and die for you!' How sweet it is to repeat these words!

23 December

Today went better than yesterday and tomorrow must go better than today, and so on, with God's grace. I must insist on a principle I have never sufficiently thought about: I must do everything, say every prayer, obey the Rule, as if I had nothing else to do, as if the Lord had put me in this world for the sole purpose of doing that thing well, as if my sanctification depended on that alone, without thinking of anything else.

This is a great principle which, if scrupulously applied, has the power to put distractions to flight, just as holy water makes the devil take to his heels; it is the principle of recollection, of the old saying: *age quod agis,* 'pay attention to what you are doing', and the practice of the presence of God. But to be effectual it must be observed from my very first actions every morning.

Tomorrow must be a day of great recollection and fervour. Jesus is at hand, he is about to issue from his mother's sacred womb; his loving voice has already been heard: 'Behold I come.'[1] I must make special preparations for his coming because I hope for immense benefits from it. I have great things to tell him and he has great and plentiful gifts to share

[1] Rev. 16: 15.

with me. My mind and heart must dwell all day tomorrow before his tabernacle, which has now been transformed into the stable of Bethlehem. 'Come, O come, good Jesus, do not delay; my soul now rests in hope.'

24 December

Night has fallen; the clear bright stars are sparkling in the cold air; noisy strident voices rise to my ear from the city, voices of the revellers of this world who celebrate with their merrymaking the poverty of their Saviour. Around me in their rooms my companions are asleep, and I am still wakeful, thinking of the mystery of Bethlehem.

Come, come Jesus, I await you.

Mary and Joseph, knowing the hour is near, are turned away by the townsfolk and go out into the fields to look for a shelter. I am a poor shepherd, I have only a wretched stable, a small manger, some wisps of straw. I offer all these to you, be pleased to come into my poor hovel. Make haste, O Jesus, I offer you my heart; my soul is poor and bare of virtues, the straws of so many imperfections will prick you and make you weep —but O my Lord what can you expect? this little is all I have. I am touched by your poverty, I am moved to tears, but I have nothing better to offer you. Jesus, honour my soul with your presence, adorn it with your graces. Burn this straw and change it into a soft couch for your most holy body.

Jesus, I am here waiting for your coming. Wicked men have driven you out and the wind is like ice. Come into my heart. I am a poor man but I will warm you as well as I can. At least be pleased that I wish to welcome you warmly, to love you dearly and sacrifice myself for you.

But in your own way you are rich and you see my needs. You are a flame of charity and you will purge my heart of all that is not your own most holy Heart. You are uncreated holiness and you will fill me with those graces which give new life to my soul. O Jesus, come, I have so much to tell you, so many sorrows to confide, so many desires, so many promises, so many hopes.

I want to adore you, to kiss you on the brow, O tiny Jesus, to give myself to you once more, for ever. Come, my Jesus, delay no longer, come, be my guest.

Alas! it is already late, I am overcome with sleep and my pen slips from my fingers. Let me sleep a little, O Jesus, while your Mother and St Joseph are preparing the room.

I will lie down to rest here, in the fresh night air. As soon as you come the splendour of your light will dazzle my eyes. Your angels will awaken

me with sweet hymns of glory and peace and I shall run forward with
joy to welcome you and to offer you my own poor gifts, my home, all
the little I have. I will worship you and show you all my love, with the
other shepherds who have joined me and with the angels of heaven,
singing hymns of glory to your Sacred Heart. Come, I am longing for
you.

26 December

He has come and he has consoled me; I was able to stay with him a
long time, to tell him all I wished. There was only one thing I did not do,
or hardly at all: I did not thank him properly, as my Spiritual Father had
told me to do.

The giving of thanks means the certainty of receiving new graces. I
have been thinking too much about myself and my needs, and this is
most unmannerly. But I will endeavour to show him my gratitude, in a
life that shall be after his own heart, and in the imitation of those virtues
of which he has given us such eloquent testimony in this most blessed
feast of his birth.

But it is just in this that I feel the need of asking him for more help,
even while I thank him. If I think of my desires and my resolutions, to
be sure I am already a saint! But if I look at what I do, alas! how ugly and
misshapen I am. I have not yet succeeded in maintaining with Jesus that
uninterrupted flow of holy desires and recollected thought which to me
ought to be like the air I breathe.

O my St Aloysius, St John Berchmans, you seem so far away from me
in your close union with God! And yet I must go on trying to go forward, a little at a time, and never get worried, as I do when I see I am
not achieving anything. Here too it is partly a question of pride. And then,
I have noticed another thing. How is it that after I have been talking to
someone for a long time, even without meaning to show myself in a
good light, I think it over and am depressed and discouraged? It is pride
weeping over pride: crocodile tears.

The fact is that the more I speak about myself the more virtue I lose;
vanity squirts out from every word, even from those which seem most
innocent. I must get it into my head that when I am with others, my
fellows or my Superiors, the best thing I can do is to preserve a becoming
silence, or say only what is necessary or opportune; at least, never to
speak about myself unless I am interrogated, and even then to say little
and not try to hold my listener's attention. I must always consider that,
because of my faults, I am unworthy to be with my companions. If I

think this, how can I have the courage to sing my own praises before them?

27 December, St Stephen, St John the Evangelist

Yesterday the Church honoured the memory of St Stephen, and I also felt impelled to honour this first glorious athlete of the faith of Jesus Christ. Until these last few years I was not in the least interested in St Stephen because I did not know him. Only after I had been able to form a less vague idea of his mission and his work did the figure of this great hero impress itself on my mind and heart, and now I feel much drawn towards him: I revere him with profound and tender affection and implore his intercession.

St Stephen was the first to show a complete understanding of the universal ideal of the new religion, and he was the first to strike a blow at Jewish exclusiveness, thus opening new channels for the regenerating love of Christ. With daring confidence he threw open a new door, which had seemed closed, so that Christianity might expand and Christ Jesus be brought to all peoples, until the final triumph of his kingdom.

That great soul St Paul had the glorious mission of spreading the new faith beyond Jerusalem, so that the Romans were able to respect and accept it. But it was Stephen who had the honour of striking the first blow and sealing his glorious initiative with his own blood—and his was the first blood spilt after the death of Jesus. A glorious primacy which sets the young martyr nearest to the divine Martyr of Golgotha and makes his noble crown more precious and revered.

You lived and died, St Stephen, a young man like me, and for the very cause for which I live and in which I hope, and I send a warm greeting of brotherly love to your bones that sleep in the great peace of Campo Verano, beside those of your great fellow martyr, blessed St Lawrence the deacon. Give me your faith, your courage, your enthusiasm and, above all, your indomitable fortitude, your heroism.

29 December

The way of humility, union with God and obedience in all my doings to the will of God and not to my own will, these are the three foundations upon which my Spiritual Father has been basing his advice for my true spiritual progress. I must keep these three principles always in view so that I can put them into practice. This and nothing else is my duty today, 'this is my task, this my labour'.[1]

---

[1] Virgil, Aeneid, VI, 129.

As for humility, I will so far as possible avoid speaking of myself in the first person; I must shun the pronouns 'I' and 'me' as if they were venomous snakes. I will beware of talking out of turn, especially in certain circumstances and about certain subjects.

My reverend Superiors have been pleased to entrust me with the office of infirmary attendant, a new opportunity for humbling myself, for practising charity and gentleness and making some little sacrifices. Even tonight I am not sure that I shall be able to sleep in peace. I would like to, not for my own sake, as I am glad to do some good, but for the sake of my poor fellow student in the room beside me, who is in a rather serious and precarious condition.

My Lord Jesus, dear Mother Mary, if any sacrifice of mine can in any way serve to lighten his sufferings and avert any danger, here I am ready for anything: send me all the sufferings you wish, it will always be a joy to me to prove to you at least once in my actions that I love you, and in you my brother who represents you.

31 December

Only a few hours more—and this year too will come to an end and pass into history. I too finish the year and await the new dawn with joy. How many more years shall I see before I too cast anchor in the harbour of eternity? Perhaps many, perhaps few, possibly not even one whole year.

My Lord Jesus, 'your years will never come to an end, and you have numbered mine'.[1] In whatever year you may call me, may I be found with my lamp full of oil, lest you cast me out into the shadow of death.

Meanwhile I go down on my knees before my God and, recalling his kindnesses to me this year, I humble myself in the dust and thank him with all my heart.

I shall always remember 1902: the year of my military service, the year of conflicts. I might, like so many other poor wretches, have lost my vocation—and I did not lose it. I might have lost holy purity and the grace of God, but God did not allow me to do this. I passed through the mire and by his grace I was kept unpolluted. I am still alive, healthy, robust as before, better than before. . . . Jesus, I thank you, I love you.

---

[1] Cf. Psalm 102(103): 18 and Hebrews 1: 12.

1903

Spiritual notes

1 January, 1903

I have seen the first dawn of a new year. I welcome it in the name of the Lord and I consecrate it to the loving Heart of Christ, that for me it may be a year really full of good works, my year of salvation, the year in which I shall at last make myself holy. Jesus, I am yours once more and for ever.

Tomorrow, the first Friday of the month and of this new year, is especially consecrated to the Sacred Heart: it shall be a day of quite extraordinary fervour and love.

Just recently, since I finished the Spiritual Exercises, I have felt a very urgent need to strengthen my resolves and to set before my soul, already beginning to sink into lethargy, some noble examples—in a word, to begin again from the beginning.

Much against my will, I must again confess my ineffectualness. I am a poor sinner, a disloyal and useless servant. I am up to my eyebrows in pride: I am scatter-brained, unmannerly, and worthless. My Jesus, mercy!

The new year has begun: let it be a new life too. I think of tomorrow's holy communion as of an event of the greatest importance: I will make my communion tomorrow as if I had just finished the Spiritual Exercises. I recall the feelings of that day, its promises and resolutions, and in particular I reflect on that aspect of myself in which I feel most weak, as is proved by the disappointing experience of the last few days.

My guiding principles remain the same: humility in everything, especially in my speech, union with God (the most important thing, of which I feel an even greater need today) and the will of God, and not my own, in all I do. I must mind my own business, think of myself and the pursuit of the devout life, without undue agitation. Intense, tranquil and recollected study now; at all times and in all things great peace and sweetness in my heart.

Tomorrow the lectures begin again as well; I feel a need and also a passionate desire to study. I will start the new term under the patronage of the Sacred Heart of Jesus, as he has given me the most propitious occasion for doing so.

Meanwhile, Jesus, I wait for you. I am tired of my long wanderings, I will return to cast myself on your bosom, to rest and restore my strength for the long road ahead. Jesus, I, your little lamb, am coming back to you; prepare some food, for I am hungry.

4 January

My studies must not be a source of distraction but powerful wings to raise myself to God and to dwell in him—a joyful prelude to the Beatific Vision. Very often when I am studying I forget my resolutions and lose my spirit of recollection; religious practices become less attractive; I miss the pure oxygen of the devout life. This is bad: my study must be continual prayer and my prayer uninterrupted study.

Above all I must beware of being superficial or inconstant, obsessed with learning or new things, new books, new systems, new people. I must watch what I say about these matters. I must take everything into consideration and follow with delight the ascending movement of Catholic culture, but all in its due proportion. 'Not too much of anything.'[1]

I will always remember some wise sayings of the good and most learned author of *The Imitation of Christ*: 'A humble knowledge of yourself is a surer way to God than profound learning. It is not learning that is at fault, nor is the simple knowledge of anything blameworthy, because it is good in itself and ordained by God; but a good conscience and a virtuous life are always to be preferred....

'Certainly on the day of judgment we shall not be asked what we have read but what we have done; not how well we have spoken but how virtuously we have lived. . . .

'He is truly great who is humble and thinks nothing of the highest honours. He is truly wise who despises as dung all earthly things, that his reward may be Jesus Christ himself. And he is truly learned who does the will of God and renounces his own will.'[2]

7 January

My life is one long sacrifice. It is no longer I who live, but Christ who lives in me.[3] These are St Paul's words, and he could say this because his great soul and generous heart were always on fire with love for God and

---

[1] Terence, *Andria*, I, I, 34.   [2] Cf. *Imitation*, I, III, 21–36.   [3] Cf. Gal. 2: 20.

his fellow men. I have only good intentions, to which my deeds fail to correspond.

Lord, give me grace so that I may show in all I do that I truly love you. I will waste no more words. As my Spiritual Father is always telling me, I am a poor beggar with my hand outstretched, piteously beseeching: Lord Jesus, you are rich and kind, give me alms.

8 January

Yesterday my learned Professor of Church history[1] gave us excellent advice, particularly useful to me: read little, little but well. And what he said about reading I will apply to everything else: little but well. When I think of all the books I have read in the course of my studies, in the vacations and during my military service! the tomes, periodicals, newspapers! And how much do I remember of all this? Nothing, or almost nothing. All those spiritual works, all those lives of the saints—and what do I remember? Nothing, or almost nothing.

I feel a restless longing to know everything, to study all the great authors, to familiarize myself with the scientific movement in its various manifestations, but in actual fact I read one book, devour another, and do not get very far with anything. 'Give up trying to know too much, for this is very distracting and may lead you astray.'[2]

9 January

My days must always be burning with zeal like the fiery heat of those desperate marches last year when, during the scorching hours of the dogdays, every hair was bathed in sweat. I am always at the disposal of my King, Jesus Christ, and I serve him by looking after my companions in the infirmary. From early morning on, after my holy communion, I bear within my breast a burning heat. It is no longer I who live, but Christ who lives in me.

O Jesus, let me gasp and sweat with love in what I do for you, my glorious Captain.

11 January

The author of *The Imitation* gives me a counsel which truly meets today's needs in my special circumstances: 'So we must watch and pray,

[1] Mgr Umberto Benigni (1862–1934). He was a famous historian, the author of *Storia sociale della Chiesa*, a social history of the Church from its origins to the eleventh century. He also wrote *Die Getreidepolitik der Päpste*, Berlin, 1900; *Historiae ecclesiasticae repertorium*, Siena, 1902.
[2] *Imitation*, I, II, 5.

lest we waste our time. If it is right and proper for you to speak, then speak of such things as uplift the heart!'[1] So, attention! I must never waste even a scrap of time in idle chatter. When I finish one thing I must start on another, without any intervening gap. And when it is right for me to speak I will make a point of never speaking about myself, either well or ill, and never in any way referring to my own affairs unless I am asked about them.

For the rest, my conversation must be pleasant, marked with a profound sense of virtue, and such as befits an ecclesiastic.

13 January

This evening, the octave of the Epiphany, I was at S. Silvestro in Capite[2] with all the seminary. It was the closing ceremony of the octave of the Child Jesus, instituted by the Venerable Pallotti. There were present Bishops representing the different Catholic rites, with great pomp and a display of the most varied vestments. In front of the artistically arranged crib, Jesus was resplendent in the sacred Host. What thoughts flocked to my mind, what emotions filled my heart at the sight of Jesus being worshipped by the shepherds and the three kings! I thought of the Gospel preached to the Gentiles, of the Christian missions scattered throughout the world, of the truly Catholic, that is, universal Church. O Lord Jesus, your star has appeared in every sky and yet so many have not yet recognized it; the voices of the apostles have reached the ends of the world, yet so many will not listen to them or else try to smother them!

Once kings came from Tarshish and the isles to bring you their gifts; today the kings of this world have no use for you at all, they no longer acknowledge your rights, they have hurled back at you the bleak refusal of Pharaoh: 'I do not know the Lord, I will not serve him.'[3] What a terrifying thought! But oh! may your promises be redeemed! Now that you are lifted up above the earth, draw all things to you. Scatter the darkness of the pagans, outshine the false lamps of heresy and put them out. May all the peoples serve you, love you and acclaim you as their Saviour. 'For yours is the power and yours the kingdom for ever and ever.'

16 January

Practical experience has now convinced me of this: the concept of holiness which I had formed and applied to myself was mistaken. In

[1] *Imitation*, I, X, 9–10.

[2] This really took place in Sant'Andrea della Valle. The young seminarist, in Rome for the first time, confused the names of the two churches.

[3] Cf. Exodus 5: 2.

every one of my actions, and in the little failings of which I was immediately aware, I used to call to mind the image of some saint whom I had set myself to imitate down to the smallest particular, as a painter makes an exact copy of a picture by Raphael. I used to say to myself: in this case St Aloysius would have done so and so, or: he would not do this or that. However, it turned out that I was never able to achieve what I had thought I could do, and this worried me. The method was wrong. From the saints I must take the substance, not the accidents, of their virtues. I am not St Aloysius, nor must I seek holiness in his particular way, but according to the requirements of my own nature, my own character, and the different conditions of my life. I must not be the dry, bloodless reproduction of a model, however perfect. God desires us to follow the examples of the saints by absorbing the vital sap of their virtues and turning it into our own life-blood, adapting it to our own individual capacities and particular circumstances. If St Aloysius had been as I am, he would have become holy in a different way.

18 January, monthly day of recollection

Yesterday I was at the funeral of Cardinal Parocchi,[1] celebrated in S. Lorenzo in Damaso. This filled my thoughts all day long, and I have not yet been able to get it out of my mind. Amid the tumult of sensations in my heart, I have felt a warm glow of admiration and love for that great man who alone would have sufficed to ennoble the Sacred College, and who kept the whole Christian world talking about him for a quarter of a century. Cardinal Parocchi was the sort of figure we very rarely come across in the records of the Church. The bare mention of his name was enough to silence those who accused the Church of ignorance; before him even unbelievers reverently bowed their heads, and men of science faltered when they had to speak in his presence. His erudition extended to every field of knowledge; at some time or other every learned scholar had met him. Equal to his love for the truth and for everything good and beautiful was his burning, unquenchable love for the Church and the Pope. Opinions may differ about Cardinal Parocchi's political views: I know that some malicious insinuations have been made—but no one

[1] Cardinal Lucido Parocchi (1833–1903) was Bishop of Pavia in 1871; in 1877 Archbishop of Bologna; in 1884 Vicar General to the Pope. He founded the review *La Scuola Cattolica* and promoted the *Opera dei Congressi*. He gave his support to the social movement and those young reformers who developed the programme of Christian democracy. 'A man of exceptionally liberal views', Toniolo says of him in a letter from Pisa on 3 May, 1892, to Mgr Giuseppe Callegari (cf. Giuseppe Toniolo, *Lettere*, vol. 1, p. 267).

will ever question his courage and his enthusiastic loyalty to Church and Pope, even when, as always happens to generous souls, his fortitude was severely tried. Oh, if only I had his learning and his fortitude, I should be well content. His death was universally mourned and was considered a sad bereavement for the Holy See. Yesterday, around his coffin, I saw the whole world represented, to render a last tribute of praise to one who had shed so much light around him. Cardinals, Bishops, prelates, generals of religious orders, illustrious scholars of our own and other lands, ecclesiastics and lay-folk, diplomatic representatives—all in such great numbers as I never saw before, besides a great concourse of people who had gathered at his tomb to pray. The solemn words with which the Church implores God to grant the glory of heaven to her departed children and announces the resurrection and the life beyond the darkness of the grave had never moved me so strongly as in that moment. May the soul of the great Cardinal be granted that radiance of eternal light of which he was a shining reflection. He believed, he loved, he hoped always —may he enjoy the resurrection and the life, in Jesus Christ, who knows how to judge the work of his faithful servants.

The funeral ceremonies for Cardinal Parocchi formed an unexpected introduction to my monthly day of recollection, which I began last night, and gave me most useful material for a meditation on death. It was very easy to apply these considerations to myself, particularly to my self-love, my vanity, etc., and the conclusions were surprisingly clear. The rest of the retreat, by God's grace, went fairly well, and I hope it will be rich in excellent results.

From an examination of my conscience with regard to my conduct during this first month since the Spiritual Exercises, I find that although the last Exercises, thanks be to God, brought much profit to my soul, much, very much, I might say *all*, still remains for me to do. Until now I have only begun to survey the ground, to decide what I have to do next. Tonight I cannot work out in detail the new resolves I have made, as it is already very late, but they may be reduced to a few words.

I must start from the beginning again, as if hitherto I had done nothing at all. I will aim at perfection in all my religious practices, in the most important as in the least. Scrupulous control over my tongue, no lengthy conversations, no heated arguments which get us nowhere—I understand very well what I mean by this. No 'I' in any of my conversations, in this world there must be no 'I' at all; delicacy and loving tact in speaking of others. Finally, the spirit of recollection and cheerfulness, even when my pride is mortified, and concentration on the single purpose of doing what has to be done here and now with the greatest perfection and, above all, courage always in the Lord Jesus.

20 January

Up to now on the whole not so badly and this is something to thank God for. Above all, I must bear in mind these two things: absolute calm at all times, especially when I have done something wrong and during my religious exercises, and a most careful watch over my speech, and the use of the 'I'.

Today St Sebastian, tomorrow St Agnes: two young people, both heroic, one a soldier, one a virgin. I think of them with love, praying that to the enthusiasm of the soldier and the stainless purity of the virgin may be added, in my soul, their constancy in martyrdom.

I greet you both, O blessed in Christ Jesus!

22 January

Outside it is pouring with rain. God forbid that my soul should rot away! It looks as if the water were beginning to seep in. I must be on the alert for certain little cracks, almost invisible but wide enough to let the enemy through. It might be a word more than is necessary, or a little self-love, or an *Actiones* or an *Agimus* carelessly recited. Beware! after the first fault comes the second and then the third, the fourth, and so on. With the stray word and the [careless] thanksgiving come the idle conversation and the [inattentive] rosary or meditation, etc. I must be on my guard. 'Check this at the beginning.'[1] May it be said of me: 'Many waters cannot quench love, neither can floods drown it.'[2]

23 January

Today I went to the Gesù,[3] and was present at the closing of the solemn Triduum in honour of the Holy Family. The question of divorce threatening calamity to Italy and the Church in this country[4] had drawn an immense throng of Christians to pray to the Holy Family that this disaster might not fall upon the families of our land.

Surely the Lord will deign to grant these fervent prayers, which are rising to him from every part of Italy. In any case, the future lies in his hands and I am certain that all things will concur for the increase of his

---

[1] Ovid, *Remedia amoris*, v. 91, quoted in *Imitation*, I, XIII.
[2] Song of Solomon 8: 7.   [3] The Church of the Jesuits in Rome.
[4] At that time there was much talk about divorce. It was even referred to in the speech from the throne of 20 February, 1902 (cf. *Encycl. Catt.* VII, p. 1847).

glory. This is enough for me and gives me new heart. Come what may, I shall continue to pray; meanwhile I shall find my joy in thinking often about the Holy Family and associating myself with their feelings, and I shall pray for their virtues and strive to imitate them, for I need them very much. Jesus, Mary, Joseph, my sweet loves, may I live in you, suffer for you and die for you.

27 January

I will observe the greatest caution and reserve in my conversation, especially when speaking of others. The dangers are increasing and the more freely the tongue wags the more numerous the faults. Free and open-hearted, yes! but always with prudence. 'Jesus, turn to me and be gracious to me.'[1]

29 January

Today was a perfect feast; I spent it in the company of St Francis de Sales, my gentlest of saints. What a magnificent figure of a man, priest and Bishop! If I were like him, I would not mind even if they were to make me Pope! I love to let my thoughts dwell on him, on his goodness and on his teaching. I have read his life so many times! His counsels are so acceptable to my heart. By the light of his example I feel more inclined towards humility, gentleness and calm. My life, so the Lord tells me, must be a perfect copy of that of St Francis de Sales if I wish it to bear good fruits. Nothing extraordinary in me or in my behaviour, except my way of doing ordinary things: 'all ordinary things but done in no ordinary way.' A great, a burning love for Jesus Christ and his Church: unalterable serenity of mind, wonderful gentleness with my fellow men, that is all.

O my loving saint, as I kneel before you at this moment, there is so much I could say to you! I love you tenderly and I will always remember you and look to you for help. O St Francis, I can say no more; you can see into my heart, give me what I need to become like you.[2]

31 January

I will esteem the least things as of the greatest value. A moment of time wasted, an idle or unnecessary word are enough to throw me into a state of agitation for twenty-four hours. All this is pride, to be sure. But

---

[1] Cf. Psalm 118(119): 132.
[2] The words 'to become like you' were added by the author in 1962.

I must learn, to my own cost and that of my pride. My good Spiritual Father is always telling me that I must constantly strive for perfection, for what may be most pleasing to God. With this undeniable principle in mind, there can be no more excuse for following my own inclinations. O Jesus, you see my helplessness; only you can raise me to yourself: I am like a dead thing in your hands. Jesus, raise me to life.

1 February

The pure, refined joy which must always fill my heart finds its most sincere expression in the humblest actions. I must take care then: it is not enough to bear vexations with patience of a sort, so that others may not notice anything; I must always feel within myself an indescribable gentleness and sweetness that will bring a smile to my lips, and an even brighter smile when I am trying hard not to lose my temper and feeling rather grim. In short I must show a cheerful, smiling patience, not too solemn or there is no merit in it. 'Jesus, meek and lowly of heart, make my heart like yours.'

2 February

My obligation to aim at sanctification at all costs must be ever present in my mind, but it must be a serene and tranquil preoccupation, not wearisome and overmastering. I must remember it at every moment, from when I first open my eyes to the morning light till I close them in sleep at night. So, no slipping back into old ways and customs. Serenity and peace, but perseverance and determination. A total distrust and poor opinion of myself, accompanied by uninterrupted and loving union with God. This is my task, this my labour. O good Jesus, help me. 'Mary, show that you are my Mother.'

3 February

Tomorrow is the first Friday of the month, a great feast because it is dedicated to the Sacred Heart of Jesus. I must have a great spirit of recollection and great fervour, and keep a strict control over my tongue. 'Heart of Jesus, burning with love for us, inflame our heart with love for you.'

6 February

It is my studies that are most on my mind during these days. All this really boils down to a question of pride. We think we cannot be really great men unless we are supremely learned. But this is to use the same standards as the world, and we must get used to taking a different view. My real greatness lies in doing the will of God, entirely and perfectly. If God required me to burn my books or to become a poor lay brother, set to do the most humiliating tasks in some out-of-the-way and despised monastery, my heart would bleed but I should have to do it, and in so doing I should become really great. So for goodness' sake let us not get too agitated about it. 'Not too much of anything.'

15 February, day of recollection

My notes show a gap of ten days. Why is this? I really do not know. Is it my fault? I do not think it is, so I should not feel too distressed about it. If I were to grieve over this it would mean that I set too much store by these scribblings. Perfection does not consist in this, but in loving God and despising the self.

Today I hardly dare to call it by that name but it was in fact a day of recollection, recollection of sorts. The whole day long I did nothing but remind myself that this was a day of recollection. I passed the time as my Superiors required: in church, at our country house, in recreation, walking, nothing else; no meditation or devotional exercises or special reflections, nothing. 'Lord, you see all things.' How is it with my conscience? Certainly, in a different state from that of a month ago. I hardly know what to say myself. Am I making any progress? To all appearances, no. I have many distractions, and the very careful control of my thoughts of the earlier days has slackened a little: here and there a quarter of an hour of wasted time and so on. Nevertheless, I feel at peace; when I try to do more I cannot find any better way; I really am at a loss to know why this is so. The only explanation that occurs to me is that the Lord leaves me in my failings so that I may humble myself more and more and, seeing my own helplessness, may draw nearer and ever nearer to his loving Heart, which is my true life. So, blessed Jesus, I cast myself upon you, with all my distractions, acts of pride, and sins. I can do nothing more. I am not making any special resolutions. May my thoughts be always with you, especially during these days of Carnival. Great tranquillity and perseverance, in spite of the failings of every moment: the Rule in everything and for everything, and thanks be to God. Jesus, hope of the longing heart, remember me.

18 February

Man is never so great as when he is on his knees. This is a fine saying, worthy of that great champion of Christ, Louis Veuillot. I must bear it well in mind, and always. Therefore it is not learning that is really the height of greatness and glory, but knowledge of ourselves, of our nothingness before God and of our need of God, without which we are but puny creatures, although we raise ourselves up to the stature of giants. O, Mary!

20 February

A great day today. Our Holy Father has completed the twenty-fifth year of his pontificate. The Catholic world has been at his feet to present him with its congratulations and homage on this happy occasion, which has occurred only twice in nineteen centuries.[1] This is an event which arouses the greatest wonder and, in such a sceptical society, has brought home to men the presence of God's power in his Church. Here is a Pope who was said to be near to death when he assumed the papal tiara, but has resisted the ravages of time for twenty-five years, making the earth ring with his glorious name. His persecutors have all passed away; their proud heads broken on the Rock on which the Apostolic Chair is erected, they have gone down one by one into the grave. He has survived them all, amazingly youthful for his ninety-three years, to explain the works of God to an astonished world. In the fervent praises with which the Lombard pilgrims, true to their traditions, greeted the venerable old man and rendered their thanks, which rose majestically beneath the dome of Michelangelo in the notes of the Ambrosian hymn,[2] could be felt the bursting enthusiasm of the nations, the loving heartbeats of mankind, overcome by the joy of this long-awaited day. I also join my voice to the voices of the whole world, I also have prayed today for the great Pope, in the midst of the crowd, over the tomb of St Peter. O Leo, may my poor prayers rise to heaven to invoke blessings, prosperity and triumph for you and your labours; accept, mingled with the praise of the whole world, the humble but fervent wishes of a youthful heart, unknown to you but full of veneration and true filial love, swearing unswerving loyalty and unshakable devotion. May the Lord preserve you, Leo, for the good of the Church and of our land; for the triumph of Christ in his flock. May he ever inspire your frail body with that powerful breath of divine life by means of which you reveal to our souls, thirsting for happiness, clearer horizons of justice and evangelical charity. May he bless you here on earth in the affection of your children, in veneration for the Apostolic See and in the abundant fruits of the Church's endeavours. May he preserve you from your enemies and his and allow you to see from afar the

[1] Leo XIII, 1878–1903. Pius IX, 1846–1878.   [2] The *Te Deum*.

shining dawn of that great day of peace when the victors and vanquished of this age-old struggle for the triumph of truth and love will embrace as brothers before your throne, while you, more like a father than a sovereign, reach out your trembling hand to caress and bless them. 'You are Peter: you are Christ.'

24 February

This evening sees the end of the holidays which, in deference to the fashion of this world, we call our Carnival holidays. During this vacation I have been particularly impressed by two things: the feast of our dear Madonna della Fiducia[1] and the visit to the seven churches. First the sweet, most gentle thought of Mary, whose sacred image is venerated upstairs, in the small chapel of the theology students, and associated with so many personal memories; then the holy penitential exercise which peoples our minds with the grand figures of so many departed souls who have taught us the right way to love Jesus Christ. This visit to the churches fills the heart with holy affections and purposeful resolves, and at the same time unites us with those glorious saints who have preceded us in this devout pilgrimage, shining examples of Christian and priestly virtues in ages not so far removed and not so different from our own. It cannot fail to arouse feelings of virtue and of sincere devotion which we hope, with God's help, may endure. Tomorrow when the amusements and comparative freedom of these days are over, we shall go back to more serious study, graver occupations and the more attentive and recollected practice of virtue. The Lord has allowed me to pass through the gaieties and diver-

[1] Pope John had a particular devotion to the Madonna della Fiducia (whose English title is 'Our Lady of Confidence'); he kept a picture of her on his writing table and went five times to venerate her at the Roman Seminary during his pontificate. The ancient image of the Madonna della Fiducia—a copy of another very old picture painted by the Venerable Clara, Isabelle Fornari, a Poor Clare nun, born 1697—preserved in the monastery of S. Francesco at Todi, was known to the young Roncalli when he became a student at the Roman Seminary, and he had a copy of it printed on the commemoration card of his ordination as subdeacon. The Madonna was in a small chapel of the Apollinare, which since 1814 had been the seat of the Roman Seminary, and was an object of particular devotion to the students of theology. When, in 1913, St Pius X gave the Seminary a new home at the Lateran Archbasilica, a new picture of the Madonna della Fiducia was painted by Caparoni; it was placed in a grand and imposing chapel which, however, lacked the quiet and intimacy of the small chapel that had been reserved for the use of the theology students, and became the protectress of the whole seminary. It was here that in 1917 the seminarists bound themselves with a solemn vow to make a gift to the Madonna della Fiducia if those of their number who had been called to the army came safely back from the war, a vow that was fulfilled in 1920. From then onwards the picture of the Madonna has become the goal of pilgrimages, of priests as well as laity. (See Plate 31.)

sions of these days without my spirit suffering from much distraction; indeed, he made me feel rather bored, as if it were all a lot of nonsense. For us ecclesiastics also I do not think that Carnival deserves any other name, unless perhaps a worse.

Thanks be to God this year also it is over. Meanwhile, in this last night of merry-making, the world carries on with its follies and its sins and its shameless behaviour in the theatres, carnival balls, houses of ill-fame, gardens, even in the squares and streets. And meanwhile the loving Heart of my Jesus is hurt, deeply hurt. O Jesus, I fall asleep grieving for your grief and thinking of your painful sacrifice. May my great desire to love you enable you to forget the diabolical passions of so many of my un fortunate brethren. I pray that tomorrow[1] all will be attentive to the solemn words of the Church, warning us, urging us to better things, reminding us of what we are in your eyes and what we shall be on the greatest day of our lives: 'Dust you are and to dust you shall return.'[2]

26 February

Lent: this means seriousness, temperance, mortification, recollection, prayer. Such is my life these days. I must also prepare myself for the sacred order of the subdiaconate. What would St Aloysius have done? O Jesus, I join you in spirit as you fast in the wilderness for forty days and with prayer prepare for your public life. May I learn something from you at this time, so that Easter Day may mark another step forward in the path of virtue, of union and glorification of the spirit with you.

3 March

A day of triumph! Long live the Holy Father! Today in St Peter's my heart was overcome in that immense sea of love for the Pope; the whole world was represented there. During the solemn Mass I could only reassert, over the tomb of the apostles, my living, burning faith and my determination to work to the limit of my strength in the service of Jesus Christ, the Church and the Pope. Holy Father, I am all yours, I present arms! Bless me so that I may become holy, worthy to be your son.

7 March

I cannot end this day without a last thought for the glorious Angelic Doctor, St Thomas Aquinas. What greatness in that poor friar! What wisdom, what holiness! He teaches every student, and me in particular,

---

[1] Ash Wednesday.   [2] Genesis 3: 19.

a great lesson: 'The fear of the Lord is the beginning of knowledge.'[1] In our enthusiasm for study it happens so often that piety has to take a back place; we behave almost as if we thought that the time consecrated to devotional exercises was wasted. And yet St Thomas, before becoming the greatest scholar of his age, was a saint, and it was just because he was a saint that he reached such a lofty height of wisdom. St Thomas, while I am poring over your precious volumes, make me thoroughly understand this truth: that if I really wish to become good in every respect, fully to realize my ideals and be of use to the cause of Christ and the Church, I must at all costs make myself holy.

18 March

Examinations, sick patients, physical lassitude, ordinations, all these have for some time prevented me from jotting down anything in these notes.

Today I tried to make my monthly day of recollection as best I could. Nothing out of the ordinary by way of resolutions. I shall draw my conclusions better tomorrow, with the help of the good St Joseph, from whom I hope for the grace of true recollection. These days I feel so strange and heavy, so full of aches and pains that I can hardly stand on my feet, and a severe toothache torments me continually. 'Lord, you see. The spirit indeed is willing, but the flesh is weak.'[2]

19 March

The thought of St Joseph is sweet, calm, gentle and serene. In the midst of my persistent listlessness I have asked him for one thing: the true spirit of the interior life, in particular the grace to make my meditation and holy communion as I ought. These are the practical results of my day of recollection, and I consider their application to be what I need most in the present state of my spiritual life. Glorious St Joseph, pray for me.

22 March

I must be on my guard against untimely thoughts and intrusive distractions, especially the first time they take me unawares. I must not weary of the admonition 'attend to yourself and to your reading, attend to yourself and to doctrine'.[3]

There must be no holidays in my spiritual life. The Spiritual Exercises will soon be upon us again—so let us prepare better to receive God's

---

[1] Cf. Proverbs 1: 7.   [2] Cf. Matthew 26: 41.   [3] 1 Tim. 4: 13, 16.

graces: my sacred ordination is at hand. O Lord, am I really yours? I am not worthy.

24 March

Tomorrow is a great feast. All round the world the bells will joyfully peal the angel's greeting to Mary. The angels will respond with their sweet singing and men will be moved to repeat the salutation.

O Mary, among the voices raised to greet you, O gentle, sweet and pious Virgin, hear my voice too. Hail, Mary!

25 March

And the Word was made flesh.[1] No words are more solemn than these. The Word made itself flesh: what humility, what love! He made himself flesh in the womb of Mary: what greatness, what glory for the Virgin! And yet, one day an equally strange thing will happen through my means. The Word made flesh will place himself in my hands, will enter my heart under the appearance of bread and wine, sacrificed once more for my salvation and that of the whole world. The time draws near. How can I think of anything else? How can I allow my mind to be diverted for a single moment from this thought? O Jesus, O Mary, may my soul yearn and melt within me!

1 April

Today saw once more the beginning of the Spiritual Exercises in preparation for the sacred order of the subdiaconate.[2] Until now we have had our ups and downs, but let us begin again. If Jesus would grant me but one grace during these days: great recollection during my meditations. And surely he will be pleased to grant me this? I consecrate these days of holy retreat to the suffering Heart of Jesus. Come, O Holy Spirit, enlighten my mind and fill my heart with the holy desire for virtue, wash away my impurities, soften my hardness, heal my wounds. Mary, Virgin of Sorrows, who in the agony of the Cross gave birth to me, your son, show you are indeed my mother. 'Show thyself a Mother, offer him our sighs, who for us incarnate, did not thee despise.'[3] St Joseph, you must obtain for me the gift of the interior life, of which you are such a shining example. Holy Apostles Peter and Paul, give me your faith, your love. My most kind protectors, St Francis de Sales, St Philip Neri, St Ignatius

[1] Cf. John 1: 14.　　　　　　　　　　[2] See page 127.
[3] Hail, Star of the Sea (Ave Maris Stella).

Loyola, St Aloysius, St Stanislaus, St John Berchmans, St Alexander the Martyr and St Charles Borromeo, intercede for me. My Guardian Angel, to you I specially entrust my spirit of recollection during these days; keep distractions far from me, rouse me from my listlessness, keep me calm, serene, and self-controlled in everything.

'Enlighten, guard, rule and direct me.' Amen.

12 April, Easter Day

'This is the day which the Lord has made: let us rejoice and be glad.'[1] Alleluia! This year Jesus has really given me a wonderful Easter of peace. Today is destined to mark an epoch in my life. After I had prepared myself in the Spiritual Exercises he was pleased to grant me a foretaste of his most loving caresses, and also to show me how true it is indeed that 'to serve God is to reign'.[2] Today as a newly ordained subdeacon, officially consecrated to his cause as a minister of Jesus, in the sight of the whole heavenly court and the whole Church, I was quite overcome by the feeling of confidence that comes from freedom, that holy freedom which he procured for us by his glorious death and Resurrection. Now I am free from all earthly ties and made more vigorous and more ready to rise to the heights of sacrifice, with him and for him. Jesus, I am trembling with reverence and love, and before this long-awaited and long dreamed of day draws to its close I cast myself at your feet to thank you once more, as all my life I shall never cease to thank you, for the happiness with which you have filled my heart to overflowing, and the divine honour you have conferred on me by admitting me to the number of your elect. Having risen again with you, and been illumined by the splendours of glory and love that flow from your Sacred Heart, I pray on this solemn day of triumph that I may ever preserve the grace you gave me as a sign of your Resurrection in yesterday's sacred ordination. May I from this day forth really go forward 'from strength to strength, until I shall be satisfied to contemplate your glory'.[3]

14 April

If I do not always feel my Jesus as near to me as during the days spent in the Spiritual Exercises, and especially on the sacred day of my ordination, I must not be surprised by this or cast down. Other occupations,

---

[1] Psalm 117(118): 24.
[2] Cf. Mass for Peace, postcommunion prayer, and Mass on the feast of St Irenaeus, collect: *cui servire, regnare est.*
[3] Cf. Psalm 83(84): 7 and 16(17): 15.

material and otherwise, such as study, recreation, etc., certainly prevent me from turning my mind and heart to God, except indirectly. God likes it best in this way and I must be content. But it is my duty not to let myself be distracted by all these occupations. The thought that Jesus is pleased with me and loves me must, as it were, suffuse all my doings with a life-giving glow, so that thinking of him frequently, all my behaviour may be prompted by the spirit of the interior life. Joseph used to work from morning to night, yet his mind and heart were always with Jesus. O beloved saint, help me to imitate you.

16 April

My relations with my neighbours will be really sanctified when I learn to control my tongue. With this in mind I must be more prudent and never allow myself for any reason to be induced to talk of my companions or of others with even the slightest sign of disapproval. During the day there are innumerable occasions for me to discipline myself in this matter. I will use them to raise my mind to God and humble myself profoundly. After all I really must persuade myself that my fellows are always superior to me, and that they are therefore worthy of the greatest respect. O good Jesus, 'set a guard over my mouth, O Lord, keep watch over the door of my lips'.[1]

19 April, Sunday in albis (Low Sunday)

Today sees the end of the Easter octave, and I have had the honour of exercising my newly acquired order in the new priest's[2] Solemn Mass in our Church of Sant'Apollinare. But for me it still is and always must be Easter, in the true resurrection of the spirit, and the long ceaseless effort to make myself holy. O my Jesus, I wish never to leave you. 'Stay with us, Lord, for it is toward evening.'[3] During my daily round I will be particularly careful about two things. First of all, I will keep myself humble, always and in all things, trying to see how wretched I am in the sight of God, and also in comparison with my fellows: that I need to make this effort is brought home to me at every moment. Secondly, I must always feel lowly in the presence of Jesus in the Blessed Sacrament, who in the radiance of his Sacred Heart sheds light on all. O my good Mother, mistress of humility, make me like you.

[1] Cf. Psalm 140(141): 3.
[2] Giulio Rossi, at present Canon and perpetual curate of St Peter's.
[3] Luke 24: 29.

22 April

'Sins and melancholy, far from my house must they flee!' I must learn to bear even with those things which offend my susceptibilities and with companions who are uncongenial to me, and I must bear with them calmly and peaceably, otherwise there is no merit in it and God is not pleased. I will always try to find some virtue in people, even when none is apparent. Above all, I must say to myself that perhaps others, because of my innumerable faults, may have to make great efforts to put up with me. Humility then, always humility, joined to cheerfulness of soul, un-alterable and blessed. O Jesus, make me humble.

26 April

Today, the second Sunday after Easter, the seminary has been honour-ing its three young patron saints[1] whose mortal remains are piously pre-served beneath the altar in the chapel. It was one of those dear family feasts which are so good for the soul. The memory of martyrs, of their faith and love for God, is an everyday thing here in this Rome of blessed memories, where the earth is still stained with Christian blood, but the memory is dearer when there are stronger links to bind us to those holy souls. These were three poor young men, as fresh and pure as three white lilies. The sword of the persecutor cut them down in the springtime of their lives, and they were indeed blessed. 'In the eyes of the foolish they seemed to have died but they are at peace.'[2] Of them we only know that they lived, and that they died for Christ, nothing more. But they are well known to God; their names and virtues are written in the book of life. Their brows are crowned with glory, their joy is supreme, their memory immortal. O beloved saints, Florentinus, Socius and Victorinus, pray for me too, that my life may be spent in obscurity and lowliness and that, unknown to the world, I may shed my blood for the love of Jesus, pro-vided that one day, robed in glory, I may join in your bliss and with you 'follow the Lamb wherever he goes'.[3]

28 April

After the martyrs comes the confessor, the saint who showed the same spirit as the martyr of Calvary, whose name and banner he assumed: St Paul of the Cross. Today I visited his glorious mortal remains, still

[1] The three boy martyrs Florentinus, Socius and Victorinus, whose precious remains were given to the Roman Seminary on 16 April, 1693 by Cardinal Gaspare de Carpineo.
[2] Wisdom 3: 2–3.   [3] Cf. Rev. 14: 4.

almost incorrupt, up there in the pleasant church dedicated to the two indomitable martyrs, St John and St Paul, on the Caelian Hill near the Colosseum, where the arena is still stained with Christian blood. I begged him to obtain for me a real love for Jesus Christ, a devotion to his Passion, and a great longing for a life of sacrifice. Ah, so many souls have been willing to shed their blood and when they had no opportunity of doing so they found some way of sacrificing their whole life for the love of Jesus. Shall I not impose on myself the slightest mortification for my sins, to the advantage of my soul and for the salvation of others? It is humiliating for me, great sinner as I am, to see such shining examples of the love of suffering and unwearying toil for the glory of God. Unless I accustom myself from now onwards to bear persecution and physical and moral suffering with joy, I shall have to convince myself that I shall never become holy, nor ever be a useful labourer in the vineyard of Jesus Christ. O Lord, through the prayers of this illustrious disciple of yours, grant me great and joyful patience in my tribulations and an ardent longing to suffer with you and for your love. 'If we suffer with him we shall be glorified with him.'[1]

29 April

Just now Rome is officially celebrating the arrival of Edward VII, King of England. Flags, festoons, decorations in the streets, glittering uniforms, plumes, soldiers, military reviews, receptions—amid the applause of a people who tomorrow would be just as ready to curse; it is a bewildering succession of events, an uproar, a racket, a confusion, a frenzy. For a time the crowd forgets its most pressing cares; even business men, serious men of the world, fall under the spell of the great novelty and join in the shouting, and for whom? For a poor man who may be morally inferior to innumerable unfortunates forgotten by the world, a man who recently on the very day appointed for his solemn coronation, eagerly awaited by all the élite of Europe, was struck down by a violent illness which made him the object of general compassion and disappointment. Tomorrow a return of this illness could cause him to disappear from the scene and from men's minds for ever.[2] This man is invested with great authority; he is King of one of the greatest nations, and so he deserves to be honoured and respected.

[1] Cf. Romans 8: 17.

[2] Edward VII (1841–1910) visited Italy in 1903. On 27 April he was received by Victor Emmanuel III and two days later by the Pope, Leo XIII. Illness and an operation had caused the postponement of his coronation from 26 June until 9 August, 1901.

The world crowds tumultuously around this man, who attracts them because he is well dressed and surrounded by a magnificent suite, and people believe this to be the summit of greatness and grandeur, and it does not occur to them that from the top of Monte Mario none of the happenings in the city can be seen or heard. Still less do they think that above Monte Mario, and above all the mountains of this earth, where nothing is known of these trifling events, there is a God who sees and hears all, in whose sight all today's revellers and this man also are like specks of dust; a God who will one day judge them, and then they will be humbled, reduced to nought, crushed. Oh how stupid are the opinions of the world and how blind its judgments! A gorgeous livery, a waving plume are enough to excite men and throw them into ecstasy, and meanwhile no one has a thought to spare for God, except to offend him and take his name in vain; even serious persons get carried away by all this, like men of the world.

I too saw the King; but all the commotion irritated me and made me sad. The swift procession of the sumptuous carriages of their Majesties and their large suites brought home to me even more forcibly the truth that 'sic transit gloria mundi'.[1] 'Vanitas vanitatum et omnia vanitas.'[2]

Yet this man, a Protestant, did one really good thing while he was in Rome. And it was this: showing himself superior to certain tendentious currents of anti-clericalism here and in other countries, in the height of his power he did not disdain, indeed he considered it an honour, to visit and pay homage to another man, a poor persecuted old man, whom he acknowledged to be greater than himself: the Pope, the Vicar of Jesus Christ.

This event today is so solemn as to make a glorious page in the history of the Roman pontificate; a highly significant event this, of a heretical King of Protestant England, which has persecuted the Catholic Church for more than three centuries, going in person to pay his respects to the poor old Pope, held like a prisoner in his own house.

It is a sign of the times that after such a night of storms we see the new dawn rising from the Vatican, a slow but real and sincere return of the nations to the arms of their common Father who has long awaited them, weeping over their foolishness, and the triumph of Christ the King who, upraised on the Cross, once more draws all things to himself.

For this reason King Edward's visit, while it convinces me of the vanity

---

[1] Cf. Imitation, I, III, 6. This phrase is repeated three times to the newly elected Pontiff, during the ceremony of his coronation.
[2] Eccles. 1: 2.

of worldly fame, moves me to thank the good God who holds the keys of men's hearts and who, through all the intrigues of politics, finds a means of making known the glory of his name and the glory of the Catholic Church.

30 April

From the transient things of this world the mind soars to the grandeur of heaven; from the vain glitter of worldly pomp to the serene splendour of virtue. It is so consoling to think of today's saint who, lowly and despised, was found worthy to do the most energetic and important work for the good of the Church. 'God chose what is weak in the world to shame the strong',[1] and we see this perfectly exemplified in the great virgin saint of Siena, St Catherine.

She who thought only of humbling herself and living in seclusion, loving her divine Spouse, was chosen to restore peace to the Church by recalling the Pope to Rome. In comparison with her, what are the wise men, the conquerors, the great ones of her age? What a sublime lesson for my pride and at the same time what a reason for confidence in God to whom all things are possible, who makes up for our failings and teaches us to be really great, in his own eyes and in the eyes of the world.

1 May. Hail Mary!

Today the working people, without religion and without God, the poor exploited by the demagogues, and the unthinking masses hold their own feast, with a great shouting of their ideals, most of which are Utopian but some of which are most just, although almost always distorted and degraded. But the faithful begin the month of May with their greetings to her who is the Mother of the Word, *that great Word which was Jesus Christ*, the Prince of Peace; they flock to their devotions around the altar of Mary. There is so much grace and gentleness in this love for the Virgin that it softens even those hearts least accustomed to feelings of faith and piety. I also, with all the impulse of my love for her, cast myself at Mary's feet, consecrating, particularly during this month, myself and all my actions to her and imploring her to obtain for me an ever more ardent love for Jesus Christ.[2]

[1] Cf. 1 Cor. 1: 27–28.

[2] In Catholic tradition the month of May is dedicated to the Blessed Virgin, and this custom goes back to the twelfth century. The practice of celebrating on 1 May the claim for an eight hour working day was introduced in America, by the American Federation of Labour, in 1890; this date was also adopted by the 1889 Congress of Paris which

I will try to keep my mind and heart full of loving thoughts and feelings for Mary, and frequently appeal to her in my invocations. It will be my delight to offer her my homage, bouquets and acts of virtue sanctified by the invocation of her name and her protection. But the best way to please my beloved Mother during her month will be by an intense but constant effort after perfection in ordinary things, for example in the punctilious observance of the Rule, and I must do this not sulkily but cheerfully and serenely, without becoming a bore to myself.

O Mary, 'you who gave birth to me, help me that I may ever imitate you in my mind, heart and works'.

4 May

I will be particularly careful not to let myself be drawn aside by things not altogether conducive to the pursuit of the interior life. The water that sinks the boat seeps in little by little through invisible cracks. Every stray thought that enters my mind breaks off a bit of my inner self. On my guard then, especially in tiny things. 'O Mary, most devout Virgin, keep my thoughts from wandering.'

8 May

The succession of festivities in honour of Emperor William of Germany was willy-nilly a source of distractions to me. The splendid spectacle of worldly pomp at its most magnificent dazzled my eyes and made inner recollection more difficult. This event is indeed extraordinary and of great significance. It is truly an act of Divine Providence, a real triumph for the papacy. A Protestant Emperor, after centuries of hostility, ascends the Vatican stairs with unusual, almost unique ceremony and splendour, and humbles himself before the greatness of the papal throne! For us young people especially this occurrence must give rise to joyful hope and pure happiness and, far from distracting us, it must ennoble our conception of God and Jesus Christ, the real King of the Church and King for ever, and inflame us with sincere and ardent love for him and for his work.

Now the Emperor, applauded and admired, who if he were not a heretic would be the Charlemagne of modern times, has also gone back to his own land, to Berlin, and things have returned to normal.[1]

---

founded the Second International. The commemoration of *Rerum Novarum*, fixed for 15 May, gathered the Christian workers together in solemn congress. In 1955, Pius XII transferred this commemoration to 1 May, and declared that day the feast of St Joseph the Worker. Now the Encyclical *Mater et Magistra*, 1961, is celebrated on 15 May.

[1] The young student Roncalli saw Emperor William II on 2 May.

I too return to the bosom of Mary, to the loving Heart of Jesus; the more urgent my need and the greater the feeling of emptiness left after these worldly festivities, the more I long to press further forward and the more closely I cling to Jesus.

15 May

In these beautiful days of Mary's month things are not going too badly with me. Every now and then the thought of Jesus and of Mary steals into my soul and I rejoice.

Today I passed a very happy quarter of an hour in the charming church of San Gioacchino, in the fields near Castel Gandolfo, the affectionate offering of the Catholic world to Leo XIII.

While in various Italian cities and in other European countries active Catholics, bold bands of youthful enthusiasts, have been commemorating the *Rerum Novarum* of the great Pope of the working people and joyfully celebrating the new conception of Christian democracy, I, who am not yet prepared for apostolic work, thought that the best way for me to celebrate the great event and offer my own modest tribute of praise and ardent enthusiasm for the great idea was to cling more closely to Jesus in love and in prayer. I prayed with fervour before the Blessed Sacrament, the real bread of heaven which will give true life to the world; at the feet of the white Immaculate Virgin, in the pretty flower-adorned chapel of the young North American States and, most fervently of all, before the beautiful statue of the Sacred Heart of Montmartre, an affectionate tribute from penitent and devout France. Oh how beautiful and majestic Jesus is in the Blessed Sacrament on the precious altar, such a loving figure amid his rejoicing saints and adoring angels! The social question is a question of life, not simply material but spiritual life. Amidst the agitation of thinking people and the lamentations of the poor, the earnest work of apostolic souls, the struggles, the disillusions and the triumphs, I find my attention and my interest are held and my fervent wishes and labour fully pledged when, in the background of this great picture, I seem to see Jesus, like the sun in spring-time, rising above the vast sea; his face is mild and serene, his arms opened wide, his Heart on fire with a flame that surrounds and suffuses everything. You, O divine Heart, are the solution of every problem, 'solutio omnium difficultatum Christus'; all our hopes rest in you, to you we look for salvation.

O Jesus, come back into our society, our family life, our souls, and reign there as our peaceful sovereign. Enlighten with the splendour of faith and the charity of your tender Heart the souls of those who work for the good of the people, for your poor; impart to them your own spirit, a spirit of discipline, order and gentleness, preserving the flame of enthusiasm ever alight in their hearts.

O Jesus, if one day with your help I can do any good, here I am in the ranks of your fighting men. Oh may my preparation in your school be really serious, profound and productive of excellent results, because it is easy to lose a sense of direction. May that day come very soon, when we shall see you restored to the centre of civic life, borne on the shoulders of your joyful people!

26 May

In these days of feverish activity my tasks in the infirmary, and above all my studies, take up every moment of time. 'Not too much of anything',[1] but may I know more and more, and 'think with sober judgment',[2] remembering that for everything there is a season.[3]

Meanwhile the lovely month of Mary is drawing to a close and the flowers I have to offer her are few and unattractive.

O Mary, I am poor and I am your son; look into my heart. Today the thought of St Philip [Neri] has kept me pleasant company all day. From a comfortable position in the choir of the church in Vallicella, I have taken part in the great ceremonies, I have enjoyed the music of Capocci and visited with a feeling of awe the saint's rooms above, and also the precious historic rooms in the church of S. Girolamo della Carita;[4] most of all my eyes, my mind and my heart were with the glorious tomb and I prayed very hard. I wish I had the time and ability to write of this holy man as I would like and as my heart would dictate. St Philip is one of the saints most familiar to me and his name is linked with so many dear and personal memories. I feel I have a special love for him and I commend myself to him most trustfully.

O my good Father Philip, you understand me even if I do not put my thoughts into words. Time is drawing on; where is that faithful copy of you I was to have made of myself? Am I a replica of your virtues? O teach me the true principles of your mystical school for the education of the soul, so that I may profit by them: humility and love. I need great concentration of mind, blessed Philip, pure and holy gaiety and enthusiasm for great works.

In this Novena of the Holy Spirit, once your Novena, I will often come back to you. Blessed Philip, help me to prepare my soul as a dwelling for

---

[1] Terence, *Andria*, I, I, 34.   [2] Cf. Romans 12: 3.   [3] Eccles. 3: 1.
[4] It was in this church that St Philip Neri lived with a group of fellow priests.

the Holy Spirit. I lean my frozen heart closer to yours which burns with love and with the Holy Spirit. Make my heart burn too.[1]

20 July

My brief evening notes show an enormous gap. The pressing cares of the infirmary, and in the midst of these the urgency of the examinations, have robbed me of any scrap of time available for these hasty jottings.

Solemn feasts, well-loved occasions, the month of the Sacred Heart of Jesus, memorable days,[2] all have slipped by without any mention. Yet I do not regret this. I do not wish to cling too much to these little things which I would be willing to cast on the fire at any moment if I ever thought they could foster my self-love.

[15]   † *Jesus, Mary, Joseph!*

Notes written during the Easter retreat in preparation
for the order of Subdeacon, 1–10 April, 1903

Jesus, here I am once more this year, in your presence, to listen to your divine teaching. I long to consecrate myself with all solemnity to you, once and for all. The Church has called me, you invite me: 'Lo, I come.'[3] I have no pretensions, I have no preconceived plans, I am trying to strip myself of all that is self, I am no longer my own. My soul is open before you, like a blank sheet of paper. Write on it what you will, O Lord: I am yours.

(1) 'Friend, why are you here?'[4] To know God, to love him and to serve him all my life, and after death to enjoy him forever in paradise. All the answers of the learned are not worth these few words from the children's catechism. The duties of my life are all contained in these three words. This is all I have to do: to know, love and serve God, always and at all costs; God's will must be mine and I must seek it only, even in the slightest things. This is the first and fundamental principle.

And what about all the other things which surround me? If God has given them to me they are extras: they have not been given to all, nor to

[1] Sequence of the *Stabat Mater*.
[2] An edifying memory of those days is found in the words printed on the back of an image of Our Lady: '*Die 2ᵃ iunii 1903 ego Angelus Roncalli Deiparae Immaculatae cor meum obtuli*' (On 2 June, 1903 I, Angelo Roncalli, offered my heart to the Immaculate Virgin).
[3] Psalm 39(40): 7, Hebrews 10: 7, 9.
[4] Matthew 26: 50.

all in equal measure. Their purpose is to serve man in the attainment of his end. Any other use I may make of them is bad, upsets the order of nature and lands me in deplorable confusion. My attitude towards them must be governed by that golden rule of detachment for which the saints were so much admired. My own St Francis de Sales speaks for them all. This detachment is not natural apathy, such as we find in certain characters, but supernatural virtue, detachment from everything, according to the will or pleasure of God; serenity, calm, nobility of soul, profound philosophy, because of which, in aiming at loftier ideals, we no longer care for these base and worthless things, or we use them in whatever way they present themselves as powerful wings to soar to God, to practise virtue and to make ourselves holy. Here I will mention a few practical examples, not without relevance to myself, which I must bear carefully in mind.

The blessings of fortune, such as wealth—the Lord could have given them to me or withheld them—I had no right to them. He was pleased to withhold them. Why should I complain about this? Their absence is a means of my sanctification. So, blessed be the name of the Lord. At times dire necessity obliges me to contract small debts with the Bursar, and I dislike very much having to do this; it makes me feel wretched. But this is not right: God permits this to happen, and that is enough.

Mind and memory are gifts from God. Why should I lose heart if others have more of these gifts than I? Might I not have received even less than God has given me? Examination results and successes are things which, whether I will or no, mean a great deal to me. Very well, when I have done all that God has required of me, what does the good or bad result of my studies matter?

Sometimes, even in my practices of piety, an intense effort to preserve stillness in my soul and to enjoy all the sweetness of conversing with God is all of no avail: my heart feels as if it were made of stone, I have a steady stream of distractions and the Lord seems to have hidden himself. Sadness and discontent take hold of me and I become agitated. Away with all these weaknesses! We must keep cheerful and calm, in all circumstances. Indeed, we must rejoice, since that is God's will.

However things may go, in rain or sunlight, cold or heat, and however my greater or lesser superiors may dispose of me, I must always stay in the same frame of mind: never a word of complaint or disapproval, in public or in private; my smile must be cheerful, frank and friendly; I must not let my head be turned in good fortune nor let myself be soured by the bitter moments of life.

This does not mean denying that the senses or the impulses of nature exist. The enjoyment of God's love, the sweet and total abandonment to his will must absorb all else in me or, rather, transform and sublimate all the desires of my lower nature.

To practise this principle must be the work of my every moment, whatever the place or circumstances, and one of the chief points of enquiry in my examinations of conscience.

O Jesus, 'gentle and lowly in heart',[1] help me to understand this truth and apply it to my life, in all its perfection. 'I am dumb, I do not open my mouth, for it is thou who hast done it.'[2] Blessed be the name of the Lord! O Mary most gentle Virgin and Mother, come to my aid!

(2) One single thought of pride was enough to hurl an infinite host of angels into hell for ever. One moment of weakness on the part of Eve, when she let herself be taken in by the serpent's wiles, brought about all the woes of mankind. What a lesson this is for me! If it is true that the slightest good deed is rewarded with a wealth of graces, it must be no less true that any neglect, however slight, of any opportunity given me by the good God for exercising virtue may cause me to be deprived of so many graces without which I can do nothing, absolutely nothing.

In the light of this truth, I must consider those failures of mine which are usually called small, and which are generally overlooked. These are the cause of the slow, halting progress of my spiritual life. It is not a question of greater or less condescension or kindness on the part of God, it is a question of man's co-operation with him. His graces are always available; it is our failings which prevent their being of use to us.

So, scrupulous attention to little things; extreme prudence in all I do. The holiness of the saints does not depend on anything sensational but on little things which seem but trifles in the eyes of the world. In this respect, Jesus Christ in the first thirty years of his life offers me a whole series of shining examples. 'Look and make it after the pattern.'[3]

(3) I return to this subject, since it has pleased the good God in the aridity and desolation of spirit of these first three days of the Exercises to give me some inkling of its importance for my present state of mind. I really cannot say whether some escapades of my early years ever attained the gravity of mortal sin. But, however that may be, for that age they were very serious and, even now, standing in the sight of God, I feel thoroughly ashamed of them. 'I weep as one guilty; my sin brings the flush of shame to my cheek.'[4] After those first sins many and much graver

---

[1] Cf. Matthew 11: 29.   [2] Cf. Psalm 38(39): 9.

[3] Exodus 25: 40.   [4] From the *Dies Irae* sequence.

sins have followed each other, every day, every hour: distractions, acts of pride, neglect of study, wasted time, lack of charity in thoughts, words and deeds, little vanities. O my God, what a heap of sins—enough to crush me!

So, I am a sinner, a great sinner. I feel it, I am convinced of it, I am ashamed. 'Spare, O Lord, thy suppliant.'[1]

Now, having granted all this, let us see what has been done about it. Have I done penance for my sins? None at all. And yet it is certain that I shall have to account for everything, to the uttermost farthing. Therefore I must always remember that I am in debt to the Lord; my scrupulous attention to even the least of my duties is therefore a strict obligation in the eyes of justice; it is not meant to be a compliment or something extra thrown in. Until I have cleared my debts I have no right to complain to God because he sends me suffering, desolation of soul and so on. When I feel ill-used, forsaken, solitary, I must humbly bow my head, quietly resign myself and say: I deserve this, so be it. Or I must say: Jesus, I bless you, I thank you, I love you.

Even in the midst of my wretchedness the Lord has continued to shower upon me great and extraordinary graces. Why have these not produced their effect? Why am I not already a saint, like St Aloysius or St Stanislaus, or even holier than they? The reason lies in my small failings.

How can I explain the almost total absence of recollection and therefore of good results in my meditations since the last retreat, or the spiritual aridity of the first days of the present Exercises, and my hardness of heart before the most solemn and tremendous truths, which made even the greatest saints tremble? Perhaps I must put the blame on those stray words uttered every now and then during the time of silence and other little infringements of rules from time to time, and so on. Oh, the little things! Everything is bound up together in my spiritual life. Just as graces call down fresh graces and so are constantly increasing, so faults also, following each other in their turn, cancel the effects of grace and, multiplying themselves indefinitely, draw me to the edge of the pit.

The conclusion is this: every disobedience, however trifling, every flaw, every idle word, every foolish remark represents a startling deficit in my spiritual life. So, let us go over our accounts well. A shrewd and strict scrutiny of everything, with a sharp eye to the first signs of weakness.

(4) 'After a storm thou makest a calm.'[2] So my good Lord, after three days of desolation and suspense, has been pleased to receive me in his

---

[1] Idem.   [2] Tobias 3: 22.

presence and has shed a ray of his own light upon me. A careful examination of myself and the motives of my self-love has enabled me to perceive that within me, besides the imagination, always the crazy inmate of the house, are two reasoning minds, as it were, both of which do their utmost to make themselves heard. They are the reasonable reasoning mind, my own real mind, and the other reasoning mind, which is my inveterate foe. When I am meditating seriously, and considering goodness in general and in practice, this other mind always discovers a lot of ifs and buts, makes fun of all my resolutions and always finds some objections or some soothing arguments in its own favour. Wonderfully aided and abetted by my imagination, it does all it can to cloud my understanding and to pour cold water over my good intentions; it gets the better of my reasonable mind and gives it no mercy, always bold and impertinent, always a tyrant.

We must take care not to get confused. Most often this is a trick of the devil, for he loves to fish in muddy waters; he tries in this way to discourage us and to undermine our better feelings and intentions. I can defend myself if I have, for example, the right thoughts of humility and hatred for my sins, which are to be loathed and detested even though, in my ignorance, I am unable to perceive and fathom all the profound reasons for doing so, and if I stand firm against every assault, holding the door of consent firmly closed. If I do this, God is content and requires no more of me.

I will always remember St Francis de Sales' advice: 'Let the devil (the other reasoning mind, that of the other self) bang and scream at the door of your heart, offering you a thousand images and untimely thoughts. As he cannot enter except through the door of consent, keep this firmly closed and put your mind at rest. Do not get anxious when the waves batter against your boat; have no fear while God is with you.'[1]

So when it is a question of thoughts of pride, of good reputation, honours, important posts and so on, as long as I do not give any encouragement to these thoughts and try instead to dismiss them, I must not feel alarmed. I must simply stand firm in my refusal to admit them, sternly, without listening to arguments or reasonings of any sort, and never get tired of refusing my consent, strengthening myself with humble thoughts and feelings—and pride will no longer have any power over me.

(5) Every time I think of the profound mystery of the obscure, humble life of Jesus, during the first thirty years, I am more and more astounded and words fail me. It is very clear that before such a shining example the

---

[1] Cf. *Spiritual Letters*, vol. II: letter to an Abbess.

judgments and way of thinking not only of this world but also of the overwhelming majority of ecclesiastics lose all value and seem in direct contradiction to it. As for me, I confess that I still cannot form an idea of what this humility must be like. However much I study it, I seem to achieve only the semblance of humility; its real spirit, Jesus Christ in Nazareth's 'love to be unknown',[1] is known to me only by name. To think that our blessed Saviour spent thirty years of his life in obscurity, and yet he was God, he was the splendour of the substance of the Father, he had come to save the world; and he did all this only to show us how necessary humility is and how it must be practised. And I, such a great sinner and so totally unworthy, think only of being pleased with myself and congratulating myself on my good results, all for the sake of a little worldly honour. I cannot conceive even the holiest thought without its being tinged with considerations of my own reputation with men; however much I affect a devout life and a spirit of charity and sacrifice, I cannot imagine the purest ideal without the other 'I' stepping in, wanting to show himself off, to be admired by all and sundry, by all the world if that were possible. And the worst of it is that, in the last analysis, it is only with the greatest effort that I can resign myself to the thought of real obscurity such as Jesus experienced and such as he has taught men to desire.

Let us at least admit this then, and it is one of the most important impressions left on me during these holy Exercises and should be remembered at every moment, that (1) the more I love obscurity the greater and worthier I shall be before God and men, and the more useful my ministry will be; (2) where true humility is concerned, I am still very far from knowing and practising the first degree; (3) I must continually beg from the loving Heart of Jesus, who is 'gentle and lowly', more and more understanding of this matter and his help, so that I may at least sincerely desire perfect humility and indifference to my reputation and my honour.

I will not forget that the Lord requires from me not only the 'love to be unknown', 'the love to be little esteemed',[2] but also the 'love to be despised'. I must be lowly enough to be able to say: 'I have been crucified with Christ.'[3] For the present, O Jesus, grant me at least the sincere desire for this.

(6) Besides being so full of myself and concerned with my reputation, I am a poor ignorant fellow; this is brought home to me every day, every hour; the more I study the more convinced I am of it. I must make a habit of thinking of myself as ignorant, and so always choose the place that

---

[1] Cf. *Imitation*, I, II, 15.   [2] *Ibid.*   [3] Gal. 2: 20.

best befits me. In this way, a certain unwise pretentiousness will be crushed.

This humble mind must accompany me everywhere, in class, in my studies, in conversation, in everything. I will take great care not to boast of any learning I may have. My motto in this also shall be 'love to be unknown'; my attitude to others, superiors or colleagues, shall be that of the divine Child Jesus, 'listening to them and asking them questions'.[1]

(7) I feel that Jesus is drawing nearer and nearer to me. During these days he has allowed me to plunge into the depths and be submerged in the realization of my wretchedness and pride, to show me my urgent need of him. When I am about to sink, Jesus my Saviour comes smiling towards me, walking on the waters. I would say to him with Peter: 'Depart from me, for I am a sinful man, O Lord,'[2] but I am prevented by his tender Heart, and his kind voice saying: 'Do not be afraid.'[3]

Oh I fear nothing more when I am with you. I rest on your bosom, like the lost sheep; I hear the beating of your Heart. Jesus, I am yours once more, forever yours. With you I am truly great; a fragile reed without you, a column of strength when I lean on you. I must never forget my own helplessness and so I shall always distrust myself. Even when I am bewildered and humiliated I must always cling most trustfully to you, because my helplessness is the seat of your mercy and your love. 'Good Jesus, I am always with you; never go away from me.'

(8) It is Holy Thursday, the great day of the Sacred Heart, the day of his wedding feast and of his testament of love.

Just as all at once a bright ray of sunlight melts the clouds in the sky and recalls us to life, so my good Master has deigned to raise me up and flood me with his light on this day, which is perhaps for me the most solemn of the whole year. I felt filled with a great peace when I went forward to receive him in the Blessed Sacrament; I felt all the joy of his presence, I listened with emotion to his last discourse, his words of farewell, and I was trembling all over with a mysterious tenderness when I accompanied him to his 'altar of repose'.

He makes it ever clearer to me that he wants me to burn with love for him in devotion to the Blessed Sacrament. Every time I receive him I must feel renewed that longing which stirs within me to live for Jesus only and to obtain the grace of preservation from so many sins which I should certainly commit if he did not come to my help. How can I remain deaf to his invitation?

During the Last Supper Jesus, the High Priest, established the priest-

[1] Luke 2: 46.   [2] Luke 5: 8.   [3] Luke 5: 10.

hood, and now he calls me too, unworthy as I am, to share in so lofty a ministry. For several years now I have been preparing, through various degrees and minor orders, for the great act, and now he wants to have me in his service with a more solemn dedication and an indissoluble promise of fidelity to him alone and of total detachment from the creatures of this world. O Jesus, I yearn for this long-awaited moment. You see that I am giving up my home, my family, my poor fishing nets, everything, to come with you. Receive me as you welcomed Peter, John, Matthew and the others. If I am not worthy to sit at your table, at least I will be at your feet, to gather the crumbs that fall to the ground. 'I would rather be a doorkeeper in the house of my God, than dwell in the tents of wickedness.'[1]

One thing only I desire, to stay always in your holy love, one with you as you are one with your Father. Alas! in your last words, in the sadness of your divine countenance, I see what is to come, the hellish kiss of Judas the traitor. Jesus, I implore you with clasped hands, shuddering with fear, that if you know that one day I am to break my promises, you will let me die on the spot, before I take this great step and swear loyalty to you.

(9) My great book, from which henceforth I must learn with greater care and love the lessons of divine wisdom, is the crucifix. I must make a habit of judging all human concerns and knowledge in the light of the principles of this great book. It is too easy for me to be deceived by empty appearances and to forget the true source of truth. When I look at the crucifix I shall feel all my difficulties dissolve—all those modern problems, theoretical and practical, in the field of study. The solution of all difficulties is Christ.

If I were to write down all the good thoughts and feelings with which my kind Lord has been pleased to inspire me while I have been meditating on the Passion of Jesus, a week would not be long enough. When my pride, profiting by some moment of inattention, starts to build its castles in the air, and tries to make me soar aloft, I will make it a rule to think of these three places: Gethsemane, the house of Caiaphas, Calvary. The crucifix must always be a source of great strength and consolation in my difficulties. Jesus stretches out his arms on the Cross to embrace sinners. When I have committed some sin or feel distressed, I shall imagine myself kneeling at the foot of the Cross, like Mary Magdalen, and receiving on my head the shower of blood and water which flowed from the Saviour's wounded Heart.

[1] Psalm 83(84): 10.

Calvary, concludes St Francis de Sales, is the hill of lovers, the school of pure affection.[1] Therefore I must get to know it very well, also because it was there that the Sacred Heart was first shown to men, with great solemnity.

Oh what gentleness of heart! My good Jesus, dying, inclined his head to kiss those he loved. We kiss Jesus as often as we make our acts of love. 'Longinus', says the great doctor, St Augustine, 'with his spear opened Christ's heart to me; I entered and safely rest therein.' 'In the arms of my Saviour I wish to live, there I long to die, there in safety will I sing.'[2] 'I will extol thee, O Lord, for thou hast drawn me up, and hast not let my foes rejoice over me.'[3]

(10) The hour approaches. Quick, let us light the lamps: 'Behold, the bridegroom comes.'[4] What joy, what consolation! I thank you, O Jesus, for allowing me this foretaste of the delight of that moment when, in the sight of the whole Church, I shall be able to dedicate myself irrevocably to your service at your altar. Do not look at my poverty but at my good will. Tomorrow, with the first light, when the bells of the whole world will be ringing for your Resurrection, you will come to meet me, in all your beauty and glory, to celebrate my espousals with you. O come Holy Spirit, in these few hours of the night that yet remain to me, inflame, burn, destroy, quicken and transform my poor weak heart; make it a vessel worthy of Christ.

Mary, my beloved Mother, dry your tears; your Son will rise again. Queen of Heaven, rejoice! I cast myself into your arms, you must lead me to him. St Joseph, chaste spouse of Mary, St John the Evangelist, in whose great temple I shall be ordained, you who felt the heart-beats of Jesus, give me some spark of your love for him. St Peter and St Paul, holy martyrs of Rome and of the whole world, gentle St Francis de Sales, all of you, my special and beloved patron saints, intercede all of you for me. Humbly I kneel before the court of heaven, I a sinner but blessed by Jesus, and beg all paradise to pray for me. You pure angels who followed the stainless Lamb, treasured the blood he shed on Calvary and announced his glorious Resurrection, join with my Guardian Angel to invoke the Holy Spirit, to give strength to my weakness, to be present at my feast, to intercede for me. Come Lord, my soul is waiting for you.

(11) The joy of my ordination was too great for me to hope to describe it. 'How lovely is thy dwelling place, O Lord of hosts! My soul longs,

---

[1] *Treatise of Divine Love*, bk. 12, chap. 13.
[2] St Augustine, *Enchiridion*, chap. 23, 2(P.L., XL, 961).
[3] Psalm 29(30): 1.　　　　　　　　[4] Matthew 25: 6.

yea, faints for the courts of the Lord! Truly, my heart and flesh sing for joy to the living God.'[1]

This morning's ceremony in St John Lateran[2] was solemn in itself, more solemn for me, and never to be forgotten. Now I am really a new man: the decision has been taken.

His Eminence the Cardinal Vicar,[3] in the name of the Supreme Pontiff and the Church, has received, blessed and consecrated my renunciation of all the things of this world, my whole-hearted, absolute, irrevocable dedication to Jesus Christ.

When, after the solemn prostration, I approached the altar, and the Cardinal, accepting my vow, robed me in my new and glorious habit, it seemed to me that the Popes, confessors and martyrs who sleep in their silent tombs in the great basilica arose and embraced me like brothers, rejoicing with me and joining in the chorus of the Resurrection angels to praise Jesus who in all his glory has deigned to raise such an unworthy creature to so great a height. Oh the tongue cannot describe all the emotion of that moment, but its memory will last for ever in my heart and I shall never cease to extol the love of my God, his greatness, his glories.

The only words my stammering tongue can utter are those of St Paul: 'It is no longer I who live, but Christ who lives in me.'[4] Now I am no longer my own, I am Christ's. This I have said so many times, but today I repeat it from my heart. I am Christ's. 'Lord Jesus, take and receive my entire liberty.'[5]

Have pity on me Lord if, exhausted as I am and confused by such an outpouring of graces, I cannot thank you as I should. This Eastertide shall be one long feast for me, in which, now with more calm in my innermost blissful soul, I shall rejoice in all your goodness and never rise from your banquet of love. I shall confide in you all my thoughts and my ideals of a new life, in which will be seen that flame of love which you were pleased to light in my heart this day. 'God robed me in the tunic of joy: alleluia, alleluia!'[6]

(12) The sacred ordination was a most happy epilogue to all these Spiritual Exercises. Armed with new weapons, transformed into a new

---

[1] Cf. Psalm 83(84): 1–2.

[2] The passage which follows explains John XXIII's great love for the glorious basilica of the Lateran. Cf. his *Discorsi, messaggi, colloqui, cit.*, vol. IV, pp. 401–6.

[3] Cardinal Pietro Respighi. [4] Gal. 2: 20.

[5] St Ignatius, *Spiritual Exercises*, no. 234. (References to the *Spiritual Exercises* are made according to the paragraph numbering, which is used in all editions.)

[6] Cf. *Pontificale Romanum*, Pars I: *De ordinatione subdiaconi*.

self, today I set out once more into the battle of life, to fight for the kingdom.

In the pure joy which fills my heart to overflowing and in my burning enthusiasm to run the race, to sacrifice myself for Jesus, I cannot formulate any special resolutions. Moreover, my Spiritual Father has expressly forbidden me to do so, and recommended me to study most closely the conclusion of the final Exercises of last Christmas. I must be most punctilious about this, and it is enough for now. In the future I will do as the Holy Spirit wills.

[16]   *During the mid-vacation retreat at*
         Roccantica, 29 August, 1903

The prolonged summer term in the seminary, preoccupations with the thought of examinations, the grave and extraordinary events of July and August[1] and, above all, my own inadequacies, weakness and inconstancy have led to a noticeable cooling of my earlier fervour. This is clearly proved by my having almost entirely given up my particular examination of conscience and by my more and more frequent distractions during meditation, which is nearly always without any real practical results. I also find less joy in saying the Divine Office. In general, too, I notice a self-confidence, an even too assured independence and a lack of circumspection and of concentration of all the faculties of the soul on my own spiritual progress. This concentration, if pushed to extremes, as happens in the first flush of enthusiasm, becomes wearisome, yet it is in a certain measure indispensable in all times and circumstances.

This day of recollection is a gentle loving invitation from the good God to return to the fervour of former times. Meanwhile past experience serves to keep me humble and to make me realize that I am incapable of doing anything really good. No reason here for losing heart but rather for more effort and courage. Death may be close at hand, and what if my lamp were found empty?

O blessed Jesus, have pity on my soul.

To come down to practical details, I am determined to pay special attention to three things: my particular examination of conscience, which will as usual review my behaviour during prayers and religious exercises, the Divine Office, to be said at the right time and place, with great rever-

---

[1] The author refers to the death of Leo XIII (20 July) and the election of Pius X (4 August).

ence and the utmost care; my visit to the Blessed Sacrament, together with countless invocations and acts of love during the day.

So may the good Jesus and holy Mary, the Novena for whose blessed Nativity I am about to begin, be pleased to take me back into their love, give me strength to overcome myself and to progress in virtue and in their sweet love. Amen.

[17]   *During the Triduum at the beginning of the academic year, Rome, 1–3 November, 1903*

The return to normal seminary life has already done me a lot of good. Nothing out of the ordinary in this Triduum, only an attempt to return to a more recollected and concentrated life.

God is watching over my spiritual progress. As I discovered during my mid-vacation retreat, I have really not improved at all, because of my indolence. Alas! Alas! what a dismal failure in true virtue and spiritual progress, after the innumerable graces which my good Lord has been pleased to grant me, especially during this last year. I thought I was a grown man, and instead I see that I am still a miserable boy.

Oh well, like a child who tries to make up for the harm he has done I return once more, but this time more seriously, to my resolutions, and now I seem to feel some confidence that, with God's help, I shall not fail again.

Above all, I intend to apply myself properly to the important practice of the daily particular examination of conscience. This is my most solemn promise to the ever-loving Heart of Jesus, as the result of this holy retreat. I place my promise in the hands of St Charles, the illustrious director of ecclesiastical training. As my Superiors have decided that I should not only attend to my own studies but, as a prefect, supervise those of others also, I place this new academic year under the noble patronage of this great Archbishop, the true model of tutors and a generous-hearted priest and apostle.

Besides my behaviour during prayers and religious practices in general, I will also set as an object of my daily examination the use I make of my tongue, for this is something which, when out of control, may most easily compromise my office and affect my new and delicate responsibilities.

My guiding principle and fixed idea, which must never for a moment be set aside, is the noble duty, now more strictly imposed on me, to set a good example in everything, even in things which in themselves seem insignificant. I will always live as if every one of my actions were performed under the eyes and critical observation of my students and as if my conduct were to be the infallible criterion for their own. After all, I am always under the eye of Jesus, who will be my judge.

[18]   † *Jesus, Mary, Joseph!*

During the retreat in preparation for the ordination
to the diaconate, 9–18 December, 1903

'Speak, Lord, for thy servant hears.' 'Teach me to do thy will.'[1]

Once more, and for the third time in the brief course of a year, the Lord calls me to himself in this holy retreat. 'The Teacher is here and is calling for you.'[2] These three courses of Exercises should have been three milestones along the path of virtue; instead, although something has been achieved, very much, everything, still remains to be done. I am humiliated, ashamed of my poor results, but I do not lose heart. Like a pilgrim on a river bank in the great heat of summer, I plunge once more into the healing waters of grace, to cleanse and refresh myself in the sweetness of love, the happier, in the words of the venerable Curé d'Ars, because the good Jesus is waiting for me, smiling, on the other bank. O God, come to my assistance.

I dedicate this course of Exercises first of all to the divine Heart and then to the most holy Immaculate Virgin, and I am glad to be able to inaugurate in this way, the best way for me, this coming golden jubilee year of the solemn dogmatic definition of her Immaculate Conception. I beg for the special protection of my good Guardian Angel, the intercession of St Ignatius and St Charles Borromeo, my very special patron in this final year of my theology studies and preparations for the priesthood, of the gentle St Francis de Sales, and of the two glorious deacons, St Stephen and St Lawrence, sublime models of loving devotion to God and their neighbours, indomitable martyrs for the Christian faith. 'Give me understanding, that I may keep thy law.'[3]

(1) Man is created by God to revere him, praise him and serve him, and by so doing to save his soul. As I do revere God, I must always have the sense of his divine presence. Certainly my behaviour must be as reverent as if God were always before my eyes, as sometimes he appeared to the

---

[1] 1 Sam. 3: 9–10 and Psalm 142(143): 10.
[2] Cf. John 11: 28.   [3] Psalm 118(119): 34.

patriarchs and prophets, leaving them stricken with awe—I must hold myself upright but without arrogance, head held high but eyes lowered, especially in places where there are many people. I must walk with an easy, measured step; my manner must be at the same time reserved and frank; my words well-considered and suitable; my expression always cheerful yet with a certain air of gravity, not affected but natural; all my external bearing must show my fellow men that I am occupied with the thought of God whom, although invisible, I contemplate at every moment.

The spirit must let itself be absorbed in this feeling. God sees me and sheds his own light upon me and observes all my least actions, even the almost imperceptible movements of my heart; my immense need of him, my memory of sins committed and innumerable graces, past and present: all these considerations must keep me habitually so united to God and so sensitive to the promptings of my conscience that I shall need no other motive.

(2) The golden and sublime conclusion of all the meditations of this first day is the great principle of detachment. In theory I succeed in this remarkably well, but in practice I am the man who abides least by this principle. When something happens here which even indirectly affects me personally, my imagination and my pride torment me to an extraordinary degree. Yet the keystone of the spiritual edifice is just this: to do not my own will but God's, to be habitually disposed to accept anything at all, however repugnant to my feelings and my pride.

In important matters there is no difficulty; I will do nothing more or less than what my Superiors and Spiritual Father require. The crux of the matter lies not in doing what I have to do, under obedience, but in conforming my understanding and my will to the wishes and advice of my Superiors, setting aside my own personal views—even if apparently fine and holy—the flights of my imagination and my other self.

No anxiety then, no castles in the air; few ideas, but they must be sound and serious, and fewer desires. 'One thing is needful.'[1] Golden dreams of working in one way rather than another, highly coloured plans of what I hope to be able to do tomorrow or next year or later: away with all these!

I shall be what the Lord wants me to be. It is hard for me to think of a hidden life, neglected, perhaps despised by all, known to God alone; this is repugnant to my pride. And yet, until I succeed in doing such violence to my own likes and dislikes that this obscurity becomes not only indifferent but welcome and enjoyable, I shall never do what God wants from me.

[1] Luke 10: 42.

(3) What should I be, if I had all the wisdom of the angels, and yet conceived in my mind thoughts of pride, like the first defaulters? I should be a devil, no more, no less.

Now, the fact is that I am immensely and unbelievably ignorant in comparison with the angels, and yet during the course of the day I entertain innumerable feelings of pride. What am I then? What should I deserve if the Lord were to punish me every time I sin? Ah God, the very thought makes me tremble. And that is why I must often think of it.

(4) Penitence is an essential element of a good life in this world, and a necessary means to secure happiness after death. So, there is no way out; in good time, during these finest years of my life, I must accustom myself to suffering and to the love of self-denial. It seems impossible for me to imitate the saints in their austerities. But I must always be prepared for some mortification, always, even in the smallest things, and especially in what I eat. I will never taste any sweet thing that does not contain its drop of bitterness. Indeed is this not the practice of divine Providence, who never sends a pleasure that is not accompanied or followed by some pain?

I shall subject my eyes to severe discipline. I can be sure of nothing, and 'concupiscence of the eyes' might lead me to disastrous consequences. My wine shall always be well watered: this is healthier and keeps my head cool.

(5) Among the things I find impossible to conceive is this: the possibility of my soul one day falling into hell. I cannot think of this without being struck with terror. And yet, there is a place there for me too. Were I to become lukewarm I should already be on the verge of the precipice; one sin could push me over, as might happen to any other poor sinner. Oh how wretched I am! This fear alone must keep me humble: I too might fall, and yet I hardly ever give it a thought.

My Lord, I say it once again, if only you will save me from that place, I am willing to do anything, even to let myself be trampled on like the dust of the high road. Burn me with the flame of your love.

(6) 'O death, how welcome is your sentence!'[1] Why am I thinking so much about tomorrow, my theses, my degrees and so many other un-important things when God does not even promise me today, let alone the future. With all my heart I must do what God desires, at each and every moment, leaving the future in his hands. I must learn to become familiar with the thought of death, which teaches us how to live. I will beware of becoming attached to anything, however unimportant—

[1] Ecclus. 41: 3.

clothes, pictures, books, writings, even devotional objects, for I shall have to leave them all behind one day, as I too shall be left behind, by all and everyone.

(7) The thought of the examinations worries me. I do not know how to face my professors and the whole assembled teaching staff, to show what I have studied. But what will my soul feel like, poor lonely sinner, when it stands before the whole court of heaven, before Jesus, the divine, severest judge? The saints trembled with fear when they thought about this, they fled to the wilderness—and they were holy men. What a fool I am! I am afraid when there is nothing to be afraid of[1] and when there is something I ought to feel terrified about I never even think of it. So, we must be a little more objective. Less fear of examinations here below, and a more determined effort to acquire merit and do good works, so as to make God's judgment less dreadful.

One more remark about this: why do I feel all this anxiety and trepidation about the results and success of my studies? At rock bottom, it all springs from caring about what public opinion may say about me, for I am a slave to the judgments of men, a slave to my own pride. What idiocy! What does the judgment of men matter to me? Is it they who will reward me? Is not God himself the end of all my striving?

I must learn to face it, this judgment of men, to cast it aside and ignore it, for very often in the exercise of my ministry as a priest I shall be obliged to oppose it and defy it, when I want to do something worthwhile. 'If I were still pleasing men,' said St Paul, 'I should not be a servant of Christ.'[2]

(8) My Spiritual Father insists that during these holy Exercises I should pay most attention to pride, the other self, because I shall never be really great and capable of good works until I am stripped of self.

Self-love! What a problem it is, when one stops to think about it! Who has ever defined it? What philosopher has dealt with it? It is the most important problem we have to deal with, truly a matter of life and death, and who cares about it? Yet, as I have seen in my recent meditations, Jesus Christ in his noble teaching is constantly showing us how in practice we must oppose this mortal enemy who corrupts all our actions.

The teaching of Christ is an unfolding, a sequence of wonderful lessons, which give me much food for thought. Although this is not the first time I have listened to him, nevertheless now he is revealing to me certain aspects which seem new with mysterious and marvellous depths. But— and here my astonishment increases—the life of our blessed Saviour, con-

[1] Psalm 13(14): 5.   [2] Gal. 1: 10.

sidered from this angle, means a complete reversal of worldly ideas, quite the contrary of the views and ways of thinking and feeling of even pious and sincerely good people.

Either we are already holy, or at least endeavouring to attain the third degree of humility, the wish to suffer and be despised, or we are nothing. If we only reach the first degree of humility the lessons taught us by Jesus Christ are almost without fruit and self-love is routed only in appearance. But if this is my conclusion, what am I doing, who am not even at the first degree of humility?

O loving Jesus, I kneel at your feet, sure as I am that you will know how to bring about what I cannot even imagine. I want to serve you wherever you wish, at any cost, at any sacrifice. There is nothing I can do; I do not even know how to humble myself. But I will say this to you, and say it very firmly: I want to be humble, I want to love humiliations and being treated with indifference by my fellows. I shut my eyes and hurl myself, with a sort of voluptuous delight, into that flood of scorn, suffering and shame which you may be pleased to send me. I feel a great unwillingness to say this to you, it tears my heart, but I give you my promise; I want to suffer, I want to be despised for you. I do not know what I shall do—indeed I do not really believe myself—but I will not give up wanting this with all my heart and soul: 'To suffer and be despised for you.'

(9) While reading that beautiful book by Father Faber, *The Blessed Sacrament*,[1] I came across a thought which he develops very skilfully and which made a great impression on me. Among the flowers for the altar, that is, among the good results of a sincere devotion to the Blessed Sacrament, spiritual joy has the first place; this joy is a most important element of the spiritual life, the atmosphere of heroic virtues; it is courage, instinct, genius and indescribable grace. Joy is to be thought of as the true source of that liberty of mind which alone is able to unite the apparently incompatible qualities of the spiritual life, giving a freer rein to natural expressions of love while remaining inseparably attached to mortification. In our joy we must be careful to keep our spirit mortified, and practise mortification in order to increase our joy.

I must therefore remain always and invariably happy, while never for one moment desisting from self-denial. It is self-love which stunts the growth of the spirit and saddens us; self-denial restores life, serenity and peace.

[1] Frederick William Faber, *The Blessed Sacrament, or the Works and Ways of God*, London, Burns & Oates, 1855.

The saints are always gay and monks and nuns so cheerful because, like St Paul, they chastise their bodies and subdue them, without mercy and with great discretion.[1] He who denies himself is happy with a purely heavenly joy.

(10) Faith is such a common virtue that it is almost overlooked, especially by ecclesiastics. It is, as it were, the air of Christian life, and who notices or pays any attention to the air we breathe? Nevertheless, I find the practical application of this virtue most important in the times in which we live.

I want to guard my faith carefully, like a sacred treasure. Most of all I want to be true to that spirit of faith which is gradually being whittled away before the so-called requirements of criticism, in the atmosphere and light of modern times. If the Lord should grant me a long life and the opportunity of being a useful priest in his Church, I want it to be said of me, and I shall be prouder of this than of any other title, that I was a priest of lively simple faith, solidly behind the Pope and for the Pope, always, even in matters not yet officially defined, in every detail of seeing and feeling. I want to be like those good old Bergamasque priests of old, of blessed memory, who neither saw nor desired to see further than could be seen by the Pope, the Bishops, common sense and the mind of the Church.

It will always be my principle, in all spheres of religious knowledge and in all theological or biblical questions, to find out first of all the traditional teaching of the Church, and on this basis to judge the findings of contemporary scholarship. I do not despise criticism and I shall be most careful not to think ill of critics or treat them with disrespect. On the contrary, I love it. I shall be glad to keep up with the most recent findings, I shall study the new systems of thought and their continual evolution and their trends; criticism for me is light, is truth, and there is only one truth, which is sacred. But I shall always try to introduce into these discussions, in which too often ill-considered enthusiasms and deceitful appearances have too much to say, a great moderation, harmony, balance and serenity of judgment, allied to a prudent and cautious broad-mindedness. On very doubtful points I shall prefer to keep silent like one who does not know, rather than hazard propositions which might differ in the slightest degree from the right judgment of the Church. I will not be surprised at anything, even if certain conclusions, while preserving intact the sacred deposit of faith, turn out to be rather unexpected. Surprise is the daughter of ignorance. On the contrary, I shall rejoice to see God doing all this in

[1] Cf. 1 Cor. 9: 27.

order to make the pure treasure of his revelation more crystal clear and free from dross.

In general, it will be my rule to listen to everything and everyone, to think and study much, to be very slow to judge, neither to talk too much nor to try to attract attention, and not to deviate by one jot or tittle from the mind of the Church. As Cicero said: 'Time destroys the inventions of public opinion; truth remains and grows ever stronger, and lives and lasts forever.'[1]

Meanwhile I shall simply do my best to observe everything, appreciate everything and sympathize with everyone, and try not to probe too deeply into anything, especially into those matters from which my own piety and the feeling of the people may draw much spiritual advantage. Here in Rome, especially, I must take into account everything, however insignificant or even not fully confirmed by facts or sound reasons, in order to nourish my faith, never allowing it to grow stale, and in order to enrich it with a vigorous and whole-hearted determination and also with indescribable tenderness and appealing simplicity. This also is where the great counsel of Jesus must be followed: 'Unless you turn and become like children, you will never enter the kingdom of heaven.'[2]

(11) When I come out from these Spiritual Exercises, what shall I do? My many ideas and feelings at this time, particularly with regard to the practice of holy humility, have left me somewhat sceptical about my spiritual advancement and my real progress in the way of Christian perfection. Nothing could be more useless than this scepticism; it is a temptation of the devil.

In order not to overload myself and get all confused without achieving anything constructive, I must do one thing only, as my Spiritual Father insists: I must live, not from day to day like St Stanislaus Kostka, but from hour to hour like St John Berchmans. What has to be done here and now, and nothing else: this must be the object of all my endeavours and my best exercise in perfection. The relation between one action and another, indeed between whole series of actions, the harmonious co-operation of all these to form in me a man, a good and worthy priest, will be the natural consequence, although this may not immediately be apparent, of the perfection with which I shall try to perform every single act. God does not consider the number of my deeds but the way in which I do them; it is the heart he asks for, nothing more. An intimate sense of the presence of God, as the final end of all creation, and a total forgetfulness of myself: these two things alone, and with these whatever I do is complete.

---

[1] *De natura deorum*, 2, 2, 5.   [2] Matthew 18: 3.

Father Faber wisely says that our actions must be like so many kneeling figures, their faces full of love, their hands clasped, and their eyes turned to heaven, lost in adoration and utterly forgetful of self.[1]

I shall attend to my tasks as they present themselves, calmly and composedly, with the greatest single-mindedness, as if I had been sent into the world to do just that, as if Jesus himself had given me the order and were present watching me. As for other tasks, I will attend to them later on, in their turn, without any sign of haste, or anxiety, without leaving anything unfinished, without brusqueness or negligence.

If I were to persevere in this way, what room would be left for self-love? Would not the holy Exercises have produced great, incalculable results?

(12) All the difficulties that seem to stand in my way when I set out boldly on the road of scorn and humiliation disappear as if by magic at the thought of the noble lessons my divine Master gives me in the anguish of his Passion. It is indeed true, and I see it ever more clearly: the solution of all difficulties is Christ, and Christ crucified. The Venerable Claude de la Colombière was amazed when he contemplated the frankness, the courage and the equanimity with which Jesus staunchly awaited the hour of his shame and welcomed it with divine eagerness. Although I am confused and speechless, I feel an indescribable joy in the desire to put myself to the same test at all costs, and in the longing to plunge into the sea of humiliations, for I am certain that in this way I shall, with the grace of God, succeed in overcoming self. During my life in the seminary, I shall have many little occasions to abase myself and to crush my self-love, and far greater occasions in my life as a priest; I shall follow the advice of my Spiritual Father, thinking of all these as so many Stations of the Cross, at the sight of which every sacrifice will seem easy to me.

Meanwhile, in the bright splendour of Christ's example I renew, as I shall never tire of renewing, my firm resolution to be humble, humble and despised. Jesus was betrayed with a kiss by a disciple who had just risen from his table; he was disowned by another, the special object of his kindness; he was abandoned by all, and he replied only with friendly words and loving looks of forgiveness. So I must be very careful not to show any sign of displeasure at the indifference, ingratitude or inconsiderateness shown me by persons to whom I may have done some kindness.

Jesus, when his teaching is distorted and he is slandered as a seducer, taunted with ignorance, exposed to the mockery and scorn of all, is meekly silent; he does not confound his slanderers; he lets himself be

[1] F. W. Faber, *op. cit.*

struck, spat upon, scourged, treated as a madman, and never loses his calm or breaks his silence.

So, I will let people say whatever they will about me, assign to me the lowest place, misunderstand my words and my actions, without ever trying to justify myself or find excuses, accepting cheerfully even the rebukes of my Superiors, without saying a word.

Jesus on his Cross, a castaway in a wide sea of suffering and infamy, does not lament, but pities his enemies and forgives them. So I also, in the trials which the Lord may wish to send me, will endeavour to say nothing. I will not even unburden myself with my friends. If I am mortified, particularly by bad results in my studies, I will bow my head without seeking any man's flattery, resigning myself to my disgrace, cheerfully and without resentment, as if I had received a gift, a kind word, or a caress from Jesus. In all circumstances 'far be it from me to glory except in the Cross of our Lord Jesus Christ'.[1]

(13) In this last but one evening of our holy retreat, I have been meditating on the Passion of Jesus Christ, and I have felt a great peace fill my soul, especially during the reading at supper time in the refectory of the life of the Venerable Claude de la Colombière, who speaks in fact of the graces he received during the Spiritual Exercises while he was in London. I felt, as it were, a burning desire to give myself wholly, energetically, to the search for true holiness, through this way of holy humility and lowliness before God and man; a powerful impulse to impart a new and more intense fervour to all my religious practices and to the performance of all my other duties, as a student and as a prefect, and the wish to renew the whole of my spiritual life on this foundation. I am very much afraid that when this first impression has worn off, I shall slip back into the same state as before, and for this reason I never cease, and will never cease, to pray to the good Jesus, in order that he may not fail to give me the same enthusiasm and the same sentiments which I experience today. May he always pity me and support me at all times.

I foresee more backslidings, alas! but they will be against my will, O Jesus, against my will. O Sacred Heart, see to it; I am worthless, but I love you, I love you.

(14) Every time I hear anyone speak of the Sacred Heart of Jesus or of the Blessed Sacrament I feel an indescribable joy. It is as if a wave of precious memories, sweet affections and joyful hopes swept over my poor person, making me tremble with happiness and filling my soul with tenderness. These are loving appeals from Jesus who wants me whole-

[1] Gal. 6: 14.

heartedly there, at the source of all goodness, his Sacred Heart, throbbing mysteriously behind the Eucharistic veils. The devotion to the Sacred Heart has grown with me all my life. Hardly had that good old man, my uncle Zaverio,[1] presented me, a new-born babe, at the baptismal font, than he consecrated me there in the little church of my own village to the Sacred Heart, so that I should grow up under its protection, a good Christian. I remember that among the first prayers I learnt at the knee of that good soul was the beautiful prayer that I love to repeat today: 'Sweet Heart of my Jesus, make me love you more and more.'

I remember too, that in my parish every year the feast of the Sacred Heart was celebrated on the fourth Sunday of September and everyone called it the feast of my uncle Zaverio, and he used to prepare himself very fervently for it, persuading me, as far as my tender age would allow, to do the same. My parents and my uncle intended me to become a good peasant, like themselves. But the Sacred Heart wanted me among its own elect, and to that end used that other good soul, my parish priest Rebuzzini of blessed memory. He also was a lover of the Sacred Heart, and had worked very hard for its triumph during his youth, in stormy times. I cannot forget the Eucharistic Congress of Milan of 1895, the year in which I received the first tonsure, which left me with such a strong attachment to the Blessed Sacrament. I cannot forget the little discourses to the clerics in the seminary, and the evening visits to my humble church at Sotto il Monte during the endless autumn holidays. Later on came my repeated consecrations to the Sacred Heart of Jesus, the laborious study in preparation for that panegyric which I never preached, and the reading of so many books and writings about this beloved devotion.

I remember these little things with great pleasure, although they may not seem much in themselves, because they were for me so many signposts which the Sacred Heart set along my difficult path to draw me here to Rome, to share in other and greater graces from the fountain which still flows.

Today everything which concerns the Sacred Heart of Jesus has become familiar and doubly dear to me. My life seems destined to be spent in the light irradiating from the tabernacle, and it is to the heart of Jesus that I must look for a solution of all my troubles. I feel as if I would be

---

[1] This was really his great-uncle, brother of his grandfather. The memorial tablet placed on the wall of his birthplace at Sotto il Monte, records that 'Pope John XXIII spent his childhood (1881–1891) close to his great-uncle Zaverio, a man and a Christian of dear and edifying memory, who was the first to impart to him, by word and example, the love of piety and heavenly things'. The text was revised by the Pope himself, who wanted, in his own words, to pay homage to his humble great-uncle.

ready to shed my blood for the cause of the Sacred Heart. My fondest wish is to be able to do something for that precious object of my love. At times the thought of my arrogance, of my unbelievable self-love and of my great worthlessness alarms and dismays me and robs me of my courage, but I soon find reason for comfort in the words spoken by Jesus to Blessed Margaret Alacoque: 'I have chosen you to reveal the marvels of my heart, because you are such an abyss of ignorance and insufficiency.'[1]

Ah! I wish to serve the Sacred Heart of Jesus, today and always. I want the devotion to his Heart, concealed within the sacrament of love, to be the measure of all my spiritual progress. The conclusion of my resolutions during the holy Exercises is in my desire henceforth to do all that I have been trying to do till now in intimate union with the Sacred Heart of Jesus in the Blessed Sacrament.

So the thought of the presence of God and the spirit of worship will in all my actions have as their immediate object Jesus, God and man, really present in the most holy Eucharist. The spirit of sacrifice, of humiliation, of scorn for self in the eyes of men, will be illuminated, supported and strengthened by the constant thought of Jesus, humiliated and despised in the Blessed Sacrament.

It will be sweet to abase myself and be ashamed, when I am one with the divine Heart, so ill-treated by men; and when the world treats me with indifference and scorn, my greatest joy will be to seek and find comfort only in that Heart which is the source of all consolations.

I impress upon my mind and will two special practices for daily observation: holy communion and the evening visit, besides the continual invocations with which, like St Aloysius, I shall make a habit of piercing the Heart of the Word. I am determined to give myself no peace until I can truly say I am absorbed into the Heart of Jesus.

O divine Heart, I can only promise, and in this way show the love I believe I feel for you today, but I feel great anxiety about the keeping of my resolves. May it never come to pass that when, some day, I read over again these thoughts of mine, I should read in them my own condemnation!

(15) In these holy Exercises the good God has lifted the veil of my worthlessness and pride and has given me most powerful motives to help me become really holy, while the Holy Spirit, in the sacred order of the diaconate, prepares to work the supernatural sanctification of my soul.

[1] *Vie et Oeuvres de la bienheureuse Marguerite-Marie Alacoque*, Paris, Tequi, 1935, vol. II, p. 336.

If I were once again to write down more detailed resolutions I should only be repeating myself, to little or no purpose. The practice of the presence of God, humility, intense love for Jesus, that is all: 'Do this and you will live.'[1]

I end my retreat at the feet of Immaculate Mary, as I was fortunate to be able to begin it under her patronage. This is the year of the feast, of the triumph of Mary, and also the last year of my theological training, the year of my ordination as a priest. What a happy coincidence for me! my heart fills with purest joy at the thought. 'Time is short; therefore we must be ready to make the most of it, hastening to do our good works.'[2]

O Jesus, O Mary, help me so that this may finally be my year of salvation, 'annus salutis'.

---

[1] Luke 10: 28.   [2] Cf. Eph. 5: 16.

1904

The Year of My Ordination as Priest

1904

Today I have been looking back over my progress this month to see
how my spiritual life is faring.

'Few and brief.' I have made progress, to be sure, but very little. In
fact I am still a sinner, and very slow to reform. My pride in particular
has given me a great deal of trouble, because of my unsatisfactory examination results. This, I must admit, was a real humiliation; I have yet to
learn my A.B.C. in the practice of true humility and scorn of self. I feel
a restless longing for I know not what—it is as if I were trying to fill a
bottomless bag.

I pray rather hurriedly, by fits and starts, without composure or
serenity of mind. I have become more remiss in the practice of self-
denial, and self-indulgent when faced with little opportunities for it. Although I mean to make the most of every scrap of time, I waste hours without achieving anything. I am less reserved in my speech and more effusive,
and also a little less cautious in my criticism. In general I need to live more
intensely and virtuously, in a finer spiritual atmosphere, and be more
determined in my character and resolutions.

I am getting down to work again, all the wiser for my own experience.
Most important of all is holy meditation. The essential is that my thoughts
should be well occupied during those precious moments: if the subject
set does not appeal to me, I may think of the Passion of Jesus, of the state
of my soul, and be frankly sorry for my sins; I may dwell on my love
for Jesus, or make practical resolutions for the day.

In the class room I must constantly exercise the strictest control over
my tongue; my doing this would give Jesus so much pleasure, every day.

In conversation, great reserve in what I say and how I say it. I must
beware of speaking ill of anyone, even indirectly. I must always preserve
a natural, not an affected, dignity. Above all, I must be extremely careful
when I am talking about our Superiors. It would also be very wise to
avoid effusions about my own affairs: I must not pour out my feelings
about everything, to everyone.

My first concern must be to make the most of every moment of time available for study, and not to read anything irrelevant. I mean to be very strict in this respect just as if every evening before going to bed I had to give Jesus an account of what I had learnt and how much time I had wasted.

For the rest, close loving communion with the Sacred Heart and with the Immaculate Virgin in my invocations, thoughts and aspirations. I will not let my mind be so much disturbed by distracting thoughts of pride, but attend whole-heartedly to whatever I am doing, without thinking of anything else.

'In thee, Lord Jesus, have I trusted.'

[20]   *Triduum Exercises of Holy Week*
            28–29–30 March, 1904

In order not to repeat the usual lamentations, the same things I have said over and over again, I will only dwell on the special significance of these brief days of holy retreat.

What is past is past: there remain only shame for my infidelities and eternal gratitude for the extraordinary graces which God has showered upon me.

The blessed day of my ordination to the priesthood approaches and I already enjoy a foretaste of its indescribable happiness. On the eve of such a solemn event I feel it behoves me to redouble all my efforts, so as to prepare myself for it as worthily as I can, because sacramental grace is imparted once only: he receives most who is most capable of receiving it.

I will try therefore to pass these last months in great recollection of soul, concentrating every thought and action on that event where Jesus awaits me. I will repeat all those dear religious practices of my early years in the seminary, in order to keep my fervour fresh, pure and fragrant; I feel a pleasure in being a schoolboy once more, as I return to the simple but ingenious piety of those happy years. I shall then, as far as my new occupations allow, take a delight in repeating those tiny but tender devotional exercises in honour of my very dear patron saints: the three youths, Aloysius, Stanislaus and John Berchmans; St Philip Neri, St Francis de Sales, St Alphonsus Liguori, St Thomas Aquinas, St Ignatius Loyola, St Charles Borromeo, etc.

[21]   † *Jesus, Mary, Joseph!*

1–10 August, 1904. Notes written during the retreat in
preparation for my ordination as a priest. Made in the
Retreat House of the Passionist Fathers of St John
and St Paul on the Caelian Hill[1]

(1) I have not achieved much during these first days. But the place I am staying in and the people I see arouse the finest feelings in me and give me much food for serious thought. I have meditated much on holy detachment, to which I have paid attention in other retreats also, but as far as its practice goes I am still at the starting line. God preserves me from falling into grave sins, which otherwise I might very easily commit. I profess to aim at perfection but in practice I like the way of perfection to be mapped out by me and not by God. In truth, all my fears and anxieties about my studies this year and about the danger of being recalled from Rome, and the reasons which I adduced for this, confirm the fact. Words are one thing, deeds another. My detachment ought to spring from a great simplicity of soul, a readiness for any sacrifice, and very little philosophizing; above all, prayer and trust in God.

I must be careful, especially when things are not going well for me, not to unburden myself to anyone, except my spiritual director or someone else who might be able to help me. In talking with others I lose all the merit I might otherwise acquire. And I must never lose holy joy, because whatever may happen 'in him we live, and move, and have our being',[2] and I must not be concerned with any other matter than the task in hand: *Age quod agis.*[3] What will become of me in the future? Shall I be a good theologian or a famous jurist, or shall I have a country parish or be just a simple priest? What does all this matter to me? I must be prepared to be none of all these, or even more than all these, as God wills. My God and my all. After all, it is easy for Jesus to scatter to the four winds my dream of cutting a brilliant figure in the eyes of the world.

I must get it into my head that, just because God loves me, there will be no plan for me in which ambition plays a part; so it is useless for me to rack my brains about it.

---

[1] The director of the retreat house from 1902–10 was Fr Ferdinando del Cuore di Gesù (Olindo Gori), born in Marlia di Lucca 2 November, 1862, died 26 November, 1925. The giver of the retreat in which Angelo Roncalli took part was Fr Martino del Volto Santo (Altomiro Simonetti), born in Lucca 31 March, 1843, died 12 May, 1928.

[2] Acts 17: 28.   [3] Cf. note 2, p. 75.

I am a slave; I cannot move without my master's consent. God knows my capacities, all that I can or cannot do for his glory, for the good of the Church and for the salvation of souls. So there is no need for me to give any advice to him, through his representatives here, my Superiors.

Is it not true that the saints, in their early years, appeared to set out on a road quite different from the one which their natural gifts and brilliant qualities had seemed to indicate? Yet they became saints, and such saints! Reformers of society, founders of famous Orders! They practised holy detachment: they were willing to listen to the voice of God who spoke to them as he speaks to me; they did not measure what they had to do by considering their pride, but cast themselves blindly into all that God wanted them to do. 'Look' then, my boy, 'look and make it according to the pattern',[1] and this means in everything. All my wanting to do and say is nothing but pride, there is no other word for it; if I go on in my own way I shall work and sweat over it . . . and in the end—what shall I be?—a wind-bag!

If I want to be really great, a great priest, I must be stripped of everything, like Jesus on his Cross; I must judge everything that happens in my life, and the decisions of my Superiors concerning me, in the light of faith. God forbid we should carry criticism into this field! O blessed simplicity!

(2) I come back to the subject of detachment because, when all is said and done, this is the hardest pill for me to swallow. Let us make a little survey: this year, generally speaking, my failings consisted in the lack of fervour, which even very solemn occasions did not arouse; in particular I must regret my aridity in prayer, especially during holy communion and meditation, and almost continual distractions, etc., as well as carelessness in reviewing my spiritual progress, etc. In short, a general lukewarmness. And the cause lay chiefly in my failure to achieve detachment. First of all, that craze for study, which was really with a view to cutting a dash in the examinations, before the worldly eyes of ecclesiastics; then the sheer intellectual effort prompted by pride, fearful and alarmed by the threat of being recalled from Rome, which would have meant the ruin of those rosy hopes conceived in happier days. All this work was excellent in itself but not without its weak side, at least as regards the way in which I went about it. God saw my heart becoming divided and agitated and let me go on like this for a little while, and then, well, we know what happened. So, let the past be a lesson for the future. I must press on, not from day to day but from hour to hour. I must let myself be ruled by God, with

[1] Exodus 25: 40.

a spirit of humility and self-denial, in order to have love and peace in my heart and make real spiritual progress.

(3) My studies! What a great many preconceived ideas I have about these! I have ended by judging them as the world does. I have let my head be turned by current ideas. Learning is always a fine thing, a secondary ingredient of a useful priestly life and also a secondary means of saving souls in these modern times. God preserve me from underestimating study, but I must beware of attaching to it an exaggerated and absolute value. Study is one eye, the left eye; if the right one is missing, what is the use of a single eye, of study by itself? After all, what am I now that I have secured my degree? Nothing, a poor ignorant fellow. What use am I to the Church with that alone? So I must revise my ideas about study. Here also I need a sense of proportion and harmony between what I think and what I do. Of course I shall always go on studying, I shall never give it up, but 'all according to order and measure; we must seek knowledge soberly'.[1] I must be learned, but as St Francis de Sales was. After all, what are they worth, even these people who are said to be so clever? What do they know? Very little. Naturally I do not mean those who are learned in the strict sense of the word. How wise the advice which our Holy Father Pius X gave to young seminarists: 'My sons, you must study, study hard; but for charity's sake be good too, very good!'

In future I shall study with even more enthusiasm than before, but I shall call things by their right names; I shall be studying not so much for the examinations as for life itself, so that what I learn will become an integral part of me.

(4) The lay brother who cleans my room and serves me at table, good Brother Thomas,[2] gives me plenty of food for thought. He is no longer

[1] Cf. Romans 12: 3.

[2] Brother Thomas of the Passion (Eugenio Viso) of the Province of Calvario (Brazil) was born at Arnioza (Orense, Spain) on 29 August, 1869, and died 9 July, 1939, in the Retreat of Curitiba in Brazil. He loved the Congregation of the Passionists and served it in a great spirit of sacrifice, first at St John and St Paul in Rome, where he remained until 1913, and then in Brazil, in the Province of Calvario. In his duties in the porter's lodge and in the church, where he passed the last fifteen years of his life, he showed singular patience and charity. It is difficult to describe the love and gentleness with which he received the poor; he did his best to send them all away happy. He was a great lover of poverty and during the last twenty years of his life would not allow any new habit or cloak to be made for himself.

His Christian piety received its solid foundation in his own family. When he became a religious he was steeped in the spirit of the Passionists. In the last months of his life he showed even more fervour in his devotions and continually expressed his gratitude to the Lord for having called him to the Congregation of the Passionists, and for having blessed the foundation of Curitiba and the Province of Calvario, of which he had seen the humble beginnings and lived to see the encouraging development.

young, his manners are refined, he is quite tall and robed in a very long black habit which he never refers to without calling it 'holy'. He is always cheerful and speaks only of God and divine love; he never raises his eyes to look anyone in the face. In church, before the Blessed Sacrament, he prostrates himself on the bare ground, as still as a statue. He came to Rome from Spain to join the Passionists and is ideally happy, at everyone's beck and call, as simple as a creature can be who has no alluring ambitions, no glowing mirages ahead, content to be a poor lay brother for the rest of his life. Before the goodness of Brother Thomas I feel my own nothingness; I ought to kiss the hem of his habit and take him for my teacher. And yet I am almost a priest, the recipient of so many graces! Where is my spirit of penitence and humility, my modesty, prayerfulness or true wisdom? Ah, Brother Thomas, what a lot I am learning from you! So many of these humble little lay brothers, so many unknown religious, will one day shine with glory in the kingdom of heaven. And why should not I too shine? O Jesus, give me the spirit of penitence, sacrifice and mortification.

(5) Our excellent Father Director has begged me to take as my companion, during the time we spend on our walks, a young Protestant who has been given hospitality while being prepared for the abjuration of his former faith. Poor young man, I feel so sorry for him! He is a good youth, but for the best nine years of his life—he is now eighteen—he has been thoroughly imbued with the instruction which the Protestants are so expert in giving. There is not a single prejudice against the Catholic Church that he does not know, not one article of heretical teaching that he has not learnt. His company, even if somewhat distracting, does me good, for it brings home to me another grave peril which is threatening the faith in Italy, now so beset with divers sects. Alas! the children of this world are wiser than the children of light.[1] Meanwhile this has convinced me of my tremendous obligation to thank God for the great gift of faith: one has only to talk to a Protestant for a few hours to understand all the importance of this. Therefore, forever, 'his praise shall be continually in my mouth'[2] for this gift too, indeed for this gift above all else. As for these poor unfortunates outside the Church, we must feel sorry for them, poor children, pray hard for them, and work with all our hearts and strength for their conversion.

(6) I must think of the priesthood, and think of it seriously. I am here in this holy retreat precisely for this purpose, for 'the work is great',[3] the most solemn act of my life. If from the heights of this mountain,

[1] Cf. Luke 16: 8.   [2] Psalm 33(34): 2.   [3] 1 Chron. 29: 1.

whose peak I shall reach within a few days, I were to turn back on my steps. . . .[1]

At this point the modest notes made during those Spiritual Exercises were interrupted, but the holy impressions of those days, so full of blessings, did not end there. After a lapse of eight years (I am writing in 1912) they are still clearly in my mind and, please God, will never be forgotten.

Above all else, there was at that time ripening in my mind a lively desire and determination to annihilate the self completely in the presence of the Heart of Jesus, in order that when I had become quite stripped of all that was myself my divine Master would find me more obedient to his commands and a worthier tool for doing some good, some great good in the Church, not in places and ways chosen by my pride but in simple, blind abandonment to the will of my Superiors. To make my retreat more profitable I also heard some very fervent sermons preached to us by one of those good Fathers. There were about ten of us ordinands, from different lands and different colleges: among others a Florentine student from the Capranica,[2] a Portuguese,[3] Don Nicola Turchi,[4] a former companion of mine at the Roman Seminary, another Roman student, etc. I found great help in the daily exercise of the Way of the Cross, which we all made together in the chapel, and in listening to the life of the recently beatified Gabriel of Our Lady of the Sorrows which we read in turn at mealtimes, in the evening service in the richly adorned chapel where lies the body of St Paul of the Cross (it was the Novena of the Assumption) and in the fine example of austere living given by the Fathers themselves. I still remember the impression made on me every night, when they rose for Matins, and I heard the sound of their footsteps and the trailing of their long black habits along the dark corridors. I was also particularly impressed by the solemn Christian associations of that venerable place. From my window I could see the Colosseum, the Lateran and the Appian Way. From the garden could be seen the Palatine and the Caelian Hill, with its crown of Christian monuments, the church of St Gregory, etc. At the side of the house where I was staying was the basilica of St John and St Paul, and I went down to it every evening, as I said, for the Novena of the Assumption. Under the basilica, inside the *Clivus*

[1] At this point and after, in the same notebook, come other reflections added in 1912.
[2] Igino Magonio.
[3] Enrico of the Most Holy Trinity, a Trinitarian.
[4] Nicola Turchi (1882–1959), Professor of the History of Religions at the University of Rome, friend and collaborator of Buonaiuti.

OB · MEMORIAM · AUSPICATISSIMI · DIEI

QUO

ANGELUS · JOSEPHUS · RONCALLI

BERGOMAS

PONTIFIGII · SEMINARII · ROMANI · ALUMNUS

AD · CORPUS · B · PETRI · IN · AEDE · VATICANA

PRIMUM · SACRUM · OBTULIT

SIBI · CHARITATEM · APOSTOLICAM

COGNATIS · BENEFACTORIBUS · AMICIS

MUNERA · CELESTIA

ECCLESIAE

LIBERTATEM · UNITATEM · ET · PACEM

ADPRECATUS

———

ROMAE · III · IDUS · AUG · MCMIV

Accendat in nobis Dominus ignem
sui amoris, et flammam aeternac cha-
ritatis.   *(Ecclesia in Liturgia).*

1344 — Jonquières & Dati - Roma

13. The card which Angelo Roncalli had printed for his family and friends to
commemorate his first Mass, celebrated at the tomb of
St Peter in the Vatican, August, 1904

14. Portrait, 1914

Scauri, was the martyrs' house; near my room was the room where St Paul of the Cross died. There every afternoon we practised saying Holy Mass. So everything up there breathed of holiness, nobility and sacrifice. O Lord, how I thank you for having sent me to that holy place for my immediate preparation for the priesthood!

On the eve of that blessed day of my ordination the good Father Luigi del Rosario who looked after the students following the course of Exercises, and who had shown me many kindnesses, was good enough to accede to my wish and accompany me to some of the most sacred places. So I went with him to St John Lateran, to pray in that basilica and to renew my act of faith; then I did the Holy Stairs on my knees, and thence went on to St Paul's Without the Walls. What did I tell the good Lord that evening, over the tomb of the Apostle of the Gentiles? It is locked in my heart.[1]

The dawn came of that most blessed feast of St Lawrence. My Vice-rector, Fr Spolverini,[2] came to fetch me from the monastery. I crossed the city in silence. The never-to-be-forgotten ceremony took place in the church of S. Maria in Monte Santo in the Piazza del Popolo. I still remember all the attendant circumstances. The ordaining bishop was His Grace Mgr Ceppetelli,[3] Vicegerent; some students from the Capranica College served at the altar. When all was over and I raised my eyes, having sworn the oath of eternal fidelity to my Superior, the Bishop, I saw the blessed image of Our Lady to which I confess I had paid no attention before. She seemed to smile at me from the altar and her look gave me a feeling of sweet peace in my soul and a generous and confident spirit, as if she were telling me she was pleased, and that she would always watch over me—in short she sent a gentle calm and peace into my soul which I shall never forget.

The good Vice-rector took me back to the seminary, which was deserted, as everyone had gone into the country to Roccantica. My first

---

[1] Cf. Isaiah 24: 16.

[2] Domenico Spolverini (1871–1939); in 1902 he was appointed Vice-rector of the Roman Seminary and in 1910 Rector. We quote from a letter written on the occasion of his death by Mgr Roncalli to Mgr Salvatore Capoferri: 'I knew Mgr Domenico Spolverini in 1901 when he was a tutor. Then he was my Vice-rector; he was present at my first private Mass down in the crypt of St Peter's and presented me to our Holy Father Pius X the same day. During his many years as Rector he always showed an affectionate interest in me; when I returned to Rome in 1921 he received me as tenderly as a mother her child. I shall never forget certain examples of his gentleness and tact, as when he accompanied me, with the whole seminary, to San Carlo al Corso, where I received the fulness of the priesthood' (cf. *In memoria di Mgr Domenico Spolverini*, Rome, 1940, pp. 23–4).

[3] Mgr Giuseppe Ceppetelli, Titular Patriarch of Constantinople, Vicegerent.

duty was to write a letter at once to my Bishop, Mgr Guindani of blessed memory.[1] I told him in a few words what, at the feet of Mgr Ceppetelli, I had said to the Lord; and to him I renewed my vow of obedience and love. With what joy, eight years afterwards, I recall and renew that promise! Then I wrote to my parents, so that they and all the family should share in the joy of my heart, begging them to thank the Lord with me, and to implore him to keep me faithful. In the afternoon I was alone, alone with my God, who had raised me so high, alone with my thoughts, my resolves, the joys of my priesthood. I went out. Utterly absorbed in my Lord, as if there were no one else in Rome, I visited the churches to which I was most devoted, the altars of my most familiar saints, the images of Our Lady. They were very short visits. It seemed that evening as if I had something to say to all those holy ones and as if every one of them had something to say to me. And indeed it was so.

So I visited St Philip Neri, St Ignatius, St John Baptist de Rossi, St Aloysius, St John Berchmans, St Catherine of Siena, St Camillus de Lellis and many others. O blessed saints, who in that hour were witnesses to the Lord of my good intentions, now you must ask him to forgive my weaknesses and to help me to keep ever alight in my heart the flame of that memorable day.

The next day it was again my dear Vice-rector who took me to St Peter's to celebrate my first Mass. The great square had much to say to me as I crossed it! I had often felt my heart moved when walking there, but never as on that morning. . . . And inside the majestic temple, among the venerable records of the history of the Church! I went down into the crypt near the tomb of the Apostle. There was a group of friends invited by the Vice-rector. I remember Mgr Giuseppe Palica, my Professor of moral theology, and Fr Enrico Benedetti, Fr Pietro Moriconi, Fr Giuseppe Baldi, Fr Enrico Fazi and others. I said the votive Mass of St Peter and St Paul. Ah, the joys of that Mass! I remember that among the feelings with which my heart was overflowing the most powerful of all was a great love for the Church, for the cause of Christ, for the Pope, and a sense of total dedication to the service of Jesus and of the Church, and of an intention, indeed a sacred oath, of allegiance to the Chair of St Peter and of unwearying work for souls. This oath, hallowed in such a special manner by the place where I was, by the act I performed and the circumstances which accompanied it, still lives and throbs within my breast, more alive than words can tell. I said to the Lord over the tomb

[1] Gaetano Camillo Guindani, a Cremonese, Bishop of Bergamo (1879–1904).

of St Peter: 'Lord, you know everything; you know that I love you.'[1] I came out from the church as if in a dream. On that day the marble and bronze Popes aligned along the walls of the basilica seemed to look at me from their sepulchres with a new expression, as if to give me courage and great confidence.

Towards midday a new joy awaited me: the audience with Pope Pius X. My Vice-rector had arranged it for me—how grateful I am to him for all he did for me in those blessed days!—and went with me. When the Pope came to where I was, the Vice-rector presented me, and the Pope smiled and bent his head to hear what I said to him. I was kneeling before him, telling him that I was glad to be at his feet repeating to him the intentions which I had offered during my first Mass over the tomb of St Peter, and I told him of these briefly, as well as I could.

The Pope then, still bending down, placed his hand on my head, and speaking almost into my ear said: 'Well done, well done, my boy . . . this is what I like to hear, and I will ask the good Lord to grant a special blessing on these good intentions of yours, so that you may really be a priest after his own heart. I bless all your other intentions too, and all the people who are rejoicing at this time for your sake.' He blessed me and gave me his hand to kiss. He passed on and spoke to someone else, a Pole I believe; but all at once, as if following his own train of thought, he turned back to me and asked when I should be back at my home. I told him: 'For the feast of the Assumption.' 'Ah, what a feast that will be,' he said, 'up there in your little hamlet (he had earlier asked me where I came from), and how those fine Bergamasque bells will peal out on that day!' and he continued his round smiling.

The evening of that blessed day found me at Roccantica, the villa belonging to the seminary. Father Giuseppe Piccirilli came to meet me at the station of Poggio Mirteto. I was most touched when I saw the villa, beautifully lit up; in the chapel the good students sang a fine 'Tu es sacerdos'. The next day wonderful celebrations. Everyone received holy communion. Mgr Bugarini, the Rector, guided me through the Mass and my kind spiritual director, Father Francesco Pitocchi, a Liguorian, preached the Gospel homily. That Father was too kind in what he said about me: his affection blinded him a little. And the happy rejoicings went on all day.

On the 13th I celebrated Holy Mass at the Santissima Annunziata in Florence. This was in fulfilment of an obligation of gratitude towards Our Lady, to whom, before beginning my military service, I had dedicated

[1] John 21: 17.

my purity. On the 14th I was in Milan, saying Mass over the tomb of St Charles Borromeo. . . . How much I had to tell him! And from then on the veneration and love which bind me to him have grown stronger.

On the 15th, the feast of the Assumption, I was at Sotto il Monte. I count that day among the happiest of my life, for me, for my relations and benefactors, for everyone.

Why have I written all this down? In order that these notes too may encourage me to keep faith with my promises, grateful to the Lord for his goodness to me. May I be reminded of my profession, should I ever be tempted to be unfaithful to it, and may everything serve to make me a priest worthy of my noble calling and not unworthy of Christ, to whom alone be the glory.

[22]   † *Jesus, Mary, Joseph!*
             4 November, 1904. Triduum before the
                  beginning of the academic year

As regards general resolutions I stand by all that I have written during the four courses of Exercises in preparation for my ordination. In order the better to control my conduct and to set up some solid props to support my spiritual progress, I intend to pay special attention to the following resolutions, which I humbly place under the protection of St Charles Borromeo, on this his precious feast day.

(1) Throughout the morning, from the first moment I awaken until some time after Mass, I will apply myself exclusively to spiritual thoughts and occupations: vocal prayers, spiritual reading, meditation, the recital of the Divine Office and so on.

(2) I shall be most scrupulous in making my particular examinations purposefully and profitably, five minutes before noon.

(3) My most important duty will be to pay my daily visit to the Blessed Sacrament, with the greatest fervour. I owe everything to the Blessed Sacrament and to the Sacred Heart of Jesus: so I will have a most loving devotion to the Blessed Sacrament.

(4) I will never go to bed without having recited at least the three nocturns of the following day. Nothing else matters so much: the Breviary must always be given pride of place.

(5) I will be inflexible about making my monthly day of recollection,

at least from the preceding evening until midday of the first Sunday of every month.

(6) I will obey all the rules of the seminary as scrupulously as if I were one of the youngest students, always bearing in mind that all my influence as a prefect over the young will entirely depend on the good example I set them.

(7) I renew more firmly my intention to behave with the greatest modesty during my walks. Being a priest does not give me immunity from grave sins. My concern for modesty will stand me in good stead in my efforts to maintain recollection and fervour in my soul.

(8) I must make the best use of my time, especially when studying. First of all the subjects set for this year and for the classes, then, with moderation, other things.

(9) In all things there must be humility, great spiritual fervour, mildness and courtesy towards everyone, continual cheerfulness and serenity of mind and heart.

Heart of Jesus, burning with love for us, inflame our hearts with love for you.

[23]   *8 December, 1904*
           Fiftieth anniversary of the proclamation of the
           dogma of the Immaculate Conception of Mary

I shall remember this day as one of the most impressive of my life. Today I rejoiced with my heart full of the purest delight when I was present at the solemn triumph of Mary, celebrated in the Vatican basilica and in all the churches of the city.

In a spirit of affectionate rivalry all Rome was determined to make a further display of its love for the Blessed Virgin. In the great church, crowded with people, in the splendour of the magnificent ceremony in that place, the most venerated on earth, the image of Mary Immaculate high up in the apse, shining in a radiance of dazzling light, seemed to be smiling at the Pope, at all the majesty of pontifical pomp, at the imposing array of Cardinals and Bishops gathered in large numbers from every corner of the earth, at the ecclesiastical dignitaries and the lay folk. The sacred mysteries were accompanied by the music of Perosi which resounded like that of heavenly choirs along the immense aisles, and rose to find nobler echoes in the immense dome. What a spectacle of faith, what a triumph for Mary!

I do not think it possible to imagine on this earth a greater or more wonderful honour. As for myself, swallowed up in the throng of young seminarists from every land, and yet near enough to the Apostle's tomb to be able to follow almost the whole course of the imposing ceremony [here these notes end].

1905—1914

Secretary to Mgr Radini Tedeschi,
Bishop of Bergamo

1905—1906

In 1905 Fr Angelo Roncalli did not make his usual annual retreat. He took part for the first time in a pilgrimage to Lourdes, from which he brought back tender and unforgettable memories, which he often lovingly recalled. On this occasion he visited other French shrines, notably the basilica of the Sacred Heart at Paray-le-Monial and the places hallowed by the Curé d'Ars.

From 19–21 April, 1905, before taking up his duties as Secretary to Mgr Giacomo M. Radini Tedeschi, Bishop of Bergamo, Fr Angelo Roncalli passed three days in retreat with the Camaldolesi of the Hermitage at Frascati. No notes remain from these Exercises. On 19 May, 1959, after he became Pope, he went to the Nursing Home of the Sisters of St Elizabeth at Frascati, to visit Mgr Paolo Pappalardo, Titular Archbishop of Apamea in Syria, who was a patient there, and took the opportunity of going up to the Hermitage. The Camaldolesi monks, in memory of this visit and of the days which he had spent there in 1905, put up a tablet inscribed (in Latin) with these words:

THIS HUMBLE STONE COMMEMORATES

POPE JOHN XXIII

WHO, HAVING ALWAYS TREASURED AN UNFADING MEMORY

OF THE HOLY HERMITAGE OF THE CAMALDOLESI MONKS,

WHERE HE HAD MADE A RETREAT OF FERVENT PRAYER

FROM 19–21 APRIL, 1905

BEFORE HOLDING FOR TEN YEARS THE OFFICE OF

SECRETARY TO THE MOST ILLUSTRIOUS AND VIRTUOUS

GIACOMO RADINI TEDESCHI, BISHOP OF BERGAMO,

RETURNED UNEXPECTEDLY TO THE TUSCULAN HILL

ON THE EVENING OF 19 MAY, 1959,

SO BRINGING THE MONKS

AN UNLOOKED FOR AND MUCH APPRECIATED JOY.

1906

From 19 September to 22 October, instead of making a retreat, he took part in the third Italian national pilgrimage to the Holy Land, led by the Bishop, Mgr Radini.

We have a few notes about this journey, written in pages full of moving piety, published in 1906 in *L'Eco di Bergamo*, from 27 September to 25 October, and in the journal of the Committee for Palestine and Lourdes. These are to be published in full in a later volume of Pope John's papers. Here are two extracts:

30 September

I am leaving Cana, but not without a heartfelt hope and prayer. At Cana Jesus worked his first miracle, gave the first proof of his divinity. But now at Cana, out of about 1,300 inhabitants, the majority are Moslems, most of the others being schismatic Greeks and very, very few, about fifty in all, Catholics, and these are more or less like all the Catholics in Palestine, not very faithful and not at all fervent. May the Lord grant that the new altar solemnly consecrated today and dedicated to the mystery of the first miracle of Jesus may call all those scattered souls and gather them together in the unity of the Catholic faith, in the whole-hearted and constant practice of the Christian life.

4 October

[Jerusalem. Pontifical Mass of Mgr Radini Tedeschi.] The Bishop compared the bewilderment of the pious women when they saw the stone of the sepulchre rolled away with the sense of amazement and grief felt by Christians from distant countries when confronted with the disorder, the confusion of people, things, languages, rites and faiths surrounding the holy sepulchre. Then he made an impassioned appeal to the risen Christ to return in all the splendour of his glory above the empty tomb not to disperse but to convert, that there may be heard again, in this place above all others, and echoed throughout the entire East, and from the Russian Steppes and Africa too, his promise of one fold and one shepherd. All eyes were on the Bishop and all hearts responded to his words and throbbed in unison with his in one great prayer, the common desire shared by all that the separated brethren should return to the true fold.

With the help of all Christians everywhere why should today's prayer not become tomorrow's reality? Meanwhile we must strive for the realization of this wonderful prayer, so magnificently expressed, and leave the rest to God, knowing that Christ's words will one day come to pass, and especially here in Jerusalem: one fold and one shepherd!

1907

24

Retreat of 1907, in the House of the Holy Family
at Martinengo,[1] 1–7 September

At last I have been able to give some time to recollection, in this retreat
which I have so long desired. I have revised my old resolutions and have
experienced once more my former impressions. My spiritual life has
been rather too much affected by the events of these first years of my
priesthood, during which I have never had time to think seriously about
myself. My soul has always been, as it were, dissipated in a thousand little
responsibilities and duties, some of them very unimportant, but which are
always there and always will be. I feel impelled to thank God, not only
for having preserved me from grave sins but for the immense, innumerable, precious, ordinary and extraordinary graces which he has never
ceased and never ceases to pour into my soul. Such graces, my God, so
strange and indescribable! This thought alone is an appeal to me to re-
kindle my fervour and strengthen my resolve truly to lead a holy priestly
life. O Jesus, I will answer your call: it might be the last, for who knows
what your plans are for my life? I return to your embrace, to your loving
Heart.

My position as secretary to the Bishop and my teaching duties, which
are heavier this year,[2] determine the character of my whole life, a life of
great recollection, prayer and study. In a word, I have gone back to being
a seminarist, and I wish to live as one. I have looked over all the notes I
wrote while I was in Rome. These certainly contain practical ideas and
impressions which are always useful. I will add a few more notes and a
few more resolutions, to which I shall often return during my examinations of conscience.

(1) My continual and pressing occupations in the house and elsewhere
have worked havoc in my religious exercises. So everything must be
put back into its proper place. I intend to be adamant on this point. I will

[1] Congregation of the Holy Family, religious congregation of the diocese of Bergamo. Director of this retreat, Fr Zamboni, S.J.
[2] See Chronology for 1907.

always recite Matins with Lauds in the evening; come what may, I must find time for a little meditation before Mass, half an hour, twenty minutes, a quarter of an hour or, if I can do no more, at least ten minutes: the meditation must on no account get left out. I will never leave the chapel before I have said the Little Hours as well. My set time for getting up in the morning must be regulated according to circumstances, so as to leave time for everything. As a general rule I will get up at half past five. This means that even if I go to bed at half past eleven I shall have six hours' sleep, which ought to be enough.

(2) During the retreat, I have once more felt a great surge of devotion to the Blessed Sacrament and the Sacred Heart of Jesus. This devotion has meant everything to me; now that I am a priest I must give it all my love. 'The heart in love goes with him, comes with him, stays with him always', Tasso said of the soul in love with God.[1] That is what my life must be, centred in the Blessed Sacrament. I will never miss my daily visit and I will try to return to Jesus frequently during the rest of the day, if only to greet him. I must treat Jesus as I would treat a guest whom I am delighted to honour. My devotion to the Blessed Sacrament and the Sacred Heart must permeate my whole life, my thoughts and affections and all I do, so that I live only by it and with it. I must take great care over my preparation for Holy Mass and my thanksgiving afterwards. I must also scrupulously hold to my monthly day of recollection on the first Sunday of every month, or the nearest and most convenient day to this, and make my examination of conscience strictly, every day in the afternoon after Vespers.

(3) One of my chief faults consists in still not having learnt to make the right use of time. I must find a way of doing much in a short time, and with this in mind I must be most careful not to waste a single moment in useless things, idle chatter, etc. Immediately after breakfast I will attend to the duties of my office, correspondence, etc. All the remaining time is for my lectures, which I shall prepare most conscientiously. I will read the newspapers at times when I have least energy for other things, after dinner, on my walks, for example, or in any odd moments. Every day, last thing at night, I will read some good books which will be of use to my soul.

(4) My post as Bishop's secretary sets me grave duties and demands the greatest tact and prudence. I will always try very hard to succeed in all this. The first thing necessary is great reverence for the Bishop, at all times, in my mind and heart, in my works, in private and in public, full

[1] Torquato Tasso, *L'anima innamorata di Dio*.

obedience and union of mind and heart with him. It is also my duty to set a good example in the eyes of men by conduct befitting a priest; to be charitable and gentle in all circumstances and to be tactful and reserved, especially in my speech. I must speak little but well, and above all know how to keep silence, but without ostentation and without becoming a bore, indeed always preserving the greatest tranquillity of soul and calm with everyone, with the finest courtesy in manners and speech so as to hurt no one. In short, I will follow the advice St Paul gave to Titus: 'Show yourself in all respects a model of good deeds.'[1] Nor will I forget what the Holy Father Pius X said to me when he came to Bergamo[2] with the Bishop: 'So, Father Angelo, you must be a faithful servant and a wise one, a wise one!'[3] As for what the world may say, let us 'rejoice and do well',[4] and let the sparrows twitter.

---

[1] Titus 2: 7.
[2] Pius X visited Bergamo when he was Cardinal Patriarch of Venice.
[3] Matthew 24: 45.   [4] Eccles. 3: 12.

1908

25

Retreat of 25–31 October, at Martinengo
with the Bishop[1]

(1) I thank God once more for having borne with me till now and for the new grace of this retreat. My first conclusion is a profound feeling of my utter worthlessness and the renewal of my old resolve to sanctify myself at all costs, beginning straight away, because these beautiful and precious years are swiftly passing.

(2) I still note in myself a lack of calm and serenity in what I do, although perhaps this is not apparent to others. The numerous tasks assigned to me leave my head and heart in a ferment of excitement and prevent my attending seriously and whole-heartedly to anything, to the grave detriment of my spirit of piety. Therefore more calm, more orderliness in everything, with my practices of piety taking precedence over everything else, cost what it may.

(3) I feel a great need of more intense prayerfulness and a closer and more trustful union with my Lord in the midst of my work. Therefore I resolve very firmly to keep to my religious practices very scrupulously.

I will always and *without fail* get up at half past five, so that I shall never lack time for meditation; and after supper I will always say Matins with the Lauds of the following day. The visit to the Blessed Sacrament, either in the house or outside, must never be omitted. Above all, I must see that I am recollected and attentive while reading my Breviary and saying the holy rosary. I will try to keep my spirit of prayer constantly alive, for this is essential if I am to preserve the fervour of my resolutions.

(4) Just lately the good Lord has been pleased to give me a clearer understanding of what it means to be a priest, and how this conception should rule my whole priestly life. I must think of myself as always in the hands of God, like a victim ready for the sacrifice of myself, my ideas, my comforts, my honour, all I have: for the glory of God, for my Bishop, for the good of my dear diocese: 'a living sacrifice, holy and acceptable to God'.[2] I will accustom myself to constant reflection on the sublime

---

[1] The preacher was Fr Zamboni, S.J.   [2] Cf. Romans 12: 1.

meaning of these words. So, without resorting to extremes, I shall find a way of practising continual mortification, especially of my self-love and my comforts, without complaining and without losing the joy in my soul, which will shine through and be seen in all my actions. This will be particularly in my thoughts when I am celebrating Holy Mass, when I will unite myself to Jesus Christ, the High Priest and divine victim for the whole world. What a fine thing that would be, to work untiringly and suffer in silence the little setbacks of every day, without ever losing my composure, always preserving pure and glowing the desire to suffer more and contribute more to the welfare of the diocese and to please my good Master Jesus Christ.

(5) I have re-read the brief notes which I still keep in various slim notebooks of the Spiritual Exercises made in Rome when I was a student, preparing for Holy Orders.[1] O my Lord, do not let me forget the good intentions of those days.

I am still what I was, a sinner, and ungrateful for the tender love you have shown me: yet I still desire to work and to make myself holy, in order that I may soon be able to do something useful for the Church.

The examples of your saints, whose lives I read, spur me on to imitate them more courageously. O good Jesus, support me in my good intentions and come to my aid.

---

[1] See pp. 154ff.

1909

[26]   † *During the retreat made at Martinengo with the*
Bishop, from 19–25 September, 1909[1]

(1) I have nothing to add to or to take away from the resolutions made during the two preceding retreats, concerning my life of prayer. It is humiliating to have to confess the same negligences over and over again, but I am bound to do so.

I shall follow more closely my spiritual director's advice to go to bed a little earlier in the evening, so as to rise punctually at half past five in the morning. Getting up at the right time and without delay makes a good start for the whole day. I shall also follow the good practice of saying the Divine Office as a rule in the chapel in the presence of the Blessed Sacrament.

(2) During this retreat I have frequently felt a strong urge to study Holy Scripture, and I have already begun, with great enjoyment, to read St Paul's Epistles. I intend to go on doing this, and also frequently to use a passage from Holy Scripture, generally from the New Testament, as matter for my meditation. Every evening, before going to bed, I shall read a chapter from the Bible, calmly and devoutly.

(3) All the things I have to do, which at times seem unending, are burdensome to me and confuse my brain. This will not do. I must do all my work with religious care but without in any way disturbing the tranquillity and peace of my soul. I will just do what I can. Above all, I will take care not to put off till the last moment the most important things and those which I am most bound to do.

(4) During these days I have decided to join the new Diocesan Congregation of the Priests of the Sacred Heart,[2] and I hope soon to be able to gratify this wish.

This act does not require of me anything more than what I have promised the Lord for a long time past, that is, 'to consider myself

[1] The preacher was Fr Rossi, S.J.

[2] Concerning this Congregation see Angelo Roncalli, *Mgr Giacomo Maria Radini Tedeschi*, cit., pp. 203–8.

entirely at the disposal of my Superiors, without ever doing anything that might influence them, one way or another, about me. However, it will be a new and constant encouragement to me to persevere in all my former intentions to sanctify myself, and also to give a good example to the other priests, especially the younger ones. Being a member of the new Congregation will serve to keep intact the spirit of utter humility and obedience, and will place me under a stricter obligation not to be self-seeking in any way, but always to follow the will of God as expressed in the will of my Bishop. May the Lord and Our Lady bless me in this joyful intention.

(5) Although I am not making any special resolutions but only renewing those made on former occasions, which are quite sufficient, when I come out of this retreat I shall have to make some adjustments in my life, if I am myself to feel in my soul the full benefits of these reforms.

However, to remind myself of my intentions and also to accustom myself a little more to the spirit of Christian mortification, which will also be good for my bodily health, I promise to practise self-denial, especially in food. Eating a little less than usual will certainly do me good. So I will cut down my portions by half, and in general drink little wine, and that mixed with water. On second thoughts, it seems to me I am promising too much. However, l hope the Lord will help me to keep my resolves faithfully and enable me to find joy in doing so.

(6) Next year there will be great celebrations in Lombardy for the third centenary of the canonization of St Charles Borromeo; I have already tried to do something for him here in Bergamo, pointing out how richly the great Archbishop has earned our gratitude. I myself will try to make this great saint more and more familiar to my heart and mind, to pray to him frequently for his help and to imitate him. If, with the Lord's help, I could inspire the souls of our clergy with the example of St Charles, it would do much to increase their eagerness for apostolic work, to the greater spiritual advantage of the whole diocese. Perhaps the work I have undertaken will be very onerous, but l will do it willingly in honour of St Charles, certain that in this way I shall be contributing more to the desired result.[1]

[1] Cf. *San Carlo Borromeo nel terzo centenario della canonizzazione MDCX–MCMX*, November, 1908–December, 1910 (26 numbers).

1910

[27] † *During the retreat made at Martinengo with the*
Bishop, from 2–8 October, 1910[1]

(1) Another year of grace has come and gone. But I have made little
progress in perfection and so once more I feel humbled and ashamed. But
I do not lose heart. I have read over word for word what I wrote and
promised last year, and I am starting again at the beginning, resolved to
carry out my religious duties with more faithfulness and precision. There
must be fewer distractions in so many things; and I must learn to be
contented with what is possible, and in all things acquire an ever more
sensitive and profound sense of humility because of my worthlessness,
and a habitual trust in God who is all and can do all things. Only by
being united to him can I do anything. I must remind myself that the
Lord takes everything into account, even the word that went unsaid, the
glance that was denied, the invocation and the stifled sigh. I shall therefore endeavour to continue in the practice of the presence of God who
strengthens, cheers and encourages me at all times.

(2) During this retreat Jesus, my blessed Lord, has deigned to give me
an even clearer understanding of the necessity of keeping whole and intact
my 'sense of faith' and my 'being of one mind with the Church', for he
has shown me in a dazzling light the wisdom, timeliness and nobility of
the measures taken by the Pope to safeguard the clergy in particular from
the infection of modern errors (the so-called Modernist errors), which
in a crafty and tempting way are trying to undermine the foundations
of Catholic doctrine.[2] The painful experiences of this year, suffered here
and there, the grave anxieties of the Holy Father and the pronouncements
of the religious authorities have convinced me, without the need of other
proof, that this wind of Modernism blows very strongly and more widely

---

[1] The preacher was Fr Moretto, S.J.
[2] The author alludes to the series of measures taken by Pius X for the reorganization of
the Roman seminaries at the Lateran and for the creation of regional seminaries in Central
and Southern Italy, the better to control the studies of seminarists and to establish a healthy
and soundly based ecclesiastical education.

than seems at first sight, and that it may very likely strike and bewilder even those who were at first moved only by the desire to adapt the ancient truth of Christianity to modern needs. Many, some of them good men, have fallen into error, perhaps unconsciously; they have let themselves be swept into the field of error. The worst of it is that ideas lead very swiftly to the spirit of independence and private judgment about everything and everyone.

I thank the Lord on my knees for having preserved me safely in the midst of such a ferment and agitation of brains and tongues.

But the experience of others and my own preservation until now are a grave warning that I must keep an even closer watch over my impressions, thoughts, feelings and words, everything that in any way might be affected by this devastating whirlwind. I must always remember that the Church contains within herself the eternal youth of the truth and of Christ, and is of all ages; it is the Church which transforms and saves the peoples and the times, not the other way round.

The most precious treasure of my soul is faith, the holy, pure, simple faith of my parents and the other good old folk in my family. I will be vigilant and strict with myself lest the purity of my faith should come to any harm.

(3) The grave responsibilities as Professor in the seminary, assigned to me by my Superiors, oblige me not only to think of the purity of my faith for my own sake, but also in order to see that in all that I teach the young clerics in the school, as in all my words and bearing, a spirit of loyalty to the Church and the Pope be apparent. In this way I shall influence them for good, and bring them up to think the same way too. Therefore I shall be most guarded in all I do and say, taking care to imbue my students with that spirit of humility and prayer in all their studies which strengthens the understanding and ennobles the heart.

1911

† *Retreat made at Martinengo with the*
Bishop, 1–7 October, 1911[1]

(1) I am always greatly encouraged by the thought of the past, but also much ashamed. I am now a liegeman in the service of Jesus Christ and his holy cause. I must seek nothing else, but try to remain cheerful and calm amidst all my various occupations, without haste but without procrastination, without fuss or over-exertion.

(2) I intend, and I hope this time with better results, to pay careful attention to orderliness and recollection in my religious exercises. This is something I really need. In the evening after supper: Matins and Lauds. I must get up at half past five, assist at the Bishop's Mass and then say my own; after the thanksgiving, the Hours. A brief visit to the Blessed Sacrament as soon as I return from my classes, another before the afternoon lesson. Vespers after my brief siesta and everything else in its right place. These are the absolute imperatives: my own fervour will suggest anything else.

This year I have joined the Association of Priest Adorers of the Blessed Sacrament, so I must be faithful to my hour.[2] Calm in everything, but combined with fidelity and precision.

(3) I confirm my last year's intention about guarding my loyalty of heart and mind to the Church and the Pope. In days of uncertainty and sadness St Alphonsus used to say: 'The Pope's will: God's will!'[3] This shall be my motto and I will be true to it. O Lord, help me, for I desire you alone!

[1] The preacher was Fr Bonetti, S.J.

[2] One hour's watching and prayer before the Blessed Sacrament.

[3] Antonio Tannoia, *Della vita ed istituto del ven. servo di Dio mons. Alfonso Liguori,* II, Naples, 1800, 282; other editions, book III, chap. 55: 'This blow [the suppression of the Society of Jesus] was really too much for Alphonsus. He seemed to freeze and lose the use of his senses when he heard of the thunderbolt which on 22 July, 1773, issued from the Vatican. Although he did not speak his face showed the bitter sorrow he felt in his heart. When he received the Brief of Suppression, he was silent for a moment, paying homage to the judgments of God shown in the orders from the Pope; then he said: "The Pope's will: God's will", and no other word ever came from his lips to express his inner suffering.'

1912

During the retreat made at Martinengo with the Bishop, from 13–19 October, 1912[1]

(1) I am about to enter the thirty-second year of my life. The thought of the past makes me humble and ashamed; the thought of the present is consoling because mercy is still being shown to me; the thought of the future encourages me in the hope of making up for lost time. How much future will there be? Perhaps a very short one. But long or short as it may be, O Lord, once more I tell you that it is all yours.

(2) I must not try to find or follow new ways of doing good. I live under obedience, and obedience has already overburdened me with so many occupations that my shoulders are sagging under the weight. But I am willing to bear this and other burdens, if the Lord so desires. My rest will be in heaven. These are the years for hard work. My Bishop sets me an example, since he does more than I. I will be most careful never to waste a single moment.

(3) I find it humiliating, but it is my duty to insist again on the resolutions already made about being absolutely faithful to my rule of life. Getting up at half past five, then meditation, the Bishop's Mass, my Mass, thanksgiving, the Hours; brief but frequent visits to the Blessed Sacrament, Vespers after my brief siesta, a very devout recital of the rosary; after supper Matins and Lauds, without fail, and a rather longer visit to the Blessed Sacrament; some spiritual reading before falling asleep. These are the fundamental points: they are my lifeline.

O Lord, I acknowledge my weakness; help me to keep strictly to these practices. Help me so that next year I shall not need shamefacedly to confess once more my infidelity.

(4) Having to keep to strict times for meals, with so many other things to think about, has discouraged any greediness over food. That is all to the good. But I must do more. My miserable body is becoming fat and heavy; I am conscious of this as it reduces the physical agility which also

---

[1] The preacher was Fr Giannini, S.J.

is very necessary to me if I am to do good; moreover, the body must be kept tamed lest it should start to kick: 'I chastise my body and subdue it.'[1]

So I must be very careful to eat slowly, not like a greedy man, and in general eat a little less, and in the evening very little. The same with drink. It is above all in the use of food and drink that I must exercise the spirit of mortification.

(5) Next month on the feast of St Charles I will place in the Bishop's hands the special promises which will make me a member (external) of the Congregation of Priests of the Sacred Heart. I confess that certain difficulties which arose almost weakened my good intentions about this. But they were due to human respect and caused, for the most part, by my pride. So I am glad to crush them underfoot and to hasten with eagerness wherever Jesus calls me and has shown that he wants me.

I care nothing for the judgments of the world, even of the ecclesiastical world. My intention, before God, is upright and pure. I want a seal, a visible seal, set on the intention conceived in the first years of my clerical life, that is the intention of being entirely and solely under obedience, in the hands of my Bishop, even in matters of no importance. I intend that the promise which I make shall be a declaration before the whole Church that it is my will to be crushed, despised, neglected for the love of Jesus and for the good of souls, and to live always in poverty and detachment from all the interests and riches of this world.

During this retreat the Lord has been pleased to show me yet again all the importance for me, and for the success of my priestly ministry, of the spirit of sacrifice, which I desire shall from now on ever more inspire my conduct 'as a servant and prisoner of Jesus Christ'.[2] And also I want all the undertakings in which I shall take part during this present year to be done in this spirit, in so far as I have a share in them; all are to be done for the Lord and in the Lord: plenty of enthusiasm but no anxiety about their greater or less success. I will do them as if everything depended on me but as if I myself counted for nothing, without the slightest attachment to them, ready to destroy or abandon them at a sign from those to whom I owe obedience.

O blessed Jesus, what I am proposing to do is hard and I feel weak, because I am full of self-love, but the will is there and comes from my heart. Help me! Help me!

(6) The keen sense of my own nothingness must ripen and perfect in me the spirit of kindness, great kindness, making me patient and forbearing with others in the way I judge and treat them. Although I am

---

[1] I Cor. 9: 27.   [2] Cf. Eph. 6: 6 and 3: 1.

only just over thirty years old, I begin to feel some wear and tear of the nerves. This will not do. When I feel irritable I must think of my own worthlessness and of my duty to understand and sympathize with everyone, without passing harsh judgments. This will help me to keep calm.

(7) The work I am doing now requires great delicacy and prudence as it frequently means dealing with women.[1] I intend therefore that my behaviour shall always be kind, modest and dignified so as to divert attention from my own person and give a richer spiritual quality to my work. Past experience is an encouragement for the future. Here again, if I think poorly of myself and distrust my own powers and raise my thoughts constantly to Jesus, returning to his embrace as soon as I have ended my task, it will be a great protection. It would be dangerous if in this work I were to presume on my own powers for a single moment.

(8) There is a great deal of tittle-tattle about just now. I will be true to my principles of love, obedience and devotion to the Holy Father and be on my guard against anything that might impair these loyalties, but I shall not let myself be distracted by idle gossip, still less get drawn into it. There is so much to do, and the words of our Holy Father Pius X are so solemn, and the opportunities he has given for apostolic zeal in the present hour so vast, that it seems to me a waste of time to get involved in journalistic questions. While remaining apart from all this and above it I will nevertheless consider it my duty always to speak well of the Holy Father and of his directives, and to inculcate in others that sense of love and veneration for him which I shall feel myself. This I will try to do, especially with my students in the seminary.

(9) I once again renew all the intentions I formed during earlier retreats. What I wrote at various times during these still reflects my needs and present conditions.

For the rest, let us proceed with confidence. A life of piety in the most profound theological sense of the word: a life of sacrifice. And all the time joy, gentleness and peace.

May the Sacred Heart of Jesus, my beloved Mother Mary, and my good patron saints, who see what I cannot say but feel most deeply in my heart, help me to be strong, good and faithful, and bless me. 'O God, receive me, thy servant, that I may live, and do not disappoint my hope.'

---

[1] When the Committee of the Union of Italian Catholic Women was constituted in Bergamo, he was appointed first ecclesiastical assistant, on 8 January, 1910.

1913

30

† *During the retreat made at Martinengo with the Bishop, from 19–25 October, 1913*[1]

(1) This is the seventh time that I have withdrawn to this dear and holy place to think of my soul. My overwhelming obligation is always the same: to bless the Lord who continues to show me his love, to preserve me from grave faults and make me feel ashamed of my own unworthiness.

I feel I need add no more, except in confirmation of all that I have written and proposed in earlier years. I say only this to the Lord: here I am, ready for everything, sufferings as well as joys. 'For me to live is Christ and to die is gain.'[2] I wanted to rid myself of some of the burden of my responsibilities and to indicate which of these I would prefer to retain. But I have decided not to do anything about it. My Superiors know everything, and that is enough. As I have not been asked about this I will be careful not to show my preference for one kind of work rather than another. I must proceed, as my spiritual director tells me, with my head in the sack of Divine Providence.

(2) Suppose the seven years that have gone by represented only the abundance of God's gifts to me, and the seven years of famine were to begin now? I should deserve them for not having made the best use of so many graces. Oh well, let the purging work of famine come, the bitterness, humiliation and suffering. I will accept them willingly as a token of the sincerity of my love for Jesus.

So I will accept with holy joy the daily occasions, great and small, for humiliation, shame and the mortification of my pride, without reacting in any way, as contented as the snail that collects the drops of dew that fall from heaven and secretly transforms them.

It does not matter to me if men humiliate me, as long as everything turns out to be for the glory of God and my own real good, the sanctification of my soul.

---

[1] The preacher was Fr Gamba, a secular priest of Cremona.   [2] Phil. 1: 21.

I will try to live in this constant awareness of my littleness and un-worthiness, and when I am hurt I will rejoice to say: 'It is good for me that I was afflicted.'[1]

(3) When I think of keeping all the resolves already made and now renewed I am alarmed. Good will is not lacking, but the uncertainty and overlapping of my occupations make me unsure of myself, especially as regards the ordering of my pious practices.

Well then, I will make a formal and solemn promise to Our Lady, my beloved Mother, that in this new year I will say the holy rosary every evening with special devotion. It is one of the great joys of my life that I have always been faithful to this practice. But alas! sometimes it has been reduced to a mere recital of the prayers aloud. The special pledge I now make, with deeper thought and devotion, will I hope win from my dear Mother the reward of an ever more powerful protection of the virtue of holy purity which, especially amid the dangers offered by my special ministry, I intend to guard most faithfully, and I hope she will help me to keep all my other intentions also.

If this were to be the last year of my life, what a joy it would be to appear before Mary with my garland of fragrant roses! This will be my best passport to heaven.

'Take, O Lord, and receive my entire liberty.'[2] 'Lord, you know every-thing; you know that I love you.'[3]

---

[1] Psalm 118(119): 71.   [2] Exercises, no. 234.   [3] Cf. John 21: 17.

1914

Groppino, 10 August, 1914

Today my heart is full of a sense of joyful contentment and at the same time full of shame.

I have received from God so many ordinary and special graces during these ten years! In the sacraments, received and administered, and in the many and varied duties of my ministry, in words and works, in public and in private, in prayer, in study, amidst the little difficulties and disappointments, successes and failures—my experience growing richer and stronger every day, in my contacts with my Superiors, with the clergy and with people of all ages and all social conditions. The Lord has indeed been faithful to the promise he made me on the day of my ordination in Rome, in the church of Santa Maria in Monte Santo, when he said to me: 'No longer do I call you a servant . . . but a friend.'[1] Jesus has been a real friend to me, allowing me to share in all the sacred intimacies of his Heart. When I think of all that he knows about me and has seen in me, I should be lacking in sincerity if I did not admit to feeling a great satisfaction in my soul. In the field which I sowed, and in which I have worked, there are in fact a few ears of corn, enough perhaps to make up a small sheaf. I bless you, Lord, for this, because it is all due to your love.

But for my own part, I can only feel ashamed that I have not done more, that I have reaped so little. I have been like barren waste ground. With all the grace I have received, or even with much less, so many others would already be holy. I have had so many good impulses which have not yet borne fruit. My Lord, I acknowledge my failings, my total worthlessness; be generous in forgiveness and mercy.

Besides this feeling of satisfaction, and this sense of my need for forgiveness, I feel gratitude too. Everything, O Lord, has been done for your glory; I thank you for it now and always.

But my dominant thought, in my joy at having accomplished ten years as a priest, is this: I do not belong to myself, or to others; I belong

---

[1] Cf. John 15: 15.

to my Lord, for life and death. The dignity of the priesthood, the ten years full of graces which he has heaped upon me, such a poor, humble creature—all this convinces me that I must crush the self and devote all my energies to nothing else but work for the kingdom of Jesus in the minds and hearts of men, as I do in my own simple way, even in obscurity; but from this time forth it must be done with a greater intensity of purpose, thoughts and deeds.

My own natural disposition, my experience and my present circumstances all indicate calm peaceful work for me, far removed from the field of battle, rather than controversial action, polemics and conflict. Ah well, if this is the case I will not try to save my soul by defacing an original painting, which has its own merits, in order to become an unsuccessful copy of someone else whose character is entirely different from mine. But this peaceful disposition does not mean pampering my self-love, seeking my own comfort, or mere acquiescence in thoughts, principles and attitudes. The habitual smile must know how to conceal the inner conflict with selfishness, which is sometimes tremendous, and when need arises show the victory of the soul over the temptations of the senses or of pride, so that my better side may always be shown to God and my neighbour.

I have now been a priest for ten years; what will my life be in the future? That remains hidden from me. It may be that but a short time remains before I am called to render my final account. O Lord Jesus, come to take me now. If I am to wait for some, perhaps many, years then I hope they will be years of intense labour, upborne by holy obedience, with a great purpose running through everything, but never a thought straying beyond the bounds of obedience. Preoccupations about the future, which arise from self-love, delay the work of God in us and hinder his purposes, without even furthering our material interests. I need to be very watchful about this, every day, because I foresee that with the passing of years, and perhaps in the near future, I shall have many struggles with my pride. Let whoever will pass before me and go on ahead; I stay here where Providence has placed me, with no anxieties, leaving the way clear for others.

I mean to preserve my peace of mind, which is my liberty. So I shall always remember those four things which Thomas à Kempis (Book III, chap. 23) says bring great peace and true freedom:

(1) Seek to do another's will, rather than your own.

(2) Choose always to have less rather than more.

(3) Always take the lowest place, so as to be inferior to everyone.

(4) Always desire and pray that the will of God may be wholly fulfilled in you.

With these resolves, O Lord, today once more I offer you the precious
chalice of my soul, hallowed by your anointing. Fill it with your strength
which made the apostles, martyrs and confessors; make use of me in
something good, noble and great, for you, for your Church, for the souls
of men. I live only, I wish to live only for this.

While I am pondering these thoughts, at the close of this holy anniversary day which has rejoiced my heart with precious memories of my
priestly ordination, my revered Bishop, who is everything to me—the
Church, the Lord Jesus, God—lies here close at hand, suffering, as he has
done for so long. How I suffer with him and for him! These days of my
vacation are so melancholy and anxious! O Lord, make my Bishop
recover soon, if it is your will; restore him to his apostolic work, to his
Church and yours, to his work for your glory, to the love of so many
children.[1]

More heart-rending than the gentle resigned grief for my Bishop is
the clamour of war now rising from every part of Europe. Lord Jesus,
I raise my priestly hands above your Mystical Body and tearfully repeat
today St Gregory's prayer with the utmost fervour: O God, 'order our
days in your peace' today.[2]

And what of the Church in this tumult? Save her, save her, O Lord.
Ten years ago, when for the first time I celebrated the sacrifice of the
Mass over the tomb of St Peter in Rome—oh blessed memory!—I had
for the Pope and for the Church one great thought, one fervent prayer.
During these ten years that thought and that prayer have grown ever
more insistent.

O Lord, in these days of storm and amidst the clash of nations, give
your Church liberty, unity and peace.

[32]   *Retreat, 27 September–3 October, 1914, with the
Priests of the Sacred Heart*[3]

(1) On 10 August last, when I completed the tenth year of my priesthood, I thought that there might be, that there must be, some change in
my circumstances as I entered this new period of my life.

[1] Cf. Angelo Roncalli, *Mgr Giacomo Maria Radini Tedeschi, cit.*, p. 161.
[2] Cf. Canon of the Mass.
[3] The preacher at Bergamo was Mgr Luigi Maria Marelli, Bishop of Bobbio, later
appointed successor to Mgr Radini.

O God, your purposes are unfathomable! Immediately afterwards, on the 22nd of the same month, you called my revered Bishop to share your heavenly joy, and here I am in an entirely new situation.

However, I do not lose heart. In the hour of dismay and grief I felt great peace and spiritual comfort. Certainly the great and holy soul of the man I loved and venerated so much is now in heaven praying for me, blessing me, protecting and sustaining me. May I follow him there when it pleases the Lord to call me, and meanwhile may I imitate him in his holy works!

(2) In my new situation I can give my whole attention to the seminary without neglecting my pastoral work. My life will therefore be one of greater calm and recollection, which is just what I wanted. This is another gift from the Lord. I am grateful, and I will make the best use of it. I shall love my own room and my seclusion, where I can be wholly absorbed in prayer and study.

(3) In particular I must see to it that I always get up at half past five. Then I will at once make my meditation in my own room, and go to the church of San Michele for Holy Mass and after that for confessions. I will not repeat the other points for my daily observance, as it is sufficient to recall the resolutions already made.

(4) I want to be exemplary in all my professional duties, in my relations with the Rector of the seminary, my colleagues and pupils. I will be very humble and friendly with everyone, doing my best to contribute to the mutual harmony and edification which are so important where such grave responsibilities are shared. Above all, I will refrain from criticizing or complaining about anything and always remember, among other things, that nowhere else could I be so comfortably situated.

(5) I shall make a special point of giving my new Bishop, whoever he may be, that reverence, obedience and sincere, generous and cheerful affection which, by the grace of God, I was always able to feel for his unforgettable predecessor. Indeed in this I shall try to set a good example, convinced as I am that in the person of the Bishop we ought to see and recognize no less a one than Jesus Christ himself.

Naturally my different position will mean a different relationship, but whatever it is, it will be inspired by those feelings of respect, prudence and exquisite delicacy which are the fine flower of love. May my behaviour give the new Bishop some satisfaction and comfort, so that my person may be not a stumbling block but a block and a tool with which to build. This respect and affection for my Bishop I will show in word and deed while I earnestly beg Jesus to keep me faithful at all costs to these good intentions.

(6) I will endeavour not to feel any anxiety about my future, nor to allow myself to be influenced in this matter by the opinions, even if benevolent, well-intentioned and apparently well-founded, of anyone else. I was born poor and I must and will die poor, sure that at the right time Divine Providence, as in the past, will provide what is needed, sending me what I require and even more. It would be very bad for me if I were to become attached, even in the slightest degree, to the things of this world.

(7) As for fantastic dreams in which my pride may indulge, thoughts of honours, positions, etc., I will be very careful not to entertain them, but will spurn them at once. They upset one's peace of mind, sap one's energy, and take all real joy and all value and merit from anything good one may do. For myself, I must think only of remaining very humble, very, very humble, leaving everything else to God.

(8) I am a priest of the Sacred Heart. Therefore what is said and proposed here has particular significance because of the special promises I made to the Lord as a member of this holy Congregation. As far as possible I shall share in the common activities of my fellow members and, by my good example before all the clergy, try to do honour to the Congregation which has accepted me, and to further its aims.

N.B. On Wednesday I had to interrupt this retreat for a short time while I paid a flying visit to Milan, to ask His Eminence the Cardinal Archbishop[1] for some advice about how to handle certain matters with the new Bishop.

This visit has consoled me and cheered me very much. Afterwards I went down and prayed for a long time over the tomb of St Charles, and there I renewed my vow of absolute loyalty to God for life and death, offering myself entirely, body and soul, to the service of God for the Church and for the salvation of souls and, according to the will of God, preparing myself for every sacrifice now and always. Amen.

---

[1] Cardinal Andrea Ferrari (1850–1921) of Pratopiano, near Lalatta, in the diocese of Parma, Bishop of Guastalla and then of Como, was Cardinal Archbishop of Milan from 1894. On 10 February, 1963, in the presence of a large number of pilgrims from Lombardy, Pope John signed the Decree introducing his beatification cause.

15. The First World War. In lieutenant's uniform, as military chaplain, with
his two brothers, Zaverio and Giuseppe

1915—1918

The War

1915

23 May, 1915

Tomorrow I leave to take up my military service in the Medical Corps.[1] Where will they send me? To the front perhaps? Shall I ever return to Bergamo, or has the Lord decreed that my last hour shall be on the battlefield? I know nothing; all I want is the will of God in all things and at all times, and to work for his glory in total self-sacrifice. In this way, and in this way only, can I be true to my vocation and show in my actions my real love for my country and the souls of my fellows. My spirit is willing and cheerful.[2] Lord Jesus, keep me always so; Mary, my kind Mother, help me 'that in all things Christ may be glorified'.

---

[1] He was recalled to the army because of the Italian declaration of war on Austria, on 24 May, 1915, and sent to the hospitals of Bergamo, where he was first a non-commissioned officer and later, from 28 March, 1916, a chaplain; he was discharged on 10 December, 1918.

[2] Cf. Matthew 26: 41.

1918—1920

Spiritual Director of the Seminary at Bergamo

1919

[34] *Retreat after the war,[1] in the house of the Priests of
the Sacred Heart, 28 April–3 May, 1919[2]*

(1) In four years of war, passed in the midst of a world in agony, how
good the Lord has been to me! He has enabled me to go through so much,
and granted me so many occasions of doing good to my fellow men!
My Jesus, I thank you and I bless you. I call to mind all those young
souls I have come to know during these years, many of whom I accompanied to the threshold of the other life; the memory of them moves
me deeply, and the thought that they will pray for me is comforting and
encouraging.

(2) While we are all re-awakening as if to the light of a new day, those
supreme principles of faith and Christian and priestly life which by the
grace of God were the nourishment of my youth are once more clear to
me and now seem even brighter and firmer than before: the glory of God,
the sanctification of my soul, paradise, the Church, the souls of men.
The contacts with the world during these four years have transformed
these principles into action, ennobled them and imbued them with a
more burning apostolic zeal. I am now of mature years: either I achieve
something positive, or I bear a terrible responsibility for having wasted
the Lord's mercies.

(3) As the foundation of my apostolate I want an inner life spent in
the search for God in myself and for close union with him, and in the
habitual and tranquil meditation on the truths which the Church teaches
me, a meditation which, according to the teaching of the Church, shall
be expressed in religious practices which will become more and more dear
to me. In the observance of these I want to be absolutely faithful, more
than I have been during these years of military life, partly because of my

---

[1] In November, 1918, the Bishop of Bergamo, Mgr Marelli, appointed him spiritual
director of the seminary to assist the young clerics who were returning from the front
and from life in barracks. He was recognized to have the intelligence and prudent friendliness necessary to treat such delicate situations.
[2] The preacher at Bergamo was the archpriest Speranza of Villa d'Adda.

own negligence and partly because of the impossibility of doing all I would.

Above all I will seek the joys of living with Jesus in the Holy Eucharist. From now on I shall have the Blessed Sacrament near my own rooms. I promise to keep Jesus company and to be worthy of this great honour.

(4) It is now some months since I set up my own home and furnished it in a suitable manner. Nevertheless, perhaps now more than ever before, the Lord gives me to understand the beauty and the sweetness of the spirit of poverty. I feel I would be willing to give it all up here and now, and without regrets. I shall always try, as long as I live, to keep this feeling of detachment from all that is mine, even from what is dearest to me.

I pledge myself especially to seek perfect poverty of spirit in absolute detachment from myself, never feeling any anxiety about positions, career, distinctions or anything else. Am I not already too much honoured in the sublime simplicity of my priesthood and in the work I am doing now, not sought by me but entrusted to me by Providence, by the voice of my Superiors?

I dwell at length on this matter because it is fundamental for my welfare. I will never say or do anything, I will dismiss as a temptation any thought, which might in any way be directed to persuading my Superiors to give me positions or duties of greater distinction. Experience teaches me to beware of responsibilities. These are solemn enough in themselves if assumed under obedience, but terrifying for whoever has sought them for himself, pushing himself forward without being called upon. Honours and distinctions, even in the ecclesiastical world, are 'vanity of vanities'.[1]

They assert the glory of a day; they are dangerous for whoever desires glory in eternity and paradise; even from the point of view of human wisdom they are worth very little. Anyone who has lived in the midst of these stupidities as I did in Rome, and in the first ten years of my priesthood, may well insist that they deserve no better name. Forward, forward, whoever wants to go ahead! I envy none of these fortunate souls. 'It is good for me to be near God, and to place my hope in the Lord God.'[2]

(5) During these last years there have been days when I wondered what God would require of me after the war. Now there is no more cause for uncertainty, or for looking for something else; my main task is here, and here is my burden, the apostolate among students.[3] When I reflect

---

[1] Eccles. 1: 2. [2] Psalm 72(73): 28.

[3] In November, 1918, Angelo Roncalli had founded the Students' Hostel (*Casa dello Studente*) at Palazzo Marenzi, Via San Salvatore 8, Bergamo.

on the manner, the circumstances and the spontaneity with which this plan of God's Providence, through the medium of my Superiors, suddenly took shape and is now evolving, my heart is touched and I feel bound to confess that truly the Lord is here. So often, in the evening, when I turn over in my mind the events of the day spent in looking after my dear students, I feel in me something of the awe which fell upon those two disciples on the way to Emmaus, as if in contact with the divine.

How true it is that if one entrusts oneself wholly to the Lord, one is provided with everything needful! 'Having nothing' yet 'possessing all things'[1] comes true every day under my eyes. I do not want to contract debts, and I have none. I am always at a loss to provide for the future, but I always receive what I need and sometimes more.

This proof of divine assistance consoles me in my poverty, but it also constitutes another bond of honour to hold me true to my vocation and to co-operate 'until the end' in the great work which Jesus has entrusted to me for his beloved young men.

All my cares, thoughts, affections, labours, studies, humiliations, griefs all must now be offered for this object only, that is for the glory of Jesus, through the formation of the new generation in his spirit. Nothing could be finer and more honourable for me than this, nothing more important, especially at this time, in the whole Church of God.

(6) To succeed in my apostolate I will recognize no other school than that of the divine Heart of Jesus. 'Learn from me, for I am gentle and lowly in heart.'[2] Experience also has confirmed the supreme wisdom of this method, which brings real success.

I shall love my young students as a mother her sons, but always in the Lord and with the intention of bringing them up as worthy sons of the Church and, if I can, as future generous apostles of truth and goodness —and at the same time I shall be cherishing in them the best hopes of our families and of our country.

I shall be particularly careful always to maintain in my house a fragrant atmosphere of purity which may influence my young men and make such a profound impression on them that it will survive in later years, even in the future conflicts of their lives. Nothing affected or superficial, but in simplicity of manners and speech the indefinable quality that made the saintly teachers of old and of our own times seem to live in an atmosphere of heaven, and enabled them to do so much good and be true builders of great souls. Lord, help me to follow, if only from afar and in my humble way, these shining examples of great teachers of the young.

[1] Cf. 2 Cor. 6: 10.   [2] Matthew 11: 29.

(7) The work I have set my hand to is enormous; the corn is already golden in the fields, but alas! the reapers are few. I will try, with prayers to God and my own endeavours, to inspire in young clerics and priests a love and enthusiasm for this form of ministry which excels all others. I will try to make it attractive, especially to those to whom nature and grace have granted a special aptitude for working with the young. Who knows but that the right word and still more a good example may succeed, and I may soon find myself surrounded with a fine circle of brothers, all eager for the apostolate among young people? I shall do all I can to get the Priests of the Sacred Heart to take up this order of ideals and works. The Congregation was instituted chiefly for this purpose and one must try to increase its numbers, for it was intended that it should permeate the whole diocese of Bergamo with its spirit of apostolic work and ecclesiastical discipline.

1921—1924

Rome, in the Service of Propaganda Fide

1924

35

Retreat, Rome, Villa Carpegna, 13–19 January, 1924
I. General reflections

(1) Today, 18 January, the Feast of St Peter's Chair, it is three years since I began, under obedience, my work as President for Italy of the Propagation of the Faith in the World.[1] You have always been with me, O Lord Jesus, and good and merciful: 'Thy decrees are very sure.'[2] To my sorrow, I left behind in Bergamo what I loved so much: the seminary, where the Bishop had appointed my most unworthy self as spiritual director, and the students' hostel, the darling of my heart. I have thrown myself, heart and soul, into my new work. Here I must and will stay, without a thought, a glance or a desire for anything else, especially as the Lord gives me indescribable happiness here.

(2) Anyone who judges me from appearances takes me for a calm and steady worker. It is true that I work; but deep in my nature there is a tendency towards laziness and distraction. This tendency must, with the help of God, be forcibly resisted. To humble myself constantly I will always tell myself that I am a lazy fellow, a beast of burden that ought to do much more work and get on with it much faster, and so deserves to be beaten. I must be particularly careful not to procrastinate but to do at once what is most urgent. In everything, however, I must keep and impart to others that calm and composure with which alone things can be done and done properly. I will not worry if others are in a hurry. He who is always in a hurry, even in the business of the Church, never gets very far.

(3) I fix the following rules as fundamental for the reorganization of my life: rising at six o'clock and saying my prayers in my room; from seven to eight, work at my desk. From eight to nine-thirty, Holy Mass and prayers (meditation, etc.). Less time to be spent after dinner and after

---

[1] On 18 January, 1921, invited by Cardinal Van Rossum with the approval of Benedict XV, who knew him personally, Fr Angelo Roncalli began his work at Propaganda Fide in Rome, as president of the Central Council for Italy of the *Pontificie Opere Missionarie*.
[2] Psalm 92(93): 5.

supper in chatter. A short walk every day, and this to include the visit to the Blessed Sacrament. To bed at eleven, never later. I will faithfully attend at least the discussion on the *casus moralis* and if possible also on the *casus liturgicus*[1] and always the priests' monthly meeting at San Claudio.[2]

(4) The Association for the Propagation of the Faith is the breath of my soul, and my life. Everything must be for this, and always: head, heart, spoken and written word, my prayers, labours and sacrifices, by day and night, in Rome and elsewhere, I repeat, everything and always. I will accept other priestly tasks only in so far as I can subordinate them and make them serve my primary mission, which is the only reason for my presence here in Rome.

(5) In order the better to succeed in developing the work and my whole programme, I will always remember and practise St Gregory's rule, which is to make others work, and not keep everything, or almost everything, in my own hands: 'Less important matters are to be assigned to subordinates, more important things are to be dealt with by the Superiors, so that the preoccupation with trifles may not, as it were, blind the eyes which should be concerned with the general plan' (*Liber Regulae Pastoralis*, II, c. 7). Fortunately, this does not go against the grain with me, and moreover the Lord has given me excellent collaborators.

(6) I shall insist on making good use of mortification in matters of choice, in order that the Lord may enfold my whole person, soul and body, in the atmosphere of priestly purity, so that I may be the 'fragrance of Christ' everywhere,[3] because I know that if God does not help me, I too am capable of anything.

(7) The Church, in view of my office, has conferred on me the dignity and honour of a prelate, which is more than I can ever deserve. I want to honour this condescension on the part of Holy Church by great spiritual humility (considering myself, as I am, the least and most unworthy of all) and by friendliness with all, especially with the poor and humble.

(8) I intend to set a special watch on my tongue, avoiding every word —I repeat, every word—which in any way might sin against charity. I shall always find something which I can at least improve in this connection, so I shall insist on it in my examinations of conscience.

(9) The care I wish to take about my conversation with my fellow men, especially with my superiors, I wish to show also in all my religious

---

[1] Scholarly exercises for priests according to Canon 131 of the Code of Canon Law.

[2] San Claudio is the Roman headquarters of the Association of Priest Adorers of the Blessed Sacrament.

[3] Cf. 2 Cor. 2: 14-15.

practices, which I shall perform 'worthily, attentively, and devoutly'[1] for my own spiritual joy and for the edification of my fellows. 'Heart of Jesus, burning with love for me, inflame my heart with love for you. Mary, Mother of grace, pray for me. St Joseph, pray for me. St Francis Xavier, pray for me. St Francis de Sales, pray for me. St Paul and all the saints, intercede for me.'

II. Special reflections

The priest assistants are Father Folli, whom I met at Siena when the arm of St Francis Xavier was taken there to be venerated, and Father Santopaolo. There are only five of us making the retreat, and so we are not given the points for the meditations; everyone looks after himself.

On my desk I have Father Bucceroni's fine commentary,[2] but I prefer to do my own thinking, humbly and fervently, on the text of St Ignatius.

I am here, unworthy as I am, 'to conquer self and set my life in order',[3] that is, to overcome my sluggishness which still hampers me, and to increase my activity and output. Everyone says that I work too hard, but I know that I really do very little, compared with so much more that I could do for my principal ministry, which is my work for the Propagation of the Faith.

St Ignatius desires to see the effort to acquire a virtue even more than the virtue itself. 'We must cultivate detachment from all created things.'[4] In the Book of the Exercises there is a remarkable example of the greater or lesser sin of the man who speaks against the Papal Bulls on the Crusades, 'in acting or causing others to act against the pious exhortations and recommendations of our Superiors'.[5]

What useful conclusions can be drawn from the Meditation on the three sins?[6]

'What have I done for Christ?' Little, little or nothing.

'What am I doing for Christ?' Something, but badly, like a sluggard.

'What should I do for Christ?' Everything, O Lord, if you do but help me with your holy grace.

The meditation on the kingdom of Jesus Christ has done me a great deal of good. I want to return to it frequently and every morning I will

---

[1] These words occur in the Prayer (now optional) before the Divine Office (Vespers): 'digne, attente, devote'.

[2] S. Ignazio di Loiola, Esercizi spirituali, by Fr Gennaro Bucceroni, for the use of the secular clergy and nuns for the annual eight day retreat, Rome, 1908.

[3] Cf. Exercises, no. 21.   [4] Cf. Exercises, no. 23.

[5] Exercises, no. 42.   [6] Exercises, nos. 46–54.

say the very beautiful and powerful prayer which concludes it, and which I have written out for my own devotions: *O aeterne Domine rerum, etc.*[1]

I have made my confession to Father Folli, and I feel a great peace in my soul.

'Let everyone consider that the more he detaches himself from his own self-love, will and self-interest, so much the more will he perfect himself in spiritual things.'[2]

So it is quite clear: to love God, not myself; to do the will of God, not my own, and work for the good of others, not for my own, and all this always, everywhere and with great joy. . . .

'Even as an angel of God, neither moved with blessing nor with cursing.'[3] What fine encouragement to despise the world for one who, Angelo by name, would like to be an angel in fact!

'Jesus Christ, rising from the dead, has made man's life one long festival of joy.' This thought of St Athanasius[4] is a fitting conclusion for these days, dear holy days, full of spiritual emotions.

Today is the third anniversary of my coming to Rome to take up my work on behalf of the Association for the Propagation of the Faith. My thoughts turn reverently to the Chair of St Peter, whence every apostolate draws its motive and life. In this beautiful place of meditation and rest, whence I can see the majestic dome, I hail that Chair of truth and pay it the fervent homage of my mind and heart.

A day of wonderful sunshine! The sparrows are chirping in the warm air. It is a delight to hear them, and the song of the bells of St Peter's.

---

[1] 'O eternal Lord of all things. . .', *Exercises*, no. 98.

[2] *Exercises*, no. 189b.   [3] Cf. 2 Sam. 14: 17.

[4] Cf. *In epistolam de incarnatione Dei Verbi*, 26 (P.G. XXVIII, 90).

16. In Bishop's robes on the eve of his appointment as Apostolic Vicar to Bulgaria, 1925. 'The Bishop's robes will always remind me of the splendour of souls which they signify.'

1925

Episcopal Consecration

1925

36

Rome, Villa Carpegna, 13–17 March, 1925
Preparation for my episcopal consecration

(1) I have not sought or desired this new ministry: the Lord has chosen me, making it so clear that it is his will that it would be a grave sin for me to refuse. So it will be for him to cover up my failings and supply my insufficiencies. This comforts me and gives me tranquillity and confidence.

(2) I am to be a Bishop: so there is no time to prepare myself; mine is a state of perfection already acquired (*acquisita*), not still to be acquired (*acquirenda*). 'It is the duty of Bishops', says St Thomas, 'to be perfect and teachers of perfection.'[1]
This is a terrifying thought for me, for I feel and know myself to be very helpless and incapable! Another reason for remaining humble, very, very humble!

(3) The world has no longer any fascination for me. I want to be all and wholly for God, penetrated with his light, shining with love for God and the souls of men.

(4) I shall often read again Chapter IX, Book III of *The Imitation of Christ*, which says that 'all things are to be referred to God as their final end'. This has impressed me most profoundly in the solitude of these days. Indeed, in these few words there is really everything.

(5) In my new state my life of prayer must take on a new aspect. The words '*digne, attente, devote*' must find expression in me and by me for the edification of souls.

(6) The intention and general programme of my life as a Bishop will be in accordance with the promise I shall make at my consecration, in the solemn and moving words of the *Pontificale*, that is:
'(*a*) To use prudence according to the meaning of Holy Scripture ... and to teach the same (Scripture) to the people by word and example.

---

[1] Cf. *S.T.*, II–IIae, 185, 8, *in corp.*

(b) Reverently to accept, teach and preserve the traditions of the Fathers and the constitutions of the Apostolic See.

(c) In all things to show fidelity, submission and obedience to the Blessed Apostle Peter and the Roman Pontiff.

(d) To preserve my actions from all evil and as far as I can, God helping me, to direct them to all good.

(e) To preserve and teach chastity and sobriety.

(f) Always to be engaged in the work of God and free from worldly affairs and the love of filthy lucre.

(g) To cherish humility and patience in myself, and teach these virtues to others.

(h) To treat with kindly charity the poor, pilgrims, and all who are in need, in the name of God.'[1]

These words will frequently be material for my examinations of conscience.

(7) The Bishop's robes will always remind me of the 'splendour of souls' which they signify, the Bishop's real glory. God forbid they should ever become a motive for vanity!

(8) Let any praise of my humble person be expressed in the words of the *Pontificale* only, 'constant in faith, pure in affection and sincere in my love of peace'. May my feet be 'swift to spread peace and the good things of God'.[2]

May my ministry be one of reconciliation 'in word and deeds', and my preaching 'not in the persuasive words of human wisdom but in the manifestation of the Spirit and power'[3] and the authority conferred on me by the Church never used for my own glory—used not to break down but to build up.

I shall try to deserve as a Bishop also the praise that Holy Father Pius X told me was the finest that could be said about a Bishop's secretary: 'a faithful and prudent servant', and become indeed, as the *Pontificale* goes on to say in the prayer of aspiration: 'Let him be tireless in well-doing' (this is just what I need to be), 'fervent in spirit; let him hate pride; let him love humility and truth and never forsake them under the influence of flattery or fear. Let him not consider light to be darkness or darkness light: let him not call evil good or good evil. Let him learn from wise men and from fools, so that he may profit from all.'[4]

(9) The Church is making me a Bishop in order to send me to Bulgaria,

---

[1] *Pontificale Romanum, cit.,* 'De consecratione electi in episcopum', p. 68 *et seq.*

[2] *Ibid.,* p. 78; cf. Romans 10: 15.

[3] *Pontificale, cit.,* pp. 78–9 and 1 Cor. 2: 4.   [4] *Pontificale, cit.,* p. 80.

to fulfil there, as Apostolic Visitor, a mission of peace. Perhaps I shall find many difficulties awaiting me. With the Lord's help, I feel ready for everything. I do not seek, I do not desire, the glory of this world; I look forward to greater glory in heaven.

(10) Now, forever, I assume also the name of Joseph, one of the names given me at my baptism, in honour of the dear Patriarch who will always be my chief protector, after Jesus and Mary, and my model. My other special protectors will be St Francis Xavier, St Charles, St Francis de Sales, the patron saints of Rome and Bergamo, and the Blessed Gregory Barbarigo.

(11) I insert in my coat of arms the words *Obœdientia et pax* (Obedience and Peace) which Cesare Baronius used to say every day, when he kissed the Apostle's foot in St Peter's.[1] These words are in a way my own history and my life. O may they be the glorification of my humble name through the centuries!

---

[1] Cf. Angelo Roncalli, *Il Cardinale Cesare Baronio* . . ., Rome, Edizioni di Storia e Letteratura, 1961, p. 46.

1925—1934

Papal Representative in Bulgaria

1926

(1) I have been a Bishop for twenty months. As I clearly foresaw, my ministry has brought me many trials. But, and this is strange, these are not caused by the Bulgarians for whom I work but by the central organs of ecclesiastical administration. This is a form of mortification and humiliation that I did not expect and which hurts me deeply. 'Lord, you know all.'[2]

(2) I must, I will accustom myself to bearing this cross with more patience, calm and inner peace than I have so far shown. I shall be particularly careful in what I say to anyone about this. Every time I speak my mind about it I take away from the merit of my patience. 'Set a guard over my mouth, O Lord.'[3] I shall make this silence, which must be, according to the teaching of St Francis de Sales,[4] meek and without bitterness, an object of my self-examinations.

(3) The time I give to active work must be in proportion to what I give to the work of God, that is to prayer. I need more fervent and continual prayer to give character to my life. So 1 must give more time to meditation, and stay longer in the Lord's company, sometimes reading or saying my prayers aloud or just keeping silent. I hope the Holy Father will grant me the boon of reserving the Blessed Sacrament in my home in Sofia. The company of Jesus will be my light, my comfort an dmy joy.

(4) I must take great care to show charity in my conversation. Even with trustworthy and venerable people I must be very chary about mentioning things which refer to the most delicate part of my ministry and concern the good name of others, especially if these are invested with authority and dignity. Even when I feel the need to confide in someone,

---

[1] The director of the course was the Abbot, Dom Ildefonso Schuster, O.S.B., later Cardinal Archbishop of Milan; also making the retreat was the Bulgarian priest Stefan Kyril Kurteff, who was consecrated Bishop, in the church of San Clement in Rome, on 5 December.

[2] John 21: 17.   [3] Psalm 140(141): 3.

[4] Cf. St Francis de Sales, *Introduction to the Devout Life*, III, 30.

in hours of solitude and loneliness, silence and meekness will make suffering for the love of God more productive of good.

(5) The brief experience of these months as Bishop convinces me that for me, in this life, there is nothing better than bearing my cross, as Jesus sets it on my shoulders and on my heart. I must think of myself as the man bearing the cross, and love the cross that God sends me without thinking of any other. All that is not to the honour of God, the service of the Church and the welfare of souls is extraneous to me, and of no importance.[1]

---

[1] The Apostolic Visitor was responsible to the Sacred Congregation for the Eastern Church and also partly to Propaganda Fide and the office of the Secretary of State.

The Congregation for the Eastern Church was then just beginning to work on its own; it had in fact been made independent of Propaganda Fide only in 1917 with the *motu proprio: Dei providentis* of Benedict XV.

The young prelate, who began his service in Sofia on 25 April, 1925, in the enthusiastic fervour of the Holy Year and of the new impulse given to foreign missions by Pius XI, at once ran into all sorts of difficulties.

1927

38

Retreat, 1927. Ljubljana (Slovenia). House of the Jesuit Fathers. 9–13 November

(1) I must, I will, become increasingly a man of intense prayer. This last year has brought some improvement in this direction. I shall continue with perseverance and fervour, giving even greater attention and importance to my religious duties: Holy Mass, the Breviary, Bible reading, meditation, examination of conscience, the rosary, the visit to the Blessed Sacrament. Jesus in the Blessed Sacrament is reserved in my house and he is my joy. May he ever find in my home and in my life something to gladden his Divine Heart.

(2) There must be more tranquillity, still more tranquillity, sweetness and peace in all my affairs. If I cannot do all the good that I think is necessary for the benefit of souls in the mission entrusted to me, I must not let myself be in the least worried or anxious about this. To do my duty in accordance with the promptings of charity, that is enough. The Lord knows how to use everything for the triumph of his kingdom, even my not being able to do more, even the effort it costs me to remain apparently inactive. By work and example I must impart this tranquillity and peace to others.

(3) I will be more and more careful to rule my tongue. I must be more guarded in the expression of my opinions, even with persons of my own household. This must once more become the object of the particular examinations of conscience. Nothing must escape my lips other than praise or the most mildly expressed disapproval or general exhortations to charity, to the apostolate, to virtuous living.

It is my nature to talk too much. A ready tongue is one of God's good gifts but it must be handled with care and respect, that is, with moderation, so that I may be welcome and not found a bore.

(4) In my dealings with all, Catholics and Orthodox, high and low, I must always endeavour to leave an impression of dignity and loving-kindness, a radiant kindness and a pleasing dignity. To these people I represent, however unworthily, the Holy Father. It must therefore be my

aim to make him loved and esteemed, even in my own person. This is what the Lord desires. What a task! What a responsibility!

(5) To make myself more useful in my ministry in Bulgaria I must apply myself with special care to the study of the French and Bulgarian languages.

(6) I have noticed certain things this year which convince me that I am growing old and that my body sometimes shows signs of its frailty. This will make the thought of death familiar to me, rendering my life more joyful, active and industrious.

(7) Jesus, Mary, Joseph, the souls in my charge, the Church and the Pope be ever in my heart! Serenity, calm and joy be mine in self-giving and self-sacrifice, according to the needs of my apostolic ministry! In my dealings with others: dignity, humility, mildness, forbearance and patience, always patience . . . for ever and ever, Amen.

1928

39

*Annual retreat at Babek on the Bosporus. Villa of
the Lazarist Fathers. 20–24 December, 1928*
Notes

(1) Today, the Feast of St Thomas the Apostle, I have made the general
confession of my twenty-five years of priesthood to Father Luciano
Proy, and God has poured a river of peace into my heart.[1]

(2) Twenty-five years a priest! I think of all the ordinary and special
graces I have received, of my preservation from grave sins, innumerable
opportunities of doing good, sound bodily health, undisturbed tranquillity of mind, good reputation among men, immensely superior to
my deserts, and the successful outcome of the various undertakings
entrusted to me under obedience. Later on have come ecclesiastical
honours, and finally the episcopate, not merely above but in contrast
to my deserts . . . all these graces, O God! This thought must keep me
habitually in a loving frame of mind, full of humility and awe.

(3) In twenty-five years of priesthood what innumerable failings and
deficiencies! My spiritual organism still feels healthy and robust, thanks to
God, but what weaknesses! What frequent little indulgences in sloth
and in satisfying my preferences for one thing rather than another! What
inner impatience with all that demands effort and toil! What countless
distractions in public and private prayers! What haste, at times, to get
these over! and what a waste of time spent in reading or in matters that
had little to do with the performance of my immediate duty! So many
petty attachments to places, to things, to details, amidst all of which I
ought rather to have passed as a pilgrim and exile.[2] How easily I have
offended against charity towards my fellows, even if in a correct and
pious form. In my imagination and in the trend of my thought, what a
mixture still remains of the human and worldly with the sacred, supernatural and divine, of the spirit of this world with the spirit of the Cross
of Jesus Christ!

[1] Cf. Isaiah 66: 12.   [2] Cf. 1 Peter 2: 11.

Therefore I must always see myself as the poor wretch that I am, the least and most unworthy of the Bishops of the Church, barely tolerated among my brethren out of pity and compassion, deserving none but the lowest place: truly the servant of all, not merely in words but in a profound inner sense and outward appearance of humility and submission.

(4) During this spiritual retreat I have felt once more, and most keenly, that it is my duty to be truly holy. The Lord does not promise me twenty-five years of episcopal life, but he does tell me that if I wish to become holy, he gives me the time I need and the necessary graces.

Jesus, I thank you, and I promise you, heaven and earth being my witnesses, that I will make every effort to succeed, beginning from now. Most holy Mary, my kind heavenly Mother, St Joseph, my dearest protector, I call upon you to be my sureties for the promise I make this day before the throne of Jesus, and I implore you to succour me, help me, that I may be faithful.

(5) It is not difficult for me now to understand that the beginning of sanctity lies in my total abandonment to the Lord's holy will, even in little things, and that is why I must insist on this. I do not wish or ask for anything beyond obedience to the dispositions, instructions and wishes of the Holy Father and the Holy See.

I will never take any step, direct or indirect, to bring about any change or alteration in my situation, but I will in all things and at all times live from day to day, letting others say and do, and suffering whoever so desires to pass ahead of me, without preoccupying myself about my future.

Let my familiar prayers be the two by St Ignatius in the Book of his Exercises: 'Take, O Lord, and receive all my liberty' and the other which begins: 'O eternal creator of all things, I make my oblation.'[1] All my heart is in those two prayers. May the Lord help me in this matter never to succumb to the fascination of any ecclesiastical circles in which love of this world may sometimes play a part.

(6) I renew my resolves concerning the life of prayer and union with God. I will be particularly careful about the sacred liturgy: the Mass and the Breviary, the well-meditated rosary, and other religious practices, the faithful observance of which is the safeguard of priestly piety.

(7) My dealings with others must always be marked with dignity, simplicity and kindness, a radiant and serene kindness. The love of the Cross must always be seen in me, a love which must wean my heart more and more from the love of the things of this world. May it make me

[1] *Exercises*, nos. 234 and 98.

patient, equable, forgetful of self, always joyful in the generous excerise of episcopal charity 'which gives birth to some, suffers with others, tries to build up some, is reluctant to offend others, gives way to some, asserts itself to others, is by turns persuasive and severe—hostile to none, a mother to all.'[1]

I shall return frequently to this in my examinations of conscience and confessions.[2]

---

[1] Cf. St Augustine, *De catechizandis rudibus*, XV, 23 (P.L., XL, 328).
[2] At the end of these reflections the author wrote: 'See the Notes: Retreat at Rustchuk, 28 April–4 May, 1930; Retreat at Bujukada, 18–21 June, 1931.'

1930

40

Retreat, 1930, at Rustchuk, in the house of the Passionist Fathers. 28 April–4 May

'Make me love thy Cross. . . .'[1]

A whole series of recent events has conferred on this retreat a special sense of loving abandonment to God, suffering and crucified, my Master and my King.

The trials, with which in recent months the Lord has tested my patience, have been many: anxieties concerning the arrangements for founding the Bulgarian seminary; the uncertainty which has now lasted for more than five years about the exact scope of my mission in this country; my frustrations and disappointments at not being able to do more, and my enforced restriction to my life of a complete hermit, in opposition to my longing for work directly ministering to souls; my interior discontent with what is left of my natural human inclinations, even if until now I have succeeded in holding this under control: all this makes it easier for me to enjoy this sense of trust and abandonment, which contains also the longing for a more perfect imitation of my divine Model.

All around me in this great house is solitude, absolute and magnificent solitude, amid the profusions of nature in flower; before my eyes the Danube; beyond the great river the rich Rumanian plain, which sometimes at night glows red with burning waste gas. The whole day long the silence is unbroken. In the evening the good Passionist Bishop, Mgr Theelen, comes to keep me company for supper.

My soul is absorbed all day in prayer and reflection. Very simple Exercises. I am following the Ignatian text, pausing or reading on as seems more helpful.

For reading matter I have a modern treatise by Father Plus: *The Folly of the Cross*,[2] and some other authors that I dip into here and there.

---

[1] From the *Stabat Mater*.

[2] Raoul Plus, S.J., *The Folly of the Cross*, English trans. by Irene Hernmann, London, Burns Oates and Co., 1927.

O Jesus, I thank you for this solitude which is giving me a real rest and great peace in my soul.

As a spiritual bouquet from this retreat, I will gather and preserve a very few conclusions:

(1) With the grace of God, I feel, I want to feel, truly indifferent to all that the Lord may decide for me, as regards my future. Worldly gossip about my affairs makes no impression on me. I am willing to live like this even if the present state of things were to remain unchanged for years and years. I will never even express the desire or the slightest inclination to change, however much this may cost me in my heart.

Obœdientia et pax. That is my episcopal motto. I want to die with the satisfaction of having always, even in the smallest things, honoured my obligation.

In truth, were I to ask myself what I would desire or do, other than what I am doing now, I would not know how to answer.

(2) For some time past, every morning after Mass I have said—and I think I say it from my heart—the prayer with which St Ignatius concludes his great meditation on the kingdom of Christ: 'O eternal Lord of all things, I make my oblation' etc.[1] To tell the truth, I find it rather hard to say this prayer. But, as I want to keep myself entirely absorbed in the holy will of God and the spirit of Jesus, crucified and despised, I will make habitual and daily use of the following protestation also, which repeats the very words in which St Ignatius describes the third degree of humility:

'O eternal Lord of all things and Heavenly Father, grant to me, your unworthy servant, that I may always be faithful to this protestation whereby, if this were equally to the praise and glory of your divine Majesty, and for the better imitation of Christ Our Lord, so that I may become more like him in all I do, I desire and choose poverty with Christ who was poor, rather than wealth; scorn with Christ who was scorned, rather than honours; and I prefer to be counted worthless and foolish for the sake of Christ who was once taken for a fool, rather than wise and prudent in this world.'[2]

I understand very well the reluctance of my nature, but I rely on the grace of God which, on this foundation of perfect humility, was able to work the sanctification of so many other souls who were to become instruments of his glory and illustrious apostles for the cause of Holy Church.

(3) I feel ever more strongly a love for my Lord's Cross, especially in

---

[1] *Exercises*, no. 98.   [2] *Ibid.*, no. 167.

these days. O blessed Jesus, do not let this be a spurt of flame to flicker out in the first shower of rain, but a burning, inextinguishable fire.

During this retreat I have come across another beautiful prayer which corresponds very well to the state of my spiritual life. It is by a recently canonized saint, St John Eudes. I humbly make it my own, and hope this is not too presumptuous on my part. In its context it is called: '*A profession of love for the Cross.*'

'O Jesus, my crucified love, I worship you in all your sufferings. I ask your pardon for all the times I have failed you in the afflictions you have been pleased to send me till now. I embrace the spirit of your Cross, and in this spirit, as in all love of heaven or earth, I welcome with all my heart, for love of you, all the afflictions of body and soul which you may send me. And I promise to find all my glory, my treasure and my joy in your Cross, that is in humiliations, privations and sufferings, saying with St Paul: "Far be it from me to glory except in the Cross of our Lord Jesus Christ" (Gal. 6:14). As for me, I want no other paradise in this world than the Cross of my Lord Jesus Christ.'[1]

I think everything will induce me to make a habit of this solemn profession of love for the holy Cross. The profound and lasting impression that I received during the whole ceremony of my consecration as Bishop in Rome in San Carlo al Corso on 19 March, 1925, and since then the difficulties and trials of my ministry in Bulgaria during these five years as Apostolic Visitor, without any consolation save that of a good conscience and the rather sombre prospect for the future, convince me that the Lord wants me all for himself along the royal road of the holy Cross, and it is along this way and none other that I wish to follow him.

So I will make more use of meditations on the Passion of Our Lord, and of those religious exercises which have to do with it; I will celebrate Holy Mass with more fervent devotion, letting my heart be filled and inebriated with the blood of Jesus, the chief shepherd and guardian of my soul.[2]

Oh if I too, poor sinner that I am, could succeed in making that great effort which St Ignatius recommends in his meditation on the sufferings of Jesus, to arouse in my heart feelings of 'grief, sadness and tears'.[3]

(4) A characteristic of this retreat has been a greater inner peace and joy, which embolden me to offer myself to the Lord for any sacrifice he may wish me to make of what is dear to me. My whole person and my

---

[1] Cf. *Oeuvres choisies de saint Jean Eudes*. I. *La vie et le royaume de Jésus dans les âmes chrétiennes*, Paris, Lethielleux, 1931.
[2] Cf. 1 Peter 2: 25.   [3] *Exercises*, no. 195.

whole life must be imbued with this tranquillity and joy. This comes easily to me now, but future difficulties and opposition may disturb me. I must do my best to preserve this cheerfulness in my soul and in my outward behaviour. One must learn how to bear suffering without letting anyone even know it is there. Was this not one of the last lessons I learnt from Mgr Radini, of revered memory?[1]

One of the similes used by St Francis de Sales, which I love to repeat, is: 'I am like a bird singing in a thicket of thorns'; this must be a continual inspiration to me. So, I must say very little to anyone about the things that hurt me. Great discretion and forbearance in my judgments of men and situations: willingness to pray particularly for those who may cause me suffering, and in everything great kindness and endless patience, remembering that any other sentiment or mixture of sentiments, à la Macédoine, as they say here, is contrary to the spirit of the Gospel and of evangelic perfection. So long as charity may triumph, at all costs, I would choose to be considered as of little worth. I will be patient and good to a heroic degree, even if I am to be crushed. Only in this way shall I deserve to be called a true Bishop and be worthy to share in the priesthood of Jesus Christ, who at the cost of his compliance, humiliation and suffering was the real and only physician and Saviour of all mankind, by whose wounds we are healed.[2]

I commend to my dear Mother Mary and to my gentle protector St Joseph these resolves for a renewed spiritual life. When I leave this holy retreat I will take up my cross once more with joy. Ever forward! How well I remember the motto of Mgr Facchinetti, of revered memory,[3] the dear spiritual director of the first ten years of my priesthood: 'always crucified, under obedience' (semper in cruce, obœdientia duce).

Offering of a crucified life: 'O my Jesus, grant me a hard, laborious, apostolic, crucified life. Deign to increase in my soul the hunger and thirst for sacrifice and suffering, humiliation and self-denial. I now no longer desire satisfaction, repose, consolations or enjoyments. What I want, O Jesus, and I implore your Sacred Heart for this, is to be always and evermore a victim, a sacrificial offering, an apostle, virgin and martyr for your sake.' (This prayer is by Father Lintelo, who was the apostle in Belgium of devotion to the Eucharist and of the need for spiritual reparation.)

---

[1] Cf. Angelo Roncalli, Mons. Giacomo Maria Radini Tedeschi, cit., p. 163.
[2] Cf. 1 Peter 2: 24.
[3] Mgr Giuseppe Facchinetti, Mgr Radini's pro-Vicar General in 1905. He was the first superior of the Congregation of the Priests of the Sacred Heart. He died in 1914.

1931

41

*Short retreat at Bujukada on the Bosporus, at the
house of the Conventual Franciscans
18–21 June, 1931*

(1) It is the octave of the feast of the Sacred Heart. The new Office for this feast seems to augur a renewal of spiritual life. I have in fact only my Breviary with me, and am reading nothing else.

(2) How I love St Augustine's description of the Heart of Jesus: the door of life.[1] Sometimes it seems as if in recent years the devotion to the Sacred Heart has almost reached the point of exaggeration. But if the Heart of Jesus is really the door, there can be nothing excessive or exaggerated about it. We needs must go in and out by this. And I want to go in by it.

(3) There is another thought which gives me great confidence. It is St Bernard's and is included in the Office: 'Where is there a safe shelter and rest for the weak, except in the wounds of our Saviour? The world rages around me, my body presses me down, the devil ensnares me, but I do not fall: I am standing on a firm rock. I have sinned greatly, my conscience is troubled, but I do not despair when I remember the wounds of Christ. . . . Through his pierced side the secrets of his Heart are laid bare; we see that great sacrament of compassion, the merciful kindness of our God, which has caused the dayspring from on high to visit us. . . . O Lord, how can we see your sweetness, meekness and great mercy more clearly than when we contemplate your wounds?'[2]

Of late I have found it very natural to feel a devotion to the sacred wounds of the crucified Jesus. It is complementary to the devotion to the Sacred Heart. I will try to do better in these.

(4) During the retreat last year at Rustchuk my circumstances led me to increase my love for the Cross and my desire to suffer with Jesus, my

---

[1] Cf. St Augustine, *Enarr. in Ps.* XXXIII, 2, 9 (P.L., XXXVI, 313).
[2] St Bernard, *Sermo 61 in Cantica Canticorum*, X, 3, 4, (P.L., CLXXXIII, 820). Cf. *Breviarium Romanum*, Friday in the octave of the Sacred Heart of Jesus, 2nd nocturn, lessons IV and VI (before the simplification decreed on 25 July, 1960).

Master and my King. By the grace of God, that profound meditation was not without its fruit. Since then I have felt, and I still feel, more composed and ready for whatever the future may bring, willing to accept the most diverse things, successes or defeats, with equal calm, considering it a great triumph for me simply to be doing my duty in the service of the Holy See.

I shall often return to these considerations, trying to foster in myself the desire and holy longing to suffer with Jesus who suffers, lovingly to accept my present inactivity without being impatient to do more, and to love this semi-obscurity in which the Lord keeps me, prevented as I am by circumstances from doing anything else, though this would be my inclination and my desire.

What does it matter in any case, this little more or less that I can do in the service of Holy Church in my present ministry? Or even in other ministries which might be entrusted to me, but of which I do not and will not think; what is it all worth? In the eyes of God nothing more than the inner disposition of my soul, known to him even in secret; in the eyes of men, 'a mist that appears for a little time',[1] often a snare and a delusion.

(5) I am in the fiftieth year of my life: therefore a mature man on the road to old age: perhaps death is near. I have achieved very little in half a century of life and of following a priestly vocation. I feel humble and ashamed before the Lord, and ask his pardon 'for my countless sins',[2] but I look to the future with imperturbable and confident serenity.

'Heart of Jesus in which the Father is well pleased.'[3] This invocation has made a great impression on me during this retreat. When the Father's voice was heard expressing his pleasure, Jesus had as yet done nothing in his life except live in obscurity, in silence and humble prayer, doing the humblest work. Oh what great comfort there is in this teaching!

(6) I go on my way once more, ever more determined to make the most of the time that yet remains.[4] I must persevere, driving my body and soul without mercy. I will, I must be of more use, even in my present ministry. Therefore, a more conscientious use of my time: everything to be done at once, speedily and well; no waiting about, no putting lesser things before the more important; always alert, busy and serene.

(7) But above all and in all things I must endeavour to express in my inner life and outward behaviour the image of Jesus, 'gentle and lowly of heart'.[5] May God help me.

[1] James 4: 14.   [2] Cf. Offertory of the Mass.
[3] From the Litany of the Sacred Heart.   [4] Cf. Eph. 5: 16.   [5] Matthew 11: 29.

1933

42

Retreat in Sofia with the Capuchin Fathers
4–8 September, 1933

Great calm and peace. I have had to do everything myself because the good preacher Father Samuele had prepared some fine discourses for his colleagues but without any knowledge of the Ignatian method.

On the first day I dwelt on the theme of holy detachment. On the second day I made my confession to my usual excellent confessor, Father Alberto. I was content, and my heart very calm and peaceful. Once more I reviewed the best resolutions of my episcopal life, and renewed them with all the fervour the Lord was pleased to grant me. I feel I am poor and helpless, but I persist in my resolve to sanctify myself at all costs, calmly and patiently, with absolute trust in Jesus, the 'shepherd and guardian of my soul'.[1]

The general character of my resolutions of these days is expressed in the simple words of *The Imitation of Jesus Christ*: 'Desire to be unknown, and little esteemed.'[2] But, with all this, I must never lose heart. On the contrary, I must always be cheerful, serene, courageous, until my last hour. Jesus, Joseph, Mary, may I breathe forth my soul at peace with you.

My prolonged mission as papal representative in this country often causes me acute and intimate suffering, but I try not to show this. I bear and will bear everything willingly, even joyfully, for the love of Jesus, in order to resemble him as closely as I can and to do his holy will in everything, and for the triumph of his grace amid these people, so simple and good but, alas, so very unfortunate! All in the service of Holy Church and the Holy Father and for my own sanctification. 'Lord, you know everything; you know that I love you.'[3]

---

[1] Cf. 1 Peter 2: 25.   [2] *Imitation*, I, II, 15.   [3] John 21: 17.

1934

[43] *Retreat in 1934 at Rustchuk, with the Passionist Fathers*
27–31 August

(1) Father Ausonio Demperat, Assumptionist, preached for us. His sermons were good and earnest but far removed from the Ignatian method. I made my confession to Father Isidoro Detin, Vicar General to Mgr Theelen, and parish priest of Oresc. I am content.

(2) My soul is tranquil. This year was remarkably calm.

I tremble when I think of how the Lord will judge me, looking at me by the light of his lantern. But when I ask myself what more I can do to please the Lord, and to make myself holy, I find no other answer than this: continue under obedience as you are now; do your ordinary things, day after day, without over-anxiety, without ostentation, but always trying to do them with greater fervour and perfection.

Be faithful to the pattern of priestly piety: Mass, brief meditation, Breviary, rosary, visit to the Blessed Sacrament, examinations of conscience, the reading of good books; but all this with a greater enthusiasm of love, with superabundant zeal, like a lamp overflowing with oil.

Do not be concerned about your future but think that perhaps you are drawing near the gateway of eternal life. At the same time be ever more content to live like this, hidden from the world, perhaps forgotten by your Superiors, and do not grieve at being little appreciated but try to find an even greater joy in 'being esteemed of little worth.'[1]

(3) The circumstances of my ministry, as it has taken shape during ten years in Bulgaria, do not advise or permit me to do anything more than I am already doing—at least for the present. So I must go on living from day to day. I will offer more lovingly to Jesus the life I lead here and the restrictions I have to set on my outward activity and my whole life of more intense prayer for the salvation and sanctification of my soul and the souls of these Bishops and priests, and for the wider diffusion and penetration of the spirit of charity in this country where everything is so harsh; for the edification and religious advancement of the Catholics and

[1] *Imitation*, I, II, 15.

17. August, 1934. At Sofia, in Bulgaria. With his clergy who were on retreat.

18. Portrait, 1942

for the enlightenment and blessing of this Bulgarian people, so sadly misled and yet so richly endowed with capacities for service in the kingdom of Christ and his Church.

(4) What has Mgr Roncalli been doing during these monotonous years at the Apostolic Delegation? Trying to make himself holy and with simplicity, kindness and joy opening a source of blessings and graces for all Bulgaria, whether he lives to see it or not.

This is what ought to be. But these are grand words and still grander things. O my Jesus, it shames me to think of them; I blush to speak of them. But give me the grace, the power, the glory of making this come true. The rest does not matter. All the rest is vanity, worthlessness and affliction of the soul.

Jesus, Mary, Joseph, my heart and soul are yours, now and for ever.

1935—1944

Papal Representative in Turkey and Greece

1935

[44]   *Spiritual Exercises in Istanbul*
                    15–22 December, 1935, with my priests

These are Spiritual Exercises in a manner of speaking. I have made them, here, at the Apostolic Delegation, in the company of my dear priests from the Cathedral. Father Paolo Spigre, the Superior of the Jesuit Fathers, has given them well, as usual.

We have done all we could, but held in this manner they have not been entirely satisfactory. One really must get away from one's usual surroundings and work. Staying at home and having to give one's mind to the usual responsibilities and at the same time trying to attend to one's soul is not possible. That will have to be for another year. This year I have only to renew the intentions of former years.

Since the end of August, 1934, what unexpected alterations in my affairs! I am in Turkey. What more do I need, by way of opportunities and the grace of God, to make myself holy?

By sending me here the Holy Father has wished to point out to Cardinal Sincero the impression made on him by my silence, maintained for ten years, about being kept in Bulgaria, without ever complaining or expressing the wish to be moved elsewhere. This was in order to honour a resolution I had made, and I am glad I was always faithful to it.

There is so much work waiting for me here! I bless God who fills me with the joys of his sacred ministry. I am determined, however, to order all my affairs with greater precision and calm.

Even the trial of having to wear civilian attire[1] has been accepted with resignation by all my clergy. I must, however, always set an example, with proper dignity and edifying behaviour.

May the Heart of Jesus set mine on fire and maintain and increase in me his own spirit. Amen.

---

[1] See Chronology for June 13, 1935.

226

1936

[45]   *Ranica [Bergamo], Villa of the Daughters of the*
Sacred Heart. 13–16 October, 1936

A brief retreat, full of peace and silence, in this magnificent villa which serves the novitiate of the beloved Institute of Mgr Benaglio and the Venerable Verzeri.

With God's help I have been able to examine the state of my soul. Alas! How far removed I still am from the perfection required by my obligations and by the graces which the Lord continues to bestow on me! But I still most keenly and fervently desire to attain it.

I have found a useful guide to my meditations during this retreat in the *Triduum Sacrum* of Father Bellecius.[1] I see that I have now formed the habit of constant union with God 'in thought, word and deed', of bearing in mind the twofold prayer: 'thy kingdom come, thy will be done', and of seeing everything in relation to these two ideals. But how unsatisfactory are my daily actions and my religious practices! Ah well, I will start again and do better.

I am pleased with my new ministry in Turkey, in spite of so many difficulties. I must better organize my days, and my nights too. Never going to bed before midnight is not a good thing. In particular these hours after supper need setting to rights. The wireless takes up too much time and puts everything else out of joint.

My fixed rule: at seven o'clock in the evening the rosary for everyone, in the chapel. Then supper and recreation: three-quarters of an hour is enough for both. Then Matins, followed by the news on the wireless and possibly listening to some good programme of music. Then everyone must retire: my secretary to his room and I to do a little work. At eleven I must go to bed. Every morning a good thought to give direction

---

[1] During this retreat he used, besides the *Triduum sacrum omnium praecipue religiosorum usui accommodatum* (Turin, Marietti, 1825), the *Medulla asceseos sive Exercitia S.P. Ignatii de Loyola* (Augsburg, 1757) of Ludwig Bellecius (1704-1757). The Italian edition of this work was prepared by Fr A. Bresciani (Turin, 1842), and reprinted by Marietti in 1915 and 1926.

and a pattern for the whole day. Meditation never to be omitted; it may be brief if it cannot be longer, but it must be alert, intelligent and tranquil. Long Audiences must be avoided: I must be very friendly with everyone, as if I had no one else to see, but my conversation must be brief and to the point.

For my health's sake I must stick to a diet as regards food. I eat little in the evenings already but now I must eat less at midday too. It will do me good to go out for a walk every day. O Lord, I find this hard and it seems such a waste of time, but still it is necessary and everybody insists that I should do so. So I shall do it, offering the Lord the effort it costs me.

I feel quite detached from everything, from all thought of advancement or anything else. I know I deserve nothing and I do not feel any impatience. It is true, however, that the difference between my way of seeing situations on the spot and certain ways of judging the same things in Rome hurts me considerably: it is my only real cross. I want to bear it humbly, with great willingness to please my principal Superiors, because this and nothing else is what I desire. I shall always speak the truth, but with mildness, keeping silence about what might seem a wrong or injury done to myself, ready to sacrifice myself or be sacrificed. The Lord sees everything and will deal justly with me. Above all, I wish to continue always to render good for evil, and in all things to endeavour to prefer the Gospel truth to the wiles of human politics.

I want to study Turkish with more care and perseverance. I am fond of the Turks, to whom the Lord has sent me: it is my duty to do what I can for them. I know that my way of dealing with them is right; above all, it is Catholic and apostolic. I must continue in this with faith, prudence and sincere zeal, at the cost of any sacrifice.

Jesus, Holy Church, the souls in my care, and the souls of these Turks too, no less than those of our unfortunate brethren the Orthodox: 'O Lord, save thy people, and bless thy heritage.'[1]

---

[1] Psalm 27(28): 9.

1937

[46]   *Retreat with my secular clergy in Istanbul, at the*
Apostolic Delegation. 12–18 December, 1937[1]

(1) This is like a dear family gathering, to discuss the gravest and most sacred questions. I notice however, as I did at the end of 1935, that for myself this staying in my ordinary everyday surroundings, and for my priests this coming and going every day, takes away much of the efficacy of the retreat.

However, it was impossible to arrange anything better. The Residence of the Jesuit Fathers is a special object of surveillance just now, so it would be dangerous to stay there as guests. We must just make the best of it.

(2) When I look over my spiritual organism, as it is right for me to do at this time, I see that, by the grace of God, all the parts are still functioning but some are covered with dust, some nearly worn out, others have gone rusty, and elsewhere the screws and springs are not working well or are working badly. So I must renew, clean . . . and bring back to life.

My holy confession for the year, which I have made to Father Spigre who is giving the retreat, leaves me with peace in my soul. But is the Lord really pleased with what I do? I tremble to think about this. I find courage only in trusting him and leaving myself wholly in his hands.

(3) In December last year in Athens,[2] I received a grave warning about my physical health. I took the necessary measures at once; a year later I feel much better, although I see signs of old age in my thinning hair. I must always keep myself familiar with the thought of death, not to sadden myself but on the contrary to fill with wisdom, joy and calm the span of life that still remains for me here below.

What made the most profound impression on me in my youth was the death of my Bishop, Mgr Radini of revered memory, at the age of fifty-seven, just my present age.[3] I always thought I might perhaps not live as

---

[1] Introduced by the Superior of the Jesuits of the East, Fr de Bonneville; the preacher was Fr Paolo Spigre, S.J.
[2] He stayed in Athens from 3-14 December, 1936.
[3] Cf. Mgr Angelo Roncalli, *Mons. Giacomo Maria Radini Tedeschi, cit.*

long as this. I am still alive and I thank God for it. But what an obligation this is for me to seek more earnestly to sanctify myself!

(4) I feel tranquil and content with my state, only sorry that I am not so holy and exemplary in everything as I should be, and as I would be. Honours and promotions in this world do not much affect me, and I think I keep the thought of them in check. But help me, Lord, because the temptation may easily arise and I am helpless without you. The Church has already done too much for me. I am 'the last of all'.[1]

(5) 'The Eucharistic man' (vir eucharisticus). I wish this could really be said of me. In this connection I must renew a former intention: always to say Matins the preceding evening; this enables me to make my meditation in the morning, after Mass and the Little Hours. Then, besides my ordinary daily visit to the Blessed Sacrament, which may be long or short but must be loving and devout, on Thursday, from ten to eleven o'clock at night, I will faithfully observe the hour of adoration, as I have already begun to do, for my own needs and those of Holy Church.

(6) The circumstances of my usual routine here, in Istanbul, only allow me two hours of undisturbed work, and these have to be at night, between ten and twelve; I shall have to get used to this. But at midnight, after the last news bulletin, I must make an absolute rule to retire, to say a few prayers and go to sleep. I notice that in general six hours of rest at night are enough for me. Later on I shall see if anything better can be done about this. What matters is that everything shall be orderly and calm, done briskly but without impatience.

(7) At supper, in the refectory, Father Giacomo Testa[2] and I read some passages from Faber on kindness.[3] I like this subject because I see that everything is there. I shall go on calmly trying to be, above all, good and kind, without weaknesses but with perseverance and patience with everyone. The exercise of pastoral and fatherly kindness, such as befits a shepherd and father, must express the whole purpose of my life as Bishop. Kindness, charity: what grace is there! 'All good things came to me along with her.'[4]

---

[1] Mark 9: 35.
[2] Giacomo Testa (1909–1962), Secretary to the Nunciature, Counsellor and Auditor successively at Sofia, Istanbul, and Paris. From 1953 to 1959 he was Apostolic Delegate in Turkey, Titular Archbishop of Eraclea in Europe. Later he was made President of the Pontificia Accademia Ecclesiastica.
[3] F. W. Faber, Spiritual Conferences, London, Burns & Oates, 1858.
[4] Cf. Wisdom 7: 11.

1939

47

Retreat, 12–18 November, 1939, Istanbul, in the Residence of the Jesuit Fathers Ayas of Pasa, 'Sacred Heart' Thoughts and Intentions

(1) At last the retreat I have so long desired! Enclosed, without contact with the outside world, and conducted with method. I have invited here with me my colleagues, Bishops and priests—all secular clergy; they are all here and they belong to every rite. However, many of them have to go home at night for their Mass the next morning. That is not so good, but it cannot be helped. I enjoy being here alone the whole week. And I bless the Lord for it.

(2) Father Elia Châd, Superior of the Jesuit Fathers, gives us the points for meditation after the method of St Ignatius, and he does it well. However he too must be giving us more than the points, because he takes half an hour instead of a quarter. Afterwards there should be private meditation in our rooms. I find it helpful to read the Ignatian text in the Latin translation annotated by Father Roothaan.[1]

I observe, however, that even for my priests and Bishops, this giving us small doses, according to the strict Ignatian method, and leaving the rest to the discretion of the individual, is not practical. We are all rather like children who need to be guided by the living voice of someone who presents us with the doctrine, already prepared. So my conclusion is: the Ignatian method, but adapted to modern requirements. Oh for those grand Bergamasque priests of ours who used to preach the Exercises to us in the seminary! And they were truly faithful to the spirit and, as far as circumstances permitted, the method of St Ignatius.

(3) In a few days' time, the twenty-fifth of this month, I shall have completed fifty-eight years. Having been present at the death of Mgr Radini, who died at the age of fifty-seven, it seems to me that any other years over and above these are granted to me as extra graces. Lord, I thank you. I still feel young in health and energy but I make no claims:

[1] *Exercitia spiritualia S. P. Ignatii de Loyola cum versione literali ex autographo hispanico*, Rome, Morini, 1870.

231

when you call me, I am here ready. In dying also, indeed especially in dying, 'thy will be done'.

There is no lack of rumour around me, murmurs that 'greater things are in store'. I am not so foolish as to listen to this flattery, which is, yes, I admit it, for me too a temptation. I try very hard to ignore these rumours which speak of deceit and spite. I treat them as a joke: I smile and pass on. For the little, or nothing, that I am worth to Holy Church, I have already my purple mantle, my blushes of shame at finding myself in this position of honour and responsibility when I know I am worth so little. Oh what a comfort it is to me to feel free from these longings for changes and promotions! I consider this freedom a great gift of God. May the Lord preserve me always in this state of mind.

(4) This year the Lord has tested me by taking some very dear persons away from me: my sweet, revered mother, and Mgr Morlani, my first benefactor; Father Pietro Forno, my close collaborator in the *Atti della Visita Apostolica di San Carlo*; Father Ignazio Valsecchi who was curate at Sotto il Monte during those years when I was at the seminary at Bergamo before going to Rome, 1895–1900; all are gone. And other acquaintances and very dear friends, especially my Rector, Mgr Spolverini. The face of this world is changing for me now. 'The appearance of this world is altered.'[1] This thought must encourage me to become familiar with the world beyond, thinking that soon I may be there myself. My beloved dead, I remember you and love you always. Pray for me.

(5) I have made my annual confession to Father Châd and I am at peace. To prepare myself well I celebrated Holy Mass and assisted at another Mass, and then got on to my knees, penitent and ashamed. 'I am alarmed at the thought of my sins and I blush before you; . . . do not condemn me.'[2]

My confessor tells me that the Lord is content with my service. Really content? Oh if this were true! I am only partly content. It is long since the 'election' of my state was made; even as regards the details of my life and activity everything is made clear and well-defined by undertaking to 'spend and be spent for souls'.[3] I do not actually neglect my episcopal duties, but alas! how badly I do them! Above all I am tormented by the disproportion between what I do and what remains for me to do, what I would do but do not succeed in doing. The fault must be partly my own. My letters are too lengthy because I am afraid of sounding cold or

[1] Cf. 1 Cor. 7: 31.
[2] Liturgy of the dead, III Lesson of the first nocturn, Office of the Dead.
[3] 2 Cor. 12: 15.

unfriendly if I say less and because I think I can serve the interests of charity and Holy Church better by saying more.

I must try to find the way of discretion which lies between, and if there still remains something to torment me, I shall have to put up with it.

(6) On All Souls Day my dear secretary, Mgr Giacomo Testa, left me finally to run his own course.[1] He was a good lad and had been with me for two years, and I loved him in the Lord. So be it.

In his place there is now another young man, Mgr Vittore Ugo Righi. My Superiors have sent him to me so that I may help to train him for the service of the Apostolic See. He seems docile and good: I shall do my best. I should like to lighten the burden of my official correspondence by assigning part of it to him. This is one way of lessening the gap between what is still to be done and what has already been done. May God help me.

(7) For refectory reading I have proposed, after the new Pope's first encyclical,[2] Le Journal Intime of Mgr Dupanloup,[3] which I found among the books belonging to the Delegation and which I know well. I see that these pages make a deep and edifying impression.

For my own part, I am most interested to see how frequently this priest of such dynamic energy insists on religious exercises and the interior life: Mass, Breviary, meditation, devotion to the Blessed Sacrament and to Our Lady, whom he calls 'Help of Christians, Help of Bishops', etc. There is comfort in being companions in suffering, comfort and encouragement for me. I must be most careful to say Matins the evening before. Mgr Righi likes to recite the Office with me, and that is what I like too and have already begun to do. Matins said the evening before means so much more precious time free for meditation the next day and greater speed and elasticity in everything else. I shall also continue with the family rosary, which I have begun. This was Mgr Radini's custom, too, and also Cardinal Ferrari's in Milan.

(8) It is my special intention, as an exercise in mortification, to learn the Turkish language. To know so little of it, after five years in Istanbul, is a disgrace, and would indicate scant understanding of the nature of my mission here, if there were no reasons for excuse and justification.

Now I will begin again with renewed energy; the mortification will become a source of satisfaction to me. I love the Turks, I appreciate the natural qualities of these people who have their own place reserved in

[1] Cf. Psalm 18(19): 6.   [2] Pius XII, Summi pontificatus, 20 October, 1939.
[3] Félix-Antoine Philibert Dupanloup, Le Journal Intime, Paris, ed. L. Braucherau, 1910.

the march of civilization. Whether I succeed or not in learning the language is of no consequence. My duty, the honour of the Holy See, the example I am bound to give: that is enough. If I were to succeed only in holding to this firm resolve I should consider I had gathered great and blessed fruit from my retreat.

(9) Other special intentions? I cannot think of any, because I feel bound hand and foot to my life as Apostolic Vicar[1] and Delegate. I must preserve my serenity, but within this serenity there must be great fervour. I must be faithful to this method which means being humble and meek at all times, whatever impulse or temptation to the contrary I may feel, but my meekness will in no sense be pusillanimity. I must be sparing in my speech and say very little about politics, and I must familiarize myself with the thought of death.

(10) Every evening from the window of my room, here in the Residence of the Jesuit Fathers, I see an assemblage of boats on the Bosporus; they come round from the Golden Horn in tens and hundreds; they gather at a given rendezvous and then they light up, some more brilliantly than others, offering a most impressive spectacle of colours and lights. I thought it was a festival on the sea for Bairam,[2] which occurs just about now. But it is the organized fleet fishing for bonito, large fish which are said to come from far away in the Black Sea. These lights glow all night and one can hear the cheerful voices of the fishermen.

I find the sight very moving. The other night, towards one o'clock, it was pouring with rain but the fishermen were still there, undeterred from their heavy toil.

Oh how ashamed we should feel, we priests, 'fishers of men',[3] before such an example! To pass from the illustration to the lesson illustrated, what a vision of work, zeal and labour for the souls of men to set before our eyes! Very little is left in this land of the kingdom of Jesus Christ. Debris and seeds. But innumerable souls to be won for Christ, lost in this weltering mass of Moslems, Jews and Orthodox. We must do as the fishermen of the Bosporus do, work night and day with our torches lit, each in his own little boat, at the orders of our spiritual leaders: that is our grave and solemn duty.

(11) My work in Turkey is not easy, but it is coming along well and

---

[1] Apostolic Vicar to the Catholics of the Latin Rite.

[2] Bairam or Beiram is the name of the only two annual Moslem feasts: the first of these, in imitation of our Easter, is celebrated at the end of the general fast, and lasts one day only. The other, called 'of the sacrifices', in memory of Abraham who was willing to offer his own son in sacrifice, lasts four days.

[3] Cf. Matthew 4: 19 and Mark 1: 17.

gives me great consolation. I see the charity of the Lord here, and the clergy united among themselves and with their humble pastor. The political situation does not allow me to do much, but it seems to me there is something gained if at least I do not worsen it through my own fault.

My mission in Greece, on the other hand, is so full of vexations! For this very reason I love it even more and intend to go on working there with heart and soul, forcing myself to overcome all my repugnance. For me it is an order: therefore it requires obedience. I confess I would not mind if it were entrusted to someone else, but while it is mine I want to honour the obligation at all costs. 'They who sow in tears shall reap in joy.'[1] It matters little to me that others will reap.

(12) This year my holidays were brief and spoilt by the need to return soon. In compensation, however, I received an extremely benevolent and encouraging welcome in Rome from the Holy Father, the Office of the Secretary of State, and the Congregation for the Eastern Church. I thank the Lord. This is more than I deserve. But I do not work for men's praises. 'The Lord has given.' If, as is quite possible, the Lord should take away,[2] I would continue to bless his name.

(13) As a constant encouragement to greater fervour at Mass, and in remembrance of this retreat, I intend from now on always to say the prayers in the Canon before my private celebration of Mass. Whoever is present will be kept waiting a little, but these prayers must be said. The only reason (opportunitas) that might dispense me from this would be the greater convenience of numerous worshippers who are kept waiting, and who must not be allowed to grow impatient. St Francis de Sales is a good master in teaching me the use of charitable discretion.

---

[1] Cf. Psalm 125(126): 6.   [2] Cf. Job 1: 21.

1940

48

Retreat, 25 November–1 December, 1940, at
Terapia on the Bosporus, the Villa of the
Sisters of Our Lady of Sion

(1) This year because of the war it was impossible to make the retreat at the Residence of the Jesuit Fathers at Ayas Pasa.

I have come here to act as chaplain to the good sisters, old and in retirement, who have fled here for shelter from their houses in Jassy and Galatz in Rumania. After me will come my priests from the Holy Spirit, one at a time, for their retreat. This solitude is really ideal and delightful. Jesus I thank you and I bless you.

(2) I have chosen these particular days for my retreat because they are the first of my sixtieth year. I am now entering that period in which a man begins to be old, and admits it. Oh may my old age be one long straining after that perfection of which, as Bishop, I ought to be master but from which I am still so far removed! It is something at least to sanctify the beginning of old age with prayer and meditation, in a penitent spirit; it is certainly pleasing to the Lord: it is an appeal for mercy.

(3) As a spiritual exercise, setting aside the usual method, I have chosen as the object of my meditation the Penitential Psalm, the Miserere, meditating on four verses each day. I have taken as my guide, because one needs a guide in these matters, even if one is growing old, the ample and well-reasoned exposition of Father Paolo Segneri, an author I admire very much.[1] It is too lengthy for my own needs and too highly wrought, with the result that the style is a little forced and ornate. But it is never-

---

[1] *Esposizione del 'Miserere' dato a considerar con accuratezza a qualunque anima pia* (vol. IV of the *Opere*), Milan, 1847, pp. 817–89. Mgr Roncalli writes in a memorandum: 'I have begun to run through the Miserere under the guidance of Fr Segneri, but this is contrary to all my former methods. Yet there is much good in it. I find Fr Segneri's Miserere somewhat lengthy, but that does not prevent me from penetrating to the profound meaning of this mysterious Psalm, and discovering interesting points of view for myself.'

theless a real treasure-house of thoughts and practical applications. I have meditated on this, and typed out some notes of what seemed to me most interesting and helpful. I shall use these notes for my own edification.

(4) What is the result of this spiritual concentration of mine? Nothing remarkable or exciting but, as it seems to me, a consolidation of my principles and positions in the eyes of the Lord and in all that regards my own humble life and my sacred ministry in the service of Holy Church. Even without exaggerating the importance of entering upon this last, possibly rapid and brief, period of my life, I feel something more mature and authoritative in me in relation to all that interests and surrounds me. I think I notice a greater detachment from all that concerns my own future, a more marked indifference 'to all created things', a slow and slight blurring of the outlines of things, persons, places and undertakings to which I was formerly more strongly attached, a more evident inclination to understand and sympathize and a greater clarity and tranquillity in impressions and judgments. I will be careful to preserve a fine simplicity in my conversation and behaviour, without any affectation; at the same time there must be apparent the gravity and lovable dignity of the elderly prelate, who diffuses an air of nobility, wisdom and grace.

(5) I have once more meditated on my episcopal duties. Above all, I have dwelt on 'cherishing humility and patience in myself and teaching these virtues to others'.[1] Every now and then a thorn pricks me, sometimes very sharply. I ought, strictly speaking, to make stern decisions. By doing so I should pull out the thorn. Would I not then deserve others, and sharper ones? And then, what about truth, charity, mercy? And the spirit of Christ in dealing with the souls of men? In dealing with my own soul?

(6) This year Providence has placed considerable sums of money in my hands for my own personal use. I have distributed it all, some to the poor, some for my own needs and the needs of members of my family, and the rest, the main part, for the restoration of the Apostolic Delegation and some of my priests' rooms at the Holy Spirit. According to this world's judgments, which can penetrate even the sacred inner recesses of clerical life, and according to the criteria of human prudence, I have been a fool.

In fact, now I am poor again. Blessed be the Lord. I think that, by his grace, I did the right thing. Again I trust in his generosity for the future. 'Give and it shall be given unto you.'[2]

[1] See *Pontificale Romanum* for the consecration of a Bishop; cf. pp. 204–5.
[2] Luke 6: 38.

(7) The study of the Turkish language. To be sure, at the age of sixty I ought not to shirk this labour. It is simply a matter of good will and energy, nothing more. If this labour served for nothing else but to set a good example it would still be most meritorious.

Notes

Monday evening, 25 November

Yesterday our Holy Father Pius XII invited the whole world to join him in the sorrowful singing of the Litany of the Saints and the penitential psalm, the Miserere.

We all, from the West and from the East, joined with him in his petition.

In my solitary retreat I am making the Spiritual Exercises, as the Holy Father himself is doing just now in the Vatican, and in this way I begin the sixtieth year of my humble life (1881 – 25 November, 1940). For myself and for the good of all, I think I cannot do better than return to the penitential psalm,[1] dividing the twenty verses into four for each day and making them the subject of religious meditation.

As a starting-point I am using Father Segneri's exposition of the Miserere, but with considerable freedom of inspiration and applications.

To understand the profound meaning of the Psalm I find it a great help to bear in mind the figure of the royal prophet himself and the circumstances of his repentance and grief. It is a king who has fallen; it is a king who rises again.

First day, Tuesday, 26 November

VERSE I: 'Have mercy on me, O God, according to thy great mercy.'

1. *The mourning of the nations.* This cry reaches my ears from every part of Europe and beyond. The murderous war which is being waged on the ground, on the seas and in the air is truly a vindication of divine justice because the sacred laws governing human society have been transgressed and violated. It has been asserted, and is still being asserted, that God is bound to preserve this or that country, or grant it invulnerability and final victory, because of the righteous people who live there or because of the good that they do. We forget that although in a certain sense God has made the nations, he has left the constitution of states to the free decisions of men. To all he has made clear the rules which govern human society: they are all to be found in the Gospel. But he has not given any

[1] Psalm 50(51).

guarantee of special and privileged assistance, except to the race of believers, that is, to Holy Church as such. And even his assistance to his Church, although it preserves her from final defeat, does not guarantee her immunity from trials and persecutions.

The law of life, alike for the souls of men and for nations, lays down principles of justice and universal harmony and the limits to be set to the use of wealth, enjoyments and worldly power. When this law is violated, terrible and merciless sanctions come automatically into action. No state can escape. To each its hour. War is one of the most tremendous sanctions. It is willed not by God but by men, nations and states, through their representatives. Earthquakes, floods, famines and pestilences are applications of the blind laws of nature, blind because nature herself has neither intelligence nor freedom. War instead is desired by men, deliberately, in defiance of the most sacred laws. That is what makes it so evil. He who instigates war and foments it is always the 'Prince of this world', who has nothing to do with Christ, the 'Prince of peace'.[1]

And while the war rages, the peoples can only turn to the Miserere and beg for the Lord's mercy, that it may outweigh his justice and with a great outpouring of grace bring the powerful men of this world to their senses and persuade them to make peace.

2. *The mourning of my own soul.* What is happening in the world on a grand scale is reproduced on a small scale in every man's soul, is reproduced in mine. Only the grace of God has prevented me from being eaten up with malice. There are certain sins which may be called typical: this sin of David's, the sins of St Peter and St Augustine. But what might I not have done myself, if the Lord's hand had not held me back? For small failings the most perfect saints underwent long and harsh penances. So many, even in our own times, have lived only to make atonement; and there are souls whose lives, even today, are one long expiation of their own sins, of the sins of the world. And I, in all ages of my life more or less a sinner, should I not spend my time mourning? Cardinal Federico's famous reply is still so eloquent and moving: 'I did not ask for praises, which make me tremble: what I know of myself is enough to confound me.'[2]

Far from seeking consolation by comparing myself with others, I should make the Miserere for my own sins my most familiar prayer. The thought that I am a priest and Bishop and therefore especially dedicated to the conversion of sinners and the remission of sins should add

[1] John 12: 31; 16: 11.
[2] Cf. Alessandro Manzoni, *The Betrothed*, London, J. M. Dent and Sons, 1951, chap. 26.
K*

all the more anguish to my feelings of grief, sadness and tears, as St Ignatius says.[1] What is the meaning of all these flagellations, or having oneself set on the bare ground, or on ashes, to die, if not the priestly soul's continual plea for mercy, and his constant longing to be a sacrificial victim for his own sins and the sins of the world?

3. *The great mercy*. It is not just ordinary mercy that is needed here. The burden of social and personal wickedness is so grave that an ordinary gesture of love does not suffice for forgiveness. So we invoke the great mercy. This is proportionate to the greatness of God. 'For according to his greatness, so also is his mercy' (Ecclus. 2: 23). It is well said that our sins are the seat of divine mercy. It is even better said that God's most beautiful name and title is this: mercy. This must inspire us with a great hope amidst our tears. 'Yet mercy triumphs over judgment.'[2] This seems too much to hope for. But it cannot be too much if the whole mystery of the Redemption hinges on this: the exercise of mercy is to be a portent of predestination and of salvation. 'Have mercy on me, O God, according to thy great mercy.'

VERSE II: 'And according to the multitude of thy tender mercies blot out my iniquity.' The Lord is said to be 'merciful and gracious'.[3] His mercy is not simply a feeling of the heart; it is an abundance of gifts.

When we consider how many graces are poured into the sinner's soul along with God's forgiveness, we feel ashamed. These are: the loving remission of our offence; the new infusion of sanctifying grace, given as to a friend, as to a son; the reintegration of the gifts, habits and virtues associated with the grace; the restitution of our right to heaven; the restoration of the merits we had earned before our sin; the increase of grace which this forgiveness adds to former graces; the increase of gifts which grow in proportion to the growth of grace just as the rays of the sun increase as it rises, and the rivulets are wider as the fountain overflows.

VERSE III: 'Wash me yet more from my iniquity, and cleanse me from my sin': holy confession.

Three verbs: to blot out, to wash and to cleanse, in this order. First the iniquity must be blotted out, then well washed, that is, every slightest attachment to it is removed; finally the cleansing, which means conceiving an implacable hatred for sin and doing things which are contrary to it, that is making acts of humility, meekness, mortification, etc., according

---

[1] *Exercises*, nos. 48 and 55.   [2] James 2: 13.
[3] Cf. Psalm 110(111): 4; 111(112): 4.

to the diversity of the sins. These three operations follow one another but to God alone belongs the first. To God, in co-operation with the soul, the second and the third: the washing and the cleansing. Let us, poor sinners, do our duty: repent and with the Lord's help, wash and cleanse ourselves. We are sure that the Lord will do the first, the blotting out; this is prompt and immediate. And so we must believe it to be, without doubts or hesitations. 'I believe in the forgiveness of sins.' The two processes which depend on our co-operation need time, progress, effort. Therefore we say: 'Wash me yet more . . . and cleanse me.'

This mysterious process of our purification is perfectly accomplished in holy confession, through the intervention of the blood of Christ which washes and cleanses us. The power of the divine blood, applied to the soul, acts progressively, from one confession to another. 'Yet more' and ever more. Hence the importance of confession in itself, with the words of absolution, and of the custom of frequent confession for persons of a spiritual profession, such as priests and Bishops. How easy it is for mere routine to take the place of true devotion in our weekly confessions! Here is a good way of drawing the best out of this precious and divine exercise: to think of Christ who, according to St Paul, was created by God to be 'our wisdom, our righteousness, sanctification and redemption' (I Cor. 1: 30).

So, when I confess, I must beg Jesus first of all to be my wisdom, helping me to make a calm, precise, detailed examination of my sins and of their gravity, so that I may feel sincere sorrow for them. Then, that he may be my justice, so that I may present myself to my confessor as to my judge and accuse myself sincerely and sorrowfully. May he be also my perfect sanctification when I bow my head to receive absolution from the hand of the priest, by whose gesture is restored or increased sanctifying grace. Finally, that he may be my redemption as I perform that meagre penance which is set me instead of the great penalty I deserve: a meagre penance indeed, but a rich atonement because it is united with the sacrament to the blood of Christ, which intercedes and atones and washes and cleanses, for me and with me.

This 'wash me yet more' must remain the sacred motto of my ordinary confessions. These confessions are the surest criterion by which to judge my spiritual progress.

VERSE IV: 'For I know my iniquity and my sin is ever before me.'

The advice of the ancient philosophers: 'Know thyself', was already a good foundation for an honest and worthy life. It served for the ordinary exercise of humility, which is the prime virtue of great men. For the Christian, for the ecclesiastic, the thought of being a sinner does not by any means signify that we must lose heart, but it must mean confident and habitual trust in the Lord Jesus who has redeemed and forgiven us; it means a keen sense of respect for our fellow men and for all men's souls and a safeguard against the danger of becoming proud of our achievements. If we stay in the cell of the penitent sinner, deep in our heart, it will be not only a refuge for the soul which has found its own true self, and with its true self calm in decision and action, but also a fire by which zeal for the souls of men is kept more brightly lit, with pure intentions and a mind free from preoccupations about success, which is extraneous to our apostolate.

David needed the shock of the prophet's voice saying: 'You are the man.'[1] But afterwards his sin is always there, always before his eyes, an ever-present warning: 'My sin is always before me.'

Father Segneri wisely points out that it is not necessary to remember the exact form of every single sin, which would be neither profitable nor edifying, but it is well to bear in mind the memory of past failings as a warning, as an incitement to holy fear and zeal for souls. How often the thought of sins and sinners recurs in the liturgy! This is even more true of the Eastern than of the Latin liturgy; but it is well expressed in both: 'My sin is always before me', just as the sins of men were before Jesus in his agony in the garden of Gethsemane, as they were before Peter at the height of his authority as Supreme Pontiff, before Paul in the glory of his apostolate, and before Augustine in the splendour of his great learning and episcopal sanctity.

I pity those unhappy men who, instead of keeping their sin before them, hide it behind their backs! They will never be free from past or future sins.

Second day, Wednesday, 27 November

VERSE V: 'Against thee only have I sinned, and have done evil in thy sight, that thou mayst be justified in thy sentence and blameless in thy judgment.'

Sin is an offence against God, and for this alone a grave evil. The other considerations are all secondary in comparison with this: a wife raped and a husband killed are things of small account compared with an outraged God. This is what David understood and what we must understand too. How differently this world thinks! People are sorry, not for having

[1] 2 Sam. 12: 7.

offended the Lord, but because they have suffered disgrace, loss or misfortune.

The saints did not feel that way. 'I said "O Lord, be merciful to me, heal my soul for I have sinned against thee"' (Psalm 40(41): 4).

Another thought: 'I have done evil in thy sight.' Sin, even if directed against one's neighbour and against oneself, directly violates God's holy law. But it is graver because it is committed in God's sight. 'God sees me': our humble grandmothers used to work this motto into their samplers of rustic embroidery: it still hangs on the old walls of our houses and it contains a stern reminder which serves to give a character of decency to all our behaviour. What a profound truth this is of the omnipresence of God, of his searching glance which penetrates even the secret recesses of our privacy. A whole treatise of ascetic doctrine could be written about this truth from which is derived the purest beauty of sanctified souls, as clear as crystal, as pure as well water, using no deceit with others or with themselves (for it happens sometimes that we are insincere even with ourselves, surely the height of folly!) even at the risk of seeming of little worth. 'The simplicity of the just man is derided.'[1] What a fine passage this is from St Gregory the Great!

VERSE VI: 'For behold I was brought forth in iniquity, and in sin did my mother conceive me.'

This might seem to be proffered as an excuse, but is really a more explicit statement of his own helplessness. David is referring to the law of original sin, of which St Paul speaks[2] and which theologians call 'natural infirmity', the law we feel in our body, in opposition to the law of the spirit, but he did not mention this in order to turn the question aside, or seek a pretext or a justification.

We must recognize that wickedness is in us because, although the temptation comes from without, the grace to resist it is entirely at our disposal and is stronger than the temptation. 'Devils? What devils?' Professor Tabarelli[3] used to say when he was expanding to us the Treatise De gratia at the Apollinare, 'We are the devils. We are the ones responsible.' Of David's case, St Augustine wisely said: 'When the woman was far away, the man's desire was at hand. What he desired to see, and the cause of his sin, were elsewhere.'[4]

Our knowledge of human frailty must be for us, physicians of souls,

[1] Moralia, 10, 29, 4 (P.L., LXXV, 947).   [2] Romans 7: 23 et seq.
[3] Riccardo Tabarelli, theologian (1859–1909). He taught philosophy and scholastic theology at the Apollinare.
[4] Enarr. in Ps., 50, 3 (P.L., XXXVI, 587).

a reason for pitying, raising and encouraging others, not for excusing ourselves.

We have the grave responsibility of guarding the grace that is always offered us to hold nature in check. In our poor nature lie hidden perverse tendencies towards ambition, pride, greed, impatience, envy, avarice, sloth and impunity. These are within us, as Segneri says, as in a vast menagerie of wild beasts, bears, wolves, tigers, lions and leopards. They cannot hurt us so long as the portcullis is down and holds them back. It is as if they were not there: grace has shut them in and holds them down. But if the barrier is raised the wild beasts, following their own natural instincts, rush to sate their appetites! 'A Saviour, a wall and a rampart shall be set therein' (Isaiah 26: 1).[1] If exterior and interior grace, the wall and the rampart, fall, what a disaster for a poor Christian, for a poor priest! 'For behold I was brought forth in iniquity, and in sin did my mother conceive me.' Not our own good natural mothers, but the ancient sinful mother of mankind.

VERSE VII: 'For behold thou hast loved truth: the uncertain hidden things of thy wisdom thou hast revealed to me.'

First of all the Psalmist wished to justify the Lord's words spoken to him by the prophet: 'that thou mayst be justified in thy sentence', and to exalt the triumph of his judgment: 'that thou mayst be blameless in thy judgment'.

Now he proclaims that his God is a lover of truth. In fact truth is in God as in its source and God is all truth; as Jesus, the divine Word, said himself: 'I am the truth.'[2] A declaration of this sort would seem that of a madman had it not come from the lips of God made man. The Roman governor was much puzzled by this declaration of Christ's and asked him: 'What is truth?'

The truth, says Father Segneri, is a transcendent virtue which enters into all well-ordered human affairs and, according to the diversity of these, assumes different names. In the schools it is called science, in speech veracity, in conduct frankness, in conversation sincerity, in actions right-eousness, in business dealings honesty, in giving advice freedom from prejudice, in the keeping of promises loyalty, and in the courts of law it has the noble title of justice. This is the Lord's truth which 'abides for ever'.[3]

The love of truth. On the day of my episcopal consecration the Church

---

[1] Cf. Lamentations 2: 8: 'He caused rampart and wall to fall together.'
[2] Cf. John 14: 6.   [3] Cf. 1 John 2: 17.

gave me a particular mandate concerning it: 'Let him choose humility and truth and never forsake them for any flattery or threats. Let him not consider light to be darkness, or darkness light; let him not call evil good, or good evil. Let him learn from wise men and fools, so that he may profit from all.'[1] I thank the Lord for having given me a natural inclination to tell the truth, always and in all circumstances and before everyone, in a pleasant manner and with courtesy, to be sure, but calmly and fearlessly. Certain small fibs of my childhood have left in my heart a horror of deceit and falsehood. Now, especially as I am growing old, I want to be particularly careful about this: to love the truth, God helping me! I have repeated this many times, swearing it on the Gospel.

The revelation of the uncertain and hidden things of divine wisdom comes by itself. The love of truth means perpetual childhood, fresh and joyful. And the Lord reveals his most sublime mysteries to children and conceals them from the learned and the so-called wise men of this world.

VERSE VIII: 'Sprinkle me with hyssop and I shall be clean: wash me and I shall be whiter than snow.'

This refers to the Mosaic rite of the cleansing of lepers. They had to let themselves be sprinkled by the priest with a bunch of hyssop dipped in blood, and then wash themselves from head to foot in pure water.[2] Here are foreshadowed the sins which defile the body and sully the soul. Hyssop is a plant of mean appearance but of great strength. It sprouts on rock and strikes roots in it. Oh how great is man's need of this cleansing! Isaiah was right when he saw Jesus as the great purifier: 'He shall sprinkle many nations (with hyssop)' (Isaiah 52: 15). In the metaphor David used we may see not only the reference associated with the Mosaic rite but also, and more significantly, the double cleansing reserved for the human race by means of the two sacraments of baptism and penance. He who cleanses us is our Redeemer himself. The altar of his sacrifice is humble, like hyssop, but his blood is powerful, sprinkled with divine generosity over the bodies and souls of believers for their purification. What a great gift this is, daily poured out all over the world, in the two sacraments of reconciliation and salvation! Through these this poor world is purified and rises again, whiter than snow.

I will make further use of this verse when I make my weekly confession: 'Sprinkle me, Lord, and I shall be cleansed.'

May the Lord cleanse me from my self-love which, as Segneri says, is attached to three things: to my will, which wants to go its own way; to

---

[1] Cf. *Pontificale Romanum*, cit.   [2] Cf. Lev. 14: 1ff.

my reputation, making me intolerant of scorn; to my own comfort, which is averse to suffering and encourages the wasteful use of time!

I think too of the Sunday aspersions with holy water in the parish churches before Mass. 'Familiarity breeds contempt.' We must return to the mystical significance of these rites, and expound it to the faithful. How can we not fail to recall the coming of Christ as the 'High Priest of the good things to come' who 'through his own blood assures for us eternal redemption' and in this way purifies his faithful people.[1]

Third day. Thursday, 28 November

VERSE IX: 'To my hearing thou shalt give joy and gladness; and the bones that have been humbled shall rejoice.'

When we hear that we are forgiven: 'The Lord has put away your sin',[2] we are full of joy and gladness. We have felt this so often when after the absolution we rise from kneeling before our confessor, especially when we are in retreat or on some other more solemn occasions in our life. The joy is in our understanding, the gladness in our heart. This two-fold sensation is expressed also in the renewed physical vigour and energy of our bodies: 'The bones that have been humbled will rejoice.' There are some most moving references to this in the Bible: Isaiah tells us 'Your heart shall thrill and rejoice' (Isaiah 60: 5), and we read in Proverbs: 'a glad heart makes a cheerful countenance' (Prov. 15: 13).

The mystery of spiritual joy, which is a characteristic of saintly souls, is seen here in all its beauty and charm. The Lord leaves us uncertain about our eternal salvation, but gives us signs which suffice to calm our souls and make us joyful.

'It is the Spirit himself bearing witness with our spirit that we are children of God' (Romans 8: 16). I ask you: is this a small thing, to feel we are God's children? This confidence, which is often in our hearts without our being able to account for it, is the inexhaustible source of our joy, the most solid foundation of true piety, which consists in desiring everything that is full and loving service to the Lord. The essential is that this desire of ours should be prompt and effective. That it should be a source of enjoyment also, that is, of tender affection, sweetness, delight and joy—this is also important, but accidental and secondary. The realization of Our Lord's goodness to us, and of our worthlessness, makes us happy and sad at the same time. But the sadness is lessened as it becomes an encouragement for our apostolate in the service of all that is sublime

---

[1] Cf. Hebrews 9: 11-12.   [2] 2 Sam. 12: 13.

and noble, to make Jesus known, loved and served, and to take away the sins of the world.

The thought of holiness, smiling amidst trials and crosses, is always with me. Interior calm, founded on the words and promises of Christ, produces the imperturbable serenity which may be seen in face, words and behaviour, the expression of all-conquering charity. We feel a renewal of energies, physical as well as spiritual: sweetness to the soul and health to the body (Prov. 16: 24). To live in peace with the Lord, to hear that we are forgiven, and in our turn to forgive others, gives the soul that feast of 'marrow and fat' of which the psalmist sang, and brings the Magnificat constantly to our lips.[1]

VERSE X: 'Turn away thy face from my sins, and blot out all my iniquities.'

The prayer of the penitent king rises once more, imploringly, and is now broadened to include all the iniquities he has committed, besides the graver sin which has inspired the Miserere. How moving is this reference to the Lord's face, that is to his eyes and features and his expression of scorn and anger! We shall see his face once more, on our last day, and unrepentant sinners will be smitten with eternal despair and horror.

I must make myself very familiar with this verse, as an expression of renewed contrition. One must not be afraid to call oneself a sinner. Any exaggerated form of expression spoils the effect; each must express himself according to his own temperament, but as we always need Our Lord's forgiveness, it is well to be imploring divine mercy, and trusting to it, at all times. 'A contrite and a humbled heart, O God, thou wilt not despise.' David was soon to say this. But we must not neglect any of the forms that may express this humble contrition.

VERSE XI: 'Create a clean heart in me, O God, and renew a right spirit within me.'

The heart is the will and the spirit is the understanding. So we need a purified will and a renewed understanding.

Alas! how many attachments and temptations assail our will, especially in the sphere of our feelings: objects, people and circumstances! The charms of certain circles, sometimes even of a chance meeting, try it sorely. The heart is helpless by itself. Once it has been spoilt, weakened by superfluities, it has to be made anew. It is not much good patching it:

[1] Cf. Psalm 62(63): 6.

the weakness reappears. The heart of Paul, the heart of Augustine, were new creations. Great God, what a miracle that was! Once they had been turned in a new direction, the wills of these two men never turned back, never faltered.   In the hour of their death they were still as true as steel.

The right spirit, that is, the understanding of what is most important to believe and to do, yes, this can simply be renewed. For this a man must have a most just conception of the chief motives of his own conduct and a more sufficient knowledge of what, in practice, he must do. The reform must be above all interior and profound, 'within me', in order to express itself externally in the various aspects of life: reform in speaking, seeing, hearing and writing; a new art of living, corresponding to a new conception of life.

VERSE XII: 'Cast me not away from thy face; and take not thy holy spirit from me.'

The gravest punishment David could impose on his son Absalom, who had betrayed him, was this: 'Let him no longer see my face.'[1] So we understand why he implores the Lord not to banish him from his sight. It is one thing for God to turn his face away from our iniquities, it is quite another for him to banish the sinner from his sight. The mystery of the Lord's face: how impressive and terrifying that is! On the other hand, one can understand the redeemed soul's supreme joy in the vision of the Lord's face. May the Lord grant me the grace not to be rejected by him at the end. May he be merciful and admit me, even if I am the last and least of all, that I may contemplate him for ever.

Another point: the presence of the Holy Spirit in the faithful soul. Here, without books or commentaries, I cannot verify whether this Holy Spirit of the Lord must be understood specifically as the third Person of the most Holy Trinity. It seems obvious to me that it must be so. The action of grace in a soul is described in the words 'and we will come to him and make our home with him'.[2] This means the three divine Persons. Each comes with his own personal characteristics. The Holy Spirit is the Lord and Giver of life, and it is he who sanctifies the soul. Is not the Christian a living temple of the Holy Spirit? And what a wealth of benefits to the soul comes with this indwelling of the Lord's Spirit! St Paul numbers these gifts: they are twenty-four. They begin with peace and joy.[3]

[1] 2 Kings 14: 24.   [2] John 14: 23.
[3] Cf. Gal. 5: 22: 'Love, joy and peace.'

Fourth day. Friday, 29 November

VERSE XIII: 'Restore to me the joy of thy salvation, and strengthen me with a perfect spirit!'

Restore to me the joyful certainty that you will save me: serene confidence in my Saviour. St Jerome uses the apt translation: 'joy of thy Jesus', instead of 'joy of thy salvation'. This is the true joy of a forgiven soul, the first fruit of the indwelling Holy Spirit, to feel numbered with the elect. And all this through the merits of Jesus who shed his blood to redeem this soul of ours and to fill it with his virtue and his life. This confidence must not be free from fear, for we bear the treasure of grace in fragile vessels; a small jolt may make us stagger: the vessel is broken again. Oh poor sinners that we are! But if we do our best the Lord continues to give us his grace, the grace of feeling we are his for ever, this foretaste of the eternal companionship with Jesus which is reserved for us, for that long day that will have no sunset. And the thought that our Saviour is Jesus himself—David in his melancholy chant sang for the New as well as for the Old Testament—oh, how it makes my heart rejoice the whole day long! The first Christians expressed this doctrine with the symbol of the fish, *IXΘΥΣ*—'Jesus Christ, Son of God, Saviour' —and placed this sign above their tombs in the catacombs as a pledge of resurrection, and also as a symbol of the Eucharistic mystery, known only to the initiated. What is more dear to me, a priest and Bishop, than daily contact with the great sacrament, the pledge of future glory?

And the 'perfect spirit'? This is the indispensable condition for our preservation of the joyous and certain hope of paradise. It is a habitual reception of continual graces, which keep the soul inclined towards good, like the saints in heaven, without any hesitations—a confirmation in grace, a very rare gift which the Lord grants without his chosen creature even knowing it, so that the uncertainty of possessing it may encourage the exercise of many virtues which derive from it, chaste fear, circumspection, humility, a perpetual recourse to God, and other virtues.

David also asked for this gift, which he called the 'perfect' spirit, that is, no common spirit but one worthy of a most noble prince, a lofty, disinterested spirit, untouched by self-love, eager only for God and his glory. St Paul too asked for it, as he subjected his body to mortification and chastisement, trembling lest 'after preaching to others, I myself should be disqualified'.[1] I also ask for it, O Lord, with David and Paul, but feeling so puny beside them. I also ask, as a great boon, for this gift which will

[1] I Cor. 9: 27.

confirm me in a low opinion of myself and my own worthlessness, and give me a selfless longing for you, for whom alone I should live since you have died for me (2 Cor. 5: 15).

VERSE XIV: 'I will teach the unjust thy ways, and the wicked shall be converted to thee.'

My priesthood means not only sacrifice for the sins of the world and for my own sins but also an apostolate of truth and love. My vocation leads me to this. The thought of the little I have done till now and the pardon I have received from the Lord for my past failings must induce greater fervour.

'Mercy and truth, the universal ways of God.'[1] It is here I must distinguish myself. I must not be a teacher of political science, of strategy, of human knowledge: there are teachers galore of these subjects. I am a teacher of mercy and truth. And by teaching these I shall also contribute a great deal to the social order. This is stated also in the Psalms: 'Mercy and truth have met together: justice and peace have kissed.'[2] My teaching must be by word and example: therefore principles and exhortations from my lips and encouragement from my conduct in the eyes of all, Catholics, Orthodox, Turks and Jews. 'Words move but examples draw.'

'The wicked shall be converted to thee.' The problem of the conversion of the irreligious and apostate world presents one of the mysteries which weigh most heavily on my soul. However, the solution is not my business but the Lord's secret. On my shoulders, on the shoulders of all priests, all Catholics, rests the solemn duty of working together for the conversion of this impious world and for the return of heretics and schismatics to the unity of the Church and the preaching of Christ to the Jews who put him to death. We are not responsible for the result. Our sole comfort, but it is enough for our peace of mind, is knowing that Jesus the Saviour is much more anxious than we are for the salvation of souls: he wants them to be saved through our co-operation, but it is his grace alone, working in their souls, which saves them; and his grace will not be lacking when the moment comes for their conversion. This moment will be one of the most joyful surprises of our glorified souls in heaven.

VERSE XV: 'Deliver me from blood, O God, thou God of my salvation, and my tongue shall extol thy justice.'

[1] Cf. Psalm 84(85): 11.   [2] Ibid.

To this verse dear Father Segneri devotes no fewer than fifteen pages of comment, in which he says some fine things, but in too ornate a manner. For me the interpretation must be more simple and practical. What is this 'blood' from which the royal Psalmist begs the Lord to deliver him? I do not know the exegetic interpretation of this. Looking at it from my own angle I choose to see in this:

(1) The internal impulses of carnal desire, the result of our 'natural infirmity', of the tainted blood which mankind has inherited from its first source in fallen Eve. Advancing years, when one is in the sixties like me, wither the evil impulses to some extent, and it is a real pleasure to observe the silence and tranquillity of the flesh, which has now become old and irresponsive to the temptations which disturbed it in the years of my youth and vigorous maturity. However, one must always be on the alert. The Bible speaks also of the foolish, doting old man, one of 'the three things my soul hates'.[1]

(2) Excessive attachment to members of one's own family which, when they are felt beyond the limits of charity, become an embarrassment and a hindrance. The law of the apostolate and the priesthood is above the law of flesh and blood. Therefore I must love my own kith and kin, and go to their assistance when their poverty makes this necessary, because this is an obvious duty for one who does so much to help strangers, but all must be done discreetly, in a purely priestly spirit, in an orderly and impartial manner. My closest relations, brothers, sisters, nephews and nieces, with very few exceptions, are exemplary Christians and give me great joy. But it would never do for me to get mixed up in their affairs and concerns, so as to be diverted from my duties as a servant of the Holy See, and a Bishop!

(3) Patriotism, which is right and may be holy, but may also degenerate into nationalism, which in my case would be most detrimental to the dignity of my episcopal ministry, must be kept above all nationalistic disputes. The world is poisoned with morbid nationalism, built up on the basis of race and blood, in contradiction to the Gospel. In this matter especially, which is of burning topical interest, 'deliver me from men of blood, O God'. Here fits in most aptly the invocation: 'God of my salvation': Jesus our Saviour died for all nations, without distinction of race or blood, and became the first brother of the new human family, built on him and his Gospel.

With what enthusiasm and liberty the tongue of the priest and Bishop, thus loosed from earthly ties, will be able to preach to all the Lord's

[1] Cf. Ecclus. 25: 4.

commands, and to praise his justice, mercy and peace, in the name of the Father who is God of all virtues, the Son who is God of salvation, and the Holy Spirit who is God of peace! In the enjoyment of this holy liberty how much more joy is felt in the sacred ministry of souls! 'Thy statutes have been my songs in the place of my pilgrimage' (Psalm 118 (119): 54). 'Come, let us praise the Lord with joy; let us joyfully sing to God our Saviour' (Psalm 94(95): 1).

VERSE XVI: 'Lord thou wilt open my lips, and my mouth shall declare thy praise.'

This is one of the best loved verses in the whole Psalm. The priest's morning prayer, his 'sacrifice of praise', opens with these words. They breathe such poetry and tenderness! The priest is also a teacher, and his lips must guard the truth. How fine it would be to begin all sermons, discourses, and all forms of teaching thus: 'Lord, thou wilt open my lips.' After the invocation comes the whole Office, distributed in the various Hours of day and night. This sets the tone for the whole sacred ministry of the Word, which is the announcement of the good tidings, an exaltation of religious truth and a hymn of glory to the Lord.

When Father Segneri reaches this verse he jumps a whole octave: omitting the literal interpretations of the exegetes, he invites the contemplative soul to see in this declaration of praise the exaltation of the Lord's greatest work, in which he employed the fulness of his powers, that is the founding of Holy Church, which came to pass ten centuries after the time of David but was foreseen by him as God's masterpiece, wrought by means of his Christ. In fact elsewhere (Psalm 47(48): 1) it is said: 'Great is the Lord and greatly to be praised.' But where? On earth, in the sea, in the air, in fire, in the sky, in the stars, in the sun? No, but in the 'city of our God, in his holy mountain'.[1] This interpretation is shared by St Robert Bellarmine who writes: 'Among those things which have been revealed to us we have hardly anything greater, or from which we may better discover the greatness of God, so as to praise it more fervently, than the founding of the Church.' Having made this point, Segneri finds reasons to infer that, as David wished to give God the greatest possible praise in return for the many benefits he had recovered with God's forgiveness, he chose this as the main theme for his ready harp. This was to be the grandest achievement of all ages and David, viewing it from afar with the spirit of a prophet, wanted to have the honour of announcing it: 'My mouth shall declare thy praise.'

[1] Psalm 47(48): 2.

When we think that these words are repeated at all Matins, in the name of Holy Church, who prays for herself and for the whole world, and repeated by innumerable lips opened by the touch of the grace they have invoked, the vision broadens, comes alive and is fulfilled. Here the Church is seen not as a historic monument of the past but as a living institution. Holy Church is not like a palace that is built in a year. It is a vast city which must one day cover the whole universe: 'With the joy of the whole earth is Mount Sion founded; in the far north the city of the great king.'[1] The building was begun twenty centuries ago, but it spreads and stretches through all lands until the name of Christ is everywhere adored. As the Church increases so new nations, hearing the good news, rejoice: 'And when the Gentiles heard this, they were glad' (Acts 13: 48). The pious and daring commentator concludes with a thought that is very fine and uplifting for every priest as he reads his Breviary: everyone must take part in this building of Holy Church. He whose work is preaching this grand enterprise must, as a messenger of his Gospel, say to the Lord: 'Lord, thou wilt open my lips and my mouth shall declare thy praise.' A priest who is not engaged in missionary work should long to co-operate in the great task of the apostolate, and when he reads the Psalms privately in his cell he also should say: 'Lord, thou wilt open my lips', because even there, through the communion of love, he must consider as his own voice any voice that is at that moment announcing the Gospel, 'the supreme praise of God which has given us the theme for this verse, more charged with hidden mysteries than with words'.

Fifth day. Saturday, 30 November: feast of St Andrew the apostle

VERSE XVII: 'For if thou hadst desired sacrifice, I would indeed have given it: with burnt offerings thou wilt not be delighted.'

These words reveal David's willingness for sacrifice, for any sacrifice. The thought of the sin he has committed still weighs on his heart. Since he has acknowledged the gravity of his twofold crime, the rape of another man's wife and the murder of an innocent man—and it took him a year to realize this—he feels that the proper expiation should be death. This would be in accordance with the Mosaic law. But since the prophet has assured him: 'The Lord has put away your sin: you shall not die',[2] he knows that he must make an offering to the Lord of all that is the expression of death, that is, the annihilation of everything, before the offended majesty of God: hence the sacrifice according to the legal requirements

---

[1] Psalm 47(48): 3.   [2] 2 Sam. 12: 13.

and, since he was inordinately rich, a more abundant sacrifice in burnt offerings and in creatures of the earth. But the Lord did not want him to offer these forms of sacrifice, prescribed for the Jews who had come from Egypt, where they had been workers with straw, earth and lime. For one who was to be a progenitor of Christ, for a man made after God's own heart, these forms of worship and expiation were too ignoble. Therefore the Lord did not want them from him, and would take no delight in burnt offerings. But David was right when he showed his willingness to offer them, in order at least to show himself ready to obey the divine commands.

Readiness for self-sacrifice, such as the Lord wants from every one of us, and in the measure he requires, this must present a great lesson and warning for me. This is what loyal and sincere devotion means. Not just shedding consoling tears during prayer but preparing a ready will for God's service, whatever it may be. 'My heart is ready, O God, my heart is ready',[1] for much or for little, to do what God wants of me and understand what he does not want, which therefore must not be done. So frequently we are deceived about this. We take pleasure in fashioning for ourselves ways of serving the Lord which really are simply ways of expressing our own taste, our own ambition, our own caprice. 'The pride of your heart has deceived you, you who dwell in the clefts of the rock' (Obadiah 3). You hardly know how to take, in God's service, one step outside your hole, in which, like a tarantula, you take refuge from the storms that rage, and yet you like to persuade yourself that you could fly like an eagle if you received a call from beyond the mountains and beyond the seas. In your piety you have unwittingly deceived yourself. Let the readiness of your will be seen in works done to carry out the will of the Lord, as this is made known to you day by day, and do not show this readiness merely by heaving fervent sighs.

VERSE XVIII: 'A sacrifice to God is an afflicted spirit: a contrite and humbled heart, O God, thou wilt not despise.'

The sacrifice that is most pleasing to God is the spirit beset by trials, indeed doubly beset because to the torment of the spirit is frequently added the suffering of the body which with the soul has played its own large part in doing evil. If we consider this doctrine apart from the particular case of David, the repentant sinner, it sets before us that great mystery of the Cross and of all suffering which is the surest way to priestly and episcopal perfection.

[1] Psalm 56(57): 8.

During my retreat in Rustchuk in May, 1930 I was entirely absorbed in this doctrine which, moreover, appeared to me with amazing clarity when I prostrated myself before the altar of San Carlo al Corso in Rome, during the ceremony of my episcopal consecration, and arose from that ceremony bearing with me a clear impression of resemblance, at least in my soul, with Christ crucified. 'Make me love thy Cross.'[1] I must frequently repeat this invocation! Until now I have suffered too little. My own happy nature, which is a great gift from God, has kept me immune from those afflictions which accompany daring and generous spirits who hurl themselves like living flames into their zealous labour for souls. But it is only to be expected that, before the end of my humble life, the Lord will send me trials of a particularly painful nature. Well, I am ready: provided that the Lord, who sends me these, will also grant me the strength to bear them with calm, dignity and sweetness. I read in the life of the last Mistress of Novices, Mother Maria Alfonsa, of these Sisters of Sion whose pleasant hospitality I enjoy, that the spirit of this Institute consists in *abnégation souriante*.[2] Oh, this motto is just right for me! I desire always to be ready for the interior sacrifice, which must be borne with humility, in a spirit of penitence and with a contrite heart— 'a contrite heart in ashes'[3] as is said of all the most famous characters of the Old Testament, and as we read of the most beloved saints of the New. It is enough to think of St Francis of Assisi, whose prayer was always the same: 'O Jesus, have mercy on me, a sinner.' To help me to acquire this contrite spirit I will be most careful and fervent in celebrating Holy Mass, which transports me to the garden of Gethsemane, to the most secret sanctuary of Christ's sufferings. I shall find the necessary trials also in the series of daily pinpricks for which I have to find a perfect answer through compliance, patience, resignation and justice, dignity and peace.

VERSE XIX: 'Deal favourably, O Lord, in thy good will, with Sion, that the walls of Jerusalem may be built up!'

Biblical exegesis has a wonderful opportunity here to exercise itself in the examination of the three meanings: literal, allegorical or mystical, and anagogic. The royal prophet, raised up again after his sin, ready for sacrifice, looks towards the future and prays that it may be one of glori-

---

[1] From the *Stabat Mater*.

[2] The Congregation of the Sisters of Our Lady of Sion, founded in Paris in 1843 by Théodore and Alphonse Ratisbonne and Madame Stoulhen, has as one of its purposes the offering of prayers and sacrifices for Israel and a direct apostolate to the Jews.

[3] These words are taken from the sequence *Dies Irae*, used in the Requiem Mass for the dead.

fication for his merciful God. The favourable treatment he begs for his house, established on Mount Sion, which will permit him to rebuild the walls of the royal city, foreshadows the appearance of Christ the Saviour: 'The goodness and loving kindness of God our Saviour appeared', says St Paul (Titus 3: 4). Sion was to see the dynasties of the kings of Judah, which gave place to Constantine and then to the more firmly established and unfailing pontifical religious monarchy. Jerusalem is Holy Church, which pitches its tents in every part of the world and has firm, massive walls, sometimes breached here and there but rebuilt and fortified more strongly than ever. From the mystic Jerusalem, or Church Militant, we raise our eyes to the heavenly Jerusalem, or Church Triumphant, which awaits us in the final consummation. The last notes of David's Miserere set the tone for St John's Apocalyptic vision which, after the description of the 'blessed vision of peace', ends with the prayer 'Come, Lord Jesus'.[1]

My poor heart too is ravished and moved by these splendours and from them I draw encouragement to do my best to co-operate in preaching the spirit of Jesus from Mount Sion, and in the extension and restoration of the walls of Jerusalem, in the service of Holy Church, as Providence has decided for me, who, though the humblest of the Bishops and representatives of the Holy See, am none the less desirous to honour my vocation.

These remaining years should be my best years of earnest, effective and worthy co-operation in the great work carried on by the Catholic Church, from the sacred heights of Sion to the ramparts of Jerusalem. May Jesus accept at least my good intention and bless it graciously, in his good will.

VERSE XX: 'Then shalt thou accept the sacrifice of justice, oblations, and whole burnt offerings. Then shall they lay calves upon thy altar.'

This speaks of the great and authentic sacrifice which Jesus offered for us when 'he delivered himself for us, an oblation and a sacrifice to God for an odour of sweetness' (Eph. 5: 2).

David, in rapt contemplation, saw this from afar, the true sacrifice of justice and universal atonement which, from the summit of the sacred hill that rises between Sion and Moriah, was to complete all other sacrifices all over the world, and also endow with divine virtue all the sacrifices that would be made by millions down through the centuries who, drawn by a passionate love for the Cross, would offer their penitence and suffering, as they shared in the Mystical Body of Christ.

Around the sacrifice of the Cross it is well to contemplate these 'obla-

[1] Rev. 22: 20.

tions and whole burnt offerings'. They are the apostles, confessors, martyrs, saints of every age. Here are the virgins whose life was and continues to be the glory of Holy Church, all fervour, all sacrifice, all blood. 'Like a sacrificial burnt offering he accepted them.'[1] A mount of oblations and burnt sacrifices, often obscure and unknown, rising towards the Most High, in propitiation for the whole world. And the calf or calves placed on the altar? The commentators are agreed in seeing in this the image of the Holy Eucharist, by means of which the sacrifice of the Cross is mystically and no less truly and perpetually renewed. What an honour for a priest or Bishop, in this ministry that has been entrusted to him, to offer the divine victim on the altar every day! But what a responsibility before heaven and earth!

Ah, Lord Jesus, I take refuge in my nothingness, I plead for pity and forgiveness for my failings, I renew the consecration of my life to your worship, your love, your altar. 'Have mercy on me, O God, have mercy on me.'

---

[1] Wisdom 3: 6.

1942

[49]   *Retreat with my clergy at the Apostolic Delegation*
from the feast of Christ the King to All Saints Day
Istanbul, 25–31 October, 1942

(1) Last year I could not make a retreat, as I was busy in Greece directing relief work, in the name of the Holy Father.[1]

This year I would willingly have made my retreat again with the Jesuit Fathers, as I did in 1939. But it is still inadvisable for many people to be seen coming and going around that house and the Fathers themselves are uncertain and afraid. So I decided to be content with making the retreat at home, as we did in 1935 and 1937. I invited their Excellencies Kiredjian, the Archbishop of the Armenians, and Varuhas, the Ordinary of the Greeks of the Byzantine rite, to join us. Varuhas brought with him his three ecclesiastics: Fathers Basil and Polycarp and Deacon Haralampoś. There are also the three Heads of the Eastern rites: Chami for the Melkites, Fakir for the Syrians and Nikoloff for the Bulgarians. The Bishops and these representatives of the three rites remain at the Delegation for dinner. In all we are fifteen this retreat, a good number. Father Folet, a French Jesuit, is preaching very well, with great fidelity to Scriptural doctrine. Silence in the house, and punctuality to the timetable: altogether a general atmosphere of good will on everyone's part, which is pleasing and edifying for us all.

(2) On the feast of St Simon and St Jude I made my confession to Father Folet, after I had celebrated my own holy Mass and attended his, in preparation for the sacrament of purification. I extended my examination and confession to cover the two years from December, 1940 until now, My penance: recital of the Miserere and the Magnificat. But alas! I must accustom myself to very different penances if I want to enter heaven easily and honourably! May the Lord grant me more and more the right spirit. The hour of greatest penance for the whole world is drawing near.

[1] In 1941 he visited Greece four times: 11–12 January, 20 April–10 May, 8 July–7 October and 14–16 December.

It is right that Bishops and priests should set the example, just as St Charles Borromeo and Cardinal Federico did in times of great calamity: they went in procession, bare-footed, with ropes around their necks and wearing hair shirts, bearing the relics of the holy Cross.

(3) I am continually disappointed, and often secretly disquieted about the same old problem: not being able to keep up with all I have to do, and having to watch myself closely to try to overcome my natural sloth, which tends to make me calm and unhurried, although I never stop working. This disappointment humiliates and almost saddens me. I must welcome and cherish everything that may be a source of humiliation but without losing my inner calm and serenity. This is my torment. My not being able to get on more quickly may be due to several reasons. It may be due to the fact that I really have too much to do, or to the particular circumstances of my position here and in Greece. But I must choose to attribute this state of things to my own insufficiency and 'at least bear it patiently, if not joyfully', as Thomas à Kempis says (bk. III, chap. 57). And remembering that other admonition of his in the same book of *The Imitation*, I must not consider myself really humble until I admit that I am inferior to everyone else.[1]

(4) The fundamental principles of the spiritual life still hold firm, thanks be to God: to feel wholly detached from my own nothingness and to remind myself that, in the words of the Ambrosian Mass, I am the least of all, and a sinner. I must abandon myself completely to the will of the Lord and desire to live for nothing else but the apostolate and the faithful service of Holy Church. I must feel no concern about my future and be ready to sacrifice everything, even life itself—should the Lord think me worthy—for the glory of God and the accomplishment of my duty; I must have a great spiritual fervour, in keeping with the mind of the Church and the best tradition, without any exaggeration of external forms or methods, but constant zeal and mildness, with an eye for everything, always with great patience and gentleness, remembering what Cardinal Mercier quotes from Gratry: gentleness is the fulness of strength. And finally, I must always be familiar with the thought of death, which helps so much to make life carefree and joyful.

(5) I find it rather mortifying to go over the same things again, but this is what my soul needs. So, I renew my resolve to observe the custom of reciting Matins in the evening, so as to be sure of having time for meditation in the morning, and I renew also my determination to study the Turkish and Greek languages. I have been studying Greek now for some

[1] Cf. *Imitation*, II, II, 13.

months, and I am pleased. As soon as I can I will take up Turkish again, not because I have any hope of becoming learned in these languages, but simply to do my duty and set a good example for my successors.

(6) My ministry in Greece is the one more beset with difficulties. For this reason I must love it more. Moreover, in recent months it has given me the greatest consolation. When I am here, in Istanbul, I never wish to leave for that country which today has become a 'place of torments', but once I get there I am like a fish in water. The thought that Mgr Giacomo Testa is working there and doing well is a great consolation to me, but cannot free me of much responsibility as long as the Holy See intends to leave it all to me.

(7) The two great evils which are poisoning the world today are secularism and nationalism. The former is characteristic of the men in power and of lay folk in general. The latter is found even among ecclesiastics. I am convinced that the Italian priests, especially the secular clergy, are less contaminated by this than others. But I must be very watchful, both as Bishop and as representative of the Holy See. It is one thing to love Italy, as I most fervently do, and quite another to display this affection in public. The holy Church which I represent is the mother of nations, all nations. Everyone with whom I come into contact must admire in the Pope's representative that respect for the nationality of others, expressed with graciousness and mild judgments, which inspires universal trust. Great caution then, respectful silence, and courtesy on all occasions. It will be wise for me to insist on this line of conduct being followed by all my entourage, at home and outside. We are all more or less tainted with nationalism. The Apostolic Delegate must be, and must be seen to be, free from this contagion. May God help me.

(8) We are living through great events, and chaos lies ahead. This makes it all the more necessary to return to those principles which are the foundation of the Christian social order, and to judge what is happening today in the light of what the Gospel teaches us, recognizing in the terror and horror which engulf us the terrible sanctions that guard the divine law, even on earth. The Bishop must be distinguished by his own understanding, and his adequate explanation to others, of the philosophy of history, even the history that is now, before our eyes, adding pages of blood to pages of political and social disorders. I want to re-read St Augustine's *City of God*, and draw from his doctrine the necessary material to form my own judgment, a wise judgment which may bring light and comfort to all who come within the scope of my ministry.

(9) Good Father René Folet, who is giving the Exercises with great

fidelity to Sacred Scripture, has for once diverged from this method to give an image of the perfect Bishop, using the words of St Isidore of Seville about St Fulgentius (*Liber II Officiorum*, chap. 5)[1]. I copy these words out as a warning to myself and in remembrance of this happy retreat. If only my own life could mirror this doctrine!

'He who is set in authority for the education and instruction of the people for their good must be holy in all things and reprehensible in nothing.... His speech must be pure, simple, open, full of dignity and integrity, full of gentleness and grace when he is dealing with the mystery of the law, the teaching of the faith, the virtue of continence and the law of justice; admonishing everyone, with exhortations varying according to that person's profession and the quality of his morals; that is, he must know in advance of what, to whom, when and how he should speak. It is his special and primary duty to read the Scriptures, to know the Canons, to imitate the examples of the saints, and devote himself to vigils, fasts and prayers, to live at peace with his brethren and never alienate any member, to condemn no one without proof, to excommunicate no one without due consideration. Every Bishop should be distinguished as much by his humility as by his authority, so that he may neither cause the vices of his subordinates to flourish, through his own excessive humility, nor exercise his authority with immoderate severity. The more strictly he fears he will be judged by Christ, the more warily should he act towards those committed to his care.

'He will also preserve that charity which excels all other gifts, and without which all virtue is nothing. For charity is the safeguard of chastity too, but this safeguard is grounded in humility. Besides all these things, he will also preserve perfect chastity, so that his mind, given to Christ, will be clean and free from all fleshly corruption. Among other things, it will be his duty to show care for the poor, with anxious steward-ship, to clothe the naked, to succour pilgrims, to ransom captives, to watch over widows and orphans and to show vigilant care for all, making provision for all with due discretion. In hospitality also he will be noteworthy in supplying the needs of all with kindliness and charity. For if all the faithful long to hear that saying of the Gospel: "I was a stranger and you took me in", all the more must the Bishop, whose house must give shelter to all.'

---

[1] St Isidorus, *De ecclesiasticis officiis*, II, 5 (P.L., LXXXIII, 785–6). In the original, the passage quoted is given in Latin.

1943—1944

Note

The year 1943 was full of uncertainty about the retreat. It was fixed and prepared for the end of 1944.

Father Lévêque, a Lazarist Father, was to have given it. Then, just before Christmas, I was ordered to Paris.[1]

---

[1] On 6 December, 1944, Mgr Roncalli received reserved information of his appointment as Apostolic Nuncio in France. In the last letter he wrote from Ankara, on 26 December, 1944, to the Chargé d'Affaires, Mgr Paolo Pappalardo, he wrote: 'If you hear anything good about me, praise the Lord as I do, for he has done all. If you hear criticisms, pray for me, that the Lord may forgive me if the criticism is just and, if it is unjust, forgive whoever utters it. The Apostolic Delegation of Istanbul affords opportunities for performing all fourteen works of mercy. "Blessed are the merciful" my dear Don Paolo! And pray for me too. Since, thank God, I never sought for or imagined what has happened, I enjoy great peace in my heart and serene trust in the Lord!' He signed the letter: 'Angelo Gius. Roncalli, Archbishop of Mesembria, now [writing] for the last time as Del. and Vic. Ap. in Istanbul.'

1945—1952

Papal Representative in France

1945

[51]   *Retreat at Solesmes during Holy Week, from*
26 March–2 April, 1945[1]

Thoughts and resolutions

(1) He that trusteth in God shall never fare the worse.[2] The events of my life during the last three months are a constant source of amazement and confusion to me. I have had to renew very frequently my good resolution not to preoccupy myself with my future or try to obtain anything for myself!

Here I am now, transported from Istanbul to Paris, with the initial difficulties of introduction overcome, I hope successfully. Once again my motto *Obœdientia et Pax* has brought a blessing. All this is a good reason for mortifying myself and seeking a more profound humility and trustful confidence, in order to consecrate to the Lord, for the sanctification of my own soul and the edification of others, the years I still have to live and serve Holy Church.

(2) I must not disguise from myself the truth: I am definitely approaching old age. My mind resents this and almost rebels, for I still feel so young, eager, agile and alert. But one look in my mirror disillusions me. This is the season of maturity; I must do more and better, reflecting that perhaps the time still granted to me for living is brief, and that I am drawing near to the gates of eternity. This thought caused Hezekiah to turn to the wall and weep.[3] I do not weep.

(3) No, I do not weep, and I do not even desire to live my life over again, so as to do better. I entrust to the Lord's mercy whatever I have done, badly or less than well, and I look to the future, brief or long as it may be here below, because I want to make it holy and a source of holiness to others.

(4) The Divine Office! Familiarity with these Benedictine monks and taking part in their liturgical services during Holy Week has given me

[1] Preacher: Abbot Germain Cozien, O.S.B. Solesmes is a Benedictine Abbey in France, renowned for its liturgical practice.
[2] Cf. Ecclus. 32: 28.   [3] Cf. 2 Kings 20: 2.

new and greater fervour in reading my Breviary. Now that I have found a study for myself near the chapel, I shall always say my Hours in the chapel, saying Matins the evening or the night before, and following the monastic rules about rising and remaining seated, especially at Matins. Even this external discipline of the body is an aid to spiritual recollection. I shall also make a more intense study of the Book of Psalms, in order to know and understand them more thoroughly. There is so much doctrine and so much poetry in the Psalms!

(5) In order to simplify everything, I shall bear in mind the theological and cardinal virtues. The first cardinal virtue is prudence. This is what Popes, Bishops, kings and commanders have found difficult, and it is in this that they frequently fail. It is the characteristic quality of the diplomat, so I must cultivate it with particular care. Every evening I must examine myself strictly on this point. My ready tongue often betrays me into saying far too much. Beware, beware! Know how to preserve silence, how to speak with moderation, how to refrain from judging people and their attitudes, except when this is an obligation imposed by Superiors, or for grave reasons.

On every occasion say less rather than more and always be afraid of saying too much, remembering St Isidore of Seville's praise of St Fulgentius. And be particularly careful to preserve charity. This is my Rule.

1947

[52]   *Retreat, 8–13 December, 1947. Paris, Clamart, at*
Villa Manresa, the House of the Jesuit Fathers[1]

Thoughts and resolutions

(1) This is the end of my third year as Nuncio in France. The sense of
my unworthiness keeps me good company: it makes me put all my trust
in God. The fact that I live constantly under obedience also gives me
courage and banishes all fear. The Lord has pledged himself to help me.
I bless him and thank him: 'his praise shall always be in my mouth.'[2]

(2) I have returned to the Exercises followed in common, according to
the old method. There are about thirty of us here, mostly secular priests,
a few religious, perhaps one missionary. The preacher is a young Jesuit,
Father de Soras, an assistant in Catholic Action, intelligent and full of
zeal. Good doctrine, expounded in an interesting way, but quite modern
in construction, speech and imagery. I made my confession to him,
covering the period from my Easter retreat at Solesmes, March, 1945,
until now. I feel content and encouraged.

(3) As regards my life, the central thought of these days is of my death,
which is perhaps near, and of my preparation for it. Now that I am in
my sixty-seventh year, anything may happen. This morning, 12 December, I celebrated Mass for 'the grace of a good death'. In the afternoon,
while adoring the Blessed Sacrament, I recited the penitential psalms
together with the Litany, and also the prayers for the departing soul.

I think this is a good devotional practice. I shall make frequent use of it.
This rendering myself familiar with the thought of death will lessen and
soften the shock when my hour comes.

(4) In view of this I have revised my will, which was drawn up in
1938, and needs to be adapted to the new circumstances of my family at
Sotto il Monte. The Lord sees my detachment, in a spirit of absolute
poverty, from the things of this world. If there is anything left it will be
given to the parish Home, and for the poor.

[1] The Superior of the House was Fr Foreau; the preacher, Fr de Soras.
[2] Psalm 33(34): 2.

(5) No temptation of honours in the world or in the Church can now affect me. I am still covered with confusion when I think of what the Holy Father has done for me, sending me to Paris. Whether I shall receive further promotion in the hierarchy or not is a matter of complete indifference to me. This gives me great peace of mind and makes it easier for me to do what I must do here, at all costs and at any risk. It will be wise for me to prepare myself for some great mortification or humiliation which will be the sign of my predestination. May heaven grant it may mark the beginning of real holiness in me, as was the case with those elect souls who, in the last years of their lives, received the touch of grace which made them truly holy. The thought of martyrdom frightens me. I distrust my resistance to physical pain. And yet, if I could bear Jesus the witness of my blood, oh what grace and what glory in heaven for me!

(6) I am fairly pleased with my devotional practices which bring me near to God. After having skimmed through the doctrine of various authors, I am now quite content with the Missal, the Breviary, the Bible, *The Imitation* and Bossuet's *Méditations sur l'Evangile*.[1] The holy liturgy and Sacred Scripture give me very rich pasture for my soul. So I am simplifying everything more and more and find it is better so. But I want to give more faithful and devout attention to the holy Eucharist, which I am blessed in being allowed to keep under my own roof, with direct access from my apartment. I shall take more pains about my visit to the Blessed Sacrament, making it more varied and attractive, with reverent and devout exercises such as the recital of the penitential psalms, the Way of the Cross, and the Office for the Dead. Are not all these contained in devotion to the holy Eucharist?

(7) I have filled my room with books which I love to read: all serious books dealing with the requirements of Catholic life. But these books are a source of distraction which often creates a disproportion between the time I must give primarily to my current affairs, to preparing reports to the Holy See and similar matters, and the time that in actual fact I spend in reading. Here a great effort is needed and I shall set about it with all my might. What is the use of all this anxiety to read and to know, if it is detrimental to my immediate responsibilities as Apostolic Nuncio?

(8) All goes well in my home. I bear with patience my own imperfections and those of my household. But I must remember St Isidore of Seville's praise of St Fulgentius, which I added to my notes of the retreat in 1942 at Istanbul. It is a wonderful passage. I select a few phrases very applicable to my life here in Paris and my relations with my colleagues

[1] Bossuet, *Méditations sur l'Evangile*, Paris, Desclée, 1903.

and my servants: 'He must live at peace with his brethren and never alienate any member', but above all it behoves the Bishop 'to be distinguished as much by his humility as by his authority, so that he may neither cause the vices of his subordinates to flourish, through his own excessive humility, nor exercise his authority with immoderate severity'. And I shall also remember to preserve charity, 'which excels all other gifts and without which all virtue is nothing'. For 'charity is the safeguard of chastity too', as St Isidore insists, and above all I must pay attention to his words: 'Besides all this he will preserve a perfect chastity', a chastity I want to obtain at all costs. So I shall keep a careful watch on conversation, which must be free from all rash judgments, and show no disrespect to anyone's episcopal dignity, or to our ecclesiastical Superiors, of high or low degree, on whom the Nunciature depends. Even if this costs me inner mortification and personal humiliation I am determined to succeed in this. My colleagues will understand and that will be a source of satisfaction. The same with regard to the 'kindness and charity' of the hospitality of the Nunciature. St Isidore says that the Bishop's house must 'give shelter to all'.

(9) My own temperament and training help me to show friendliness to all and forbearance, with courtesy and patience. I will not give up this way of behaving. St Francis de Sales is my great teacher. Oh if I could really be like him, in everything! In order not to disobey the Lord's great precept, I will be ready to endure even scorn and mockery. To be 'meek and lowly of heart'[1] is still the brightest glory of a Bishop and a papal representative. I leave to everyone else the superabundant cunning and so-called skill of the diplomat, and continue to be satisfied with my own *bonhomie* and simplicity of feeling, word and behaviour. In the end, all turns out for the good of those who are faithful to the teaching and example of the Lord.

(10) The longer I stay in France the more I admire this great country, and the more sincerely fond I grow of 'this most noble Gallic people'. I am, however, aware of a contrast, which sometimes gives me a twinge of conscience. I am delighted to praise these dear brave Catholics of France, but I feel it is my duty, one inherent in my mission, not to conceal, through a desire to be complimentary and not to give displeasure, a certain disquiet concerning the real state of this 'elder daughter of the Church' and certain obvious failings of hers. I am concerned about the practice of religion, the unsolved question of the schools, the insufficient numbers of the clergy and the spread of secularism and Communism.

---

[1] Matthew 11: 29.

My plain duty in this matter may be reduced to a question of form and measure. But the Nuncio is unworthy to be considered the ear and eye of Holy Church if he simply praises and extols all he sees, including even what is painful and wrong.

This means a continual watch over what I say. A gentle silence, without severity, kind words full of mercy and forbearance, will do more than statements, even if made in confidence and for a good purpose. For the rest, 'there is one who discerns and judges'.[1]

May the Sacred Heart of Jesus, in this land which he has especially honoured and blessed, the Holy Virgin, 'Queen of France', St Joseph, patron saint of diplomats and my special 'light and guide', with all the saintly protectors of France, be to me a help, comfort and blessing!

---

[1] Cf. John 8: 50.

1948

[53] *Annual retreat, 23–27 November, 1948. Benedictine*
monastery of the Sacred Heart at
En Calcat [Dourgne][1]

Notes

(1) This 25 November I enter the sixty-eighth year of my age. Yesterday evening I made my confession to the Father Prior, Germain Barbier of Auxerre. My mind is at peace. From my small Benedictine bed I have made my preparation for a good death, reciting very slowly the eight prayers set by Bossuet for this exercise.[2] I now consider my life has come to its end. Whatever else the Lord may send me, be it years or days, I shall receive as something extra. I must often repeat the words of St Paul, and live them: 'For I have died, and my life is hid with Christ in God' (cf. Col. 3:3).

(2) This state of mystical death now means, more decidedly than ever, absolute detachment from all earthly ties: from myself, my own pleasures, honours, successes, material and spiritual benefits, and complete indifference to and independence of all that is not the Lord's will concerning me.

(3) During this retreat I have read over again the notes written last year when I was with the Jesuit Fathers at the Villa Manresa at Clamart. I find they correspond entirely to my present circumstances. It is not necessary to repeat them. It will be enough if I re-read them every now and then, in order to correct myself and to find encouragement for further effort.

(4) The more mature I grow in years and experience the more I recognize that the surest way to make myself holy and to succeed in the service of the Holy See lies in the constant effort to reduce everything, principles, aims, position, business, to the utmost simplicity and tranquillity; I must always take care to strip my vines of all useless foliage and spreading tendrils, and concentrate on what is truth, justice and charity, above all charity. Any other way of behaving is nothing but affectation

---

[1] The retreat was given by the Abbot de Floris.
[2] 'Préparation à la mort', in *Méditations, cit.*, pp. 29–41.

and self-assertion; it soon shows itself in its true colours and becomes a hindrance and a mockery.

Oh, the simplicity of the Gospel, of *The Imitation of Christ*, of the *Little Flowers* of St Francis and of the most exquisite passages in St Gregory, in his *Moralia*: 'The simplicity of the just man is derided',[1] and the words that follow! I enjoy these pages more and more and return to them with joy. All the wiseacres of this world, and all the cunning minds, including those in Vatican diplomacy, cut such a poor figure in the light of the simplicity and grace shed by this great and fundamental doctrine of Jesus and his saints! This is the surest wisdom, that confounds the learning of this world and, with courtesy and true nobility, is consistent, equally well and even better, with the loftiest achievements in the sphere of science, even of secular and social science, in accordance with the requirements of time, place and circumstance. 'This is the height of philosophy, to be simple with prudence',[2] as was said by St John Chrysostom, my great patron saint of the East.

Lord Jesus, preserve in me the love and practice of this simplicity which, by keeping me humble, makes me more like you and draws and saves the souls of men.

(5) My own temperament inclines me towards compliance and a readiness to appreciate the good side of people and things, rather than to criticize and pronounce harsh judgments. This and the considerable difference in age, mine being more full of experience and profound understanding of the human heart, often make me feel painfully out of sympathy with my entourage. Any kind of distrust or discourtesy shown to anyone, especially to the humble, poor or socially inferior, every destructive or thoughtless criticism, makes me writhe with pain. I say nothing, but my heart bleeds. These colleagues of mine are good ecclesiastics: I appreciate their excellent qualities, I am very fond of them and they deserve all my affection. And yet they cause me a lot of suffering. On certain days and in certain circumstances I am tempted to react violently. But I prefer to keep silence, trusting that this will be a more eloquent and effective lesson. Could this be weakness on my part? I must, I will continue to bear this light cross serenely, together with the mortifying sense of my own worthlessness, and I will leave everything else to God, who sees into all hearts and shows them the refinements of his love.

(6) In this connection I reaffirm all that I wrote in no. 8 of my notes written during the Exercises at Villa Manresa at Clamart last year. How

---

[1] *Moralia*, 10, 29, 3 (P.L., LXXV, 947).
[2] *Hom. LXII al. LXIII in Matt.*, 4 (P.G., LVIII, 594-5).

well I remember, after more than forty years, the edifying conversations in the Bishop's residence at Bergamo with my revered Bishop Mgr Radini Tedeschi! Never was there a single reference to a Vatican official, from the Holy Father downwards, that was lacking in reverence, affection or respect. As for women, and everything to do with them, never a word, never; it was as if there were no women in the world. This absolute silence, even between close friends, about everything to do with women was one of the most profound and lasting lessons of my early years in the priesthood; and I am grateful still to the kind and illustrious man who taught me this discipline.

(7) I have not been able to read much Holy Scripture during this time. But I have carefully meditated upon the General Epistle of James the Less. Its five chapters are a wonderful summary of Christian life. The teaching about the exercise of charity, the right use of the tongue, the power of the man of faith, collaboration for peace, respect for others, the awful fate awaiting the rich, unjust and hateful man, and finally the appeal for trust, hopefulness and prayer . . . all this and more make it an incomparable treasury of directives and exhortations, particularly and alarmingly applicable to those of us who are ecclesiastics, and to lay folk of all times. One should learn it by heart and return to it from time to time to enjoy the heavenly doctrine line by line. At my time of life, on the threshold of my sixty-eighth year, there is nothing but old age before me. But wisdom is there in the divine book. Here is an example:

'Who is wise and understanding among you? By his good life let him show his good works in the meekness of wisdom. But if you have bitter jealousy and selfish ambition in your hearts, do not boast and be false to the truth. This wisdom is not such as comes down from above, but is earthly, unspiritual, devilish. For where jealousy and selfish ambition exist there will be disorder and every vile practice. But the wisdom from above is first pure, then peaceable, gentle, open to reason, full of mercy and good fruits, without uncertainty or insincerity. And the harvest of righteousness is sown in peace by those who make peace' (James 3 : 13–18).

19. In France, as Papal Nuncio, with President Auriol

20. Cardinal Patriarch of Venice. Arriving with Mgr Montini for the celebrations for the centenary of St Lawrence Guistiniani, 1956

1950

[54]   *Spiritual notes written during my brief retreat at*
Oran (Algeria), 6–9 April, 1950, Thursday,
Friday, Holy Saturday and Easter Day

Three days of rest at the end of my long journey in North Africa which
began on 19 March, the twenty-fifth anniversary of my episcopal consecration, and ends on 9 April, Easter Day.

The Bishop of Oran, Mgr Lacaste,[1] has welcomed me with brotherly
hospitality, for which I am grateful to him. In my prayers, meditations
and silences I share in the immense yearning of loving souls who, all over
the world and in all churches, are gathered around Jesus, suffering and
victorious, during these three holy days of prayer before Easter. It is now
a quarter of a century since Holy Church made me, poor and unworthy
as I am, a Bishop, and I like to think of my past, my present, and my
future.

Holy Thursday: my past

I have brought with me on this journey the bundles of spiritual reflections made during these years, 1925–1950, to jolt me out of any complacency and inspire me with repentance and an increase of episcopal
fervour, notes written on the various retreats that I was able to make
from year to year in Bulgaria, Turkey and France. I have read them all
over again, with calm, as if in a confession, and I recite the Miserere,
which is all my own, and the Magnificat, which is entirely the Lord's,
as my penance and as an exercise in sincere and trustful humility. At a
distance of twenty-five years I have re-read no. 4 of the first notes I
made at Villa Carpegna, 13–17 March, 1925, while preparing for my
impending episcopal consecration which took place on 19 March, the
feast of St Joseph, at San Carlo al Corso.[2] I then resolved: I will often

[1] Mgr Bertrand Lacaste, born in Accous, diocese of Bayonne (France), appointed
Bishop of Oran on 29 December, 1945.
[2] See pp. 204ff.

re-read chapter IX, book III of *The Imitation of Jesus Christ*: 'That all things are to be referred to God as to their final end.' This has impressed me profoundly in the solitude of these last few days. Indeed, in these few words there is everything! It was on the eve of my new life that I wrote this; I feel the same way now, and so I enjoy returning to that time and reconsidering this teaching of Christ's after a quarter of a century of trials, weaknesses and recoveries, although, thanks to the Lord, my will has remained firm, faithful and convinced, in spite of all the seductions and temptations of the spirit of this world.

O Jesus, how much I thank you for having kept me faithful to this principle: 'From me, as from a living fountain, the humble and the great, the poor and the rich draw the water of life.'[1] Ah, I am numbered among the humble and the poor! In Bulgaria, the difficulties of my circumstances, even more than the difficulties caused by men, and the monotony of that life which was one long sequence of daily pricks and scratches, cost me much in mortification and silence. But your grace preserved my inner joy, which helped me to hide my difficulties and distress. In Turkey the responsibilities of my pastoral work were at once a torment and a joy to me. Could I not, should I not, have done more, have made a more decided effort and gone against the inclination of my nature? Did the search for calm and peace, which I considered to be more in harmony with the Lord's spirit, not perhaps mask a certain unwillingness to take up the sword, and a preference for what was easiest and most convenient for me, even if gentleness has indeed been defined as the fulness of strength? O my Jesus, you search all hearts: the exact point at which even the striving after virtue may lead to failure or excess is known to you alone.

I feel it is right not to boast of anything but to attribute all to your grace 'without which man has nothing, and very strictly do you demand my thanks in return'.[2] So my Magnificat is complete, as it should be. I like so much the expression: 'My merit, your mercy' and St Augustine's words: 'When you crown our merit you are crowning your own gifts.'[3]

My gratitude to you will never cease, Jesus: 'For divine charity overcomes all and enlarges the powers of the soul. I judge rightly, I rejoice in you alone, in you alone I hope, "for none is good save God alone" (Luke 18: 19), who is to be praised above all else, and blessed in all things.'[4] So, as the conclusion of my twenty-five years as Bishop, I put the last

---

[1] *Imitation*, III, IX, 6.   [2] *Ibid.*, III, IX, 8–9.
[3] Cf. *Sermone ad populum CLXX*, 10 (P.L., XXXVIII, 392).
[4] Cf. *Imitation*, III, IX, 12–13.

words of the same little chapter of *The Imitation* with which I began them. I still have, to the proper mortification of my spirit, the memory of my faults, 'in thought, word and deed', which are so many, so very many in twenty-five years. But I still have also my unalterable faith in my daily Sacrifice, the divine and immaculate Host, offered 'for my countless sins, offences and negligences'. Twenty-five years of episcopal Masses, offered with all the splendour of good intentions, and all the dust of the road, oh, what a mystery of mingled grace and shame! The grace of Jesus' tender love given as 'Bishop and Shepherd' to his chosen priest, the shame of the priest who finds his consolation only in trustful self-surrender.

Good Friday: my present

Last night I said Matins by myself; this morning in chapel I said the Hours with the Miserere four times and today's liturgy, uniting myself in spirit as I followed it in my Missal, as if I were attending the ceremony in some great church, or as if I were still presiding over it in Sofia, or in the Cathedral of the Holy Spirit at Istanbul.

My present: here I am then, still alive, in my sixty-ninth year, prostrate over the crucifix, kissing the face of Christ and his sacred wounds, kissing his heart, laid bare in his pierced side; here I am showing my love and grief. How could I not feel grateful to Jesus, finding myself still young and robust of body, spirit and heart? 'Know thyself': this keeps me humble and without pretensions. Some people feel admiration and affection for my humble person; but thanks be to God, I still blush for myself, my insufficiencies and my unworthiness in this important position where the Holy Father has placed me, and still keeps me, out of the kindness of his heart. For some time past I have cultivated simplicity, which comes very easily to me, cheerfully defying all those clever people who, looking for the qualities required in a diplomat of the Holy See, prefer the outer covering to the sound, ripe fruit beneath. And I keep true to my principle which seems to me to have a place of honour in the Sermon on the Mount: blessed are the poor, the meek, the peacemakers, the merciful, those who hunger and thirst for righteousness, the pure in heart, the suffering and the persecuted.[1] My present, then, is spent in faithful service to Christ, who was obedient and was crucified, words I repeat so often at this season: 'Christ was made obedient.'[2] So I must be meek and humble like him, glowing with divine charity, ready for sacrifice or for death, for him or for his Church.

[1] Cf. Matthew 5: 3-10.   [2] Cf. Phil. 2: 8.

This journey in North Africa has brought home to me more vividly the problem of the conversion of the peoples without the faith. The whole life and purpose of the Church, of the priesthood, of true and good diplomacy is there: 'Give me souls; take all the rest.'[1]

Holy Saturday: my future

When one is nearly seventy, one cannot be sure of the future. 'The years of our life are three score and ten, and even if we are strong enough to reach the age of eighty, yet these years are but toil and vanity; they are soon passed and we also pass away' (cf. Psalm 89: 10–11). So it is no use nursing any illusions: I must make myself familiar with the thought of the end, not with dismay which saps the will, but with confidence which preserves our enthusiasm for living, working and serving. Some time ago I resolved to bear constantly in mind this reverent expectation of death, this joy[2] which ought to be my soul's last happiness when it departs from this life. I need not become wearisome to others by speaking frequently of this; but I must always think of it, because the consideration of death, the *judicium mortis*, when it has become a familiar thought, is good and useful for the mortification of vanity and for infusing into everything a sense of moderation and calm. As regards temporal matters, I will revise my will once more. I am poor, thank God, and I mean to die poor.

As for my soul, I shall try to make the flame burn more brightly, making the most of the time that remains as it passes more swiftly away. Therefore, total detachment from the things of this world, dignities, honours, things that are precious in themselves or greatly prized. I want to redouble my efforts to complete the publication of the *Visita Apostolica di San Carlo Borromeo a Bergamo*, but I am also ready to accept the mortification of having to give this up.

There are some who, to flatter me, speak of the Cardinalate. Nothing here of any interest to me. I repeat what I have already written. Were this not to happen, as is quite possible, I shall think this also was predestined, and thank God for it.

For the rest, on my return to Paris I shall resume my ordinary life without impatience, but with absolute fidelity to my duty and to the service of the Holy See, with care, with charity and patience and in close union with Jesus, my King, my Master, my God, with Mary, my sweet Mother, and with St Joseph, my dear friend, model and protector.

---

[1] Cf. Gen. 14: 21.
[2] St Gregory the Great, *Hom. in Evang.*, XIII, 3 (P.L., LXXVI, 1124).

I must comfort myself with the thought that the souls that I have known, loved and still love are now almost all in the other world, waiting and praying for me. Will the Lord call me soon to the heavenly fatherland? Here I am, ready. I beg him only to take me at a good moment. Has he perhaps reserved for me many more years of life? I will be grateful for them, but always implore him not to leave me on this earth when I have become an encumbrance and of no further use to Holy Church. But in this also the Lord's holy will, that is enough.

I end these notes to the sound of the Easter bells ringing from the Cathedral of the Sacred Heart near by, and I remember with joy my last Easter homily in Istanbul,[1] when I preached on the words of St Gregory Nazianzen, 'the will of God is our peace'.

[1] 9 April, 1944.

1952

55

Retreat at Montmartre, with the Carmelite nuns
Thursday, Friday and Saturday in Holy Week
10–12 April, 1952

Three days that have been rather like the days Our Lord spent in the tomb, because I thought it best to admit my nuns of the Nunciature to the Maundy Thursday Mass. In the afternoon I visited on foot four churches of the sacred city: Saint-Pierre, Saint-Jean, Notre Dame de Clignancourt, and the Martyrium. On Friday two more hours in the afternoon were spent presiding at the liturgy in the Byzantine rite at Saint-Julien-le-Pauvre, and making my confession to Father Fugazza at the Church of the Lazarist Fathers. However, the continuity of recollection was not too greatly disturbed. I am particularly happy to have sought shelter, like a swallow, under the roof of the great basilica of the Sacred Heart and to be about to end this retreat in the splendours of the holy eve of the Resurrection, according to the ancient ceremonial of the recently restored Easter Vigil. The circumstances of this retreat have prevented me from making many notes, either for my examination of conscience or for meditation. I will just put down a few thoughts that may be good for my soul if I re-read them every now and then.

(1) Let us give thanks. The ordinary term of human life, seventy years, is now completed. I think back on all my seventy years, I must admit, 'in bitterness of soul'.[1] Alas! I still feel shame and grief for my 'countless sins, offences and negligences', for the little I have achieved and the much more that I could, and should, have done in the service of the Lord, of Holy Church and of souls. But at the same time I cannot forget the wealth of graces and mercies which Jesus has lavished so generously upon me, contrary to all my deserts: 'Therefore His praise shall be always in my mouth.'[2]

(2) 'Simplicity of heart and speech!' The older I grow the more clearly I perceive the dignity and the winning beauty of simplicity in thought.

[1] Cf. Isaiah 38: 15.   [2] Psalm 33(34): 2.

conduct and speech: a desire to simplify all that is complicated and to treat everything with the greatest naturalness and clarity, without wrapping things up in trimmings and artificial turns of thought and phrase. 'To be simple with prudence'—the motto is St John Chrysostom's.[1] What a wealth of doctrine in these two phrases!

(3) Friendliness, serenity and imperturbable patience! I must always remember that 'a soft answer turns away wrath'.[2] What bitterness is caused by a rough, abrupt or impatient manner! Sometimes the fear of being underestimated as a person of little worth tempts us to give ourselves airs and assert ourselves a little. But this is contrary to my nature. To be simple, with no pretensions, requires no effort from me. This is a great gift that the Lord has bestowed on me: I want to preserve it and to be worthy of it.

(4) I must have a great understanding and respect for the French people. My prolonged stay with them enables me to appreciate the very noble spiritual qualities of this people and the fervour of Catholics of every school of thought. At the same time, however, it has enabled me to see their failings and excesses also. This means I have to be very careful in what I say. I am free to form my own judgment, but I must beware of any criticism, however slight and friendly, that might wound their susceptibilities. Oh, this never doing or saying to others what we would not wish to have done or said to us! We are all rather remiss about this. Great care then to avoid the slightest expression that might lessen the effectiveness or the dignity of our conduct. I say this for myself, but I must be the guide and example of those around me, my colleagues. In every case, a caress is always better than a scratch.

(5) Greater alacrity in the more important business, especially the nominations of Bishops, relations with the Holy See, and dealing with timely and important information. No haste, but no delay. I will make this the special object of my daily examinations.

(6) In all things 'consider the end'.[3] The end is drawing nearer as my days follow one another. I must be more concerned with the thought of imminent death, and with dying well, than with lulling myself with dreams of a longer life. But I must not be sad about this or talk too much about it. 'The will of God is our peace', always, in life and, still more, in death.

(7) The thought of what lies in store for me, honours, humiliations, opposition, etc., nothing of all this causes me any anxiety or preoccupation.

[1] Cf. note 2, p. 271.   [2] Cf. Proverbs 15: 1.   [3] Cf. Aesop, *Fabulae*, 22: 5.

This year I hope to complete the publication of the *Atti della Visita Apostolica di San Carlo Borromeo a Bergamo*. This satisfies my ambition as a good Bergamasque, and I desire nothing else.

(8) My only wish is that my life should end in a holy manner. I tremble at the thought of having to bear pain, responsibilities or difficulties beyond my poor capacity, but I trust in the Lord, without claiming any successes or extraordinary or brilliant merit.

(9) My spiritual life must be intensified. No overloading with devotions of a novel and secondary character, but fidelity to those which are fundamental, with passionate fervour. Holy Mass, the Breviary, the rosary, meditations, the reading of good books, close and frequent union with Jesus in the Blessed Sacrament.

(10) This retreat has not been marked by laborious meditations and practices, but in re-reading my notes of past retreats I have found in them a motive and encouragement to 'gather speed as I near the end'. I think my conscience is quiet, and I trust in Jesus and in his glorious and well-beloved Mother who is my Mother too, in my darling St Joseph, and in St John the Baptist around whom I like to see my own kith and kin gathered.[1] And now I get ready to go up to the Church of the Sacred Heart, where they are awaiting me for a solemn, splendid night that is meant to be the symbol of the resurrection of souls, of Holy Church and all nations. The Cross of Jesus, the Heart of Jesus, the grace of Jesus: these are everything in this world, and this is the beginning of future glory, reserved for the elect for evermore. 'Heart of Jesus, our life and our resurrection, our peace and our reconciliation, the salvation of all who hope in you, the hope of all who die in you, the joy of all the saints. Heart of Jesus, have mercy on us.'

---

[1] His father's name was Giovanni Battista (John Baptist).

1953—1958

Cardinal Patriarch of Venice

1953

56

Retreat with the Bishops of the Province of the Three Venetias, at Fietta, in the Villa of the Venetian Seminary, 15–21 May, 1953 Preacher, Father Federico da Baselga, Capuchin[1]

Notes and jottings

(1) In April last year I sought shelter under the roof of the Sacred Heart at Montmartre in Paris, and May this year finds me here at the foot of the Grappa, Cardinal and Patriarch of Venice. What a transformation in all that surrounds me! I hardly know what to dwell on more: on how 'I rejoiced when they said to me . . .'[2] with all that follows, or on the sense of insufficiency which inspires feelings of humility and trust in the Lord. It is he who has really done all, and done it without my help, for I could never have imagined or desired such greatness. I am happy also because this meekness and humility do not go against the grain with me but come easily to my nature. Why should I be vain or proud of anything, my Lord? Is not 'my merit' all 'God's mercy?'

(2) It is interesting to note that Providence has brought me back to where I began to exercise my priestly vocation, that is to pastoral work. Now I am ministering directly to souls. To tell the truth, I have always believed that, for an ecclesiastic, diplomacy (so-called!) must be imbued with the pastoral spirit; otherwise it is of no use and makes a sacred mission look ridiculous. Now I am confronted with the Church's real interests, relating to her final purpose, which is to save souls and guide them to heaven. This is enough for me and I thank the Lord for it. I said so in St Mark's in Venice on 15 March, the day of my solemn entry. I desire and think of nothing else but to live and die for the souls entrusted to me. 'The good shepherd gives his life for his sheep . . . I am come that

---

[1] The heading also contained a list of those present: the Archbishops of Trent and Gorizia, the Bishops of Vicenza, Padua, Chioggia, Belluno, Vittorio Veneto, Concordia and Rovigo, and the Cardinal Patriarch.
[2] Psalm 121(122): 1.

they may have life, and may have it more abundantly' (John 10: 11 and 10).

(3) I am beginning my direct ministry at an age—seventy-two years —when others end theirs. So, *I find myself on the threshold of eternity.* O Jesus, chief Shepherd and Bishop of our souls, the mystery of my life and death is in your hands, close to your heart. On the one hand I tremble at the approach of my last hour; on the other hand I trust in you and only look one day ahead. I feel I am in the same condition as St Aloysius Gonzaga, that is, I must go on with what I have to do, always striving after perfection but thinking still more of God's mercy.

In the few years I have still to live, *I want to be a holy pastor,* in the full sense of the word, like the Blessed Pius X, my predecessor, and the revered Cardinal Ferrari, and my own Mgr Radini Tedeschi while he lived, and as he would have remained had he lived longer. 'So help me God.'

(4) During this retreat I have been reading St Gregory and St Bernard, both of them concerned with the *interior life* of the pastor, which must not be affected by external material cares. My day must be one long prayer: prayer is the breath of my life. I propose to recite all fifteen decades of the rosary every day, if possible in the chapel before the Blessed Sacrament, with the intention of recommending to Our Lord and to Our Lady the more urgent needs of my children in Venice and in the diocese: the clergy, young seminarists, consecrated virgins, public authorities and poor sinners.

I have already two painful problems here, amidst all the splendour of ecclesiastical state, and the veneration shown to me as Cardinal and Patriarch: the scantiness of my revenue and the throng of poor folk with their requests for employment and financial help.

As for the revenue, there is nothing to prevent me from improving it, both for my own sake and for my successors. But I prefer to bless the Lord for this poverty, which is rather humiliating and often embarrassing. It draws me closer to Jesus, who was poor, and to St Francis and, after all, I am sure I shall not die of hunger. O blessed poverty, which ensures for me a greater blessing on everything else and on what is most important in my pastoral work!

(6) My triumphal entry into Venice and these first two months' contact with my children make me realize the natural goodwill the Venetians feel for their Patriarch: they give me great encouragement. I do not want to set myself any new precepts to follow. I shall continue on my own way and according to my own temperament. Humility,

simplicity, fidelity to the Gospel in word and works, with unfaltering gentleness, inexhaustible patience and fatherly and insatiable enthusiasm for the welfare of souls. I see that they like to listen to me and that my simple words go straight to their hearts. But I will take great care to prepare my sermons well, so that what I say may not be lacking in dignity and may be more and more edifying.

(7) My episcopal household will gradually take shape. If the Holy Father grants me the Auxiliary Bishop that I need I shall be able to arrange everything for the good of all.

(8) Sometimes the thought of the short time still left to me tempts me to slacken my efforts. But with God's help I will not give in. 'I neither fear to die nor refuse to live.'[1] The Lord's will is still my peace.

The arc of my humble life, honoured far beyond my deserts by the Holy See, rose in my native village and now curves over the domes and pinnacles of St Mark's.

I want to add to my will the request that I should have a resting place reserved for me in the crypt of the basilica, near the tomb of the Evangelist, who has now become so dear and familiar to my soul and to my prayers. Mark, son to St Peter, and his disciple and interpreter.

---

[1] Cf. *Sulpicii Severi Epistola III ad Bassulam socram suam*, 14 (P.L., XX, 182): '*Nec mori timuerit, nec vivere recusarit.*'

1954[1]

57

Retreat at Torreglia in 1954, 6–12 June
Preacher, Mgr Landucci

No notes.

I have made my will instead. For everything else I have returned to the conclusions drawn from last year's Exercises. In fact during these days I have found very helpful the meditation well divided among the twelve chapters of the second book of *The Imitation of Jesus Christ*: 'Admonitions concerning the inner life'.

(1) Of the inner life of the soul.
(2) Of humble submission.
(3) Of a good, peaceable man.
(4) Of a pure mind and simple intention.
(5) Of the consideration of one's self.
(6) Of the joy of a good conscience.
(7) Of the love of Jesus above all else.
(8) Of close friendship with Jesus.
(9) Of the lack of all comfort.
(10) Of gratitude for the grace of God.
(11) Of how few there are who love the Cross of Jesus.
(12) Of the royal road of the holy Cross.

---

[1] On 10 August, very simply, Cardinal Roncalli celebrated the fiftieth anniversary of his priestly ordination, in the peace of Sotto il Monte. That day he made the following note: 'My golden jubilee as a priest at Sotto il Monte, 10 August, 1954. A wonderfully bright sky after beneficial night showers. The sound of the Angelus from S. Giovanni roused me at once with a "Laus tibi, Domine". There followed an hour of prayer in the chapel, with the Breviary Lessons about St Lawrence in my hand, on my lips, in my heart: pages that are a poem. What is my poor life of fifty years of priesthood? A faint reflection of this poem: "My merit—God's mercy." '

1955

[58]   *Retreat with the episcopate of the Three Venetias*
Villa Immacolata of Torreglia (Padua)
from 20–25 May, 1955[1]
Preacher, Father Riccardo Lombardi, S.J.

Notes and resolutions

(1) I am seventy-four years old. The same age as St Lawrence Giustiniani, the first Patriarch of Venice, when he died (8 January, 1456). I am preparing the celebration of the fifth centenary of his blessed death. Is not this a good way of preparing for my own?

A grave and salutary thought for me. 'I neither fear to die nor refuse to live.'[2] But the life still left to me will be a joyful preparation for death. I accept death and await it with confidence—not in myself, for I am a poor sinner, but in the infinite mercy of the Lord to whom I owe all that I am, all that I have. 'I will sing of the mercies of God for ever.'[3]

(2) The thought of death has kept me good, if melancholy, company since the day of my nomination as Cardinal and Patriarch of Venice. In seventeen months I have lost three dear sisters; two of them especially dear because they lived solely for the Lord and for me; for more than thirty years they looked after my house in tranquil expectation of spending their last years with their brother the Bishop. Losing them has been a great blow to me: it is my heart, not my reasoning mind, that has grieved. Although I never cease praying for them, I love to think of them in heaven praying for me, even more delighted than of old to help me and await me there. O Ancilla, O Maria, now reunited in the joyous radiance of eternity with the other two, Teresa and Enrica, so good and God-fearing all four of you, I remember you always, I mourn for you and at the same time I bless you.[4]

[1] This heading also contained a list of those present: 'Roncalli, De Ferrari, Ambrosi, Urbani, Mantiero, Mazzocco, Bortignon, Zaffonato, Zinato, Piassentini, Muccin, Gargitter, Santin, De Zanche, Cicutini.'

[2] Cf. note 1, p. 284.   [3] Psalm 88(89): 2.

[4] Enrica died in 1918; Ancilla and Teresa in 1954; Maria in 1955. Ancilla and Maria looked after Pope John's home at Sotto il Monte.

Now I clearly see that this separation too was decreed by the Lord so that, as I devote myself to the spiritual welfare of my Venetian children, I may seem to them to be like Melchisedech, with 'no father, no mother, no genealogy'.[1]

My relations I must of course love in the Lord, all the more so because they are poor, and very worthy Christian folk everyone of them, and they have never given me anything but respect and joy, but I must always live apart from them, as an example to these good Venetian clergy who, for various reasons, some of them valid, have with them too many members of their families, who are a considerable encumbrance to their pastoral ministry in life, in death, and after death.

(3) Of my pastoral life, my only life now, what can I say? I am content because it really gives me great joy. I do not need to use harsh measures to keep good order. Watchful kindness, patience and forbearance get one along much farther and more quickly than severity and the rod. I have no illusions or doubts about this.

But I am dismayed at the thought of not being able to look into everything, and more thoroughly—not being able to get everything done; I am always tempted to indulge my peaceable instincts which lead me to prefer a quiet life rather than risk making precarious moves. Cardinal Gusmini's[2] principle: 'A Bishop should never give an order unless he is sure it will be obeyed' may perhaps accord too easily with my natural inclination to fear that the reaction may cause an increase rather than a reform of the evils that are to be corrected.

But the shepherd must above all be good, very good. On the other hand, although he does not, like the hireling, leave his flock to the wolf, he runs the risk of becoming useless and ineffective if he nods over his task. O Jesus, good shepherd, pour your own spirit into me, that these last years of my life may be a sacrifice and burnt offering for the souls of my beloved Venetians.

(4) I will renew once more, and now more earnestly than ever, my effort to attain a more intense interior and supernatural life. The passing of years makes everything in my life of prayer more enjoyable: Holy Mass, the Breviary, the rosary, the company of the Blessed Sacrament in my home. To be close to God from morning to night, and during the night also, always with God or the things of God, gives me constant

---

[1] Hebrews 7: 3.

[2] Mgr Giorgio Gusmini (1855-1921), a native of Bergamo; a parish priest in his own diocese, where he promoted social services; Bishop of Foligno in 1910; Archbishop of Bologna in 1914; Cardinal in 1915.

joy, and helps me to be calm and patient at all times. But the work of my ministry, and of all that more or less concerns it, takes up too much of my time, almost stifling me and robbing me of the calm and tranquillity I need for my pious exercises or devotions. I shall lay more stress on these practices, at least on the rosary which I mean to have recited in common with all the members of my household. This will serve as a remembrance of this retreat of mine. The family rosary with my secretary, nuns, household staff and guests.

(5) These Exercises with Father Lombardi have been conducted by him from the point of view not of the individual Bishop but of the episcopate in general, and the Venetian episcopate in particular, confronted with the problems of the 'Better World'.

[. . .] Here also it is well to 'test everything: hold fast what is good'.[1] I must not lose myself in details and points of secondary importance. This Movement bears the seal of the approval and encouragement of the Holy Father, Pius XII, who initiated it. So we are on the right road. Here also are the seven lamps of sanctification: the theological and cardinal virtues. Ah my soul, your time on this earth is drawing to a close: your steps are turned towards the sunset. Go bravely forward: you will not be left without light, grace or joy. In the expectation of heaven even the Cross will be welcome and a source of strength.

(6) One of the first fruits of these reflections with Father Lombardi is my resolution to occupy myself more busily with religious schools of all kinds. For this I shall avail myself of the help of my Auxiliary Bishop[2] who already presides over the diocesan religious education office.

---

[1] 1 Thess. 5: 21.

[2] Mgr Augusto Gianfranceschi, Titular Bishop of Emeria in 1953; transferred to Cesena in 1957.

1956

[59]   *Retreat in the seminary at S. Maria della Salute*
(Venice), 11–15 June, 1956

Brief notes

(1) My pilgrimage to Fatima[1] prevented me from joining in the course of Exercises arranged for the excellent Bishops, my colleagues of the Venetian provinces, held at Torreglia and preached by Mgr Bosio, Archbishop of Chieti.

I have taken the opportunity to join my diocesan priests who are gathered here in the seminary for the Exercises preached by Mgr Pardini, Bishop of Jesi. He is an excellent preacher of the Exercises to the clergy.

But being with my dear priests and sharing their perplexities has robbed me of the tranquillity I needed in order to think of myself. So another time I shall endeavour to visit my priests and stay with them at their various courses or wherever they may be, and more at my leisure. But for my retreats I shall stay with the Bishops, to attend exclusively to my own soul.

(2) With regard to practical proposals for the year I have confirmed my renewed resolution to achieve what has been the object of so many of my efforts, so frequently repeated, to improve my spiritual life: the perfection of mildness, patience and charity in my prayers as a priest and in my work for souls and for Holy Church, day by day. And this at all costs, at the risk of seeming to be and being considered a person of little worth, with little to give.

(3) This sense of my own insufficiency, which is always with me and preserves me from vanity, is a great gift from the Lord: it keeps me simple and saves me from making a fool of myself.

I would not mind being thought a fool if this could help people to understand what I firmly believe and shall assert as long as I live, that the Gospel teaching is unalterable, and that in the Gospel Jesus teaches us to be *gentle and humble*; naturally this is not the same thing as being weak

[1] 9–15 May.

and easy-going. Everything that smacks of pretentiousness and self-assertion is only selfishness and comes to nought.

(4) I am convinced that it is not right for me to make the Exercises together with my priests. I have to listen to the requests of every one of them, and so I have no time or tranquillity left to look after my own spiritual needs. And yet I should so much like to preach the Exercises myself, but with time for calm and long preparation, 'proximate and remote'.

The memory of Fatima and of the joy I felt there makes me feel an even greater veneration for the Lord's command 'to preach the good news to the poor and to comfort the broken-hearted'.[1]

---

[1] Cf. Luke 4: 18.

1957

*Retreat with the episcopate of the Province of the
Three Venetias, 2–7 June, 1957, at Torreglia
Preacher, Mgr van Lierde, Sacristan to His Holiness*

Personal notes

(1) 'Give me more light as evening falls.'[1] O Lord, we are now in the
evening of our life. I am in my seventy-sixth year. Life is a great gift
from our heavenly Father. Three-quarters of my contemporaries have
passed over to the far shore. So I too must always be ready for the great
moment. The thought of death does not alarm me. Now one of my five
brothers also has gone before me, and he was the youngest but one, my
beloved Giovanni. Ah, what a good life and what a fine death! My health
is excellent and still robust, but I cannot count on it. I want to hold myself
ready to reply *adsum*[2] at any, even the most unexpected moment.

(2) Old age, likewise a great gift of the Lord's, must be for me a
source of *tranquil inner joy*, and a reason for trusting day by day in the
Lord himself, to whom I am now turned as a child turns to his father's
open arms.

(3) My poor life, now such a long one, has unwound itself as easily as
a ball of string, under the sign of simplicity and purity. It costs me nothing
to acknowledge and repeat that *I am nothing* and *worth precisely nothing*.

The Lord caused me to be born of poor folk, and he has seen to all my
needs. I have left it to him. As a young priest I was struck by the motto
Obœdientia et Pax of Cesare Baronius,[3] who used to say it as he bowed
his head to kiss the foot of St Peter's statue—and I have left everything
to God and have allowed myself to be led in perfect obedience to the
plans of Providence. Truly, 'the will of God is my peace'. And my hope
is all in the mercy of God, who wanted me to be his priest and minister.

---

[1] From Sunday Office, for Nones (*ad nonam*), hymn: *Rerum, Deus, tenax vigor*.

[2] *Adsum*, 'I am here,' is the response the young cleric makes to the call of his Bishop at
his ordination to each of the minor orders he receives on the way to the priesthood.

[3] Cf. A. Roncalli, *Il Cardinale Cesare Baronio, cit.*, p. 46.

He has been too kind about my 'countless sins, offences and negligences'[1] and he still keeps me full of life and vigour.

(4) I think the Lord Jesus has in store for me, before I die, for my complete mortification and purification and in order to admit me to his everlasting joy, some great suffering and affliction of body and spirit. Well, I accept everything and with all my heart, if it is for his glory and the good of my soul and for the souls of my dear spiritual children. I fear my weakness in bearing pain; I implore him to help me, for I have little faith in myself, but complete faith in the Lord Jesus. 'The white-robed army of martyrs praise you.'[2]

(5) There are two gates to paradise: innocence and penance. Which of us, poor frail creatures, can expect to find the first of these wide open? But we may be sure of the other: Jesus passed through it, bearing his Cross in atonement for our sins, and he invites us to follow him. But following him means doing penance, letting oneself be scourged, and scourging oneself a little too.

My Jesus, amidst the many joys of my episcopal ministry there are also continual opportunities for mortification. I welcome them. Sometimes they hurt my pride a little, but I rejoice at this suffering and repeat before God: 'It is good for me to be humiliated.' St Augustine's great saying is always in my mind and comforts me.

---

[1] Roman Missal. Offertory prayer.   [2] From the *Te Deum*.

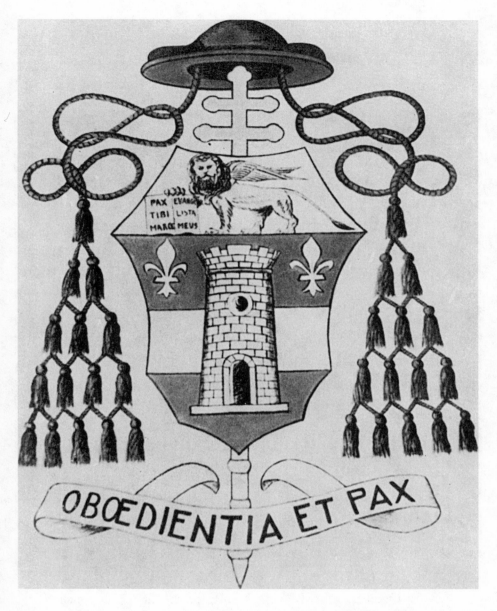

PAX EVAN
TIBI LISTA
MARCE MEVS

OBŒDIENTIA ET PAX

21. His coat of arms as Cardinal Patriarch of Venice. 'I insert into my coat of
arms the words *Oboedientia et pax* . . . . These words are in a way
my own history and my life.'

22. 12 October, 1958. Leaving Venice for the Conclave which
was to elect him Pope

1958

[61]   *Retreat at [Col Draga di] Possagno, House of the*
Sacred Heart, with the Cavanis Fathers
22–26 September, 1958. The preacher, invited by
me, was Mgr Aurelio Signora, Archbishop,[1]
Prelate of Pompei

(1) This is a most pleasant situation, high up on the slopes of the Grappa.
I was welcomed by these excellent Fathers of the Istituto Cavanis.
Father Pellegrino Bolzonello, the Superior, most friendly and courteous.
With me are the pro-Vicar, Mgr Gottardi, Mgr Capovilla and the staff
of the Curia and several parish priests. Among the Canons, Mgr Vecchi,
Mgr Spavento, etc. Many of my young priests too. Mgr Signora is good
and preaches well. His voice was a little difficult for me, as I had to listen
from where I was placed at the side, but his doctrine was excellent, well
expressed and presented with obviously profound and sincere conviction.
There were also some priests from Vittorio Veneto. Altogether a serious
and worthy group.

(2) Alas! I found, and for the second time, that I need a 'lonely place'
to 'rest a while'.[2] To please those present I also had to speak to them. The
first evening: the office of the priesthood;[3] the second: the mind of a
priest; the third: the five points from my talk at Faenza;[4] the fourth:
the priest's heart, character and conversation, strongly emphasizing
meekness and humility, character and conversation, with references to
courtesy and to preaching.

No, this will not do. For the Exercises I must be alone, free from curial
business and in silence and tranquillity, occupied only with myself and
my own soul.

---

[1] Titular Archbishop of Pompei.   [2] Cf. Mark 6: 31.
[3] Ecclus. 45: 19.
[4] Cf. Angelo Giuseppe Cardinal Roncalli, *Scritti e discorsi, cit.*, vol. III: *1957–1958*,
Rome, Edizioni Paoline, 1959, pp. 634–44.

(3) My advanced age means that I should now be much more chary of accepting engagements to preach outside my own diocese. I have to write everything down first, and this is a great effort, besides the constant humiliation of feeling my own insufficiency. May the Lord help me and forgive me.

1958—1963

Pope

1958

62

Retreat at the Vatican[1] for Advent
30 November–6 December, 1958
Preacher, Father Messori Roncaglia, S.J.

Sunday, 30 November, in the evening
Quotation from Mgr Radini's little book: *Principio e Fondamento*. Difference between 'e' (and) and 'o' (or).[2]

Monday, 1
The Father, Creator. First Sermon: cancelled for the visit of the Shah of
Persia, Reza Pahlevi.

Second sermon: man, God's creature.

Third sermon: the curve and the end of the arc, in
the relations between God and
man.

Tuesday, 2
1. The law of God.
2. Sin.
3. Gravity of sin.
4. Hell.

Wednesday, 3 December
1. The mercy of God.[3]

---

[1] In the Matilda chapel of the Apostolic Palace.

[2] Mgr Giacomo Maria Radini Tedeschi, in his little book, *Gli Esercizi spirituali secondo S. Ignazio di Lojola. Commento*, Milan, Gattoni, 1914, pp. 91–2, in the chapter 'Principio e Fondamento' (Principle and foundation) says: '. . . the truth is expressed, not in a disjunctive but in a conjunctive way: not with an "or" but with an "and". We say "Principle *and* foundation" not "Principle *or* foundation".'

[3] The next sheet is blank. Probably the author wished to add more to this note.

Thursday, 4

1. The two standards: the work of the devil and how to resist him.
2. The apostolate: its motives, the example of Jesus, principles to be followed.
3. The priest at prayer.
4. The holy Eucharist makes the priest.

Friday, 5

1. The Passion of Christ, physical suffering.
2. The Passion of Christ, moral suffering.
3. The glory of Christ and for us paradise.
4. The love of God which kindles and consumes all things.

1959

63

Retreat in the Vatican
29 November–5 December, 1959. Preacher at my
invitation, Mgr Giuseppe Angrisani, Bishop of
Casale, who made an edifying impression on all

Ignatian inspiration. As the general foundation for meditations and instructions: Holy Scripture, the Gospel, St Paul and St John. Simple, transparent, encouraging. Unfortunately my own attention was again somewhat distracted by the circumstances, from which I could not altogether free myself. But everything helps my main work. 'Thanks be to God, and in all things blessing and peace.'

At mealtimes I had Mgr Loris read me several pages of the *De consideratione* which St Bernard wrote for Pope Victor.[1] There could be nothing more suitable and useful for a poor Pope like myself, and for any Pope at any time. Certain things which did not redound to the honour of the Roman clergy in the twelfth century still survive today. Therefore 'one must watch and correct', and bear in patience.

(1) My first duty: to set my will in order, in preparation for my death, which may be near; the thought of it is never far from me. I shall take care to arrange everything in an orderly manner; even when it is written down, it will still be the will of a poor and simple Pope. I have only a few details to add and these are already substantially accounted for. I want the Pope's example to be an encouragement and an admonition to all the Cardinals. It is quite wrong for any ecclesiastic to die without leaving a will in good order, and not having done so may be a terrifying thought when he is face to face with eternity.

(2) Since the Lord chose me, unworthy as I am, for this great service, I feel I have no longer any special ties in this life, no family, no earthly country or nation, nor any particular preferences with regard to studies or projects, even good ones. Now, more than ever, I see myself only as the humble and unworthy 'servant of God and servant of the servants of

[1] This was in fact written for Pope Eugenius II.

God'.[1] The whole world is my family. This sense of belonging to everyone must give character and vigour to my mind, my heart and my actions.

(3) This vision, this feeling of belonging to the whole world, will give a new impulse to my constant and continual daily prayer: the Breviary, Holy Mass, the whole rosary and my faithful visits to Jesus in the tabernacle, all varied and ritual forms of close and trustful union with Jesus.

The experience of this first year gives me light and strength in my efforts to straighten, to reform, and tactfully and patiently to make improvements in everything.

(4) Above all, I am grateful to the Lord for the temperament he has given me, which preserves me from anxieties and tiresome perplexities. I feel I am under obedience in all things and I have noticed that this disposition, in great things and in small, gives me, unworthy as I am, a strength of daring simplicity, so wholly evangelical in its nature that it demands and obtains universal respect and edifies many. 'Lord, I am not worthy. O Lord, be always my strength and the joy of my heart. My God, my mercy.'

(5) The welcome immediately accorded to my unworthy person and the affection still shown by all who approach me are always a source of surprise to me. The maxim 'Know thyself' suffices for my spiritual serenity and keeps me on the alert. The secret of my success must lie there: in not 'searching into things which are above my ability'[2] and in being content to be 'meek and humble of heart'. Meekness and humbleness of heart give graciousness in receiving, speaking and dealing with people, and the patience to bear, to pity, to keep silent and to encourage. Above all, one must always be ready for the Lord's surprise moves, for although he treats his loved ones well, he generally likes to test them with all sorts of trials such as bodily infirmities, bitterness of soul and sometimes opposition so powerful as to transform and wear out the life of the servant of God, the life of the servant of the servants of God, making it a real martyrdom. I always think of Pius IX of sacred and glorious memory and, by imitating him in his sufferings, I would like to be worthy to celebrate his canonization.

---

[1] Cf. note 2, p. 65. [2] Ecclus. 3: 22.

1960

[64]
Retreat in the Vatican
from 27 November–3 December, 1960
Preacher, Mgr Pirro Scavizzi, Imperiari missionary[1]

I knew him [Mgr Pirro Scavizzi] and esteemed him during my years as a priest in Rome, from 1921 to 1925, when he was parish priest of Sant' Eustachio. He is good and able. He took as his themes for meditation and instruction various considerations from the New Testament, and developed them well, touching the fundamental principles of ecclesiastical life as regards the clergy who work in close collaboration with the Holy See. There were present at his sermons in the Matilda Chapel eighteen Cardinals and fifty-eight prelates, including a few Vatican functionaries; in all, with myself, seventy-seven ecclesiastics. All invisible to me but, I have heard, attentive and devout.

At the end of the retreat, before the Apostolic Blessing, I added three points:

(*a*) Gratitude to the edifying preacher whose sermons were varied, made interesting with panoramic visions of Palestine and always full of fervour, containing some shrewd but respectful home-thrusts.

(*b*) He was particularly effective in his references to the Roman Synod, the New Testament, and the universal vision of Holy Church in the world.

(*c*) He spoke gently and lovingly of the adoration and love for the Blessed Sacrament, 'God with us', and for Our Blessed Lady. Altogether very substantial and uplifting.

[1] John XXIII, in a note dated 29 November, writes: 'The day was inspired by Mgr Scavizzi's four penetrating addresses, all in conformity with the requirements of a good priestly character. The rest of the time in my room, revising the diaries of my humble life, from 1900–1921, when, acting under obedience, I left everything at Bergamo and devoted myself to missionary work. Oh, I have always been conscious of being of little worth in God's house.'

23. Figure of Pope John XXIII, from *The Door of Death* in St Peter's, Rome, by Giacomo Manzu

24. 25 June, 1960. 'Since the Lord chose me for this great service, I feel I have no longer any special ties in this life, no family, no earthly country or nation. . . .'

Some thoughts to encourage a priest in unfailing fervour

The course of my life over these two last years—28 October, 1958–59–60—shows a spontaneous and whole-hearted intensification of union with Christ, with the Church and with the heaven which awaits me.

I consider it a sign of great mercy shown me by the Lord Jesus that he continues to give me his peace, and even exterior signs of grace which, I am told, explain the imperturbable serenity that enables me to enjoy, in every hour of my day, a simplicity and meekness of soul that keep me ready to leave all at a moment's notice and depart for eternal life.

My failings and incapacities, and my 'countless sins, offences and negligences' for which I offer my daily Mass, are a cause of constant interior mortification, which prevents me from indulging in any kind of self-glorification but does not weaken my confidence and trust in God, whose caressing hand I feel upon me, sustaining and encouraging.

Nor do I ever feel tempted to vanity or complacency. 'What little I know about myself is enough to make me feel ashamed.' What a fine saying that is, which Manzoni put in the mouth of Cardinal Federico![1]

'In thee, O God, have I hoped; let me never be confounded.'[2]

At the beginning of my eightieth year it is all-important for me to humble myself and lose myself in the Lord, trusting that in his mercy he will open for me the gate to eternal life. Jesus, Mary, Joseph, may I breathe forth my soul in peace with you!

[1] Cf. *The Betrothed*, cit., chap. 26.   [2] Psalm 30(31): 2.

1961

My retreat in preparation for the completion of the
eighteeth year of my life. Castel Gandolfo
10–15 August, 1961

10 August, 1961

I have called for silence and a halt in the customary occupations of my
ministry. My sole companion is Mgr Cavagna, my usual confessor.

At dawn on this feast of St Lawrence, at a quarter to six in the morning,
I said the Divine Office on the terrace looking towards Rome.

My heart is touched when I think of this anniversary of my ordination
as a priest—10 August, 1904—in the church of Santa Maria in Monte
Santo, Piazza del Popolo. The prelate who ordained me was Mgr Ceppetelli, Vicegerent of Rome, Archbishop and titular Patriarch of Istanbul.
I remember it all, at a distance of fifty-seven years. Ever since then I have
felt ashamed of my worthlessness. 'My God, my mercy.'[1]

This form of spiritual retreat has a purpose beyond the usual scope.
My heart rejoices at the memory of all the Lord's goodness, in spite of
my shame that the effort I have put into my work for him has been so
disproportionate to the gifts I have received. This is a mystery which
moves me deeply and makes me afraid.

After my first Mass over the tomb of St Peter I felt the hands of the
Holy Father Pius X laid on my head in a blessing full of good augury for
me and for the priestly life I was just entering upon; and after more than
half a century (fifty-seven years precisely) here are my own hands extended
in a blessing for the Catholics, and not only the Catholics, of the whole
world, in a gesture of universal fatherhood. I am successor to this same
Pius X who has been proclaimed a saint, and I am still living in the same
priestly service as he, his predecessors and his successors, all placed like
St Peter at the head of the whole Church of Christ, one, holy, Catholic
and apostolic.

These are all sacred words, which have a loftier meaning than that of

[1] Psalm 58(59): 18.

any unimaginable self-glorification of my own, and they leave me still in the depths of my own nothingness, though I am raised to the sublime height of a ministry which towers far above the loftiest human dignity.

When on 28 October, 1958, the Cardinals of the Holy Roman Church chose me to assume the supreme responsibility of ruling the universal flock of Jesus Christ, at seventy-seven years of age, everyone was convinced that I would be a provisional and transitional Pope. Yet here I am, already on the eve of the fourth year of my pontificate, with an immense programme of work in front of me to be carried out before the eyes of the whole world, which is watching and waiting. As for myself, I feel like St Martin, who 'neither feared to die, nor refused to live'.[1]

I must always hold myself ready to die, even a sudden death, and also to live as long as it pleases the Lord to leave me here below. Yes, always. At the beginning of my eightieth year I must hold myself ready: for death or life, for the one as for the other, and I must see to the saving of my soul. Everyone calls me 'Holy Father', and holy I must and will be.

My own sanctification

I am very far from attaining this holiness in fact, although my desire and will to succeed in this are whole-hearted and determined. This particular way of sanctification, which is the right way for me, has once again been shown to me here at Castel Gandolfo, in a passage in a book and in a picture.

The passage I came across unexpectedly in a little volume: *La perfezione cristiana. Pagine di ascetica* by Antonio Rosmini,[2] page 591: 'In what does sanctity consist?':

'Reflect on this thought, that sanctity consists in being willing to be opposed and humiliated, rightly or wrongly; in being willing to obey; in being willing to wait, with perfect serenity; in doing the will of your Superiors without regard for your own will; in acknowledging all the benefits you receive and your own unworthiness; in feeling a great gratitude to others, and especially to God's ministers; in sincere love; in tranquillity, resignation, gentleness and the desire to do good to all, and in unceasing work. I am about to leave and can say no more, but this is enough' (Stresa, 6 September, 1840).

I find it comforting to note that these are simply the applications of

[1] Cf. note 1, p. 284.
[2] Antonio Rosmini, '*La perfezione cristiana, Pagine di ascetica*, ed. M. F. Sciacca, Turin, S.E.I., 1948. (The quotation occurs in a letter written by Rosmini from Stresa, 1 January, 1850, to Don Pietro Bertetti in England: translator's note.)

my own special motto, which I took from Baronius: *Obœdientia et Pax*. Jesus, this shows me that you are always with me! I thank you for this doctrine, which seems to follow me wherever I go.

The picture. This work is in the oldest and most private chapel of this Apostolic Palace. Today I showed it to my spiritual director, Mgr Alfredo Cavagna, as the most precious hidden jewel of this country residence. It dates from the time of Urban VIII (1636–1644). It served for his devotions and was used also by Pius IX who used to say his Mass here. Immediately after his own Mass he was present at his secretary's, in the small adjoining oratory that can still be seen, decorated entirely by the painter Lagi Simone, 'painter and gilder'. Over the altar is a very pious picture, a *Pietà*, the dead Jesus with Our Lady of Sorrows. Nothing could be more suitable: paintings and decorations. All round are scenes of the sufferings of Jesus: a permanent training school for any pontificate.

All this, the written words and the paintings, helps to confirm me in the doctrine of suffering. Of all the mysteries of the life of Jesus this is the most suitable and most familiar thought for the Pope's constant meditation: 'To suffer and be despised for Christ and with Christ.'[1]

This is the first light shed upon this exercise in perfection, while I prepare myself to enter upon old age: 'God's will, my sanctification in Christ.' Jesus, 'you have been my helper: I will rejoice under the cover of your wings. My soul has clung to you: your right hand supports me.'[2]

11 August, 1961

First of all: 'I confess to Almighty God.'

During my whole life I have kept faithful to my practice of weekly confession. Several times during my life I have renewed my general confession. So now I content myself with a more general examination, without precise details, but in the words of the offertory prayer of my daily Mass: thinking of my 'countless sins, offences and negligences', all of which have already been confessed in their turn but are still mourned and detested.

Sins: Concerning *chastity* in my relations with myself, in immodest intimacies: nothing serious, *ever*.

In relations with others, 'through the eyes, or through touch, in the time of puberty, or youth, or maturity, or old age or in the reading of books or newspapers, or in looking at statues or pictures. God's grace, God's grace I say, never once permitted temptation and failure, never, never; he always came to my help, with great and infinite mercy, in

[1] Cf. note 1, p. 28.   [2] Cf. Psalm 62(63): 8–9.

which mercy I trust that I shall always be preserved till the end of my days.'

Concerning *obedience*. I have never felt any temptation against obedience, and I thank the Lord that he has never permitted me to feel this even when obedience was a great effort, as it still is now that I am made 'the servant of the servants of God'.

Concerning *humility*. I make a special point of cultivating this and practising it. This does not mean I no longer feel hurt by what I consider to be a lack of respect shown to me. But for this also I rejoice before God, as if it were an exercise in forbearance, or the wearing of an invisible hair shirt for my own sins and to obtain from God forgiveness for the sins of the whole world.

Concerning *charity*. This is the virtue which comes most easily to me; yet even this sometimes costs me some sacrifice and I feel tempted and roused to show an impatience from which, unknown to me, someone may suffer.

Offences. Who knows how many, many times I have offended against the law of God and the laws of Holy Church! Times without number. But these offences have all been against the regulations of the Church and never in matters involving mortal or venial sins. I feel in my heart and soul a love of those rules, precepts and regulations, and obedience to all this ecclesiastical and human legislation, and I always keep a careful watch over myself where they are concerned, above all so that I may be an example for the edification of the clergy and all the faithful.

All these offences too have been confessed, all together and with the purpose of amendment and, as I grow older, a greater daily effort to achieve precision and perfection.

Negligences. These must be considered in relation to the sum of the various functions of my life as pastor, and the spirit of pastoral service must be pre-eminent in an apostle and successor of St Peter, as today I am regarded by all.

The vivid memory of the failings of my life, eighty years long, and of my 'countless sins, offences and negligences' was the general matter for the holy confession which I renewed this morning to my spiritual director, Mgr Alfredo Cavagna, here in my bedroom where my predecessors Pius XI and Pius XII slept, and where in fact Pius XII died on 9 October, 1958, until now the only Pope to die here at Castel Gandolfo, in the summer residence.

Lord Jesus, as you assure me of your great and eternal forgiveness, so continue to have pity on me.

Still 11 August, the afternoon of forgiveness

Holy confession, well prepared and repeated every week on Friday or Saturday, still remains a solid foundation for the progress of sanctification; and it gives me peace and encouragement as I hold myself ready to make a good death at any hour and any moment of the day. This serenity of mine, this readiness to depart and appear before the Lord whenever he wills, seems to me to be such a sign of trust and love as to deserve from Jesus, whose Vicar on earth I am called, the final gesture of his mercy.

So let us continue moving slowly towards him, as if he stood waiting with outstretched arms.

To strengthen my usual trust in God I see that Rosmini quotes that wonderful Father Caraffa who was the seventh General of the Society of Jesus, and who used to say he was always meditating on three letters that had become very familiar to him: a black letter, a scarlet one and a white; the black letter for his sins; the scarlet letter for the Passion of Jesus our Saviour; and the white letter for the glory of the blessed souls in heaven.

These three symbols truly contain the fine flower of good Christian meditation.

The black letter teaches me to know myself and urges me to cleanse my soul; the scarlet makes me familiar with the thought of the sufferings of Jesus, racked in body and soul, and the white letter helps me to resist discouragement, desolation and sadness, while all the time the saints do their duty of strengthening me for suffering, reminding me truly that 'the sufferings of the present time 'are not worth comparing with the glory that is to be revealed to us'.[1]

Moreover this thought is in any case in line with all the ascetic teaching of the *Spiritual Exercises* of St Ignatius, whose admirable book Rosmini said he always kept by him.

12 August, Saturday. Jesus crucified and his sorrowing Mother

So this retreat of mine is an attempt to make some progress in personal sanctification, not only as a Christian, priest, and Bishop, but as Pope, the 'good Father of all Christians', the good shepherd which the Lord has called me to be, despite my insufficiency and unworthiness.

At other times and frequently I ponder the mystery of the Precious Blood of Jesus, a devotion which, as Pope, I at once felt bound to en-

---

[1] Romans 8: 18.

courage, as complementary to the devotions to the Name and Heart of Jesus which, as I said, are already fairly well known and wide-spread.

I admit: this was a sudden inspiration for me. I saw private devotion to the Precious Blood of Jesus when I was a boy, little more than a child, as it was practised by my old great-uncle Zaverio, the eldest of the five Roncalli brothers. In fact he was the first person to train me to that practice of religion from which my priestly vocation was to spring, very early in my life and, I think, quite spontaneously. I remember the prayer books he kept on his *prie-dieu*, and among them *The Most Precious Blood* which he used during July. Oh sacred and blessed memories of my childhood! How precious they are to me in this sunset hour of my life, for they confirm the fundamental points of my search for holiness, and offer a consoling vision of what lies before me, as I humbly trust, in my eternity. The crucifix and eternity: the Passion of Christ in the light of never-ending eternity. Oh what sweetness and what peace! So must it always be, and increasingly so: the life still left for me to live here below must draw its strength at the foot of the Cross of Jesus crucified, bathed in his most Precious Blood and in the bitter tears of Our Lady of Sorrows, Mother of Jesus and my Mother too.

This inspiration, which has lately taken me by surprise, is like a new impulse, a new spirit in my heart, a voice that imparts courage and great fervour. I wish to express what I feel in three distinctive ways:

(1) Total detachment from everything, with absolute indifference to both praise and blame, and to any grave event that may happen in this world, as far as it affects me personally.

(2) In the eyes of the Lord I am a sinner and nothing but dust: I live by the mercy of Jesus, to whom I owe everything and from whom I expect everything. I submit to him even if he wishes me to be wholly transformed by his pains and his sufferings, in the entire abandonment of absolute obedience and conformity with his will. Now more than ever, and as long as I live, and in all things, *obœdientia et pax*.

(3) Perfect readiness to live or die, like St Peter and St Paul, and to endure all, even chains, sufferings, anathema and martyrdom, for Holy Church and for all the souls redeemed by Christ. I feel the awesomeness of this promise and I tremble, knowing myself to be weak and back-sliding. But I trust in Christ crucified and in his Mother, and I fix my eyes on eternity.

13 August, Sunday. The practice of prudence by the Pope and by the Bishops
Faith, hope and charity are the three stars of the episcopal glory. The

Pope as the head and as an example, and the Bishops, all the Bishops of the Church, with him. The sublime work, holy and divine, which the Pope must do for the whole Church, and which the Bishops must do each in his own diocese, is to preach the Gospel and guide men to their eternal salvation, and all must take care not to let any other earthly business prevent or impede or disturb this primary task. The impediment may most easily arise from human judgments in the political sphere, which are diverse and contradictory according to the various ways of thinking and feeling. The Gospel is far above these opinions and parties, which agitate and disturb social life and all mankind. The Pope reads it and with his Bishops comments on it; and all, without trying to further any worldly interests, must inhabit that city of peace, undisturbed and blessed, whence descends the divine law which can rule in wisdom over the earthly city and the whole world.

In fact, this is what wise men expect from the Church, this and nothing else.

My conscience is tranquil about my conduct as newly elected Pope during these first three years, and so my mind is at peace, and I beg the Lord always to help me to keep faith with this good beginning.

It is very important to insist that all the Bishops should act in the same way: may the Pope's example be a lesson and an encouragement to them all. The Bishops are more exposed to the temptation of meddling immoderately in matters that are not their concern, and it is for this reason that the Pope must admonish them not to take part in any political or controversial question and not to declare for one section or faction rather than another. They are to preach to all alike, and in general terms, justice, charity, humility, meekness, gentleness and the other evangelical virtues, courteously defending the rights of the Church when these are violated or compromised.

But at all times and especially just now, the Bishop must apply the balm of sweetness to the wounds of mankind. He must beware of making any rash judgment or uttering any abusive words about anyone, or letting himself be betrayed into flattery by threats, or in any way conniving with evil in the hope that by so doing he may be useful to someone; his manner must be grave, reserved and firm, while in his relations with others he must always be gentle and loving, yet at the same time always ready to point out what is good and what is evil, with the help of sacred doctrine but without any vehemence.

Any effort or intrigue of a purely human nature is worth very little in these questions of worldly interest.

Instead, he must with more assiduous and fervent prayer earnestly seek to promote divine worship among the faithful, with religious practices, frequent use of the sacraments, well taught and well administered, and above all he must encourage religious instructions because this also will help to solve problems of the merely temporal order, and do so much better than ordinary human measures can. This will draw down divine blessings on the people, preserving them from many evils and recalling minds that have strayed from the right path. Help comes down from above: and heavenly light disperses the darkness. So wrote Antonio Rosmini from Villa Albani, Rome, on 23 November, 1848.[1]

This is my pastoral thought and care, which must be for today and for ever.

Still Sunday, 13 August. Ideas for a good apostolate

Everyone must be treated with respect, prudence and evangelical simplicity.

It is commonly believed and considered fitting that even the everyday language of the Pope should be full of mystery and awe. But the example of Jesus is more closely followed in the most appealing simplicity, not dissociated from the God-given prudence of wise and holy men. Wiseacres may show disrespect, if not scorn, for the simple man. But those wiseacres are of no account; even if their opinions and conduct inflict some humiliations, no notice should be taken of them at all: in the end everything ends in their defeat and confusion. The 'simple, upright, God-fearing man' is always the worthiest and the strongest. Naturally he must always be sustained by a wise and gracious prudence. He is a simple man who is not ashamed to profess the Gospel, even in the face of men who consider it to be nothing but weakness and childish nonsense, and to profess it entirely, on all occasions, and in the presence of all; he does not let himself be deceived or prejudiced by his fellows, nor does he lose his peace of mind, however they may treat him.

The prudent man is he who knows how to keep silent about that part of the truth that it would be inopportune to declare, provided that this silence does not affect the truth he utters by gainsaying it; the man who knows how to achieve his own good purpose, choosing the most effective means of willing and doing; who, in all circumstances, can foresee and measure the difficulties set before him, and knows how to choose the middle way which presents fewer difficulties and dangers; the man who,

[1] *Op. cit.*, pp. 19–21. A letter written by Rosmini from Rome (Villa Albani), 23 November, 1848, to Mgr Claudio Samuelli, Bishop of Montepulciano.

having chosen a good, or even a great and noble objective, never loses sight of it but manages to overcome all obstacles and see it through to the end. Such a man in every question distinguishes the substance from the accidentals; he does not allow himself to be hampered by the latter, but concentrates and directs all his energies to a successful conclusion; he looks to God alone, in whom he trusts, and this trust is the foundation of all he does. Even if he does not succeed, in all or in part, he knows he has done well, by referring everything to the will and greater glory of God.

Simplicity contains nothing contrary to prudence, and the converse also is true. Simplicity is love: prudence is thought. Love prays: the intelligence keeps watch. 'Watch and pray': a perfect harmony. Love is like the cooing dove; the active intelligence is like the snake that never falls to the ground or bruises itself, because before it glides along it first probes with its head to test the unevenness of the ground.

Tranquillity on all occasions

The Lord Jesus, the Founder of Holy Church, directs all that happens with wisdom, power and indescribable goodness according to his own pleasure and for the greater good of his elect who form his Church, his beloved mystical Bride.

No matter how much events seem to be working against the good of the Church I must preserve a perfect tranquillity, which however will not dispense me from grieving and from imploring that 'thy will be done on earth, as it is in Heaven'.

I must beware of the audacity of those who, with unseeing minds led astray by secret pride, presume to do good without having been called to do so by God speaking through his Church, as if the divine Redeemer had any need of their worthless co-operation, or indeed of any man's.

What is important is to co-operate with God for the salvation of souls, and of the whole world. This is our true mission, which reaches its highest expression in the Pope.

'In all things look to the end.' I am not thinking here of death but of the purpose and divine vocation to which the Pope has been summoned by a mysterious decree of Providence.

This vocation is shown in a three-fold splendour: the personal sanctity of the Pope which gives its own glory to his life; the love which the holy universal Church bears to him, in the measure of that heavenly grace which alone can inspire him and assure his glory; finally, his obedience to the will of Jesus Christ, who alone rules through the Pope and governs the Church according to his own pleasure, for the sake of that glory which is supreme on earth as in the eternal heavens.

The humble Pope's most sacred duty is to purify all his own intentions in this light of glory, and to live according to the teaching and grace of Christ so as to deserve the greatest honour of all, the imitation, as his Vicar, of the perfection of Christ; of Christ crucified and, at the price of his blood, Redeemer of the world, of Christ the *Rabbi*, the Master, the only true Teacher of all ages and peoples.

14 August, Monday. Six maxims of perfection

Considering the purpose of my own life I must:

(1) Desire only to be virtuous and holy, and so be pleasing to God.

(2) Direct all things, thoughts as well as actions, to the increase, the service and the glory of Holy Church.

(3) Recognize that I have been set here by God, and therefore remain perfectly serene about all that happens, not only as regards myself but also with regard to the Church, continuing to work and suffer with Christ, for her good.

(4) Entrust myself at all times to Divine Providence.

(5) Always acknowledge my own nothingness.

(6) Always arrange my day in an intelligent and orderly manner.

My life as a priest, or rather—as I am called to my honour and shame—as Prince of the whole priesthood of Christ, in his name and by his power, unfolds before the eyes of my divine Master, the great Lawgiver. He looks down on me as he hangs on the Cross, his body torn and stained with blood. His side is wounded, his hands and feet are pierced. He looks at me and invites me to gaze on him. Justice led him straight to love, and love immolated him. This must be my lot: 'The disciple is not above his master.'[1]

O Jesus, here I am before you. You are suffering and dying for me, old as I am now and drawing near the end of my service and my life. Hold me closely, and near to your heart, letting mine beat with yours. I love to feel myself bound for ever to you with a gold chain, woven of lovely, delicate links.

The first link: the justice which obliges me to find my God wherever I turn.

The second link: the providence and goodness which will guide my feet.

[1] Matthew 10: 24.

The third link: love for my neighbour, unwearying and most patient.

The fourth link: the sacrifice that must always be my lot, and that I will and must welcome at all times.

The fifth link: the glory that Jesus promises me in this life and in eternity.

O crucified Jesus, 'my love and my mercy now and for ever'. 'Father, if thou art willing, remove this cup from me; nevertheless not my will, but thine be done' (Luke 22: 42).

Thoughts. I: Purpose of tribulations

Turning my thoughts in on myself and on the varied events of my humble life, I must admit that hitherto the Lord has spared me those tribulations which make the service of truth, justice and charity hard and distasteful for so many souls. I have lived through my childhood and youth without feeling the effects of poverty, with no anxieties about my family, my studies or situations of danger, such as my military service, for example, at the age of twenty, and again during the Great War, from 1919 to 1921.[1]

Humble and unpretentious as I know myself to be, I was always warmly welcomed wherever I went, from the seminaries of Bergamo and Rome through the ten years of my life as a priest with my Bishop in my native city, and from 1921 until now, 1961, that is from Rome and back to Rome again, to the Vatican. O God, how can I thank you for the kindness always shown to me wherever I went in your name, always in simple obedience, not to do my own will but yours? 'What shall I render to the Lord for all the things that he has rendered to me?' I know that my answer, to myself and to the Lord, is always the same: 'I will take the chalice of salvation, and I will call upon the name of the Lord.'[2]

As I have already indicated in these pages: if and when the 'great tribulation befalls me', I must accept it willingly; and if it delays its coming a little longer, I must continue to nourish myself with the Blood of Jesus, with the addition of all those great and little tribulations which the good Lord may send me. The short Psalm 130 has always made, and still makes, a great impression on me: 'O Lord, my heart is not lifted up, my eyes are not raised too high; I do not occupy myself with things too great and too marvellous for me. But I have calmed and quieted my soul,

---

[1] The author refers also to the difficulties of the immediate post-war period, before his summons to Rome.

[2] Cf. Psalm 115(116): 12 and 13. The priest says these words at Mass, before receiving communion in the Blood of Christ.

like a child quieted at its mother's breast.'[1] Oh, how I love these words! But even if they were to lose their comfort for me towards the end of my life, Lord Jesus, you will strengthen me in my suffering. Your Blood, your Blood which I shall continue to drink from your chalice, that is, from your Heart, shall be for me a pledge of eternal salvation and happiness. 'For this slight momentary affliction is preparing for us an eternal weight of glory, beyond all comparison' (2 Cor. 4: 17).

Thoughts. II: Contentment with my daily apostolate, without wasting time in predicting the future

'Jesus Christ, yesterday and today and the same for ever.'[2]

Not to try to predict the future, indeed not to count on any future at all: that is my rule of conduct, inspired by that spirit of tranquillity and constancy from which the faithful and my collaborators must receive light and encouragement from the Pope, the head priest.

The source of all priesthood is Christ, as St Thomas assures us (*S.T.*, III, q. 22, ad. 4): 'The priest of the Old Testament was a figure of Christ, the priest of the new law functions in the person of Christ himself.' This must be said in the first place of the Pope, both because of the Pope's conscience, which is felt to be invested with the presence, the grace and the light of Christ, and because of the fact that he entrusts everything to Christ, all the thoughts and operations of his many-sided apostolic activity. It is enough to take thought for the present: it is not necessary to be curious and anxious about the shape of things to come. The Vicar of Christ knows what Christ wants from him and does not have to come before him to offer him advice or to insist on his own plans. The Pope's basic rule of conduct must be always to content himself with his present state and have no concern for the future; this he must accept from the Lord as it comes, but without counting on it or making any human provision for it, even taking care not to speak of it confidently and casually to anyone.

My experience during these three years as Pope, since 'in fear and trembling' I accepted this service in pure obedience to the Lord's will, conveyed to me through the voice of the Sacred College of Cardinals in conclave, bears witness to this maxim and is a moving and lasting reason for me to be true to it: absolute trust in God, in all that concerns the present, and perfect tranquillity as regards the future.

The various initiatives of a pastoral character which mark this first stage of my papal apostolate have all come to me as pure, tranquil, loving, I

---

[1] Cf. Psalm 130(131): 1.   [2] Hebrews 13: 8.

might even say silent, inspirations from the Lord, speaking to the heart of his poor servant who, through no merit of his own save that very simple merit of mere acquiescence and obedience, without discussion, has been able to contribute to the honour of Jesus and the edification of souls.

My first contacts with high and low; the charitable visits here and there; the meekness and humility shown in the approaches made to clarify ideas and give warm-hearted encouragement; my Lenten visits to new parishes; the unexpectedly successful outcome of the Diocesan Synod, the closer links between the papacy and the whole Christian world, achieved by the repeated creation of new Cardinals and Bishops from every nation and of every race and colour, and now this vast activity, of unforeseen and most imposing magnitude, for the General Council—all this confirms the wisdom of the principle of waiting on God and expressing with faith, modesty and confident enthusiasm the good inspirations of the grace of Jesus, who rules the world and guides it according to the supreme purposes of the creation, redemption, and final and eternal glorification of souls and peoples.

15 August, 1961. Feast of the Assumption

Here we are on one of the most solemn and beloved occasions for religious devotion. My immediate predecessor Pope Pius XII proclaimed this dogma of faith on 1 November, 1950. As Nuncio to France, I was one of the fortunate ones present at that ceremony in St Peter's Square. I felt no anxiety about this doctrine, having always believed it; during my years in Eastern Europe my eyes were constantly drawn to images of the 'falling asleep of the Blessed Virgin Mary', in churches of both the Greek and Slav rites.

On the feast of the Assumption I think with tender affection of Sotto il Monte, where I loved so much to venerate Mary represented in her two statues: the very devout robed statue by Sansi at Brusico, the church of my baptism, and the other fine and powerful statue by the sculptor Manzoni in the new parish church. This was a gift from the beloved parish priest Father Carlo Marinelli,[1] one of the priests best known to me and most helpful in my ecclesiastical training, and very dear to my grateful heart.

The political atmosphere of the world in general just now arouses some anxieties about the problem of preserving peace. I thought it good to celebrate my Assumption Mass here, in the parish of Castel Gandolfo, inviting everyone to it, regular parishioners as well as casual visitors. It

[1] Parish priest at Sotto il Monte, 1919–24.

was a great and imposing gathering. There were present also Cardinal Agagianian with Mgr Sigismondi and a considerable group from the Seminary of Propaganda. My prayer after the Mass came straight from my heart, moved with emotion and full of fervour. Yesterday I had broadcast throughout the world information concerning the significance of this ceremony: it was an invitation to all Catholics of all nations, Bishops, priests and lay folk, to join with the Pope in collective prayer to the glorious Virgin, the Queen of Peace and Peacemaker of the whole world.

This brief and satisfactory ceremony served as the introduction to this last day of my retreat.

My dominant thought at its close is expressed in the familiar but precious phrase: 'To Jesus through Mary.'

In fact, this life of mine, now nearing its sunset, could find no better end than in the concentration of all my thoughts in Jesus, the Son of Mary, who holds him out to me in her arms for the joy and comfort of my soul.

So I shall concentrate with great care and intimate joy on these three highly significant and glorious words which must summarize my efforts to attain perfection: piety, meekness, charity.

I shall go on trying to perfect my pious practices: Holy Mass, the Breviary, the whole rosary, and a great and constant friendship with Jesus, contemplated as the Child and as the Crucified, and adored in the Blessed Sacrament. The Breviary at all times uplifts my soul; Holy Mass sanctifies it in the Name, the Heart and the Blood of Christ. Oh what tenderness of love and what refreshing happiness I find in my morning Mass!

The rosary, which since the beginning of 1953 I have pledged myself to recite devoutly in its entirety, has become an exercise of constant meditation and tranquil daily contemplation, keeping my mind alert in the vast field of my teaching office and my ministry as supreme Pastor of the Church and common Father of souls.

As my retreat draws to an end, I see very clearly the substance of the task which Jesus in his Providence has allowed to be entrusted to me.

'Vicar of Christ?' Ah, I am not worthy of this name, I, the humble child of Battista and Marianna Roncalli, two good Christians to be sure, but so modest and humble! Yet that is what I must be; the Vicar of Christ. 'Priest and victim'; the priesthood fills me with joy, but the sacrifice implied in the priesthood makes me tremble.

Blessed Jesus, God and man! I renew the consecration of myself to you, for life, for death, for eternity.

When I turn from considering the events of my life and my circumstances it comes naturally to me to linger frequently on the hill of Calvary, there to speak with the dying Jesus and his Mother, and from Calvary to return to the holy tabernacle where Jesus dwells in his Sacrament. I find it easier to read my Breviary, and I enjoy it more, at my ordinary working desk, but the rosary and my meditation on its mysteries, with the intentions which for some time now I love to add to each decade, I enjoy more on my knees before the sacred veil of the Eucharist.

As a reminder of the fervour and the happy inspirations of these days, I wish to make a note of the three most important points arising from my daily talks with Jesus:

(1) In the morning, recitation of the Breviary followed by holy Mass; before Mass, the Hours up to Sext, after Mass Sext and None and the first five mysteries of the rosary.

(2) After dinner I must never omit the brief visits to the Blessed Sacrament as soon as I leave the dining-room. Then a short rest.

(3) In the afternoon and after my brief rest—never in bed but lying on a sofa—recitation of Vespers and Compline and the next part of the rosary: the sorrowful mysteries. This form of prayer may well take the place of a visit to the Blessed Sacrament.

(4) In the evening, at seven-thirty, the third set of mysteries of the rosary, with the whole papal household, secretary, nuns and domestic staff. If convenient, a last visit to the Blessed Sacrament, as a prayer for protection during the night hours.

As for the practice of meekness, I add nothing more. I am grateful to the Lord for helping me to keep 'meek and humble of heart' in word and deed.

The same as regards charity. It is the Holy Spirit who 'lives, speaks and works in us, and is poured out on the clergy and faithful people as great patience and charity unfeigned'.[1]

I have enriched with a Plenary Indulgence (11 March, 1960) the so-called 'Universal Prayer' (Oratio Universalis) of Pope Clement XI: 'I believe, O God, but make me believe more firmly, etc.' The memory of this Pope, Giovanni Francesco Albani (1700–1721), is especially dear to me also because of his piety and his devotion to St Joseph, on whose feast (19 March, 1721) he died. I shall make a habit of saying his prayer more often. Pastor calls it 'a monument more lasting than bronze or marble' (Pastor XV, p. 410).[2]

---

[1] Cf. 1 Cor. 12: 11; 2 Cor. 6: 4, etc.

[2] The reference is to L. von Pastor, The History of the Popes. (English translation, vols. 1–35, London, Kegan Paul and Co., 1891 ff.)

'Simon, son of John, do you love me more than these? Do you love me? . . . Do you love me?' (John 21).

Conclusion of my retreat

For this my good Mgr Cavagna suggests to me the episode of the miraculous draught of fishes, ending in the dialogue between Jesus and Peter, with Peter's replies and the ensuing command: 'Feed my lambs, feed my sheep.'[1]

There is great authority in these words: the investiture of the Pope with his task as universal shepherd, in answer to his thrice repeated assurance of love, an assurance he gives to Jesus, who has deigned to ask for it with gentle insistence. It is love, then, that matters: Jesus asks Peter for it, and Peter assures him of it.

Peter's successor knows that in his person and in all that he does there is the grace and the law of love, which sustains, inspires and adorns everything; and in the eyes of the whole world it is this mutual love between Jesus and himself, Simon or Peter, the son of John, that is the foundation of Holy Church, a foundation which is at the same time visible and invisible, Jesus being invisible to the eyes of our flesh, and the Pope, the Vicar of Christ, being visible to the whole world. When I ponder this mystery of intimate love between Jesus and his Vicar I think what an honour and what a joy it is for me, but at the same time what a reason for shame for my own littleness and worthlessness!

My life must be filled with the love of Jesus and also with a great out-pouring of goodness and sacrifice for individual souls and for the whole world. From the Gospel episode which proclaims the Pope's love for Jesus, and through him for souls, it is but a short step to the law of sacrifice.

Jesus himself foretold this to Peter: 'Truly, truly, I say to you: when you were young you girded yourself and walked where you would, but when you are old you will stretch out your hands and another will gird you and carry you where you do not wish to go' (John 21: 18).

By God's grace I have not yet entered upon helpless old age; but having now completed my eighty years, I am on the threshold. So I must hold myself ready for this last phase of my life, in which restrictions and sacrifices await me, until the sacrifice of my bodily existence and the opening of eternal life. O Jesus, I am ready to stretch out my hands, now weak and trembling, and allow others to dress me and support me along the way.

O Lord, to Peter you added 'and to carry you where you do not wish to go'.

After so many graces, showered upon me during my long life, there is nothing now that I can refuse. You have shown me the way, O Jesus. 'I will follow you wherever you go',[1] to sacrifice, to mortification, to death.

'Not till death's hour is passed do other men obtain

The meed of holiness, and glorious rest attain.'

The thought of death, perhaps very near, certainly not far away, brings me back to my beloved St Joseph, rightly venerated among his other titles as Protector of the Dying, because, just as his whole life had been spent with them, so he enjoyed the company of Jesus and Mary at his blessed and happy death. The Church's hymn continues:

'Thou like to angels made, in life completely blest,

Didst clasp thy God unto thy breast.'

Oh what joy I feel in concluding the last notes of my retreat[2] with the final verse of this liturgical hymn which Holy Church dedicates to the most holy and august Trinity, from whom, as we remember St Joseph, Mary's spouse, flow all blessings and all assurances of radiant and eternal life.

---

[1] Matthew 8: 19.

[2] On 16 August, 1961, at the conclusion of this course of Exercises in preparation for his eightieth birthday, from Castel Gandolfo Pope John wrote to Mgr Alfredo Cavagna the following letter, full of a profound significance which defines and encourages one of the most important elements of Christian asceticism:

My dear Monsignor and revered Spiritual Father. At the conclusion of our retreat, which has brought me so much comfort and encouragement, I beg you to accept my heartfelt thanks. Alas! even on this occasion circumstances have not permitted us to realize our mutual desire and purpose of absolute and tranquil solitude. The departure for the highest spheres of two Cardinals, both most distinguished servants of the Holy See [Tardini and Canali] has caused me many grave preoccupations, inherent in my ministry, that of the servant of the servants of God. Fed by other unexpected sources of inspiration we found ourselves meditating upon the fundamental principles of ecclesiastical sanctification. We shall continue along this good road which, thanks to the Lord, has been well known and familiar to us from the beginnings of our vocation. I thank you, dear Monsignor, for the precious service you have rendered to what I am glad to acknowledge, the humble and innocent simplicity of my soul, which I hope to render to God as not unworthy of his infinite mercy. Meanwhile let us promise each other another spiritual meeting, apart from our usual meetings every week, for next year, and may it be in circumstances which give more assurance of solitude, but ever and always according to the will of God. During this retreat we have read together some pages of ascetic writing and found the sublime and beautiful prayer composed by that devout priest: 'Make me, O God, subject to you, as your Father made you subject to himself.' Again I thank you, dear Monsignor. Joy and peace. Blessing and peace. Most affectionately yours in the Lord, Joannes XXIII, the unworthy successor of Peter in God's Holy Church.

'O Holy Trinity, thy suppliant servants spare,
Grant us to rise to heaven for Joseph's sake and prayer,
And so our grateful hearts to thee shall ever raise
Exulting canticles of praise. Amen.'[1]

[66]   *Retreat in the Vatican*
                    26 November–2 December, 1961
            Preacher, Father Ilarino da Milano, Capuchin

Short notes

(1) I return again to the meditations and notes I wrote for the occasion of my eightieth birthday, when I was alone at Castel Gandolfo with Mgr Alfredo Cavagna, my confessor (cf. the manuscript of my *Soliloquies*).

(2) To have entered and now to have completed my eightieth year does not cause me any anxiety: in fact, it helps to keep me serene and confident. As always: I desire nothing more or less than what the Lord continues to give me. I thank and bless him every day and I am ready for anything.

(3) I notice in my body the beginning of some trouble that must be natural for an old man. I bear it with resignation, even if it is sometimes rather tiresome and also makes me afraid it will get worse. It is not pleasant to think too much about this; but once more, I feel prepared for anything.

(4) It gives me joy to keep faithful to my religious practices: Holy Mass, the Divine Office, the whole rosary, with meditation on the mysteries, constant preoccupation with God and with spiritual things.

(5) In order that what I say may be not superficial but full of substance, I wish to become more familiar with the writings of the great Popes of old. In recent months I have felt very much at home with St Leo the Great and with Innocent III. It is a pity that so few ecclesiastics study these writers, who abound in theological and pastoral doctrine. I shall never tire of drawing from these sources, so rich in sacred learning and sublime and delightful poetry.

(6) But above all I must endeavour to seek closer union with the Lord and to keep myself in serene and loving converse with him. He is 'the Word of the Father made flesh': the centre and life of the Mystical Body,

[1] Roman Missal, Hymn for Solemnity of St Joseph. Second Vespers, third Wednesday after Easter.

and a continuation of divine brotherhood, divine and human, through which I am his brother by adoption and, like him, the son of Mary his Mother.

(7) On this kinship is based the mission and office of the chief Pontiff of the Holy Catholic Church, the 'Vicar of Christ', as I am called. Oh how profoundly I feel the meaning and the emotion of the 'Lord I am not worthy' which I say every morning, in token of humility and love, when I take the sacred Host in my hands.

(8) A great deal of my daily work is in preparation for the Second Vatican Council. There begin to take shape in my mind the desire and idea of gathering around me in my daily prayer the prayers of all the secular and regular Catholic clergy, and of the women's religious Congregations, in some official and world-wide form. I shall await a happy inspiration to invite [the sentence ends abruptly].

1962

This retirement to Castel Gandolfo for my usual, and rather better organized, work, still concerned with the daily occurrences in the life of Holy Church, has enabled me to follow the preparatory work for the Council. The large Audiences were very useful for this purpose. They were perhaps too crowded, as they included representatives from every country in the world, but full of spiritual and religious fervour, and a sincere and pious enthusiasm which is edifying and encourages optimism. What seems clear and providential is that all these crowds of Italians and still more of 'foreigners' who come to Rome know at once how to distinguish between the sacred and the profane; that is, Rome the capital of Catholicism and seat of the universal Roman pontificate, and the Rome of ancient ruins and the whirlwind of secular and ... worldly living which rages even on the banks of the Tiber. All this however with mutual respect among the various human elements, and no unfriendliness between Italians and non-Italians.

For his part the Pope has been able to press on with his purpose, which is fairly well understood, of spending himself in all that is a service of faith, grace and pastoral spirituality, holding himself aloof from questions of a political character of whatever sort or degree.

The Biblical references to the attitude of the old patriarch Jacob who, when his sons were railing at their brother Joseph, pondered silently over the meaning of Joseph's dream,[1] have had a salutary effect: everyone has kept to his place and behaved with moderation [. . .].

Government and municipal authorities are now busily co-operating with the twofold intent that the Council shall be worthy of Rome as the spiritual centre of the world, and that Rome's arrangements for accommodation, civic hospitality and the honourable treatment of her guests gathered from all over the world may excel all the finest achievements of her past. This is far better than might have been feared, considering the unwillingness of certain spirits who are to be

[1] Genesis 37: 11.

found everywhere, but most of all in Rome, in the service of the 'Prince of this world'.

The personal preparation of the Servant of the Servants of God before the summoning of the Ecumenical Council, which was entirely his own initiative and *in capite* under his own jurisdiction, is briefly outlined here. His activity from 25 January, 1959, when the first communication was made about the Council, till 11 October, 1962, the official commencement of the great event, is recorded in the story of these three years of preparation. These acts and documents are already well known.

Here are indicated only the last characteristic expressions—*ora et labora*—of the Pope's own spiritual state immediately before the opening of the Council, with a few brief indications of dates and other details.

[68] *The Pope's private retreat for the week 8–16 September*

Saturday, 8 September: A day of loving prayer to Mary, on this feast of her nativity; careful reading of the final regulations for Council procedure; the first session to be from the feast of the Divine Maternity to the feast of the Immaculate Conception of Mary (11 October–8 December).

I have carefully studied the seventy articles of these regulations, to which it will be well frequently to refer.

Sunday, 9 September: Preparations in the Vatican for my retreat in the Torre San Giovanni where I intend to withdraw and stay all this week. The only persons to be admitted: the Cardinal Secretary of State if necessary, and every day at eleven o'clock Father Ciappi, Master of the Sacred Apostolic Palace, so that I may practise speaking correct Latin with him in case it may be necessary for me to do so during the general meetings presided over by me in the Council; and also every day from four till five in the afternoon the Very Reverend Father Cavagna, my usual confessor.

Monday, 10: At an early hour and in silence I accompanied Mgr Loris Capovilla as he carried the Blessed Sacrament from the Vatican chapel to the chapel of the Torre San Giovanni, where I joyfully began my private pre-Conciliar retreat.

This retreat began with great fervour last night during the almost unexpected visit I agreed to make to the church of Santa Maria degli Angeli. This was to have been a private visit, but the great concourse of people turned it into a most impressive occasion.

25. 14 April, 1963. In the Torre San Giovanni, reading his breviary

26. John XXIII receives the homage of Cardinal Rugambwa. Detail from *The Door of Death* in St Peter's, Rome, by Giacomo Manzu

Although my soul is well disposed for this retreat I am making in preparation for the Council, present circumstances compel me to make inevitable alterations to the usual meditations on these Exercises. This time everything is with the intention of preparing the Pope's soul for the Council: everything, including the preparation of the opening speech which the whole world gathered in Rome awaits, just as it listened most attentively to the speech which was broadcast this very evening to the whole world.

Therefore, to help me to fix my thoughts on spiritual matters, I have resolved to fix my mind on the three theological virtues: faith, hope and charity, and the four cardinal virtues: prudence, justice, fortitude and temperance; precisely seven points, altogether worthy of concentrated meditation, not only on the part of every good servant of the Lord but above all for the perfection of the holy and sanctifying virtue of a Bishop, and especially of the Bishop of Bishops, whose virtue must shine like the chief point of splendour in the glory of a Council.

This then is the order of the dates and points for thoughtful concentration:

Sunday, 9 September, under the heavenly auspices of Our Lady of the Angels

Monday, 10: Faith and Hope
Tuesday, 11: Charity
Wednesday, 12: Prudence
Thursday, 13: Justice
Friday, 14: Fortitude
Saturday, 15: Temperance

[69]   *Beginning of my private retreat before the Council,*
in the Torre San Giovanni

Monday, 10 September, St Nicholas of Tolentino

Holy Mass at home, with prayer to my Holy Family in the chapel, that Jesus, Mary, St Joseph and the little St John may protect and inspire me during this week of spiritual solitude. After Holy Mass, and in complete silence, Mgr Loris took the Blessed Sacrament from the tabernacle, and I accompanied him along the way, to place it here in the Tower, in the new chapel, on the 'Chinese' altar[1] which will always remind me

[1] A gift from the Chinese Catholics to John XXIII on the first anniversary of his election, 28 October, 1959.

of the missionary activity to which the Pope is called. At eleven o'clock appeared Father Ciappi, Master of the Sacred Palace, with whom I began to practise Latin conversation, and at four o'clock came Mgr Cavagna, my confessor. I realize that my desire to serve the Council will cause some alteration in the customary forms of the so-called Spiritual Exercises. But what is the Pope's life if not a daily continuation of true spiritual exercise for the salvation of his soul and the souls of all the redeemed of Jesus Christ, the Saviour of the world?

Wednesday, 12 September, feast of the Most Holy Name of Mary

> Quanto è soave al cuore
> il nome tuo, Maria.
> Ogni dolcezza mia
> Da quel tuo nome vien.
> Che bella idea di amore
> da quel tuo nome appresi,
> che bei desiri accesi
> mi vien destando in sen.

[How sweet is your name to my heart, Mary! Every joy I have is linked with your name, from which I learnt the beauty of love. You arouse such noble desires in my heart.]

These lines are the beginning of the first poem I learnt as a child, and I learnt it from the Second Reader then in use in the village school. I did my first year's schooling in the old village schoolhouse at Camaitino,[1] the first house on the right-hand corner of the so-called Piazza, as you come from the Guardina. Opposite was the shop (*bütiga*) of Rose Bonanomi and her sister Marianna, who was an invalid. That must have been in 1886 or 1887. The next year, with the completion of the new municipal buildings, the new school was opened at Bercio, and for two years I was among the first to attend it.

Thursday, 13, St Maurilius

'Justice is a common virtue.' This virtue may be exercised in many ways, as I once read in a passage written by Cardinal Mercier; and in Ecclesiasticus 4: 33 we read: 'Strive for justice for thy soul; and even to death fight for justice, and God will overthrow your enemies for you.'

[1] See Appendix I, p. 407.

This fourth chapter is indeed very fine, and full of instruction for personal, private and public life.

Meanwhile I continue my Latin conversation about religious matters with my good Father Ciappi, and in the afternoon I speak with Mgr Cavagna, my confessor. Alas! the cares which follow me even here do not permit me to go into it very thoroughly. But all helps to give me courage and a sense of spiritual meaning in everything. And this is what I need in my ministry.

Saturday, 15, St Nicomedus

My retreat, with only Father Ciappi and Mgr Cavagna to see me, in immediate and personal preparation for the Council, today comes to an end, although I have not been able to use it, as I wished, solely and entirely for the purpose I had set myself.

But it set a good example; it prevented me from being distracted by any exterior matters, business, literature or anything else. It was a more intense effort to find union with the Lord, in prayers, thoughts, and a calm and determined will. It leaves me with an increased fervour in my heart for all that concerns the substance of my ministry and my apostolic mandate. Lord Jesus, supply what I lack. 'Lord you know all; you know that I love you.'

[70]   *Summary of great graces bestowed on a man who thinks poorly of himself*

A summary of great graces bestowed on a man who has a low esteem of himself but receives good inspirations and humbly and trustfully proceeds to put them into practice.

First grace. To have accepted with simplicity the honour and the burden of the pontificate, with the joy of being able to say that I did nothing to obtain it, absolutely nothing; indeed I was most careful and conscientious to avoid anything that might direct attention to myself. As the voting in Conclave wavered to and fro, I rejoiced when I saw the chances of my being elected diminishing and the likelihood of others, in my opinion truly most worthy and venerable persons, being chosen.

Second grace. To have been able to accept as simple and capable of being immediately put into effect certain ideas which were not in the least complex in themselves, indeed perfectly simple, but far-reaching in their effects and full of responsibilities for the future. I was immediately successful in this, which goes to show that one must accept the good inspirations that come from the Lord, simply and confidently.

Without any forethought, I put forward, in one of my first talks with my Secretary of State, on 20 January, 1959, the idea of an Ecumenical Council, a Diocesan Synod and the revision of the Code of Canon Law,[1] all this being quite contrary to any previous supposition or idea of my own on this subject.

I was the first to be surprised at my proposal, which was entirely my own idea.

And indeed, after this everything seemed to turn out so naturally in its immediate and continued development.

After three years of preparation, certainly laborious but also joyful and serene, we are now on the slopes of the sacred mountain.

May the Lord give us strength to bring everything to a successful conclusion!

---

[1] We give a note written by Pope John in 1959: 'This is the mystery of my life. Do not look for other explanations. I have always repeated St Gregory Nazianzen's words! "The will of God is our peace." The same thought is contained in that other expression which is dear and familiar to me: obedience and peace, *obœdientia et pax*.

'The statue of St Peter is still here, awaiting the homage of us all, a never-ending source of joy and blessing.'

II

Four Letters

1901—1961

[71]   *Letter to his parents*[1]

† J.M.J.[2]   Rome, 16.1.1901

My beloved parents, brothers, sisters, grandfather and uncle,

When you read this letter of mine you will all have benefited spiritually from the Mission you are attending, which will soon be over. I rejoice with you and from my heart congratulate you on having this fine and enviable opportunity of once more devoting some serious thought to the salvation of your souls and to your eternal happiness in paradise.

This is what I most desire for you, for I have never wished or implored from heaven for my family the good things of this world—wealth, pleasures, success—but rather that you should all be good Christians, virtuous and resigned in the loving arms of divine Providence, and living at peace with everyone.

In fact what use would it be for us to possess even all the gold in the world at the price of losing our souls? Keep this truth firmly fixed in your minds and never forget it.

We must never feel saddened by the very straitened circumstances in which we live;[3] we must be patient, look above and think of paradise.

Paradise, paradise! We shall find our rest there, do you understand? There we shall suffer no more; we shall receive the reward of our works and of our sufferings, if we have borne them with patience.

Direct all your actions and your sacrifices to this end: that they may all serve to make you more happy and content in paradise.

[1] This is the first letter extant in manuscript.
[2] Jesus, Mary, Joseph.
[3] Poverty was the distinctive and shining characteristic of Pope John's childhood. 'We were poor,' he used to say, 'but content with our condition and full of confidence in the Lord's help. There was never any bread on our table, only *polenta* [a dish of maize flour]; no wine for the children or young people, and seldom meat; only at Christmas and Easter did we have a slice of home-made cake. Clothes, and shoes for going to church, had to last years and years. . . . And yet when a beggar appeared at the door of our kitchen, where the children—twenty of them—were impatiently waiting for their bowl of *minestra*, there was always room for him, and my mother would hasten to seat that unknown person beside us!' (See also 'Spiritual Testament', p. 343.)

Think of what the good Jesus did and suffered for us. He endured great poverty, he worked from morning to night, was slandered, persecuted and ill-treated in every way and crucified by the very people whom he loved so much.

We must learn from him not to complain, not to get angry, and not to lose our tempers with anyone, and not to nurse in our hearts any dislike for those we believe have injured us, but to have compassion for one another, because we all have our faults, some of one kind, some of another, and we must love everyone. You understand what I mean? Everyone, even those who injure, or have injured us; we must *forgive*, and pray for these too. Perhaps in God's eyes they are better than we are.

This is the real lesson you should learn from the Mission, and this is the only way to live happily, even in this world, even in the midst of so many hardships. And then you must pray, pray always and pray well, and go frequently to confession and to holy communion and have a great love for the Sacred Heart of Jesus and for Our Lady. Hear Holy Mass every day, never miss the homily and the explanation of doctrine; never stay out of doors after the Angelus, and so on.

The Lord wants me to be a priest: that is why he has lavished so many gifts upon me, even sending me here to Rome, to be near his Vicar, the Pope, in the Holy City, near the tombs of so many illustrious martyrs and so many holy priests. This is a great good fortune for me and for you, for which you must always thank the good God.

But I am not going to be a priest just to please someone else, or to make money, or to find comfort, honours or pleasures. God forbid! It is simply because I want to be able later on to be of some service to poor people, in whatever way I can. And that is why I would like you to be the first to benefit from this, you who have done so much for me, you whose spiritual welfare is so dear to my heart and for whom I pray every day, I might say every hour.

Will you give me the great joy of knowing that you have all received great good from the holy Mission, and that you have become better Christians than before? I hope this is so, indeed I am quite sure of it, knowing so well your excellent intentions.

Please remember me, all of you, at the general communion. Meanwhile accept my wishes and my greetings, and share these with all our relations and friends.

Your seminarist, ANGELO.

My health is flourishing. Greetings to the parish priest and the curate.

To the Rector of the Roman Seminary[1]

These two letters to Mgr Vincenzo Bugarini form part of a series of a hundred and sixteen letters to the Rectors of the Roman Seminary, written during the years 1901–1957, all preserved in the archives at that Institute.

The second of these is particularly interesting. It describes the undoubtedly difficult situation of a seminarist called to do his military service, while at the same time it bears witness to the courtesy of the officer commanding the Regiment and to the good nature of the Italian soldier. This letter bears out what the seminarist Roncalli wrote in his notes 'after the Babylonian captivity' (cf. pp. 84ff.) with all the frankness of an innocent soul brought face to face with the reality of the moral crisis in which most young men, especially those who live the communal life of the barracks, find themselves involved. In such circumstances the weaker and less noble, one might say the most melancholy, characteristics of youth come to the fore. We must also remember that at the beginning of the century there were no military chaplains to give spiritual assistance in the barracks.

[72] † J.M.J.   Sotto il Monte, 19.8.1901

Most Reverend Monsignor,

It is now several days since I left Rome, with a heavy heart, and I feel more strongly than ever my duty to present to Your Reverence my most respectful greetings, with my heartfelt gratitude for the great benefits I enjoyed while with you, and I want especially to express to you my warm

[1] Letters sent to Mgr Vincenzo Bugarini, Rector of the Roman Seminary, after Angelo Roncalli's departure from Rome to do his military service, which began on 30 November.

Mgr Vincenzo Bugarini, born in Rome on 26 December, 1852, and ordained priest in 1875, held many offices, among them that of official interpreter of Propaganda Fide, Professor of Hebrew, Syriac and Arabic. From 1893 to 1910 he was Rector of the Roman Seminary. Angelo Roncalli was his devoted friend from the time when he was a student at the Apollinare, and was presented by him to Mgr Radini in 1905.

In 1921 when Mgr Roncalli was transferred to Rome, to the service of Propaganda Fide, he took Mgr Bugarini into his own house at Santa Maria in Via Lata and looked after him most lovingly until the day of his death, 14 February, 1924. In a commemorative sermon preached thirty days afterwards, Mgr Roncalli said: 'On this day of commemoration we think of him, not as a distinguished scholar of extraordinary culture, not as famous for the eminent posts he held in the Church nor celebrated because of events to which he gave his name, but because he was simple, friendly, pious, above all very humble, always serene and cheerful in the various happenings of life and active in works of charity. Every one of us has, as it were, found himself again in these most sacred memories of our ecclesiastical training, and of our numerous contacts with him and the impressions we received during those years in which by word and example he trained us for the tasks and responsibilities of the priesthood.'

and sincere affection for Your Reverence, from whom I received more than a father's care.

When I left the Holy City, which had given me such indescribable happiness, and parted from so many good people for whom I feel a great respect, I felt as if I were leaving in Rome and in the Roman Seminary a large part of myself.

After all the kindness I had already received and all the loving counsels and wise suggestions which you have given me along my way, and with the help of that modicum of heavenly grace with which the good God is wont to comfort his poor seminarists, I can say that I am content and very happy, even in the midst of my tribulations. I have now accustomed myself to regarding this interruption of my studies and the necessity of adapting myself to a life which is certainly most undesirable, as the most natural thing for me, profoundly convinced as I am that in this way the Lord is preparing great blessings for me and will make me more whole-hearted and persevering in the service of that cause to which I have now consecrated all my youthful energies, my whole self.

But this serenity of mind does not mean that I do not long to return as soon as possible to my beloved Roman Seminary, or that I do not think of the dear persons and associations which I have left behind, more often and more lovingly than Your Reverence can imagine.

I will not add anything about my excellent health or my studies because I think you have already received information about these from other sources.

I conclude by renewing once more to Your Reverence and the other Reverend Superiors the expression of my heartfelt gratitude and my most sincere affection, recommending myself most earnestly to your prayers.

May the divine Heart of Jesus and our good Madre della Fiducia deign to bless Your Reverence and all the Seminary with me, as I, an unworthy son, pray every day from my heart.

Affectionately kissing your hand, I have pleasure in professing myself,

Yours with filial love,

Seminarist ANGELO RONCALLI.

[73] † J.M.J.   Bergamo, 23.12.1901

Most Reverend Monsignor,

I have waited until today to send you my news, because I was not sure of what was to happen and I was waiting for the approaching Christmas festivities in order to have a more favourable opportunity of writing to you.

And now, after living for some time in what is to me an alien land, I am glad to be able to tell Your Reverence that once more I have seen in myself the clear confirmation of all that you have already told me, in order to encourage me to resign myself to what has happened. I am here as God wills, in his hands, but almost completely liberated, to my good fortune, from my preconceived ideas of life in the army.

My life is one of great suffering, a real purgatory; and yet I feel the Lord is very close to me, with his holy and provident care, beyond all my expectations. Sometimes I am amazed at myself, at the happy solution of this difficult and terrifying problem, and I can only explain it to myself by the thought of so many good and dear people who are certainly praying for me, as they promised, and of my beloved Madonna della Fiducia, whose beautiful image I always wear on my breast, and of the Sacred Heart of Jesus, the shining focus of all my fervent ideals as a young man and as a seminarist who does at least desire to do a little good one day.

What more, what better can I say?

I have found excellent superior officers[1] who seem very fond of me; they treat me with consideration and insist on my being respected as a seminarist; in fact they show me a high regard which I really cannot understand and, which is more important, allow me the most ample liberty to pursue my religious practices.

My fellow soldiers, mostly from Bergamo or Brescia, also know my situation and from them I have until now received only marks of respect and affection: they compete in doing those little services for me which at least save me a lot of bother. Every evening when I leave the barracks I go to the seminary to see my beloved Rector, who welcomes me like a father and has given me a short Rule, similar, if I am not mistaken, to the Rule proposed for students from the Roman Seminary who are in the army. In short, it would be most unreasonable of me to complain of my situation. I dislike this life intensely, I long for that blessed moment when I shall be able to return to my happy life in Rome, but nevertheless I feel perfectly

---

[1] In the 73rd Infantry Regiment 'Lombardia', whose motto was: *acerrimus hostibus* (most fierce to the foe); commanding officer: Col. Enrico Campi, Umberto I Barracks.

resigned and tranquil. Every day I am more convinced of the great benefit I shall draw from this year's experience, for the glory of God and to the advantage of the Church, and I console myself with the thought of all those dear persons whom I take a delight in remembering every day and whom I love deeply, who are waiting for my return and whom I desire —oh how ardently!—to see again and to gladden with my presence.

I am sorry that my occupations and military exercises, very arduous and tiring, especially during the early days, do not leave me time to express to each Superior of the Roman Seminary individually my feelings of gratitude, esteem and affection., It is perhaps enough to say that I began this poor letter of mine about a week ago, and have never been able to finish it till now. So I hope you will be kind enough to pass on all those greetings that I would like to be able to write myself to all the Reverend Superiors, Mgr the Bursar, Canon Borgia, the Vice-rector and Mgr Spolverini.

I end by once more commending myself to your prayers and those of the seminary. When time permits, I will not fail to send you my news. Believe me,

Your Reverence's most devoted son,

Seminarist ANGELO RONCALLI.

[74]   *Spiritual testament 'to the Roncalli family'*[1]

Vatican, 3 December, 1961

My dear brother Severo,

Today is the feast of your great patron saint, who bore your own real Christian name, which is Francesco Zaverio, the same as that of our dear great-uncle, our '*barba*',[2] and now, happily, the name of our nephew Zaverio.

I think it is now three years since I last used a typewriter. I used to enjoy typing so much and if today I have decided to begin again, using a machine that is new and all my own, it is in order to tell you that I know I am growing old—how can I help knowing it with all the fuss that has been made about my eightieth birthday?—but I am still fit, and I con-

---

[1] Pope John XXIII regarded this letter as his spiritual testament to the Roncallis. It was published in *L'Osservatore Romano*, 7 June, 1963.

[2] See below, pp. 405-6.

tinue on my way, still in good health, even if some slight disturbance makes me aware that to be eighty is not the same as being sixty, or fifty. For the present at least I can continue in the service of the Lord and Holy Church.

This letter which I was determined to write to you, my dear Severo, contains a message for all, for Alfredo, Giuseppino, Assunta, our sister-in-law Caterina, your own dear Maria, Virginio and Angelo Ghisleni, and all the members of our large family, and I want it to be to all of them a message from my loving heart, still warm and youthful. Busied as I am, as you all know, in such an important office, with the eyes of the whole world upon me, I cannot forget the members of my dear family, to whom my thoughts turn day by day.

It is pleasant for me to know that, as you cannot keep in personal correspondence with me as you did before, you may confide everything to Mgr Capovilla, who is very fond of you all, and speak to him just as you would to me.

Please bear in mind that this is one of the very few letters that I have written to any of my family during these first three years of my pontificate, and do your best to understand why it is that I cannot do any more, even for people of my own blood. But this self-denial too, that I impose upon myself with regard to my contacts with you all, does you and me more honour, and gains more respect and sympathy, than you can believe or imagine.

Now the great manifestations of reverence and affection for the Pope, on the occasion of his eightieth birthday, are at an end and I am glad, because, rather than receive the praises and good wishes of men, I prefer to enjoy the mercy of God who has chosen me for so great a task and who, I trust, will uphold me until the end of my life.

My own personal serenity, which makes such an impression on people, derives from this: the obedience in which I have always lived, so that I do not desire or beg to live longer, even a day beyond that hour in which the Angel of Death will come to call me and take me, as I trust, to paradise.

This does not prevent me from thanking the Lord for having deigned to choose from Brusico and Colombera the man who was called to be the direct successor of the Popes of twenty centuries and to assume the title of Vicar of Jesus Christ on earth.

Because of this choice the name Roncalli has become known, loved and respected all over the world. You are very wise to keep yourselves very humble, as I too try to do, and not let yourselves be influenced by the insinuations and tittle-tattle of the world. All the world wants is to make money, enjoy life, and impose its own will at all costs, even with violence, if this should unhappily seem necessary.

My eighty years of life completed tell me, as they tell you, dear Severo, and all the members of our family, that what is most important is always to keep ourselves well prepared for a sudden departure, because this is what matters most: to make sure of eternal life, trusting in the goodness of the Lord who sees all and makes provision for all.

I wish to express these sentiments to you, my beloved Severo, so that you may pass them on to our closest relatives at Colombera, Gerole, Bonate and Medolago, and wherever else they may be—I do not know the exact whereabouts of them all. I leave it to your discretion to do this. I think Enrica could help you, and Don Battista too.

Go on loving one another, all you Roncallis, with the new families growing up among you, and try to understand that I cannot write to all separately. Our Giuseppino was right when he said to his brother the Pope: 'Here you are a prisoner *de luxe*: you cannot do all you would like to do.'

I like to remember the names of those among you who have most to bear: dear Maria, your good wife, bless her, and the good Rita who with her sufferings has earned paradise for herself and for you two, who have cared for her so lovingly, and our sister-in-law Caterina who always makes me think of her Giovanni and ours, who looks down at us from heaven—and all our Roncalli relations and nearest connections, like those who have 'emigrated' to Milan.

I am well aware that you have to bear certain mortifications from people who like to talk nonsense. To have a Pope in the family, a Pope regarded with respect by the whole world, who yet permits his relations to go on living so modestly, in the same social condition as before! But many know that the Pope, the son of humble but respected parents, never forgets anyone; he has, and shows, a great affection for his nearest kin; moreover, his own condition is the same as that of most of his recent predecessors; and a Pope does not honour himself by enriching his relations but only by affectionately coming to their aid, according to their needs and the conditions of each one.

This is and will be one of the finest and most admired merits of Pope John and his Roncallis.

At my death I shall not lack the praise which did so much honour to the saintly Pius X: 'He was born poor and died poor.'

As I have now completed my eighty years, naturally all the others will be coming along after me. Be of good heart! We are in good company. I always keep by my bedside the photograph that gathers all our dead together with their names inscribed on the marble: grandfather Angelo, 'barba' Zaverio, our revered parents, our brother Giovanni, our sisters Teresa, Ancilla, Maria and Enrica. Oh what a fine chorus of souls to await us and pray for us! I think of them constantly. To remember them in prayer gives me courage and joy, in the confident hope of joining them all again in the everlasting glory of heaven.

I bless you all, remembering with you all the brides who have come to rejoice the Roncalli family and those who have left us to increase the happiness of new families, of different names but similar ways of thinking. Oh the children, the children, what a wealth of children and what a blessing!

JOANNES XXIII PP.

27. Christmas Day, 1958. Visiting the Roman prison

III

Spiritual Testament

28. June, 1962. With a group of octogenarians

Spiritual Testament

It is known that Pope John intended to draw up a spiritual testament of a more universal character, that should sum up the ideals of his whole life and be preceded by an *Epistola ad clerum universum* (Letter to the clergy of the whole world), the substance of which is contained, as he said himself, in *Journal of a Soul*.

Here we give the spiritual testament as it was published in *L'Osservatore Romano* on 7 June, 1963. It is in two parts: the first dated 29 June, 1954, and confirmed in 1957, and the second dated 12 September, 1961, with the addition of two codicils, dated respectively 17 September, 1957, and 4 December, 1959.

The most recent manuscript, now widely known, re-confirms Mgr Loris Capovilla as executor of the will and bears the date 7 October, 1960. It is deposited in the archives of the Secretary of State's office.[1] In this Pope John says, among other things, 'In carrying out this last will of mine he (Mgr Loris Capovilla) is asked to consult two persons, witnesses worthy of respect, known to me by blood relationship and friendship, that is the priest Don Battista Roncalli, son of my deceased brother Giovanni, and His Excellency Most Reverend Angelo Dell'Acqua, Titular Archbishop of Chalcedon, formerly my secretary at Istanbul.'

Not all the versions of the testament, written between 1925 and 1961, have survived. As this is no place for a critical edition, we restrict ourselves to adding

---

[1] When Pope John died, in obedience to his wishes and requests, personal gifts from him were sent to famous churches and shrines all over the world: chalices, crosses, rings, reliquaries and vestments.

Apart from Bergamo, Rome, Sofia, Istanbul, Athens, Paris and Venice, places dear to him and in all of which in turn he served and ministered, we mention Notre Dame in Paris, Lyons, the Church of Peace in Hiroshima, the Black Madonna of Czestochowa, St Stephen's Cathedral in Vienna, Guadalajara, Toledo, Lisbon, Leiria, Buenos Aires, Saõ Sebastiaõ of Rio de Janeiro, Munich, Utrecht, Malines, Sydney, Bukoba (Tanganyika), Washington, Boston, Bombay, Montreal; and in Italy: Milan, Padua, Brescia, Piacenza and elsewhere.

Although the dispositions contained in pp. 345–54 (1954 and 1939–1944) were later abrogated, some were carried out to the letter and others in a different manner but with the same meaning and intention. Finally, as is well known, with Pope John's consent, very many objects have been placed permanently in the house at Camaitino (Sotto il Monte) and others are about to be placed there. In fact, this house, used by Pope John XXIII from 1925 to 1958 and furnished by him, is today the most eloquent witness to his service for God and for souls.

to the spiritual testament those final provisions of a material nature (Section II) which Pope John himself called 'My final dispositions' and which completed the spiritual testament of 29 June, 1954. The first part of this testament was used for the more recent final version of 1957. The variations between the 1954 and 1957 versions are hardly noticeable. These provisions were annulled consecutively on 28 October, 1958, and 30 April, 1959.

Finally we give (Section III) two pages, all that has survived, of a will drawn up between 1939 and 1944, probably a revision of the one that Mgr Roncalli wrote in 1925 and of which nothing now remains. These two pages were later inserted, with a few adjustments, in the 1954 will.

I

[75]   *Spiritual testament and my final dispositions*

Venice, 29 June, 1954

On the point of presenting myself before the Lord, One and Three, who created me, redeemed me, chose me to be priest and Bishop and bestowed infinite graces upon me, I entrust my poor soul to his mercy. Humbly I beg his pardon for my sins and failings; I offer him what little good, even if imperfect and unworthy, I was able with his help to do for his glory and in the service of Holy Church and for the edification of my fellows, and I implore him finally to welcome me, like a kind and tender father, among his saints in the bliss of eternity.

I wish to profess once more my complete Christian and Catholic faith, belonging and submitting as I do to the holy, apostolic and Roman Church, and my perfect devotion and obedience to its august head, the supreme Pontiff, whom it was my great honour to represent for many years in the various regions of East and West, and who finally sent me here as Cardinal and Patriarch, and for whom I have always felt a sincere affection, apart from and above any dignity conferred upon me. The sense of my littleness and worthlessness has always kept me good company, making me humble and tranquil, and permitting me the joy of putting my best efforts into a continual exercise of obedience and love for souls and for the interests of the kingdom of Jesus, my Lord and my all. To him be all the glory: for me and for my own merits, only his mercy. 'God's mercy is my only merit. Lord, you know all things: you know that I love you!' This is enough for me.

I ask forgiveness from those whom I have unknowingly offended, and those whom I have not influenced for good. I feel that for my own part I have nothing to forgive anyone, because in all those who knew me and had dealings with me—even if they have offended or despised me or, no doubt justly, had little regard for me, or given me cause to suffer—I recognize only brothers and benefactors, to whom I am grateful and for whom I pray and will pray always.

Born poor, but of humble and respected folk, I am particularly happy to die poor, having distributed, according to the various needs and circumstances of my simple and modest life in the service of the poor and of the holy Church which has nurtured me, whatever came into my hands—and it was very little—during the years of my priesthood and episcopate. Appearances of wealth have frequently disguised thorns of frustrating poverty which prevented me from giving to others as generously as I would have wished. I thank God for this grace of poverty to which I vowed fidelity in my youth, poverty of spirit, as a priest of the Sacred Heart, and material poverty, which has strengthened me in my resolve never to ask for anything—positions, money or favours—never, either for myself or for my relations and friends.

To my beloved family according to the flesh, from whom moreover I have never received any material wealth, I can leave only a great and special blessing, begging them to preserve that fear of God which made them always so dear and beloved to me, and to be simple and modest without ever being ashamed of it: it is their true title of nobility. I have sometimes come to their aid, as a poor man to the poor, but without lifting them out of their respected and contented poverty. I pray and I will ever pray for their welfare, glad as I am to see in their new and vigorous shoots the constancy and faithfulness to the religious tradition of the parent stock which will always be their happiness. My most heartfelt wish is that not one of my relations and connections may be missing at the final joyful reunion.

About to leave, as I hope, on the heavenward path, I greet, thank and bless the infinite number of souls who made up, successively, my spiritual family in Bergamo, in Rome, in the East, in France, and in Venice, my fellow citizens, benefactors, colleagues, students, collaborators, friends and acquaintances, priests and lay folk, men and women of the Religious Orders, to all of whom, by the decree of Providence, I was the unworthy brother, father or shepherd.

The kindness shown my humble person by all those I met with along my way has made my life a peaceful one. Now, in the face of death, I remember all and everyone of those who have gone before me on the last stretch of the road, and those who will survive me and follow me. May they pray for me. I will do the same for them from purgatory or paradise where I hope to be received, not, I repeat, through my own merits but through the mercy of my Lord.

I remember them all and will pray for them all. But my Venetian children, the last the Lord has given me, for the final joy and consolation of my priestly life, shall here receive special mention as a sign of my admiration, gratitude and very special love. I embrace them all in the spirit, all, everyone, clergy and lay folk, without distinction, as without distinction I loved them all as belonging to the same family, the object of the same priestly love and care. 'Holy Father, keep them in thy name, whom thou hast given me, and that they may be one, even as we are one' (John 17: 11).

In the hour of farewell or, better, of leave-taking, I repeat once more that what matters most in this life is: our blessed Jesus Christ, his holy Church, his Gospel, and in the Gospel above all else the Our Father according to the mind and heart of Jesus, and the truth and goodness of his Gospel, goodness which must be meek and kind, hardworking and patient, unconquerable and victorious.

My children, my brothers, I take leave of you. In the name of the Father, the Son and the Holy Ghost. In the name of Jesus our love; of Mary, his sweet Mother and ours; of St Joseph, my first and most beloved protector. In the name of St Peter, of St John the Baptist, and of St Mark; of St Lawrence Giustiniani and St Pius X. Amen.

CARD. ANG. GIUS. RONCALLI PATRIARCH.

(The text contains, in the Pope's handwriting, the following codicils):

These pages written by me are valid as proof of my final dispositions in case of my sudden death.

ANG. GIUS. CARD. RONCALLI.

Venice, 17 September, 1957.

And they are valid also as my spiritual testament, to be added to the testamentary provisions here enclosed, under the date of 30 April, 1959.

JOANNES XXIII PP.

From Rome, 4 December, 1959.

29. Receiving a little girl suffering from leukemia

30. On a visit to a parish Church in Rome

My will

Castel Gandolfo, 12 September, 1961

Under the dear and trustworthy auspices of Mary, my heavenly Mother, to whose name the liturgy of this day is dedicated, and in the eightieth year of my age, I hereby set down and renew my will, annulling every other declaration concerning my wishes, made and written previously, on divers occasions.

I await the arrival of Sister Death and will welcome her simply and joyfully in whatever circumstances it will please the Lord to send her.

First of all I beg forgiveness from the Father of mercies for my 'countless sins, offences and negligences', as I have said and repeated so many, many times when offering my daily sacrifice of the Mass.

For this first grace of forgiveness from Jesus for all my sins, and for his acceptance of my soul in his blessed and eternal paradise, I commend myself to the prayers of all who have known me and followed my whole life as priest, Bishop, and most humble and unworthy servant of the servants of the Lord.

It is with a joyful heart that I renew wholly and fervently the profession of my Catholic, Apostolic and Roman faith. Among the various forms and symbols in which the faith finds its expression I prefer the Creed of the Mass, said by priest and Pontiff, resounding and sublime, in union with the universal Church of every rite, every century, every land: from the 'Credo in unum Deum patrem omnipotentem' to the 'et vitam venturi saeculi'.

II

[76]   *My final dispositions*

(a) *My last will concerning things which belong to me as Patriarch of Venice*

I direct that those things which I brought with me to Venice from my property at Bergamo: the suite of furniture consisting of large sideboard, table and chairs, with the articles of silver and tableware acquired by me or given me by the people of Bergamo on the occasion of my being made Cardinal and making my solemn entry into the town, shall remain after my death in the patriarchal palace, as table furnishings for the use of my successors. It will be well to affix a little plate engraved with my name. My sister Maria and my niece Enrica may keep as a legacy or give away, as they think best, my personal garments, underwear, cassocks and cloaks of whatever colour, red, purple and black. The Morlani rochet is to go, as indicated below, to the venerable Chapter of the Cathedral of Bergamo. Let the other rochets be sold in the most profitable way and the proceeds in cash given to the poor of Venice, as I have nothing else to give to these people who are Christ's poor and therefore the dearest to the heart of their Bishop, and I beg them to accompany me to eternity with their prayers. My crosses and rings likewise are to be sold so as to fetch the highest possible price and the proceeds from these also given to the poor in whatever seems the most suitable form.

This distribution to the poor, with a special thought for nuns, seminarists and needy priests, is also to be made from what remains in my credit after the liquidation of the income attached to the patriarchate, to be calculated at the moment of my death according to the usual procedure. If there are any stipends assigned for Masses not yet celebrated, these with their respective intentions are to be divided between my secretary and the members of the patriarchal Curia, who will say the Masses.

I appeal to the charity of the executor of my will to see that this request is carried out with the greatest care, lest my poor soul should suffer purgatory for lack of precision in this sacred matter. First the Mass obligations: then the poor.

I desire also that there should be sent to the Apostolic Nunciature of Paris—in case I have not done this myself before my death—the crozier in gilt metal which I brought thence, and I would like to have engraved on it the words: CARDINALIS ANGELUS JOSEPH RONCALLI SUCCESSORIBUS SUIS IN NUNTIATURA APOSTOLICA PARISIENSI 1945–1952.

The other crozier, silvergilt, the gift of the people of Bergamo, I offer to the church of S. Maria della Salute in Venice, as a mark of filial devotion to the dear image of Our Lady venerated there, and of fatherly affection for the patriarchal seminary which promotes devotion and honour to her.[1]

(b) *My last dispositions concerning my goods and material possessions at Sotto il Monte*

My share of the property, fields, terraces or woods, which came to me when the property was divided among us all, sisters and brothers, and which are now in the hands of my brother Giuseppino, who has always worked them and is still doing so, paying the relative taxes,

---

[1] The two croziers were actually given to the Nunciature in Paris and the church of S. Maria della Salute in Venice in 1958.

without my drawing any profit from them, shall remain for him and his family as a gift from me and in his inalienable possession.[1]

For my brother Giovanni I have already done much in other ways and in various circumstances, especially by maintaining as a student at the college of Romano and the seminaries of Bergamo and Faenza his son and my dear nephew Don Battista, now very near to attaining the priesthood. My care for him was a source of anxieties and suffering, but I was always sustained by the confidence I had and still have in his earnestness and goodness, and in his success as a priest. I commend him to the charity of my sister Maria and his sister Enrica with regard to the furniture and books at Camaitino.

It is to this sister of mine, Maria, who has outlived our never-to-be-forgotten Ancilla, and to her niece and mine, Enrica, Giovanni's daughter, that I leave the largest share, for their use and possession, of my furniture at Camaitino, because these two blessed creatures, together with our mourned and much loved Ancilla, after parting from my brothers, have formed part of my most intimate family, have given me so much loving and patient service, and therefore deserve to be treated with special and particular respect. I will be grateful from heaven for any kindness shown to my sister Maria and my brother Alfredo, especially to this latter, because, as he grows older, he needs more assistance and affection.

I desire also that at my death there shall be given, out of the money that belongs to me, a small token of ten thousand Italian lire to each of my beloved brothers, Zaverio, Alfredo, Giovanni and Giuseppino, as well as to the families of my sisters Teresa, now dead, and Assunta. I have always loved all my brothers and sisters, with equal affection. And let each of them be given also some household object belonging to me in remembrance of me, chosen, however, exclusively from the furniture at Camaitino.

I request also that a little remembrance should be given to our dear cousin Elisa Mazzola, to her brother Giovanni and to our Magni cousins of Carvico, in memory of our revered mother who was a Mazzola, and of our aunt Felice, her sister who married into the Magni. Small objects, but such as to serve as a sign of my respectful and faithful remembrance.

(c) *Dispositions regarding any money that might still belong to me at my death*

The money deposited in my name in the Institute Opere di Religione

---

[1] In all, five acres of land.

in the Vatican consists of the sum, my private property, remaining from the salaries paid to me by the Holy See during my diplomatic service abroad. It has served as my current account, and I desire that at my death it shall be distributed as follows:

To the Bank 'Piccolo Credito Bergamasco' as much as I owe it, with warm thanks and with my blessing and good wishes for success in furthering the charitable purpose of that Institute.

To the Holy Father 50,000 lire[1] (fifty thousand lire) as a slight but significant offering of filial love.

To the Diocesan Curia of Bergamo 500,000 lire (five hundred thousand lire) so that the annual interest may serve as a contribution to the expenses of the holy Forty Hours' Devotion in my parish church of Sotto il Monte, the building of which was begun and continued during my priesthood and which was solemnly consecrated by me,[2] with the obligation that at least one of the Holy Masses celebrated during those days of adoration should be for my soul and for the souls of my relations who die before or after me.

I desire that there shall likewise be paid to the same Curia a sum that, according to the current value of money, is a generous alms for the celebration of twelve Holy Masses each year, one a month, and of an Office for the Dead to be sung in a seemly manner on the anniversary of my death in this same native parish of mine, Sotto il Monte, in suffrage for my soul, as above. The Holy Masses of the Office and of the Forty Hours' Devotion may be included in the twelve Masses mentioned above.

To the Central National Committee of the Pontifical Society for the Propagation of the Faith, of which Providence made me the first President of the Council for Italy, as a positive contribution to the general reconstitution of that organization as a Pontifical Society for the whole world, for the encouragement and edification of the clergy, shall be assigned 100,000 lire (one hundred thousand lire.)

As for the money that might still remain to my credit after all the above expenditure has been deducted, I desire that a part of it should go to my sister Maria and my niece Enrica for any eventual necessities of theirs, with the request that the poor should not be forgotten, especially those who are really poor and most shy about coming forward. Charity to the poor is a tradition in our family, as I remember it to have been from my

---

[1] At 1954 values, there were approximately 1750 lire to the £ sterling, 620 to the U.S. $.

[2] 21 September, 1929.

childhood. To honour this tradition will draw down many blessings on them also for the future.

For the poor I intend to reserve—within the limits of what is possible and suitable—a sum that it will be well to fix as soon as my humble possessions are liquidated, and hand over to the Diocesan Curia of Bergamo on behalf of the orphanage of Sotto il Monte which, together with the worthy parish priest, Father Giovanni Birolini, I always tried to help as much as my slender resources would permit, and which was especially dear to my heart. The blessing of a parish begins in the orphanage.

(d) *Various dispositions regarding books, objects, pictures, etc., belonging to me and destined for persons, institutions and places*

To the Holy Father, for the Vatican Library, my entire collection of books and prints of Bergamasque interest, not only as an act of homage but so that my example may serve as an encouragement to others of other dioceses, in Italy and abroad, to do the same for the increase and adornment of that famous library.

To the Bishop pro tempore of Bergamo, to adorn his residence where I spent the first happy years of my priesthood (1905–1914) as private secretary to Mgr Radini Tedeschi of revered memory, to whom I owe so much: the large canvas 'Our Lady with the Child and the little St John' which I bought from the antiquarian Carlo Ceresa in 1915; the other excellent painting from the same source, 'St Alexander the martyr with the Child bearing the dish full of flowers, blossoming from the miraculous blood of the martyr', as well as the large picture given me by the Marchese Pino Terzi di Sant' Agata, the portrait of Bishop Gerolamo Ragazzoni of Bergamo (d. 1591), formerly Apostolic Nuncio in Paris.

To the Cathedral of Bergamo, of which I enjoyed the cherished privilege of remaining a Canon, although an unworthy one, even after I was made Bishop and Cardinal, I bequeath my ceremonial cope of purple silk with the ermine and the precious rochet of old Burano lace. The ermine once belonged to Mgr Radini Tedeschi, Vatican Canon and Bishop; I bought the rochet for 20,000 lire from the Morlani family, after the death of my great and charitable benefactor Mgr Giovanni Morlani, to whom it had belonged, having come to him apparently from the family of the Counts Benaglio, the brothers Giuseppe and Mgr Gaetano, Bishop of Lodi. This cope may be used on the funeral catafalque of Bishops and Canons.

To the diocesan seminary of Bergamo, so dear to me, where I remained twenty-five years as student and teacher, the small panel portrait of Mgr

Radini Tedeschi by the painter Spinelli; all my manuscripts and correspondence—which really do not amount to much because the greater part is in the Roman archives of Propaganda Fide and in the Vatican: in the Apostolic Delegations in Bulgaria, Turkey and Greece and the Nunciature in Paris. Everything is useful for archives: even the most humble notes or papers about private matters and the letters preserved at Camaitino and here in Venice (provided that they have nothing to do with the diocesan administration). All these private papers, then, are to be sent to the seminary of Bergamo.

It is my particular and deliberate wish that the library of the seminary of Bergamo to which, with the help of His Excellency Most Reverend Gustavo Testa, Archbishop of Amasea, I gave in 1943 the entire collection of Migne's *Patrologia Latina* and *Graeca*, together with the later addition of more volumes that I had had bound, should also receive the entire collection of books and prints which I brought from Paris to Venice in 1953 and augmented here with my own acquisitions.

Above all, I declare that I leave to the seminary of Bergamo the absolute possession of my publication, *Gli Atti della Visita Apostolica di S. Carlo Borromeo (1575)*, with the request that the seminary will see to its distribution in a form that shall be advantageous to general ecclesiastical and secular studies, placing copies in the principal historical institutes in Italy and abroad. Until now, except for a few private subscriptions, I have borne the whole cost of this myself and the expenses for the first four volumes have been very considerable. I hope, with God's help, to complete this work before I die. In any case it will be well to seek instructions concerning this from the Prefect of the Biblioteca Ambrosiana in Milan and the well-deserving Società Editrice S. Alessandro, to both of which I wish to send, even in my last hour, a message of good wishes, gratitude and blessing, so that all may be successfully arranged in agreement with the seminary. Any eventual profits shall go to the increase of sound ecclesiastical studies for the clergy of Bergamo.

To the priests of the Sacred Heart in Bergamo, my beloved brothers, the large canvas portrait, under glass, of Mgr Radini Tedeschi by the painter Lussana, which is at Camaitino, and the large desk which the same prelate used until his death and bequeathed to me.

To the parish church of Sotto il Monte, to which I would have liked to make a more generous offering, besides the various gifts I have already made, I bequeath the chasuble embroidered in gold on silver lamé, which I brought from France. Also my mitres, so that they may be placed on the credence table on solemn occasions, if and when this is allowed or tolerated by the liturgical rules. The church may have the small wooden altar of mine which is now used provisionally for Our Lady of Sorrows.

To the little shrine of the Madonna delle Caneve, all the furnishings from my private chapel, if this is no longer used for worship after my death, and the baroque chalice, given me by Count Vittorio Mappelli on the occasion of my episcopal consecration.

To my nephew Don Battista, the silver chalice bequeathed to me by the late Mgr Vincenzo Bugarini, formerly my Rector at the Roman Seminary, who died in my house at S. Maria in Via Lata. Don Battista may do what he likes with the books I have left at Camaitino, eventually giving some share in these to his cousin Beltramino, if he also continues till the end in his training for the priesthood.

To the church of S. Maria at Brusico, the church of my baptism and of my childhood, the other chalice which I use here in Venice, a gift from Signora Eugenia Volpi, widow of Dott. Gerolamo.

To my brother Alfredo, as a mark of special affection, my gold watch and chain.

To my brothers Zaverio, Giovanni and Giuseppino, one each of the three largest paintings of the Madonna that are at Camaitino, not including the one left to the Bishop, as mentioned above, but including the Greek Madonna that is now in my study in Venice and that I bought in Istanbul.

(e) *My wishes and requests concerning my burial*

I now express one final consideration and desire to my beloved children of Venice concerning the last resting-place of my bones in expectation of the final resurrection. I deserve no special regard or consideration. But since to bury the dead is a work of mercy I implore this mercy for myself from those who loved me and whom I loved so well, namely, that there may be found a place for my body in the crypt of St Mark's near the tomb of the Evangelist, according to the prescribed rules and venerable traditions of the Catholic Church throughout the world, and that my most recent predecessors, whose mortal remains are left forgotten in the small chapel of the Most Holy Trinity in the patriarchal seminary or in the island of San Michele, may be associated with me, in tombs raised from the ground, around the tomb of the great Patron of Venice. I submit this meek and modest request to the gentlemen who form the glorious *Procuratoria* of St Mark's, with whom it has been such a pleasure for me to share the care for the beauty of this incomparable basilica, and I assure them of my prayers, from the world beyond too, and special blessings for them and their families.

Were it found impossible to accede to my wishes in this matter, then I desire to indicate as the last resting-place for my body before the resurrection the church of S. Maria della Salute under the compassionate gaze of the Mother of both living and dead, and near my patriarchal seminary, where the dearest hopes of Holy Church in Venice bloom and flourish. Amen.

Finally I commend the carrying out of these my wishes to the charity of Mgr Loris Capovilla, my beloved, distinguished and faithful secretary, whom I shall never cease to thank on earth and in heaven for the intelligent and affectionate service which with incomparable devotion he has been pleased to render to me personally and to my episcopal ministry. I am sure that he will do honour to himself and to me, knowing my way of thinking about meekness, discretion and patience in his relations with the various persons, especially the humblest members of my own family, named in this will. He may if he so wishes seek advice from one of his friends, but he must remain the sole judge and arbiter, to decide and carry out all that is contained in these pages concerning my last wishes.

I leave him free to choose among my belongings one or more souvenirs that he may keep in token of my gratitude, and as a pledge of the great blessing that I promise to send him from paradise, where I shall be awaiting him for our reunion and eternal happiness. Amen. Amen.

Once more and evermore:
  Glory be to the Father and to the Son and to the Holy Ghost.
  Hail Holy Queen, Mother of mercy.
  St Joseph, pray for me.

                              Cardinal ANGELO GIUSEPPE RONCALLI,
                                           Patriarch of Venice.

Venice, 29 June, 1954, feast of St Peter.

III

[77]   *[From the will drawn up between 1939 and 1944]*

To the Holy Father for the Vatican Library my whole collection of things of Bergamasque interest, not only as an act of homage but so that my example may serve as an encouragement to others, in other dioceses in Italy and abroad, to do the same for the increase and adornment of that famous library.

To the Bishop of Bergamo, to adorn his residence where I spent the first happy years of my priesthood as secretary to Mgr Radini Tedeschi of revered memory, to whom I owe so much, the large canvas, 'Our Lady with the Child and the little St John', which I bought from the antiquarian Ceresa, and the other excellent painting from the same source: 'St Alexander the Martyr with the divine Child bearing the dish full of flowers blossoming from the miraculous blood of the martyr', as well as the little inlaid panel by Fra Topolino representing the Blessed Gregory Barbarigo.[1]

To the Cathedral of Bergamo, where I always enjoyed the cherished privilege of remaining a Canon, although an unworthy one, even after I was made a Bishop, I bequeath my ceremonial cope of silk with the ermine. This ermine belonged to the late Mgr Radini Tedeschi and was considered valuable. If this is so it may also be sold and the money used for some other purpose for the church. The cope may be used on the funeral catafalque of Bishops or Canons.

To the seminary of Bergamo, so dear to me, where I remained for twenty-five years a student and teacher, my silver crozier, the small panel portrait of Mgr Radini Tedeschi by the painter Spinelli, and all my manuscripts, which really do not amount to much because the greater part is in the Roman archives, Propaganda Fide, and the Apostolic Delegations of Bulgaria, Turkey and Greece. All is of use to archives: even the most humble private papers.

To the Priests of the Sacred Heart in Bergamo, my beloved brothers, the large canvas portrait under glass of Mgr Radini Tedeschi by the artist Lussana, my desk used by the same prelate until his death and bequeathed to me, and all the books that are at Sotto il Monte at the time of my death, except for the collection of Bergamasque works already destined as above.

To the parish church of Sotto il Monte, which I should so much have liked to help more generously, my gold watch and chain, and two crosses, also of gold with gold chains, so that they may be sold and the proceeds used to provide a large, well-designed, artistic silver chalice, with my Archbishop's arms engraved upon it, and the date of my death, for the use of this church on the most solemn occasions.

To the same church I bequeath also my mitres so that they may be placed on the credence table on solemn occasions, if and when this is allowed or tolerated by the rubrics. The church may also keep the same wooden altar of mine which is now used, on the right-hand side, for Our Lady of Sorrows.

[1] On the death of Pope John this panel of inlay was given to Cardinal Amleto Giovanni Cicognani, as a mark of special and most grateful affection.

To the little shrine of the Madonna delle Caneve all the furnishings from my private chapel, including the baroque chalice given me by Count Vittorio Mappelli on the occasion of my episcopal consecration.

To the chapel of the Madonna della Fiducia in the Major Lateran Pontifical Roman Seminary, the silver chalice bequeathed to me by the late Mgr Vincenzo Bugarini, formerly Rector of the said seminary.

To the church of S. Maria at Brusico, the church of my baptism and of my childhood, the other chalice, a gift from Signora Eugenia Volpi, widow of Dott. Gerolamo.

I beg my sisters to leave to my brother Alfredo, as a sign of special affection, my silver watch which is already in his room at Camaitino, and to let my three brothers, Zaverio, Giovanni and Giuseppino choose, one for each, out of the three largest paintings of the Madonna at Camaitino, painted on canvas, or the panel painting which is now at Istanbul and will be sent from there or from wherever it is at the time of my death. I want these pictures to stay with members of the family in remembrance of their late uncle the Archbishop.

All the books that I myself have acquired and possess at the time of my death shall stay in Istanbul. They will be of use to my successors.

As for my body, I beg the Holy Father to have the kindness to arrange for it to be transported to my native place, Sotto il Monte, and buried there in the parish church near the steps that lead to the sanctuary, in the place where they are wont to set the bier of the humble dead for the funeral and for the Office, so as more easily to remind those good and simple faithful, my relations and compatriots, to pray for my soul, and so that I may pray with them and forever bless them and their descendants.

On the stone which will cover me forever, and over which will pass the feet of all, I want my humble name inscribed, with the dates and details of the offices I have held in the service of Holy Church, and also the words which I would wish to sum up my life and death: *Obœdientia et pax*. I want a special gift to be bestowed in remembrance of me on the parish priest of Sotto il Monte, and I desire that these dispositions of mine should be valid, apart from eventual modifications or additions.

In the name of the Father and the Son and the Holy Ghost. Amen. Jesus, Mary, Joseph, may I breathe forth my soul in peace with you.

ANGELO GIUS. RONCALLI
Archbishop of Mesembria

preced. pp. 1, 2 and 3 all typewritten by myself.

IV

The Holy Rosary

The Rosary

I

Apostolic Letter of H.H. John XXIII to the
Bishops and faithful of the whole
Catholic world[1]

Venerable brothers, beloved children, health and apostolic benediction.

The religious ceremony at Castel Gandolfo on Sunday, 10 September, attended by an impressive and numerous gathering of Cardinals, prelates, members of the diplomatic corps and a great throng of the faithful from all parts of the world, was wholly concerned with the general feeling of acute anxiety about the problem of peace.

The fact that we were there in our own humble person, our voice trembling with emotion, was the central, guiding and shining point of that meeting. Our consecrated and blessed hands raised aloft the Eucharistic Sacrifice, Jesus, our Saviour and Redeemer, the Saviour and Redeemer of the whole world, the King of peace for all ages and all peoples.

Every nation was represented there, thus giving our gathering a worldwide significance. Among other groups there was a large number of students from the Collegio Urbano di Propaganda, reminding us that all peoples, even those who are not Christian, are praying for peace.

With our heart full of emotion and of trust in God we announced on that inspired evening our intention of encouraging further gatherings, as suitable occasions present themselves, to pray about our fundamental duty of trying to preserve the peace of the world and civilization itself. It was for this intention, and to offer an initial example, that we went a few days ago to the catacombs of San Callistus, those being the nearest to our summer residence, in order to pray: surrounded by sacred memories

---

[1] The apostolic letter and the meditations were published in *L'Osservatore Romano*, on 10 February, 1962, and reprinted in book form with the title *Il Santo Rosario. Pensieri di S.S. Giovanni XXIII* (Turin, 1962: the 'offering of the workers of the Fiat factory to His Holiness John XXIII'). Cf. also *Giovanni XXIII, Discorsi, messaggi, colloqui, cit.,* vol. III, pp. 753-72.

of our predecessors, of at least fourteen Popes, and Bishops and martyrs famous in history, we prayed for their intercession in heaven to assure for all nations, since all belong in some way to Christ, the great treasure of peace: 'That God would vouchsafe to give peace and unity to all Christian people.'[1]

Here we are now in October which is, by trustful, pious tradition and Christian love, dedicated to the customary veneration of Our Lady of the Rosary, and now appears to us as a new and most suitable opportunity for universal prayer to the Lord for the same great intention, of vital interest to individuals, families and peoples.

Last May, inspired by the example of Pope Leo XIII of glorious memory, we again recommended the teachings contained in his *Rerum Novarum* and further developed these in our encyclical *Mater et Magistra*, with the purpose of adapting Catholic teaching still more closely to the new requirements of human and Christian society.

We recall that this great Pope, who was the light and guidance of our soul in our boyhood, when we were preparing for the splendour of the priestly ministry, frequently invited the Christian world to say the holy rosary, presented to all the Church's children as an exercise in holy and profitable meditation, for the uplifting of their souls and as an intercession for heavenly graces for the whole Church.

His successors were always faithful to this pious and affecting tradition. And we also intend humbly to follow these great and most revered shepherds of the flock of Christ, not only in ever more devoted care for the interests of justice and brotherhood in this earthly life, but also in fervent endeavours for the sanctification of souls, for in this lies our real strength and our assurance of success; it is like a voice from heaven answering the voices that rise from this earth, from sincere souls longing for truth and love.

Already, at the beginning of October, 1959, we addressed to the whole Catholic world the encyclical *Grata Recordatio*[2] and in the following year, with the same intention, we wrote a letter[3] to the Cardinal Vicar of our Roman diocese.

For this reason, venerable brothers and beloved children, scattered throughout the world, we wish once more this year to set before you some simple and practical considerations which the devotion of the holy rosary suggests to us, for the nourishment and strengthening of vital principles intended to guide your thought and prayer. All this as an

---

[1] Cf. the Litany of the Saints.   [2] A.A.S., LI (1959), pp. 673–88.
[3] *L'Ottobre che ci sta innanzi*, cf. A.A.S., LII (1960), pp. 814–17.

expression of perfect and tranquil Christian piety, and with the purpose of world-wide supplication for the peace of all men and of all peoples.

The rosary, as an exercise of Christian piety among the faithful of the Latin rite, who form a large part of the Catholic family, takes its place, for ecclesiastics, after Holy Mass and the Breviary, and for lay folk after their participation in the sacraments. It is a devout form of union with God, and always has a most uplifting effect on the soul.

It is true that, in the case of some souls who have not been trained to rise above mere lip service, it may be recited as a monotonous succession of the three prayers: the Our Father, the Hail Mary, and the Gloria, arranged in the traditional order of fifteen decades. Even this, to be sure, is something. But, we must repeat, it is only the beginning or the external expression of trustful prayer, rather than the joyful flight of the soul in converse with God in the sublime and tender mysteries of his merciful love for all mankind.

The real substance of the well-meditated rosary consists in a threefold chord which gives its vocal expression unity and cohesion, revealing in a vivid sequence the episodes which bind together the lives of Jesus and Mary, with reference to the various conditions of those who pray and the aspirations of the universal Church.

Every decade of Hail Marys has its own picture, and every picture has a threefold character which is always the same: *mystical contemplation, private reflection,* and *pious intention.*

First of all the *contemplation,* pure, clear and immediate, of every mystery, that is of those truths of the faith which speak to us of the redeeming mission of Christ. As we contemplate we find ourselves in close communion of thought and feeling with the teaching and life of Jesus, Son of God and Son of Mary, who lived on this earth redeeming, teaching, sanctifying: in the silence of his hidden life, all prayer and work; in the sufferings of his blessed Passion; in the triumph of his Resurrection; in the glory of heaven, where he sits on the right hand of the Father, ever assisting and with his Holy Spirit giving life to the Church founded by him, which proceeds on its way throughout the centuries.

The second element is *reflection,* which out of the fulness of Christ's mysteries diffuses its bright radiance over the praying soul. Everyone finds in each mystery a good and proper teaching for himself, for his sanctification and for the conditions of his own life; under the constant guidance of the Holy Spirit, which from the depths of the soul in a state of grace 'intercedes for us with sighs too deep for words',[1] everyone con-

[1] Romans 8: 26.

fronts his own life with the strength of the doctrine he has drawn from the depths of those same mysteries, and finds them of inexhaustible application to his own spiritual needs and to the needs of his daily life too.

Finally there is the *intention*: that is intercession for persons, institutions, or necessities of a personal or social nature, which for a really active and pious Catholic forms part of his charity towards his neighbour, a charity which is diffused in our hearts as a living expression of our common sharing in the Mystical Body of Christ.

In this way the rosary becomes a world-wide supplication of individual souls and of the immense community of the redeemed, who from all parts of the world meet in a single prayer, either in private petitions imploring graces for each one's personal needs, or in sharing in the immense and general chorus of the whole Church praying for the supreme interests of all mankind. The Church, as the divine Redeemer has ordained, lives amid the difficulties, conflicts and storms of a social disorder that frequently becomes a frightening menace; but her eyes and her natural and supernatural energies are directed towards her supreme destiny of fulfilling the eternal purposes of God.

This is the rosary of Mary, considered in its various elements, which are linked together in vocal prayer and woven into it as in a delicate and rich embroidery, full of spiritual warmth and beauty.

Vocal prayers thus take on their full significance: above all the Our Father, which gives the rosary its tone, substance and life and, coming as it does after the announcement of the individual mysteries, marks the passing from one decade to another; then the angel's greeting, echoing the joy of heaven and earth and accompanying the various scenes from the lives of Jesus and Mary; and finally the Gloria, repeated in profound worship of the Most Holy Trinity.

Oh how beautiful it always is when said in this way by innocent children and by the sick, by virgins consecrated to cloistered seclusion or to the apostolate of charity, always to a life of complete humility and self-denial; of men and women who are fathers and mothers of families, and are sustained by a lofty sense of their noble and Christian responsibilities; of humble families faithful to their old family traditions; of souls recollected in silence, aloof from the life of the world they have renounced, but in which they are still obliged to live, like anchorites, amidst doubts and temptations.

This is the rosary of pious souls, who are deeply conscious of their own particular lives and circumstances.

While we respect this ancient, customary and affecting form of Marian devotion, responding to everyone's individual circumstances, we wish at the same time to point out that the transformations that have appeared in every sector of modern society, the scientific inventions, even the improvements in the organization of labour, which enable man to get a broader and clearer view and understanding of the state of the world today, are arousing a new awareness even of the functions and forms of Christian prayer. Now every man who prays no longer feels alone, occupied exclusively with his own interests of a spiritual and temporal order, but perceives, more clearly and better than in the past, that he belongs to a social body, sharing its responsibilities, enjoying its advantages and fearing the common uncertainties and dangers. This is moreover characteristic of the liturgical prayer of the Missal and Breviary; every time we say 'Let us pray', this implies a concourse of people, not only of those who are praying now but also of those who have prayed and await the answer to their prayers; it is the whole throng that prays in common supplication for the whole brotherhood of man, in religious or in social life.

In this way the rosary of Mary assumes the dignity of a great public and universal prayer, to express the ordinary and extraordinary needs of Holy Church, of the nations and of the whole world.

In the history of the most powerful states of Europe there have been some periods of great, indeed of the greatest danger, because of series of events which have stained them with tears and blood.

Those who study the developments of political events from the historical point of view know well the influence exerted by Marian devotions in preserving the nations from the calamities which threatened them, in the restoration of prosperity and social order and in the achievement of spiritual victories.

We are always mindful of our beloved city of Venice, where for six years we had so many precious opportunities for good pastoral work, and we wish to mention as an occasion of great joy, which touches our heart, the now completed restoration of the richly adorned Chapel of the Rosary, the glory of the Dominican Fathers' basilica of St John and St Paul.

This is a monument which shines most honourably, even among the many in Venice which attest the victories of the Faith through the centuries, and represents those years, 1563–1575, which followed the Council of Trent and were characterized by the fervour diffused throughout all Christendom in honour of the rosary of Mary, who since then has been invoked under the name of 'Help of Christians'.

O blessed rosary of Mary! what joy to see it raised in the hands of innocent children, of holy priests, of the pure in heart, young and old, of all who understand the value and efficacy of prayer; raised aloft by countless pious multitudes as an emblem or standard of that peace in men's hearts and among peoples for which we all hope.

When we speak of peace in the human and Christian sense we mean that sense of truth, justice and perfect brotherhood among the nations which, once it has penetrated the minds of men, dissipates all danger of discord and confusion; which sets the wills of one and all in harmony with the teaching of the Gospel and the contemplation of the mysteries and lives of Jesus and Mary, which are familiar to the piety of all; every soul will then practise perfect obedience to that holy law which, ruling in men's secret hearts, will direct the actions of all towards the attainment of Christian peace, the delight of men's lives and the foretaste of unfailing and eternal joys to come.

Beloved brothers and children, concerning this subject of the rosary of Mary, we could find in our heart other devout considerations of moving and persuasive power, presenting it as a world-wide supplication for the peace of the Lord and for the happiness of men and peoples even in this world. But we choose to offer for your attention, as the complement of this Apostolic Letter, a short sequence of devout considerations, arranged for every decade of the rosary, with reference to the threefold emphasis —mystery, reflection and intention—which we have mentioned above.

These simple notes, which come from our heart, may be found useful to many who are particularly desirous to overcome the monotony of mere recitation: they are useful and timely thoughts for the heightening of personal piety and for giving more fervour to our prayer for the salvation and peace of all men.

My last thought is for St Joseph. His beloved figure appears several times in the joyful mysteries of the rosary. And we must remember that the great Pope Leo XIII most fervently commended him three times— in 1885, 1886 and 1889—to the veneration of the faithful, teaching us that prayer: 'To you, O Blessed Joseph' (*A te, O beato Giuseppe*) which is all the more dear to us because it was learnt in the fervour of our happy childhood.

Once more we also commend it to you, as we beg the guardian of Jesus and the chaste spouse of Mary to strengthen with his intercession our prayers and our hopes.

Finally, with all our heart we hope that this month of October may be for loving souls what it is intended to be, a constant, delightful intercourse in mystical union with her who at the end of the Office for the feast of the

Most Holy Rosary is still and always acclaimed as 'Blessed Mother and inviolate Virgin, glorious Queen of the world', for the peace and happiness of all.

JOANNES XXIII PP.

Castel Gandolfo, 29 September, 1961, Feast of St Michael the Archangel.

II

[79] *A brief sequence of devout considerations arranged for each decade of the rosary*

THE JOYFUL MYSTERIES

1. *The Annunciation*

This is the first shining point of union between heaven and earth: the first of those events which were to be the greatest of all time.

The Son of God, Word of the Father, 'without whom was not anything made that was made'[1] in the order of creation, in this mystery takes on human nature and becomes a man, in order to save and redeem all men, all mankind.

When Mary Immaculate, the finest and most fragrant flower of all creation, said in answer to the angel's greeting: 'Behold the handmaid of the Lord'[2] she accepted the honour of divine motherhood, which was in that moment realized within her. And we, born once in our father Adam, formerly the adopted sons of God but fallen from that high estate, are now once more brothers, adopted sons of the Father, restored to his adoption by the redemption which has already begun. At the foot of the Cross we shall all be children of Mary, with that same Jesus whom she has conceived today. From today onwards she will be Mother of God (*Mater Dei*) and our Mother (*mater nostra*) too.

What sublimity, what tender love in this first mystery!

When we reflect on this we see that our chief and constant duty is to thank the Lord who deigned to come to save us and for this purpose made himself man, our brother man; he has joined us by becoming the son of a woman and by making us, at the foot of the Cross, the adopted sons of this woman. He wanted us who were the adopted sons of his Heavenly Father to be sons of his own Mother.

[1] John 1: 3.   [2] Luke 1: 38.

Let the intention of our prayer, as we contemplate this first picture offered to our thoughts, be, besides a constant feeling of gratitude, a real and sincere effort to acquire humility, purity and ardent love for the Blessed Virgin who provides the most precious example of all these virtues.

2. *Mary's Visit to her Cousin Elizabeth*

What gentleness and charm in this three months' visit made by Mary to her beloved cousin! Each of them is about to bear a child, but for the Virgin Mother this is the most sacred maternity that it is possible to imagine on earth. Their two songs mingle and respond in a sweet harmony: 'Blessed are you among women'[1] on the one hand, and on the other: 'God my Saviour has regarded the low estate of his handmaiden: for behold, henceforth all generations will call me blessed.'[2]

What takes place here, at Ain-Karim on the hill of Hebron, sheds a light, both very human and divine, on the relations that bind Christian families, brought up in the ancient tradition of the holy rosary: the rosary recited every evening at home, in the family circle; the rosary recited not just in one or a hundred or a thousand families but by every family, by everyone, everywhere in the world, wherever there is one of us 'suffering, fighting and praying',[3] someone who has answered another call to the priesthood or to missionary service or to a dream which will turn out to be an apostolate; or wherever men are constrained by those legitimate if obligatory demands of labour or trade, military service, study, teaching or any other occupation.

There is a beautiful reunion, during the ten Hail Marys of the mystery, of so many countless souls, linked together by blood or by domestic ties, in a relationship which hallows and thereby strengthens the love that binds our dearest ones together: parents and children, brothers and relations, people from the same locality, people of the same race. All this with the purpose and intention of sustaining, increasing and irradiating that universal charity, the exercise of which is the most profound joy and supreme honour of our lives.

3. *The Birth of Jesus in the Stable at Bethlehem*

At the hour appointed by the laws of the human nature he had assumed, the Word of God, now made man, issues from the holy shrine, the immaculate womb of Mary. He makes his first appearance in this world in a manger: the cattle are there, chewing their straw, and all

[1] Luke 1: 42.   [2] Luke 1: 48.   [3] A. Manzoni, *La Pentecoste*, v. 6.

around are silence, poverty, simplicity and innocence. Angels' voices are heard in the sky, announcing peace, that peace which the new baby has brought to us. His first worshippers are Mary his mother and Joseph, thought to be his father, and after these some humble shepherds who have come down from the hills, led by angels' voices. Later on comes a caravan of distinguished persons guided from far, far away by a star; they offer precious gifts, full of a mysterious meaning. Everything that night at Bethlehem spoke a language that the whole world could understand.

Pondering this mystery every knee will bow in adoration before the crib. Everyone will look into the eyes of the divine Infant which gaze far away, almost as if he could see one by one all the peoples of the earth, one after the other, as if he were reviewing them all as they pass before him, recognizing and identifying them all and greeting them with a smile: Jews, Romans, Greeks, Chinese, Indians, the peoples of Africa and of every region of the world, of every age of history, the most desolate, deserted lands, and the most remote, secret and unexplored; past, present and future ages.

The Holy Father, as the intention of these ten Hail Marys, wishes to commend to the new-born Jesus the infinite number of babies—and who could count them all? who in the last twenty-four hours, by night or day, have been born, some here, some there, all over the world. An infinite number indeed! And all, whether baptized or not, belong by right to Jesus, to this Child who is born in Bethlehem; they are his brothers, called to establish this rule of his which is the most sublime and the most gentle that can be found in man's heart or in the history of the world, the only rule worthy of God and man: a rule of light, a rule of peace, the 'kingdom' for which we pray when we say the Our Father.

4. *The Presentation of Jesus in the Temple*

Jesus, carried in his mother's arms, is offered to the priest, to whom he holds out his arms: it is the meeting, the contact of the two Covenants. He is already the 'light for revelation to the Gentiles',[1] he, the splendour of the chosen people, the son of Mary. St Joseph also is there to present him, an equal sharer in this rite of legal offerings according to the law.

This episode is continually repeated in the Church, indeed is perpetuated there in forms which vary but are similar in the substance of the offering. As we repeat the Hail Marys, how beautiful it is to contemplate the growing crops, the rising corn: 'Lift up your eyes, and see how the fields are already white for the harvest.'[2] These are the joyful and rising hopes of

---

[1] Luke 2: 32. [2] John 4: 35.

the priesthood, and of those men and women who co-operate with the priests, so numerous in the kingdom of God and yet never enough: young people in the seminaries, in religious houses, in missionary training colleges, also, and why not? are they not Christians also, called likewise to be apostles?—in the Catholic universities. There are also all the other young shoots of the future and indispensable apostolate of the laity, this apostolate which, increasing in spite of difficulties and opposition, even within nations tormented by persecution, offers and will never cease to offer such a consoling spectacle as to compel expressions of admiration and joy.

This child is the 'light for revelation to the Gentiles,'[1] and the glory of the chosen people.

5. *Jesus Found among the Doctors in the Temple*

Jesus is now twelve years old. Mary and Joseph have brought him with them to Jerusalem, for the ritual prayers. Without warning he disappears from their sight, although they are so watchful and so loving. Great anxiety and a fruitless search for three days. Their sorrow is followed by the joy of finding him again, there, under the porches of the Temple. He is speaking with the doctors of the Law. How significant is the account given us by St Luke, with his careful precision! They found him then, sitting in the midst of the doctors 'listening to them and asking them questions'.[2] In those days an encounter with the doctors was very important and meant everything: learning, wisdom, and the direction of practical life by the light of the Old Testament.

Such, in every age, is the task of the human intelligence: to garner the wisdom of the ages, to hand down the good doctrine and firmly and humbly to press ahead with scientific investigation. We die, one after the other, we go to God, but mankind moves towards the future.

Christ, in natural as in supernatural revelation, is never absent; he is always in his place, in the midst: 'For you have one master, the Christ.'[3]

This is the fifth decade of Hail Marys, the last of the joyful mysteries. Let us keep it as a very special invocation for the benefit of those who are called by God, because of their natural gifts, or the circumstances of their lives, or the wishes of their Superiors, to the service of truth, in research and in teaching, in the imparting of ancient learning or modern skills, by means of books or wireless and television—for all these too are called to follow Jesus. They are the intellectuals, the professional classes and the journalists; the journalists especially, who have the particular task of

[1] Luke 2: 32.   [2] Luke 2: 46.   [3] Matthew 23: 10.

honouring the truth, must transmit it with religious fidelity and great discretion, without fantastic distortions or inventions.

We pray for them all, priests or laity; we pray that they may listen to the truth, and for this they need great purity of heart; that they may understand it, and for this they need profound humility of mind; that they may defend it, and for this they need what made the strength of Jesus and of his saints: obedience. Only obedience wins peace, which means victory.

THE SORROWFUL MYSTERIES

1. *Jesus in the Garden of Gethsemane*

Our heart is moved as we continually return to the image of the Saviour, in the place and hour of his supreme anguish: '... and his sweat became like great drops of blood falling down upon the ground.'[1] Suffering of the innermost soul, extreme bitterness of loneliness, exhaustion of the broken body. His suffering can only be measured by the imminence of his Passion which now Jesus sees, no longer as far away, or even as near at hand, but as present in that hour.

The scene in the garden strengthens and encourages us to force all our will to an acceptance, a full acceptance, of suffering sent or permitted by God: 'Not my will but thine be done.'[2] Words which tear the heart and heal it again, for they teach us what passionate fervour the Christian can and must feel if he is to suffer with Christ who suffers, and give us the final certainty of the indescribable merits he obtained for us, the certainty of the divine life, a life which today is lived in grace and tomorrow in glory.

A special intention should be borne in mind as we dwell on this mystery: the 'anxiety for all the Churches',[3] an anxiety which torments us, as the wind tormented the lake of Gennesaret, 'for the wind was against them',[4] the daily prayer of the Holy Father, the anxiety of the highest pastoral ministry in the most critical hours; the anxiety of the Church, scattered all over the earth, which suffers with him, and which he bears with the Church, present and suffering in him; anxiety for countless souls, whole portions of the flock of Christ, who are subjected to persecutions directed against liberty of belief, thought and life. 'Who is in trouble, and I not in trouble with him?'[5]

[1] Luke 22: 44. [2] Luke 22: 42. [3] 2 Cor. 11: 28.
[4] Matthew 14: 24. [5] Cf. 2 Cor. 11: 29.

To share in our brothers' pain, to suffer with those who suffer, to weep with those who weep,[1] will confer a blessing, a merit on the whole Church. Is this not what we mean by the 'communion of saints', everyone of us sharing in common the blood of Jesus, the love of the saints and of good people, and also, alas! our sins and failings? Do we ever think of this 'communion' which is union, and almost, as Jesus said, unity: 'That they may be one'?[2] The Lord's Cross not only raises us up but draws the souls of men, always: 'And I, when I am lifted up, will draw all men to myself.'[3] All things, all men.

2. *The Scourging*

This mystery reminds us of the merciless torture of the many stripes inflicted on the pure and holy body of Jesus.

Man is made up of body and soul. The body is subjected to the most humiliating temptations: the will, which is weaker, may easily be overcome. In this mystery then there is a call to practise penance, a salutary penance, since it is important for man's true health, which is health in the bodily sense and also health in the sense of spiritual salvation.

There is a great lesson here for us all. We may not be called to endure a cruel martyrdom, but we are called to the exercise of constant discipline and the daily mortification of our passions. This way, a real 'Way of the Cross,' our daily, unavoidable and indispensable duty, which at times becomes even heroic in its requirements, leads us step by step towards a more and more perfect resemblance with Jesus Christ, and a share in his merits and in the atonement through his innocent blood for every sin in us and in all people. We cannot do this in any other way, by facile enthusiasms, or by a fanaticism which, even if innocent, is always harmful.

His Mother, sorrowing, saw her Son scourged in this way: what pain she too must have felt! There are so many mothers who would like to have the joy of seeing their children grow up, initiated by them into the discipline of a good training and a healthy life, and who instead have to mourn the vanishing of so many hopes and weep that so much care and anxiety have come to nothing.

So our Hail Marys of this mystery must implore the Lord to give purity of morals to our families and to society, especially to our young people who are most exposed to the temptation of the senses. At the same time they will beg him to give them strength of character and fidelity at all costs to the teachings they have received and the resolutions they have made.

[1] Romans 12: 15.   [2] John 17: 22 and cf. John 10: 30.   [3] John 12: 32.

3. The Crowning with Thorns

The contemplation of this mystery is particularly indicated for those who bear the weight of grave responsibilities, in the government of society; hence it is the mystery for rulers, law-givers and magistrates. This King wears a crown of thorns. They too wear crowns, which have their own undeniable dignity and distinction, crowns representing an authority which comes from God and is divine; nevertheless they are so mixed with burdensome and hurtful elements that sometimes we are perplexed and almost disheartened by these pricking thorns and pre-occupations, as well as by all the suffering caused by the misfortunes and sins of men; this suffering is the greater the more we love men, and it is our duty to represent to them their Father who is in heaven. Then love itself becomes, as it did for Jesus, a crown of thorns woven by cruel men for the head of one who loves them.

Another useful way of thinking about this mystery would be to consider the grave responsibilities of those who have received greater talents and are therefore bound to make them yield greater fruit, through the continual use of their faculties and intelligence. The ministry of the mind, that is the service required of those most richly endowed with intelligence, in order to be a light and guide to all others, must be undertaken with great patience, resisting all the temptations of pride, selfishness and the disintegration which is destructive.

4. The Way of the Cross

The life of men is a pilgrimage, continual, long and wearisome. Up and up along the steep and stony road, the road marked out for all upon that hill. In this mystery Jesus represents the whole race of men. Every one of us must have his own cross to bear; otherwise, tempted by selfishness or cruelty, we should sooner or later fall by the roadside.

From the contemplation of Jesus climbing up to Calvary we learn, first with our hearts and then with our minds, to embrace and kiss the Cross, and bear it bravely and with joy, as we read in *The Imitation of Christ:* 'In the Cross is our salvation, in the Cross is our life, in the Cross is our defence against our foes, and our heavenly sweetness.'[1]

And how can we fail to include Mary in our prayers, Mary who followed Jesus sorrowing, sharing so intimately in his merits and his sufferings.

The mystery should set before our eyes a vast vision of poor suffering

---

[1] *Imitation,* Book II, XII, 2.

souls: orphans, old people, the sick, the weak, prisoners and exiles. We pray for strength for all these, and the consolation which alone brings hope. We repeat with emotion and, we must admit, with secret tears, 'Hail, O Cross, our only hope.'[1]

5. The Death of Jesus

'. . . in strange and awful strife
Met together death and life.'[2]

Life and death are the two significant and decisive elements of Christ's sacrifice. From his smile at Bethlehem, the same smile which lights up the faces of all the children of men when first they appear on earth, to his last gasp and sob on the Cross, which gathered all our sufferings into one to hallow them, and wiped away all our sins by atoning for them, we have seen how Christ lived in this our earthly life. And Mary is still there, beside the Cross, as she was beside the Babe at Bethlehem. Let us pray to her, this Mother, pray to her so that she too may pray for us 'now and at the hour of our death'.

In this mystery we might see foreshadowed the mystery of those who —what sadness in this thought!—will never know anything about the blood that was poured out for them too by the Son of God; and above all the mystery of obstinate sinners, of unbelievers, of those who have received, still do receive and then refuse the light of the Gospel! With this thought our prayer expands in a vast longing, in a sigh of heartfelt reparation, the longing to reach to the ends of the earth with our apostolate; and we earnestly pray that the Precious Blood, poured out for all mankind, may at long last bring to all, to all men everywhere, salvation and conversion, that the Blood of Christ may be to all the pledge and promise of eternal life.

THE GLORIOUS MYSTERIES

1. The Resurrection of Our Lord

This is the mystery of death challenged and defeated. The Resurrection marks the greatest victory of Christ, and likewise the assurance of victory for the holy Catholic Church, beyond all the adversities and persecutions of past yesterdays and tomorrow's future. 'Christ conquers, reigns and rules.' We do well to remember that the first appearance of the risen

---

[1] Roman Breviary, Vesper Hymn for Passion Sunday.
[2] Roman Missal, Sequence from the Easter Mass.

Christ was to the pious women, who were near to him during his humble life, who had accompanied him in his sufferings as far as Calvary, and stayed with him there.

In the splendour of this mystery we see with the eyes of faith, as living and united with the risen Jesus, the souls who were most dear to us, the souls of those who lived with us and whose sufferings we shared. How vividly the memory of our dead rises in our hearts in the light of the Resurrection of Christ! We remember and pray for them in the very sacrifice of our crucified and risen Lord, and they still share the best part of our life, which is prayer and Jesus.

The Eastern liturgy wisely concludes the funeral rite with the 'Alleluia!' for all the dead. While we implore the light of eternal habitations for our dead, at the same time our thoughts turn to the resurrection which awaits our own mortal remains: *Et exspecto resurrectionem mortuorum.* Learning to wait, trusting always to the precious promise of which the Resurrection of Jesus gives us a sure pledge—this is a foretaste of heaven.

2. *The Ascension of Jesus into Heaven*

In this picture we contemplate the 'consummation', that is the final fulfilment of the promises of Jesus. It is his reply to our longing for paradise. His final return to the Father, from whom one day he came down among us in this world, is a surety for us all, to whom he has promised and prepared a place above: 'I go to prepare a place for you.'[1]

Above all, this mystery brings light and guidance for those souls who are absorbed in the study of their own vocations. We see within it that spiritual longing, that yearning to soar upwards, which burns in the hearts of priests who are not hampered or distracted by the wealth of this world but intent only on opening the way, for themselves and others, to holiness and perfection, to that degree of grace which is to be attained, privately and in common, by priests, men and women in Religious Orders, men and women missionaries, lay people who love God and his Church, and numerous souls, those souls at least that are like 'the aroma of Christ',[2] who make the presence of Jesus felt wherever they are, for indeed they are already living in constant communion with the life of heaven.

This decade of the rosary teaches and urges us not to let ourselves be hampered by things that burden and encumber us, but to abandon ourselves instead to the will of God which draws us heavenward. As Jesus ascends into heaven to return to his Father, his arms are open to bless

[1] John 14: 2.　　　　　　　　　　[2] Cf. 2 Cor. 2: 15.

his first apostles, to bless all those who in the footsteps of the apostles continue to believe in him, and his blessing is in their hearts a tranquil and serene assurance of their final reunion with him and with all the redeemed, in everlasting bliss.

3. *The Descent of the Holy Spirit*

At the Last Supper the apostles received the promise of the Spirit; later, in that very room, in the absence of Jesus but in the presence of Mary, they received him as Christ's supreme gift. Indeed, what is his Spirit if not the Consoler and Giver of life to men? The Holy Spirit is continually poured out on the Church and within it every day; all ages and all men belong to the Spirit, belong to the Church. The Church's triumphs are not always externally visible, but they are always there and always rich in surprises, often in miracles.

The Hail Marys of the present mystery have a special intention during this year of great enthusiasm when the whole Holy Church, a pilgrim on this earth, is preparing for the Ecumenical Council. The Council must succeed in being a new Pentecost of faith, of the apostolate, of extraordinary graces for the welfare of men, and the peace of the world. Mary the Mother of Jesus, always our own sweet Mother, was with the apostles in the upper room for the miracle of Pentecost. Let us keep closer to her in our rosary, all this year. Our prayers, united with hers, will renew the miracle of old. It will be like the rising of a new day, a radiant dawn for the Catholic Church, holy and growing ever more holy, Catholic and growing ever more Catholic, in these modern days.

4. *The Assumption of Mary into Heaven*

The queenly figure of Mary is illuminated and glorified in the highest dignity which a creature may attain. What grace, sweetness and solemnity in the scene of Mary's 'falling asleep', as the Christians of the East imagine it! She is lying in the serene sleep of death; Jesus stands beside her, and clasps her soul, as if it were a tiny child, to his heart, to indicate the miracle of her immediate resurrection and glorification.

The Christians of the West, raising their eyes and hearts to heaven, choose to portray Mary borne body and soul to the eternal kingdom. The greatest artists saw her thus, incomparable in her divine beauty. Oh let us too go with her, borne aloft by her escort of angels!

This is a source of consolation and faith, in days of grief or pain, for those privileged souls—such as we can all become, if only we respond to grace—whom God is silently preparing for the most beautiful victory of all, the attainment of holiness.

The mystery of the Assumption brings home to us the thought of death, of our own death, and gives us a sense of serene confidence; it makes us understand and welcome the thought that the Lord will be, as we would wish him to be, near us in our last agony, to gather into his own hands our immortal soul.

'May your grace be always with us, Immaculate Virgin.'

5. *Coronation of Mary above all the Choirs of Angels and Saints*

The meaning of the whole rosary is summed up in this scene of joy and glory, with which it ends.

The great mission which began with the angel's announcement to Mary has passed like a stream of fire and light through the mysteries in turn: God's eternal plan for our salvation has been presented to us in one scene after another, accompanying us along our way, and now it brings us back to God in the splendour of heaven.

The glory of Mary, Mother of Jesus and our Mother too, is irradiated in the inaccessible light of the august Trinity and reflected in dazzling splendour in Holy Church, triumphant in heaven, suffering patiently in purgatory in the confident expectation of heaven, and militant on earth.

O Mary, you are praying for us, you are always praying for us. We know it, we feel it. Oh what joy and truth, what sublime glory, in this heavenly and human interchange of sentiments, words and actions, which the rosary always brings us: the tempering of our human afflictions, the foretaste of the peace that is not of this world, the hope of eternal life!

V

Some Prayers

1929

To the Child Jesus[1]

O heavenly Child, our almighty Lord, we believe that you grant the requests of those who turn to you with pure hearts and that you also hear the prayers of those who are silent; we thank you for having called us today to share in the holy mysteries offered to our souls, to strengthen us ever more in the faith, to preserve our piety and to obtain for us forgiveness of our sins. Your name has been invoked over us.

Keep us closely united among ourselves and with those who are dedicated to your service. Confirm us in your truth, through the grace of the Holy Spirit; reveal to us the truths of which we are still ignorant, supply what we lack and strengthen our faith in what we know. Preserve priests in purity for the service of your altar, and protect kings and governments in peace and magistrates in justice; give us tranquil skies and the fruits of the earth in abundance and keep the whole world in your almighty care. Calm aggressive minds, convert the erring, make your people holy, preserve the purity of virgins, guard the faithfulness of married men and women, fortify the chaste; enlighten those who have only just begun to follow your teaching, and confirm them, make them worthy of loftier attainment, and may we at the last all be eternally reunited in your kingdom, O Jesus, together with you, with the Father and the Holy Spirit, to whom be glory, honour and blessing for ever and ever. Amen.

[1] Prayer taken from his Christmas homily, Sofia, 1929.

1940

[81]   *For the safety of the city of Istanbul*[1]

O God, Saviour of souls, Saviour of nations, of all nations, Saviour of
the world! You see the storm that is raging over the peoples of the
west and that threatens to engulf families, states, and enormous sections
of mankind.

O Jesus, stretch out your powerful hand over this mighty conflict and
bring it to an end. Give to the hearts of men a lively understanding, in
which all shall share, of the sacred rights of social justice, which is inspired
by the evangelical principles of mutual respect, true brotherhood and the
co-operation of all in the common good and in the promotion of material
prosperity also.

Give us your peace, the just peace, the lasting peace, that the world
cannot give, in which there will be room for all, because first of all there
will be room for you and for your Gospel, for your Church.

It is only right that while we share in the sufferings of the sister nations,
to which many of us belong, and which are today officially at war with
one another, we should also be anxious and fearful about what concerns
us most closely. Permit us therefore, dear Lord, to implore you to deliver
us from the evils and dangers that war, if unhappily it were to spread
from the West to the East, might bring to us, to our lives, our families,
our possessions, to the whole of this land where Providence has placed us.
And what we ask for ourselves we ask with equal purity of intention for
all with whom we live, under the same skies, all brothers together, even
if of diverse religion, race, historical traditions and social position.

Lord Jesus, have pity on us and spare this most noble city, founded in
your name and still dear to you.

We implore you in the name of Holy Church: 'From plague, famine
and war, deliver us, O Lord.'[2]

[1] Prayer composed and spoken in Italian and French by Mgr A. G. Roncalli, Apostolic
Vicar and Delegate, for the transferred Feast of St Anthony, after the Procession of the
Lilies, on Thursday, 15 June, 1940, to beg for the preservation of the city of Istanbul from
air raids and other acts of war.
[2] Cf. Litany of the Saints.

From the dangers that threaten us, deliver us, O Lord.

And since today is the feast of your illustrious servant Anthony of Padua, whom you so often chose as your minister to distribute your graces and favours, permit us to place in his blessed hands our common and solemn supplication, sure as we are that he will add his own intercession to our humble prayers.

Requests however are more acceptable when accompanied by a gift. Here then is our gift, Lord Jesus, and this also we present to you by the hands of St Anthony.

First of all a promise of renewed and more intense Christian life, by avoiding sin, showing charity to all and bearing peacefully and calmly the troubles and crosses that you have laid on our shoulders. And then a vow, a public and solemn vow: IF THE CITY OF ISTANBUL IS SPARED THE BOMBARDMENTS AND DESTRUCTIONS OF WAR, a generous offer of bread for the poor, for our most needy brothers and all who are ill; and for St Anthony, your servant, a silver statue which shall remain here in your church and his, in remembrance of your mercy which we have seen shown to us, and also of the purity of our devotion to your beloved saintly dispenser of graces and blessings.

O Jesus, Saviour of the world, have pity on us.

Jesus, Mary and Joseph, help us, protect us, save us.

O St Anthony, intercede for us.

1954

[82]   *O Holy Father Pius X*[1]

On the day of my first Mass your hands were laid on my head, the head of a newly ordained priest kneeling as you passed by in the Vatican.

I have always treasured in my heart the memory of that gesture and of the gentle words of good wishes and blessings which accompanied it.

Now fifty years have passed. You are a citizen of the heavenly Jerusalem, you rejoice in the glory of the saints, and all Christians pray to you.

The humble young priest of long ago has been placed in the Chair of St Mark, where you, too, presided with such splendour of doctrine, virtue and example.

O Holy Father Pius X, I put my trust in you. I do not fear to die. I do not refuse to work. May your powerful arm assist me, so that all that is still left for me to do in my life may be to the edification, the blessing and the joy of these beloved children of Venice, your children and mine, with whom it is sweet to live but still more precious and joyful to sacrifice myself in an outpouring of loving-kindness and pastoral care.

[83]   *To the Madonna del Bosco*[2]

O beloved Madonna del Bosco, here you are now crowned by my own humble hands. The revered Cardinal Schuster of Milan is here in the spirit with me, and I am his representative.

I have loved your dear shrine since my childhood, with a devoted heart, so I welcome with joy this privilege which has been granted me of solemnly crowning and ceremoniously greeting you here, Mother and Queen!

The royal title belongs of right to your Son Jesus because of his nature,

[1] Prayer for the fiftieth anniversary of his ordination as priest: 1904 – 10 and 11 August, 1954. Cf. Cardinal Roncalli, *Scritti e discorsi, cit.*, vol. I, p. 259. See Plate 32.

[2] Prayer recited by the Cardinal Patriarch on 29 August, 1954, on the occasion of the crowning of the statue of Our Lady at the shrine of the Madonna del Bosco, in the territory of Imbersago (Como), not far from Sotto il Monte. Cf. *Scritti e discorsi, cit.*, vol. II, pp. 620–1.

31. The Madonna della Fiducia

O SANTO PADRE PIO X

Nel giorno della mia prima Messa le tue mani si stesero sopra il mio capo di novello sacerdote chinato sul tuo passaggio in Vaticano.

Conservai sempre nel cuore il ricordo di quel gesto e delle soavi parole beneauguranti e benedicenti che lo accompagnarono

Eccomi ora dopo 50 anni. Tu, cittadino della Gerusalemme celeste, esulti nella gloria dei Santi, e tutto il popolo cristiano ti invoca.

L' umile levita di un tempo fu posto sulla cattedra di S. Marco, dove tu sedesti con tanto splendore di dottrina, di virtù, di esempi.

O Santo Padre Pio X. In te confido. Non temo di morire: non ricuso di lavorare. Mi assista il tuo braccio potente, e tutto volga, quanto ancora mi resta a compiere nella vita, ad edificazione, a benedizione, a letizia di questi carissimi figli di Venezia, figli tuoi e miei, coi quali mi è dolce il vivere, ma è più prezioso e gradito sacrificarmi in effusione di mitezza e di apostolato pastorale.

32. Card commemorating the fiftieth anniversary of his ordination to the priesthood. The translation of this prayer will be found on p. 380

33. Pope John was buried with this little gilded cross, given him in 1925

34. He kept his crucifix always with him, from 1925 until his death

both human and divine. It belongs to you by grace, the grace of Jesus, who has magnified you by choosing you for his mother.

How wonderful, how beautiful and precious is this golden crown we have placed on your head, and the one we have given to Jesus also, your blessed Son! With this you are adorned like Aaron in the splendour of his most sacred priestly vestments.

Your crown is a token of supreme holiness, the honourable symbol of superhuman beauty, an ornament of honour (Ecclesiasticus 45: 14), an expression of power, of power to intercede for us with Jesus your Son, for those graces which we here implore with prayers and hymns.

O Madonna del Bosco, today crowned Queen, we beg you now to bless more generously than ever your children who from both banks of the Adda come to you with so much faith, so much love and so much trustful longing for prosperity and peace.

[84] *O Mary, Queen of the Lebanon*[1]

Now, O Mary, Queen of the Lebanon and recently proclaimed Queen of the World, hear my prayer. The archangel who was the first to greet you called you 'full of grace'. A great Doctor of the Church, St Bernard, commented: 'You are full of grace and your grace overflows to us: you have more than enough grace for yourself, enough to spare for us.'

O Mary, pour out the superabundance of your grace over this beloved nation of yours. For the first time in its long history it enjoys full liberty and political and social independence. May its decrees be ever inspired by principles of respect and fidelity for its glorious ancestral traditions; may its social life be characterized by those mystical gifts of unity and peace which are the most fervent intention of the holy Sacrifice of the Mass which I am now celebrating under your loving gaze, O Mother, O Queen of the Lebanon, in close sacrificial union with blessed Jesus, your Son and our Brother.

One more prayer, O Mary. In answer to the prayer of Jesus that all his brothers should be united among themselves and with him, as he is united with the Father (cf. John 17: 23), the promise of one fold under the pastoral staff of one shepherd (John 10: 16) will surely be fulfilled; let the attainment of this unity for which all believers in Christ are longing

---

[1] From the concluding homily of the Marian celebrations, Beirut, 24 October, 1954. Cf. *Scritti e discorsi, cit.*, vol. IV, pp. 63–5.

begin here, in the land of the Lebanon, through your intercession, O Mary!

The restoration of the catholicity of faith in all its breadth and perfection will be the most important event of modern times. May it be ascribed to your name, O Queen of the Lebanon, as our Holy Father says in the words which I shall transmit to these your faithful people in his name. The Pope will say to the Lebanese: 'Your fervour, renewed in these devotions to Mary, must be the salt that does not lose its savour, the light set on a candlestick so that its flame may be a light to all that are in the house; may the warmth of your charity be shown above all in welcoming your separated brethren, whose deep devotion to Mary is well known to us, and to whom in our encyclical *Fulgens Corona* we have sent a fatherly invitation to join with us in appealing to Mary, and begging most earnestly for this unity.'[1]

My dear Lebanese brothers, nothing is beyond the reach of prayer. The Archangel Gabriel is still here with us. The last word of his message is precisely this: 'With God nothing will be impossible' (Luke 1: 37).

So, courage and faith!

On the summit of the holy mountain the ancient cedars are still growing, ever growing, and their branches are still wide and robust enough to gather in a mystical embrace all who worship Christ 'in spirit and in truth'.[2] This will be the future glory of Lebanon, the glory of Mary, her Mother and Queen. Amen.

---

[1] Letter to the Cardinal Legate for the celebrations of the National Marian Congress of the Lebanon; cf. A.A.S., XLVI (18 November, 1954), p. 653.

[2] Cf. John 4: 23.

1955

[85]   *Mary, Fountain of Mercy and Mother of Joy*[1]

We crown you together with your divine Son, O Madonna di Siponto, we crown you as our Queen, and may the golden crown that encircles your brow glow as the sign of the highest holiness to which a human creature may rise, as an 'ornament of honour' that surpasses all other dignity and merit in the Holy Church, both militant and triumphant, and finally as a symbol of your most powerful intercession with your Son for our needs. These are the individual needs of every one of us, of our families, and the whole of this noble archdiocese of Manfredonia, most fortunate in having been for centuries past under your heavenly protection, and which the presence of St Michael, unconquered prince of the heavenly hosts, at your command defends in many and various ways against the forces of disorder and evil, a sure safeguard against all the temptations and misfortunes of life.

O Madonna di Siponto, come, let us crown you Queen. The crown is of purest gold, like the hearts of your children who offer it to you, like the heart of their pastor[2] who procured it for you. '. . . and a crown of gold upon her head, a sign of holiness, an ornament of honour and a work of power'.

O Queen of Siponto, I beg two special graces of you: peace of mind and the spirit of peace in our families, in our parishes, and all this diocese which loves and honours you; peace in Italy, our own blessed land, in all her endeavours to achieve the loftiest ideals of human and social life in the light of the Gospel and in faithfulness to the teaching of the apostles, today, yesterday and always the only shining beacon of truth, justice and true Christian brotherhood.

Ah my brothers! I speak of true Christian brotherhood and, after peace, this is the second grace for which I intend to pray, and for which I

[1] This prayer is taken from the homily preached by the Patriarch of Venice for the Pontifical Mass at Manfredonia, 28 August, 1955, on the occasion of the crowning of the Madonna di Siponto. Cf. *Scritti e discorsi, cit.*, vol. II, pp. 169–71.

[2] Archbishop Mgr Andrea Cesarano, consecrated Bishop at Istanbul in 1931 by Mgr Carlo Margotti. Mgr Roncalli was one of the two consecrating Bishops.

ask you all to pray to Jesus during this solemn evening ceremony, under the auspices and with the help of the prayers of the newly crowned Queen of Siponto.

This holy image comes to us almost certainly from the eastern shores of our sea. Those other numerous and similar images of Our Lady which are so greatly revered in our peninsula came to Italy from the east, during the first half of the thirteenth century. First of all our own sweet Madonna Nicopeja in St Mark's in Venice. Here, in these parts, we have St Mary of Constantinople in the Cathedral of Bari, the Madonna of the Fountain in Trani, the Virgin of the Martyrs in Molfetta, the Madonna della Guardia in Bologna, Santa Maria Valleverde in Bovino, the Madonna of Grottaferrata and others, all from the East and Byzantine in character and style.

O Mary, why should not your Eastern children be reunited with us, in the house of our common Father who awaits them, and so restore the 'one fold and one shepherd', for which Jesus asked in his last prayer, when he was about to offer himself in sacrifice for our redemption and the peace of the whole world?

We pray that the vast regions where faith in Christ, formulated in the same apostolic Creed, still groans and suffers may find a way of peaceful return to that source of true unity of all peoples in the embrace of our common mother, in Jesus her blessed firstborn Son, and in the embrace of the other Mother we all share in common, the holy Catholic Church, to which it is our joy to belong, and which awaits the return of all.

O newly crowned Madonna di Siponto, may this your image and all the others which represent you in Italy, in the Near East and in the vast lands of Russia, inspire our prayers for this return to unity, which will be the joy and exultation of continents and seas, of earth and heaven, in Christ Jesus your Son and our Brother, to whom in our emotion we dedicate the prayers of our lips and the throbbing of our grateful and joyful hearts, in the glorification of his blessed Mother and ours.

1956

To Our Lady of Fatima[1]

Bless, O Mary, this noble Portuguese land of yours which you have chosen as a new sanctuary for your miracles, and which was the first country you called to enjoy the blessings of your protection.

Bless all Europe, now more than ever tormented by profound divisions between those who think they can build a new world without your Son, the Saviour of the world, the Way, the Truth and the Life, and without remaining true to the glorious tradition of their fathers.

Noble Christian explorers and conquerors have set sail from these shores throughout the centuries: the first to spread the Gospel of Christ and his peace where it was till then unknown. Here the dear and miraculous name of Fatima is venerated.

And do not forget, O Mother, O Queen of all lands and seas, this humble servant of Holy Church who today enjoys the great privilege of paying you homage where your feet have trod! His title of Patriarch of Venice is like an affectionate and brotherly link, in the sharing of a common conviction and faith in the mission of Fatima, with the Patriarch of Lisbon, who has welcomed him so cordially, together with the venerable Bishop of Leiria and the worthy prelates of the Portuguese episcopate.

You know how great and fervent is the devotion to you, O Mother, on the shores of the Venetian lagoon. The Madonna della Salute and the Madonna Nicopeja, those two incomparable ikons, objects of great veneration, one in her own church and the other over the precious altar near the tomb of St Mark, both from Chios and old Byzantium, are like two kind and shining eyes with which you look at us with smiling motherly love. Your love for the old Christians of the East is equalled, I think, by your love for your Venetian children today, who have been the possessors of these great treasures for more than seven centuries. Lady

---

[1] From the homily preached by the Patriarch of Venice at Fatima on 13 May, 1956, for the twenty-fifth anniversary of the consecration of Portugal to the Immaculate Heart of Mary. Cf. *Scritti e discorsi, cit.*, vol. II, pp. 430–2.

of Fatima, I will now add to these ikons, for the veneration of my people and in memory of this pilgrimage of mine, a remembrance of all my prayers to you for all that lies nearest to my pastor's heart in the present particularly difficult circumstances. And so I shall once more unite East and West in your love across these two seas 'from the rising of the sun until its setting'.

Salute means safety from the evils of this world, and *Nicopeja* means Queen of Victories. But I am not thinking of military victories, which always mean violence, the ferocity of men, and blood. I am thinking of spiritual conquests for the truth, for the Gospel, for the Holy Catholic Church and her august head, for justice, liberty of souls and nations, and of the whole world.

I wish to say once more in my name and in the name of this enormous throng, gathered here from every land: O, Our Lady of Fatima, through the virtue of your Immaculate Heart, obtain for us from blessed Jesus, the fountain of every grace, justice, charity and peace! Amen.

[87]   *The Glory of Mary*[1]

From your throne of glory, O Queen, O Mother, turn your merciful gaze on those of us who are unhappy; obtain forgiveness for us; may the justice of your Son turn to mercy for us all. May our trust in you be equal to our hope, and strengthen the good principles of Christian life which must be inspired by warm and sincere charity.

O Mary! O Mary! Four precious gifts we ask of you, we, the first Patriarch, St Mark, and his very humble successor, both united in a prayer that is a sorrowful and tearful request for your Venice. First of all we pray for purity of mind, a clear understanding of doctrine which is a gift of the intellect; then modesty of body. O Mary, you see what a scandal of shameless nakedness of men and women we have around us, profaning the churches, the squares and the ways of the city, for the corruption of innocent youth and the perversion of our people, with the threat of terrible punishment to follow.

Thirdly, we beg for holiness of life, because this is what matters most on earth and in heaven; finally, brotherly love, that is the peaceful agree-

---

[1] From the homily for the Feast of the Assumption, Venice, 15 August, 1956. The Cardinal paraphrases and comments upon some passages of St Lawrence Giustiniani about the Assumption of Mary into heaven. Cf. *Scritti e discorsi, cit.*, vol. II, pp. 469–70.

ment among citizens which is the secret of prosperity, the perfection of Christianity and an inexhaustible source of joy and peace.

These are the riches and the virtues—I repeat the very words of our own St Lawrence Giustiniani—which are pleasing to God; they reform morals, convert men, raise them from the depths, and lift them on high, to where the Virgin assumed into heaven rejoices and exults in her glory and prays for the whole Church to her Son Christ the Lord, who with the Father and Holy Spirit lives and reigns for ever. Amen.

1958

To the Virgin of Lourdes[1]

O holy Virgin, O Immaculate, for so you have been proclaimed by the earthly Vicar of your Son Jesus, O Queen of Lourdes, grant us, O, from the fulness of your grace grant us your gifts. Renew the miracles of a century and let new wonders follow the old. In this place add new glory to your hand and your right arm.

Above all protect our august Pope, who shines in the same light of holiness as Pius his predecessor: preserve him and inspire him and keep him in safety here on earth.

Protect your blessed city of Lourdes, whose name is identified with yours all over the world. 'Have mercy on your people over whom your name is invoked.'

Keep your special love for this land of France, this people glorious throughout the ages, 'whom you have called, like Jesus, your firstborn'.

In the light of your motherly eyes, O Mary, you see gathered around France all the Catholic peoples, all the souls who throughout the world can boast of the name of your blessed Son.

In the course of European history, many, alas! too many of these people have contented themselves with the name of Christians, in some places rejecting the lofty and holy meaning of this name, that is the spiritual unity of understanding and of faith, whole and entire, expressed in the 'I believe in God, the Father Almighty,' and so on to the 'life everlasting'.

As your Son one day spoke to all these peoples who were ripening for the harvest, so we beg of you, O Mother of Jesus and our Mother too, to call them and gather them together in homage to the word of Jesus: 'Fill Sion with a great number in your name.'

Show your loving care especially to all those who rejoice in their own faithfulness and that of their fathers to the truth that has been handed

[1] From the speech the Cardinal Patriarch delivered in French at Lourdes, on 25 March, 1958, for the consecration of the Church dedicated to St Pius X. Cf. *Scritti e discorsi, cit.*, vol. III, pp. 519–21.

down to them: to those who have been your creatures from the beginning. May the confident messages you repeated to your beloved Bernadette find here, O Immaculate Virgin, more ample proof of your generosity in the appeals you make, here and elsewhere, for the return of the scattered children to their Father's home, which is still your home, our own precious home; may these pilgrimages continue, for the uplifting of souls, the healing of bodies and the ripening of golden fruits of patience, kindness and self-dedication.

I dare to present to you the beloved children of my own Venice, who are so delighted with the honour rendered in the person of their humble Patriarch to the dear and famous diocese of which St Pius X was shepherd and father, and the individual and numberless intentions of all who charged me with their prayers and gifts. I commend them all to your kind and motherly heart.

'Holy Mary Immaculate, help all who are in trouble.' Help all who are in trouble: give courage to the faint-hearted, console the sad, heal the infirm, pray for the people, intercede mercifully for the clergy, have a special thought for nuns; may all feel, all enjoy your kind and powerful assistance, all who now and always render and will render you honour, and will offer you their petitions through the intercession of Pope St Pius X. Hear all our prayers, O Mother, and grant them all.

We are all your children: 'Grant the prayers of your children.' Amen for ever.

1959

[89]   *Prayer for the Diocesan Synod of Rome*[1]

O Lord, who has granted to us the privilege of living in this Rome of ours, empurpled with the blood of the holy apostles Peter and Paul and of your martyrs, and chosen to be the seat of your Vicar on earth, help us always to be worthy of the holiness of this blessed place.

Enlighten and sustain the labours of the Diocesan Synod, that it may make the Christian character of our city shine more brightly.

Prepare, open and warm our hearts with the outpouring of your spirit, in order that the decrees of the Synod may find every one of us ready to obey, swift to act and generous in sacrifice.

O Lord! Through the intercession of your Immaculate Mother 'the Salvation of the People of Rome', of St Peter and St Paul and so many pious and glorious Popes, their successors, and all our patron saints, grant that the renewal of our spiritual life for which we pray may correspond to the desires of your divine Heart and to the hopes of your Vicar, our Bishop and pastor. Amen.

[90]   *To the Immaculate Virgin of Lourdes*[2]

O Mary Immaculate of Lourdes! we beg you to listen to our prayers, by whatever title we, and our fathers before us, have chosen to invoke you. O Immaculate Lady, we thank you and we are delighted with the acts of homage and love which you have inspired and helped us to make during this year which marks the centenary of your apparitions. We shall continue to greet you, O Mary, by the titles most dear and blessed to us and to you: as our ancestors invoked you here in this great church of Pope Liberius, under these arches which glow with memories of our devotion to you and your divine Motherhood.

[1] 2 February, 1959.
[2] From the speech delivered at Santa Maria Maggiore for the close of the celebrations for the centenary of the apparitions of Our Lady of Lourdes, 15 February, 1959. Cf. *Discorsi, messaggi, colloqui, cit.*, vol. I, p. 150.

35. Camaitino, the house in Sotto il Monte where Pope John
spent many of his vacations

36. Study at Camaitino, showing the desk bequeathed to him by Mgr Radini Tedeschi

In this magnificent church you are always called the 'Salvation of the Roman People'. Still be our salvation, always our salvation, O Mother, O Queen.

At the end of the first world war our predecessor Benedict XV of revered memory desired that there should be added to the ancient image above your altar the white marble statue which shows you offering us, by the hand of your divine Child, the olive branch of peace, and decreed that you should be called and prayed to as Queen of Peace.

We join these two titles together, O blessed Mother of Jesus, O sweet Mother of ours: O Mary, salvation of the Roman people, pray for us. O Mary, Queen of Peace, protect your people from all wars and all snares of the devil; ensure peace for your Rome, and your beloved Italy, the peoples of the whole world, and your holy, Catholic and apostolic Church. Amen.

[91]   *Prayer for the Second Ecumenical Vatican Council*[1]

O divine Spirit, sent by the Father in the Name of Jesus, give your aid and infallible guidance to your Church and pour out on the Ecumenical Council the fulness of your gifts.

O gentle Teacher and Consoler, enlighten the hearts of our prelates who, eagerly responding to the call of the Supreme Roman Pontiff, will gather here in solemn conclave.

May this Council produce abundant fruits: may the light and power of the Gospel be more widely diffused in human society; may new vigour be imparted to the Catholic religion and its missionary function; may we all acquire a more profound knowledge of the Church's doctrine and a wholesome increase of Christian morality.

O gentle Guest of our souls, confirm our minds in truth and dispose our hearts to obedience, that the deliberations of the Council may find in us generous consent and prompt obedience.

We pray to you again for the lambs who are no longer part of the one fold of Jesus Christ, that they too, who still glory in the name of Christians, may at last be reunited under one Shepherd.

Renew in our own days your miracles as of a second Pentecost; and grant that Holy Church, reunited in one prayer, more fervent than before, around Mary the Mother of Jesus, and under the leadership of Peter, may extend the kingdom of the divine Saviour, a kingdom of truth, justice, love and peace. Amen.

[1] 23 September, 1959.

1960

To St Joseph the Worker[1]

O St Joseph, guardian of Jesus, chaste spouse of Mary, you who spent your life in the perfect accomplishment of duty, maintaining with the work of your hands the Holy Family of Nazareth, grant your kind protection to those who, full of trust, turn to you now! You know their desires, their difficulties, their hopes; they pray to you because they know that in you they find one who understands and protects them. You also have known trials, toil and fatigue; yet, in the midst of the material cares of life, your soul, full of the most profound peace, rejoiced with indescribable happiness in the close companionship of the Son of God who was entrusted to your care, and of Mary, his sweet Mother. May those whom you protect understand that they are not alone in their toil: may they perceive Jesus by their side, receive him with grace and guard him faithfully, as you did. And with your prayers obtain that in every family, in every factory or work room, and wherever a Christian works, everything may be sanctified in charity, patience and justice, and in the search for righteousness, so that the gifts of heavenly love may be showered upon them.

[93] *Prayer for the Bishops*[2]

O Jesus, Eternal Priest, you who have lit in this world an undying flame, enable those whom you have chosen for the episcopate to share in the purposes of your divine Heart.

Give to these generous hearts upon whom you have bestowed the fulness of your priesthood the grace of honouring you in your Holy Church, and multiply around them evermore new and fervent apostles of your kingdom, for the salvation of all peoples.

[1] From the message broadcast to the workers, Sunday, 1 May, 1960. Cf. *Discorsi, messaggi, colloqui, cit.*, vol. II, p. 326.

[2] For the consecration, in St Peter's, of eight Bishops, 28 October, 1960.

O Lord, grant that as they work in peace and enjoy tranquillity of order, the peoples and nations may prosper under your most generous blessings, and the Church extend ever more widely her redeeming mission.

Save your people, Lord: and bless your inheritance. And govern them and lift them up for ever.

[94]   *O sweet Child of Bethlehem*[1]

O sweet Child of Bethlehem, grant that we may share with all our hearts in this profound mystery of Christmas. Put into the hearts of men this peace for which they sometimes seek so desperately and which you alone can give them. Help them to know one another·better, and to live as brothers, children of the same Father.

Reveal to them also your beauty, holiness and purity. Awaken in their hearts love and gratitude for your infinite goodness. Join them all together in your love. And give us your heavenly peace. Amen, Amen.

[1] From the message to the Diplomatic Corps after Midnight Mass, 25 December, 1960. Cf. *Discorsi, messaggi, colloqui, cit.,* vol. III, p. 103. The original of this prayer is in French.

1961

[95]   *To the Child Jesus*[1]

O Lord Jesus, who became a child for love of us, we still contemplate
you in Bethlehem, and we place around you and around Mary, your
Mother and ours, around Joseph, that just man, and around the good
simple shepherds, these young hopes of our Christian families, who have
come from all over the world. Every one of these offers, for our joy and
encouragement, melodious singing, a pure heart and the fervent and
heartfelt intention to do honour to Holy Church and to the fine traditions of the peoples of various continents so brilliantly represented
here. Bless them, O Jesus, as we bless them in your name. Be with them
along the road, so rich in promise, that opens before them. May they
bring joy and beauty wherever they go. Following your example, may
they grow in years, in grace, in wisdom, in the sight of God and men.
Amen. Amen.

[96]   *Seminarists' prayer to the Madonna della Fiducia*[2]

O holy Virgin, our Madonna della Fiducia, kind and pious Mother of
seminarists all over the world, once in the Upper Room you cheered
with your presence the first apostles of the Gospel, gathered in happy and
anxious expectation of the divine Spirit. Look down now on us, trembling
in the same expectation of grace and priestly fervour, holy and sanctifying.

You were our Morning Star and you still remain the serene joy of
our vocation, the protection of our purity, the inspiration of our good

[1] Prayer recited during Mass on New Year's Day for the *Pueri Cantores* (Boy Singers)
of many nations, 1 January, 1961. Cf. *Discorsi, messaggi, colloqui, cit.*, vol. III, p. 119.

[2] Prayer composed by the Supreme Pontiff on 7 April, 1961, as a remembrance of his
visit (12 September, 1960) to the summer residence of the Roman Seminary, Roccantica
(Rieti). Cf. *Discorsi, messaggi, colloqui, cit.*, vol. III, p. 859. For Madonna della Fiducia, see
note, p. 114, and Plate 31.

work in the service of Jesus, of the souls redeemed by his blood, and of his Church, suffering at times, yet ever unconquered and glorious.

What joy for each one of us and for us all together, seminarists of the whole world, to be able to repeat: 'We are your work, O Mary!' What bliss to be able to answer in every event of our lives, ever and always: 'We fear nothing, because you, O Mary, are, and always will be, our confidence, our Mother in time and in eternity.'

[97]   *To Mary, Queen of the World*[1]

We turn to you, O blessed Virgin Mary, Mother of Jesus and our Mother too. How could we, with trembling hearts, concern ourselves with the greatest problem of all, that of life or death, now overshadowing all mankind, without trusting ourselves to your intercession to preserve us from all dangers?

This is your hour, O Mary. Our blessed Jesus entrusted us to you in the final hour of his bloody sacrifice. We are sure that you will intervene.

On 8 September, Holy Church celebrated the feast of your most blessed birth, hailing it as the beginning of the salvation of the world, and a heavenly omen for lasting peace.

And now indeed we beseech you for this, O most sweet Mother and Queen of the world. The world does not need victorious wars or defeated peoples but renewed and strengthened health of mind, and peace which brings prosperity and tranquillity; this is what it needs and what it is crying out for: the beginning of salvation and lasting peace. Amen. Amen.

[98]   *Prayer for the students of the college of*
                              Propaganda Fide[2]

O Lord Jesus, supreme and eternal priest, look upon these sons of yours whom you have chosen and gathered from all parts of the world. Increase and sanctify the gifts with which they are already endowed, and which are characteristic of the nobility and wealth of their respective

[1] From the broadcast prayer for peace among the nations, Sunday, 10 September, 1961. Cf. *Discorsi, messaggi, colloqui, cit.*, vol. III, p. 414.

[2] Prayer taken from the Holy Father's talk to the students of Propaganda Fide on 25 November, 1961, his eightieth birthday. Cf. *Discorsi, messaggi, colloqui, cit.*, vol. IV, p. 65.

countries, so that the grace of the priesthood may urge them with angelic fervour along the ways which are open to their apostolate; sustain their faith, nourish their ideals, so that on returning to their own lands they may respond to the needs and desires of those immense flocks which will find in you their one fold and one Shepherd.

O Mary, Mother of priests, our comfort in hours of anxiety, dispenser of grace and hope, preserve in these young men the joy of the Magnificat, so that all, in every hour of their lives, may be generous and faithful in the performance of their duties, ready to overcome the inevitable difficulties of their ministry. Mother of Good Counsel, Virgin Mother of our trusting hearts, be close to every one of them so as to form in them your Jesus, the model of priestly sanctity.

Peter and Paul, princes of the apostles, and you, apostles of the Lord, martyrs of old and recent times, doctors, confessors and virgins and all you saints in heaven, accompany these young souls with your prayers, so that the fervour of these years of training may not dwindle but may grow every day 'from one degree of glory to another' to 'the measure of the stature of the fulness of Christ'.[1] Amen. Amen.

---

[1] Cf. 2 Cor. 3: 18; Eph. 4: 13.

1962

[99]   *Prayer for the daily offering of the Breviary for*
the success of the Council[1]

May this sacrifice of praise which I offer to your divine majesty for the success of the Second Ecumenical Vatican Council be acceptable to you, Lord God, and grant that what we, together with our Pope John, implore of you, we may effectively attain. Amen.

[On the Feast of the Epiphany, 1962.]

[100]   *Prayer to the Holy Ghost*[2]

O Holy Ghost, Paraclete, perfect in us the work begun by Jesus: enable us to continue to pray fervently in the name of the whole world: hasten in every one of us the growth of a profound interior life; give vigour to our apostolate so that it may reach all men and all peoples, all redeemed by the Blood of Christ and all belonging to him. Mortify in us our natural pride, and raise us to the realms of holy humility, of the real fear of God, of generous courage. Let no earthly bond prevent us from honouring our vocation, no cowardly considerations disturb the claims of justice, no meanness confine the immensity of charity within the narrow bounds of petty selfishness. Let everything in us be on a grand scale: the search for truth and the devotion to it, and readiness for self-sacrifice, even to the cross and death; and may everything finally be according to the last prayer of the Son to his heavenly Father, and according to your Spirit, O Holy Spirit of love, which the Father and the Son desired to be poured out over the Church and its institutions, over the souls of men and over nations. Amen. Amen. Alleluia, Alleluia!

---

[1] From the apostolic exhortation: '*De divino officio pro felici exitu Concilii Oecum. Vat. II impensiore pietate recitanda*'. Cf. A.A.S., LIV (28 February, 1962), p. 74. Original in Latin.
[2] From the homily for Pentecost, Sunday, 10 June, 1962. Cf. *Discorsi, messaggi, colloqui, cit.*, vol. IV, p. 350.

[101]   *Prayer for Boy Scouts*[1]

O Mary, your name has been on my lips and in my heart from my early infancy.

When I was a child I learnt to love you as a Mother, turn to you in danger, and trust to your intercession.

You see in my heart the desire to know the truth, to practise virtue, to be prudent and just, strong and patient, a brother to all.

O Mary, help me to keep to my purpose of living as a faithful disciple of Jesus, for the building up of Christian society and the joy of the holy Catholic Church.

I greet you, Mother, morning and evening; I pray to you as I go upon my way; from you I hope for the inspiration and encouragement that will enable me to fulfil the sacred promises of my earthly vocation, give glory to God, and win eternal salvation.

O Mary! Like you in Bethlehem and on Golgotha, I too wish to stay always close to Jesus. He is the eternal King of all ages and all peoples. Amen.

[102]   *To Jesus in the eucharistic mystery*[2]

O Jesus, you see how from every altar and every Christian heart, prayer ascends this day with more warmth and more emotion!

O Jesus, look upon us from your Sacrament like a good Shepherd, by which name the Angelic Doctor[3] invokes you, and with him Holy Church. O Jesus, good Shepherd, this is your flock, the flock that you have gathered from the ends of the earth, the flock that listens to your word of life, and intends to guard it, practise it and preach it. This is the flock that follows you meekly, O Jesus, and wishes so ardently to see, in the Ecumenical Council, the reflection of your loving face in the features of your Church, the mother of all, the mother who opens her arms and heart to all, and here awaits, trembling and trustful, the arrival of all her Bishops.

O Jesus, divine Food of the soul, this immense concourse turns to you. It wishes to give to its human and Christian vocation a new, vigorous

[1] 10 July, 1962.

[2] Thursday, 21 June, 1962, Corpus Christi. Prayer recited after the procession of the Blessed Sacrament in St Peter's Square. Cf. *Discorsi, messaggi, colloqui, cit.,* vol. IV, pp. 395–6.

[3] St Thomas Aquinas.

power of interior virtue, and to be ready for sacrifice, of which you were such a wonderful pattern in word and in example.

You are our elder Brother; you have trodden our path before us, O Christ Jesus, the path of every one of us, you have forgiven all our sins; you inspire us each and all to give a nobler, more convinced and more active witness of Christian life.

O Jesus, our true Bread, and the only substantial Food for our souls, gather all the peoples around your table. Your altar is divine reality on earth, the pledge of heavenly favours, the assurance of a just understanding among peoples, and of peaceful rivalry in the true progress of civilization.

Nourished by you and with you, O Jesus, men will be strong in faith, joyful in hope, and active in the many and varied expressions of charity.

Our wills will know how to overcome the snares of evil, the temptations of selfishness, the listlessness of sloth. And the eyes of men who love and fear the Lord will behold the vision of the land of the living, of which the wayfaring Church militant is the image, enabling the whole earth to hear the first sweet and mysterious voices of the City of God.

O Jesus, feed us and guard us, and grant that we may see the good things in the land of the living! Amen. Alleluia.

[103]   *To Mary, Queen of Missions*[1]

O Mary, once more we draw near to that great feast which celebrates your assumption into heaven.

Our way of confiding in and honouring you has not changed at all. There is still the same trust and simplicity of the far-away days of our childhood and our life in the seminary. But our responsibilities have increased with the passing years. Above all, we feel our share of responsibility for the training of future priests.

Here before you are the elect students of the Society for the Propagation of the Faith. The diversity of the countries from which they come testifies to the catholicity of the church. Their presence is a witness to the missionary fervour and enthusiasm of their families and dioceses.

O Queen of Missions, be a Mother to the Collegio Urbano, and to all the Institutes that are the honour and wealth of the Catholic Church in Rome and in the world.

[1] From the speech delivered by the Holy Father on 10 August, 1962, to the students of numerous seminaries and colleges, on the occasion of the fifty-eighth anniversary of his ordination as priest. Cf. *Discorsi, messaggi, colloqui, cit.*, vol. IV, p. 469.

Enlightened piety, innocence of life, wise doctrine and ardent charity are what they, and we, ask you to obtain for them from your divine Son, so that in every one of these young men he may appear to the world again, transfigured, ever active and blessing. Amen. Amen.

[104]   *To Our Lady of Loreto*[1]

O Mary, O Mary, Mother of Jesus and our Mother too, we have come here this morning to pray to you as the first star above the Council that is about to be held, as the light that shines propitiously upon our way as we proceed trustfully towards the great ecumenical gathering which the whole world awaits.

We have opened our heart to you, O Mary, our heart that has not changed with the passing years, since our first meeting at the beginning of the century; the same tender heart as then, the same imploring look, the same prayer.

In almost sixty years of priesthood every step of ours on the ways of obedience has been marked by your protection, and we have never asked anything else of you but the obtaining from your divine Son of the grace of a holy and sanctifying priesthood.

Even the summoning of the Council came about, as you know, O Mother, in obedience to a plan that seemed to us truly to correspond to the will of the Lord.

Today, once more, and in the name of the entire episcopate, we beg you, most sweet Mother whom we hail as Help of Bishops (*Auxilium Episcoporum*), for ourself, the Bishop of Rome, and for all the Bishops in the world, to obtain for us the grace that will enable us to enter the Council chamber of the basilica of St Peter's as the apostles and first disciples of Jesus entered the room of the Last Supper: one single heart, one single throb of love for Christ and men, one single intention to live and sacrifice ourselves for the salvation of individuals and peoples.

So, in future years and centuries, may it be said that through your motherly intercession the grace of God prepared,. accompanied and crowned the work of the Twenty-first Ecumenical Council, imparting to all the children of Holy Church new fervour, generosity, and firmness of intention.

To the glory of God Almighty, Father, Son and Holy Ghost, through

[1] From the speech delivered on the occasion of his pilgrimage to the shrine of Loreto, 4 October, 1962. Cf. *Discorsi, messaggi, colloqui, cit.*, vol. IV, pp. 561–2.

the power of the Precious Blood of Christ, whose peaceful rule is supreme liberty and grace for all peoples, all civilizations and institutions, and for all men. Amen. Amen.

[105]   *Prayer for the Council*[1]

Almighty God, in thee, distrusting our own strength, we place all our trust. Look kindly upon these pastors of your Church. May the light of your supernatural grace be with us as we deliberate, and as we draw up its laws; and be pleased to grant the prayers we utter with one faith, one voice and one mind.

O Mary, Help of Christians, Help of Bishops, whose love we have recently experienced in a special way in your church at Loreto, where it pleased you to cause the mystery of the Incarnation to be venerated, bring everything, by your aid, to a joyful, favourable and successful conclusion. With St Joseph your spouse, with the holy apostles Peter and Paul, with St John the Baptist and St John the Evangelist, pray to the Lord our God for us.

To Jesus Christ, our most loving Redeemer, the eternal King of all peoples and all ages, be love, power and glory for ever and ever, Amen.

[1] Original in Latin. From the Holy Father's opening address at the Second Ecumenical Vatican Council, Thursday, 11 October, 1962. Cf. *Discorsi, messaggi, colloqui, cit.*, vol. IV, p. 590.

1963

[106]   *Prayer to St Vincent Pallotti*[1]

We wish to offer a very special and confident prayer to you, our own St Vincent Pallotti, glory of the Roman clergy, now shining in all the splendour of your virtues. Deign to intercede for this humble Bishop of Rome, to whom your glorification brings such joy; intercede also for his collaborators of the Curia and the Vicariate, for all the priests, and particularly for the Congregation of the Catholic Apostolate, to whom you lend a ray of brightest glory. We beg you, who were an indefatigable apostle, a director of consciences, an inspirer of holy enthusiasms, magnificent in your many and varied activities, to kindle with new fervour all ministers of the Lord and these precious collaborators of the Catholic apostolate; make them ready and eager to answer every appeal from their brothers. Always and everywhere the 'salt of the earth and the light of the world' (cf. Matthew 5: 13–14) intent on spreading 'the good odour of Christ' (cf. 2 Cor. 2: 15). May they be apostles of truth, love and mercy, and educators of exemplary Christians, consoling the humble and poor in the light that streams from Christ, the Good Shepherd, Saviour of souls and peoples. Amen, Amen.

[107]   *Prayer for the beginning of Lent*[2]

O Lord Jesus, you who at the beginning of your public life withdrew into the desert, we beg you to teach all men that recollection of mind which is the beginning of conversion and salvation.

Leaving your home at Nazareth and your sweet Mother, you wished to experience solitude, weariness and hunger. To the tempter who proposed

---

[1] From the homily for the canonization of St Vincent Pallotti, published in *L'Osservatore Romano*, 21–22 January, 1963.

[2] From the broadcast of 28 February, 1963, published in *L'Osservatore Romano*, 1 March, 1963.

to you the trial of miracles, you replied with the strength of eternal wisdom, in itself a miracle of heavenly grace.

It is Lent.

O Lord, do not let us turn to 'broken cisterns', that can hold no water (Jer. 2: 13), nor imitate the unfaithful servant or the foolish virgins; do not let us be so blinded by the enjoyment of the good things of earth that our hearts become insensible to the cry of the poor, of the sick, of orphan children and of those innumerable brothers of ours who still lack the necessary minimum to eat, to clothe their nakedness and to gather their family together under one roof.

You also, O Jesus, were immersed in the river of Jordan, under the eyes of the crowd, although very few then were able to recognize you; and this mystery of tardy faith, or of indifference, prolonged through the centuries, is a source of grief for those who love you and have received the mission of making you known in the world.

O grant to the successors of your apostles and disciples and to all who call themselves after your Name and your Cross, to press on with the work of spreading the Gospel and bear witness to it in prayer, suffering and loving obedience to your will!

And since you, an innocent lamb, came before John in the attitude of a sinner, so draw us also to the waters of the Jordan. To the Jordan will we go to confess our sins and cleanse our souls. And as the skies opened to announce the voice of your Father, expressing his pleasure in you, so, having successfully overcome our trial and lived austerely through the forty days of our Lent, may we, O Jesus, when the day of your Resurrection dawns, hear once more in our innermost hearts the same heavenly Father's voice, recognizing us as his children.

O holy Lent of this mystic year of the Ecumenical Council!

May this prayer rise, on this evening of serene religious recollection, from every house where people work, love, and suffer. May the angels of heaven gather the prayers of all the souls of little children, of generous-hearted young men and women, of hard-working and self-sacrificing parents, and of all who suffer in body and mind, and present their prayers to God. From him will flow down in abundance the gifts of his heavenly joys, of which our Apostolic Benediction is a pledge and a reflection.

[108]   *Prayer to Elizabeth Seton*[1]

O Blessed Elizabeth Seton, shining today in splendour in the sight of all the nations because of your faithfulness to the promises made at your baptism, look lovingly upon your own people, who boast of you as their first flower of sanctity! Obtain for them from God the grace that they may preserve their most sacred inheritance which is fidelity to the Gospel, firmness of faith, and enthusiastic charity, so that they may joyfully fulfil their own particular vocation. And protect the whole Church, offering her the example of your warm-hearted generosity and love which carried you onwards from one degree of glory to another (cf. 2 Cor. 3: 18) to the final glory of today.

[109]   *Prayer to the Blessed Louis Palazzolo*[2]

O Blessed Louis Maria, now shining in eternal light, irradiate your native diocese, which is also our own, and the entire church, with your examples of charity, eager pastoral zeal and humble service.

O heavenly intercessor, obtain from God that the stream of holy fervour may be kept flowing among Christians, and especially among the young candidates for the priesthood; and that the fields ploughed for centuries may continue to bear their young and promising shoots.

May the Lord hear your prayers for the consecrated virgins of the Institute, to which you have shown the many opportunities for heroic dedication.

Through the grace of God may your example attract priests and religious, both men and women, scattered throughout the world, to the honour of ever-renewed apostolic labour; so that they may give light to all that are in the Father's house (cf. Matthew 5: 15) and become the most enthusiastic co-operators in that hoped-for spiritual progress which the Church of this age, strengthened by the Ecumenical Council, wishes to achieve for the good of mankind.

---

[1] Elizabeth Anna Seton Bayley, foundress of the American Sisters of Charity, beatified on 17 March, 1963.

[2] Louis Maria Palazzolo, a Bergamasque priest, founder of the Institute of the *Suore delle Poverelle* (Sisters of the Poor), beatified on 19 March, 1963.

VI

Appendices

Appendix 1

Notes for a biography of Pope John Roncalli[1]

It is certainly of some interest to find out who are these Roncalli from whose family stock was to spring such a precious branch.

The name of this family is found in the oldest records of Bergamasque history, especially in the Valle Imagna and more particularly in the communes of Corna and Cepino, each of which has a district called Roncaglia (perhaps from the term '*ronchi*', in Bergamasque dialect '*rüc*' or '*roncai*', given to the characteristic terraces cut into the mountain sides in order to utilize the ground for the cultivation of vines). In both these villages can be seen documents dating from the beginning of the fourteenth century, which speak of de Roncallis or de Ronchalis. From Roncaglia di Cepino, in the fifteenth century, there came down to Sotto il Monte a certain Martino Roncalli, called Maitino, who built his home at the foot of a hill. Even today Sotto il Monte is not so much a village as a cluster of farms and hamlets, scattered between the hill and the plain, where the land begins to slope down from Canto Basso towards the Adda. But every single isolated house, and every group of dwellings, has its own name.

The house built by Martino Roncalli, called Maitino ('*dictus Maytinus*'), newly arrived in Sotto il Monte from Valle Imagna, was at once called Camaitino, and has been so called ever since.

We find mention of Martino Roncalli in a document of 26 August, 1418 ('*Martinus dictus Maytinus filius quondam Tomasi de Roncallis*'— 'Martino, called Maitino, the son of the late Tomasi de Roncallis') among the papers of the notary Gualmino de Grecis preserved in the episcopal archives of Bergamo. We learn also from notarial documents (8 September, 1429, of the notary Giovanni da Corte; 22 March, 1429, of the notary Gianfranco Salvetti; and 16 March, 1443, of the notary Gian Antonio

[1] Unfortunately these notes, written by Pope John himself, and begun in 1959, stop short at the years he spent at the seminary (1892–1904). He showed himself willing to co-operate in the recording, in the third person, of his own documented biography. He had the idea after reading, or rather revising, the first proofs of a volume about himself which was never published. Here we give an extract from this volume, in his corrected version.

Vavassori da Medolago) that Martino had three sons—Tonolo, Pedrino and Giovanni—and that because of this the Roncalli family began to spread out in Sotto il Monte and, to a certain extent, from there to that surrounding area of the Bergamasque territory which is called Isola, stretching from the Adda to the Brembo.

Other Roncallis became detached from the main stock of Valle Imagna and were dispersed here and there over the Bergamasque territory and to other parts of Italy, under various names. So we have, besides the Maitini of Sotto il Monte, the Bragini, Piretti, Parolini, Frosio, and Quadri Roncallis, scattered more or less everywhere, at Bergamo, Brescia, Udine, Rovigo, in Tuscany, in Foligno, Rome and Venice.

The first house built by Martino, called Maitino, the first of the Roncallis to come to Sotto il Monte, which was also called Berzio, still survives. In the course of the centuries it has passed through the hands of various owners; Roncalli, De Vecchi, Macassoli, Mangili, Scotti, and by these last owners it was let for more than thirty-five years to Mgr Roncalli, as his summer residence, from 1925 to 1958.

Just when this prelate was taking up his residence there, it happened that the work of restoration brought to light on a wall, which must have been the external façade of the original building, some fifteenth century frescoes or paintings, with figures of St Antony the Abbot, a Madonna and Child, and St Bernardino of Siena, the great saint of that century. And all these were surmounted by a coat-of-arms, a tower on a field of red and white bars: precisely the arms of the Maitini of Sotto il Monte, which, after this discovery and with a few additions, became the arms of the Archbishop, later Patriarch and Cardinal and now Supreme Pontiff, Angelo Giuseppe Roncalli, who took the name of John XXIII.

As they appear now, quartered with the arms of St Mark, these papal arms certainly do not aim at gratifying any desire to prove a noble origin; they testify to the Pope's loving and studious interest in the ancient history of his native region.

If anything, one sees here the joy of a man who loves to feel rooted in his native land, rather than a search for heraldic gratifications. This much is certain, that the family of Pope Roncalli is derived from no mean origins but from worthy and respected folk who can be traced right back to the beginning of the fifteenth century, to the first *Martinus* Roncalli, called Maitino, of Valle Imagna, and from this first Roncalli of Sotto il Monte further back to a certain Bonadio, in the middle of the thirteenth century, who was followed by a Teubaldo who appears during the years 1257–1285.

OBŒDIENTIA ET PAX

37. His three brothers, under a plaque of his arms
as Cardinal Archbishop of Venice

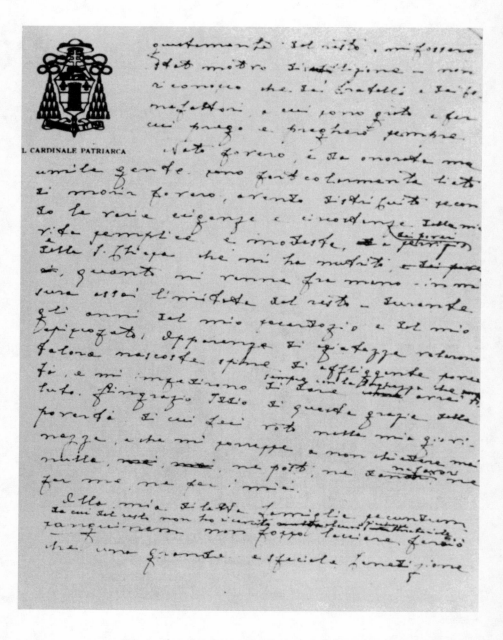

L. CARDINALE PATRIARCA

38. Facsimile of one page of his spiritual testament

Starting with the first Roncalli of Sotto il Monte—the *Martinus dictus Maytinus*—the line descends without interruption until 1616, when we notice in the parish archives the names of Donato (1616), Donato (1637), Giovanni (1659), Bartolomeo (1682), Giovanni Battista (1714), Antonio (1735), Giuseppe (1768), Giovanni Battista (1797), Angelo (1826), and Giovanni Battista (1854), the father of Pope John.

As soon as the latter was born, on the morning of 25 November, 1881, he was at once taken to the baptismal font. By chance the parish priest, Father Francesco Rebuzzini, a saintly priest and recognized as such by all who knew him, had gone into the town. So the baptism had to wait until his return, while the father of the family, delighted at the birth of his first son after three daughters, hastened to the municipal office to register his birth.

The baptism took place without any special ceremony, that very evening, 25 November, in the church of Santa Maria of Brusico, very near to the home of the Roncallis—an old church that was then used as the parish church in the place of the more ancient edifice, since then demolished, of San Giovanni Battista, which was on the hill of that name and very difficult to approach. It is interesting to see the record of the baptism in the parish register:

'In the year 1881, 25 November, I, Francesco Rebuzzini, the priest of this church of San Giovanni Battista of Sotto il Monte, baptized the infant born today of the lawfully married couple Giovanni Battista Roncalli and Marianna Mazzola, from Brusico in this parish. The infant was given the names *Angelo Giuseppe*. The godfather was Zaverio Roncalli, the son of Giovanni Battista of this parish. Signed by the parish priest Francesco Rebuzzini.'

The name of the godfather, Zaverio, is worth noting. He was the eldest of five brothers whose names were: Zaverio, Angelo, Alessandro, Giovanni and Giuseppe. This old man, the eldest son, never married: he died at the age of eighty-eight. He was a pious and most devout man, well instructed in things pertaining to God and religion. Without any intention of making him a priest, he gave his godson the most edifying and effective preparation for the training, not merely of a simple priest, but of a Bishop and Pope, such as Providence had wished and decreed he should be. As regards his religious culture, it is enough to say that he was familiar with the Meditations of Father Louis da Ponte.[1] He always read

[1] *Meditazioni* of the Venerable Luis da Ponte, of the Society of Jesus, translated from the Spanish by G. Cesare Braccini, edited by Fr Giacomo Bonaretti, S.J., 6 vols., Milan, Librario Ernesto Oliva, 1853.

the *Bollettino Salesiano* and the Catholic newspapers of Bergamo, in that period when Catholic Action was being started from Bergamo. It was this great-uncle Zaverio who, as soon as the child no longer needed his mother, took him into his own charge and by word and example imparted to him the happiness of his own religious soul. The same sentiments were instilled into the child, in all the circumstances of family life (and the family became more numerous every year), by his devoted parents, his father Giovanni Battista and his pious, innocent and most hardworking mother, Marianna Mazzola. Oh what a mother! Oh what a simple, pure conscience, remaining pure and simple until her death at an advanced age, loved and venerated by her ten children and by the whole parish! One must point out that with this Roncalli family there also lived Battista's cousin, Luigi, the son of Alessandro, with his wife who was called Angelina Carissimi, also the mother of ten children. So in the Roncalli family, the most numerous of the village, there were thirty mouths to fill, three times a day. But God provided for all: the well-cultivated cornfields and vineyards yielded their harvest, the cattle in their stalls gave milk and its products; the fear of God provided all that was needful, maintaining order and the tranquillity of a life shared in common, with all engaged in the same hard work and in doing good, and all respecting one another, so that domestic and Christian peace was never disturbed. In the evening, and every evening, it was he, the old uncle Zaverio, who intoned the rosary; and all the rest responded in unison, a music which still has power to move the heart as memory recalls it across such a great distance of years. All this was in the years between 1880 and 1892, after which date the large family was forced of necessity to divide. There were twenty children altogether, brothers and sisters and cousins, and exactly ten boys and ten girls. The eldest boy was Angelino, the future Pope, who was then eleven.

The great-uncle Zaverio—the head of the family, the '*barba*', as they say in the Bergamasque speech—and his four brothers Angelo, the father of Battista and grandfather of the future Pope; Alessandro, with three sons, Luigi, Giuseppe Filippo and Pietro; Giovanni, who later went to Carvico, also with three sons: Francesco, Pasquale and Antonio; and Giuseppe, who had no children and whose wife Anna Ghisleni was an invalid for about thirty years: these were the senior members of this large Roncalli family which always enjoyed great respect and affection in the whole parish and the surrounding countryside.

Of the grandsons who appeared one after the other, sons of the two cousins Battista and Luigi, Angelino was the firstborn, and because he was immediately and spontaneously attracted by everything to do with the Church, and because of his innocent and peaceful appearance and behaviour, he was and remained the darling of all, the object of eager and special attention. Outside his own home other boys of his own age called him Angelino, the little Roncalli angel, the little priest.

He was confirmed in 1887[1] at Carvico by the venerable Bishop, Mgr Gaetano Camillo Guindani, his first meeting with a Bishop, one moreover who was an impressive and much loved prelate and was later to confer on him the sacred tonsure in the seminary at Bergamo in 1895, and the minor orders in 1899.

He made his first communion when he was eight years old, a simple ceremony on a cold morning in Lent, in the church of Santa Maria of Brusico, which was being used as the parish church.

There were only the boys and girls present, with the parish priest Rebuzzini and his curate, Father Bortolo Locatelli.[2] In future years the Pope loved to recall the great simplicity of this ceremony and the following detail which remained engraved in his heart. After Mass, the first communicants went to the presbytery to be enrolled, one by one, in the Association of the Apostolate of Prayer, and the parish priest Rebuzzini gave to no other than Angelino the honour of writing the list of the Christian names and surnames of his boy companions and of the little girls. This was the first writing exercise that he remembers, the first of the innumerable sheets of paper he was to fill, in more than half a century of living pen in hand.

His schooling began in his childhood, in the elementary classes at Sotto il Monte, in the old school of Camaitino, and later in the new one opened at Bercio, as soon as the new town hall had been built. The first instruction in correct Italian was given him by the curate of Carvico, Father Luigi Bonardi; he learnt Latin from the parish priest there, Father Pietro Bolis, a somewhat strict tutor of the old school. However, some months of instruction, rather hard going for a small boy of nine years of age, enabled him to pass successfully a first Latin examination which, after two more months of study, assured him a place in the third elementary class of the seminary school. He profited by this in being allowed to attend, in 1892,[3] as an external pupil, the school of the Episcopal College of Celana. But those few months did not produce any solid educational results.

[1] Writing these notes down as they came into his head, the author made a mistake. He was confirmed on 13 February, 1889.

[2] Curate at Sotto il Monte from 1845 to 1895.

[3] Actually, November, 1891 and the first months of 1892.

His experience at Celana was however particularly valuable for him because it was there that his mind was brought into contact with wise religious education and training, with civil and social life from the practical angle, because there he made his first acquaintance with the life of St Charles Borromeo, the founder and patron saint of that Institute.

When for the first time Angelo saw a statue of St Charles, on the ancient door of the College of Célana, the saint took such possession of his ingenuous and innocent heart as to become his light and inspiration in all that Providence set him to do in the study and imitation of that great master of the episcopate of the universal Church. For this reason Pope John XXIII has always retained a most pleasant and grateful memory of Celana.

He finally entered the seminary at Bergamo as a boarder, at the beginning of November, 1892, and remained there until the end of 1900, eight whole years.

When he started his classical studies at the age of eleven, he found them difficult, and the effort must have cost him dearly, although he remained tranquil and determined. In fact he proceeded by slow stages. He had entered the third elementary year with satisfactory but only average marks, yet two years later he was already among the first of the class. In fact, he was so promising that when he was barely fourteen years old he was admitted to the sacred tonsure, a very rare occurrence for those, or for any, times. It was the eve of the feast of St Peter, that year 1895.[1] The next day he was present at the solemn consecration of Mgr Abbondio Cavadini,[2] a missionary Bishop at Mangalore in India. He was a Jesuit from Calcinate. The consecrating Bishop was Mgr Guindani, assisted by two prelates from Brescia, Mgr Corna Pellegrini, Bishop of Brescia, and Mgr Rota, Bishop of Lodi. This was a moving and unforgettable ceremony, in the cathedral of Bergamo, for the young seminarist Roncalli who from that time seemed to make great strides in his studies as well as in his spiritual training. In fact, barely three years later his Professor of Literature, Father Giovanni Floridi of blessed memory, who had become Vice-rector, appointed him to be the prefect of the courses of rhetoric, in charge of students several of whom were older than he. From the secondary school he passed on to theological studies [sentence un-

---

[1] Actually, 24 June, so not the eve of the Feast of St Peter.

[2] Mgr Abbondio Cavadini, born at Calcinate (Bergamo) in 1846; he died at Codialbail (India) in 1910. He was consecrated Bishop on 28 June, 1896. Evidently, with the passing of time, the two events, with a year's distance between them, became confused in the author's mind.

finished]. The Jubilee Year, 1900, saw the opening of a new horizon in the life of the seminarist Angelo Roncalli.

In September a pilgrimage for the obtaining of the great Indulgence revealed to him all the majesty of papal Rome, which from that time on was never far from his mind.

During the vacation of the preceding year, 1899, at the Ghiaie di Bonate Sopra, in the company of Father Alessandro Locatelli, who was curate there, he had met the very distinguished prelate Mgr Giacomo Radini Tedeschi, Canon of the Vatican, who had been given the grave 'burden and heat of the day' as director of the great Jubilee pilgrimages in Rome. In his youth he had been a pupil at the same Seminary of S. Alessandro at Bergamo, where he had made his elementary and secondary studies, and he had always remained a devoted friend of the prefect of his year. This was in fact Father Alessandro who, meanwhile, by means of a persevering and edifying pastoral ministry, had become the real father of the hamlet of the Ghiaie, where he built the church, initiated devotion to Our Lady of Lourdes, and began to form the new parish, so the young Roman prelate was able to continue a friendship with him that permitted a mutual exchange of good priestly services for the benefit of souls. It was thus that the seminarist Roncalli, a fellow parishioner of Father Locatelli, for both had been born at Sotto il Monte, found himself un-wittingly involved in a train of events ordered by Providence, that was five years later to result in the composition of the episcopal family of Mgr Radini Tedeschi, the new Bishop of Bergamo, consisting of the Bishop himself, Father Alessandro as the administrator of his household, and Father Angelo Roncalli as his private secretary.

The five years that elapsed between the first meeting at the Ghiaie in 1899 and the solemn entry of Bishop Radini into Bergamo in April, 1905, were the busiest and most fruitful years in the ecclesiastical training of the future servant of the servants of God, chosen to rule the universal Church.

The diocese of Bergamo, by virtue of a precious will of the year 1640, drawn up by one of its most distinguished prelates, Mgr Flaminio Cerasola (d. 1640), but put into execution at the end of the eighteenth century, had its own College in Rome, the Nobile Collegio Cerasola, for ecclesiastical studies for the benefit of certain young citizens of Bergamo chosen by the Bishop, and nominated by a special committee of the venerable Arciconfraternita dei Bergamaschi in Rome. The confused and sad events which occurred after 20 September, 1870, tempted certain people to question the purpose of the Flaminio Cerasola Foundation, and to divert in favour of lay students the income that had been fixed by that worthy ecclesiastic for the exclusive advantage of seminarists from Bergamo. This led to a suspension of this income for ten years, during which time the question of the precise intention of Cerasola's bequest was debated in the law courts. Naturally the verdict of the courts, pronounced and confirmed, was entirely in favour of the Bishop of Bergamo, who thus vindicated the rights of the whole diocese.

Therefore in 1900 students were once more sent from Bergamo to the Pontifical Roman Seminary. By a surprising coincidence it happened that the first student called and chosen for this privilege was in fact the seminarist Angelo Roncalli, with two other seminarists from Bergamo, Achille Ballini of Boltiere (who unfortunately died at an early age) and Guglielmo Carozzi of Curnasco (now for more than forty years the worthy and hard-working archpriest of Seriate); and these three once again set in motion the procession of Cerasolian students, already made noteworthy by a series of most distinguished ecclesiastics, who had made a most remarkable contribution to the work of the diocese of Bergamo and of the universal Church. Let it suffice to mention the names of Cardinals Agliardi, Cavagnis, Gusmini, of the Archbishops Signori of Genoa and the two brothers, Gustavo and Giacomo Testa, Apostolic Nuncios and Delegates, of Sigismondi, who occupies the very important post of Secretary of the Sacred Congregation of Propaganda Fide, and of Bishops Arcangeli of Asti and Battaglia of Faenza, not to mention other and most distinguished ecclesiastics who, in the various spheres of work of the sacred ministry, in the Sacred Congregations in Rome or in diocesan Curias, in seminaries and in parishes, have won tributes of great respect and praise to the diocese of St Alexander.

This second series of Cerasolian students, led by the seminarist Roncalli and his companions Ballini and Carozzi, soon showed signs of being greatly blessed. Father Achille Ballini's life was cut short, but not before he had given in social work and Catholic Action, and in the sacred pastoral ministry—he was at one time parish priest at Loreto and at Borgo Canale (Bergamo)—a wonderful example of admirable priestly zeal. Father Guglielmo Carozzi, already distinguished in Rome for remarkable successes in theological and juridical subjects, was able to give his diocese, from the time of his first service in seminary and Curia, forty years of pastoral work as archpriest of Seriate; he was universally admired and beloved and always full of lively and intense spiritual energy.

The seminarist Roncalli's Roman studies were suspended for a full year while he completed his military service in Bergamo, from November,

1901, to November, 1902, first as an infantryman in the 73rd regiment of the Lombardia brigade, then promoted Corporal on 31 May, 1902, and Sergeant from 30 November of the same year. He will always cherish the most precious memory of these twelve months, as an experience of strict discipline, a means of getting to know the souls of the young sons of Italy, and of finding out the best practical ways of drawing them to all that is good, to the loftiest summits of human and Christian feeling and living.

Having resumed his studies in Rome with excellent success, calmly and enthusiastically, he attained the various degrees of Bachelor and Doctor, receiving his Doctorate at the beginning of July, 1904. He will always remember having had as invigilator at the written examination for his Doctorate the young Roman priest Father Eugenio Pacelli, who just fifty years later was to bestow upon him his Cardinal's hat, and five years later bequeath to him his papal tiara.

Equally worthy of note were the successive, more intense and more fervent preparations for holy orders. He was made a subdeacon at the Lateran by the Cardinal Vicar, Pietro Respighi, on 11 April, 1903; a deacon by the same Cardinal, again at the Lateran, on 18 December of the same year; he attained his priesthood before his time (*extra tempus*), because of his unusually early age, on 10 August, 1904. The ceremony was in the church of Santa Maria in Monte Santo in the Piazza del Popolo, and the officiating prelate was Mgr Ceppetelli, Vicegerent of the Roman Vicariate.

When he returned from his military service the Superiors of the Roman Seminary entrusted to Roncalli the office of prefect of the 'young theologians' (*teologi piccoli*), as they were then called, and in this charge also he was much esteemed and beloved. These young students had found themselves in difficult circumstances when the Holy Father, Pius X, decreed that all the seminarists of Rome, many of whom lived with their own families, should be obliged to share the common life in the seminary, and that if they did not fulfil this obligation they would not be allowed to receive holy orders.

The life of the young Bergamasque priest at the Roman Seminary, so happy and so full of blessings, looked as if it were to be prolonged through the course of juridical studies which he had begun in November of that year; but, after a few months, the first summons to obedience opened to him the door to an unexpected future in his own diocese, as secretary to the new Bishop, Mgr Radini Tedeschi, who began his distinguished and memorable episcopate at the beginning of April.

When the Holy Father, Pius X, at the end of December, 1904, confided to Mgr Radini Tedeschi his intention of sending him to Bergamo as successor to Mgr Guindani of revered memory, he said to him: 'I thank you for having accepted. Go to Bergamo. In all that can rejoice a Bishop's heart, Bergamo is the first diocese of Italy.'

The chief characteristic of the diocese of Bergamo was its very fervent religious tradition fostered by the zeal of a clergy intent on the training [sentence left unfinished. Here these 'Notes' end].

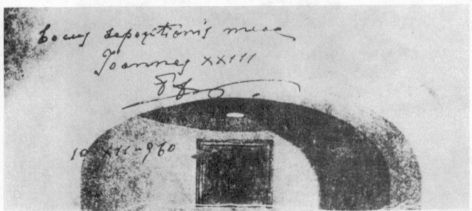

39. The inscription reads: 'This is the place for my tomb.
John XXIII Pp. 10 December, 1960.'

40. October, 1962. Addressing the crowds on the occasion of his pilgrimage to Loreto.

Appendix 2

The 'Little Rules' of ascetic life

One of the characteristic institutions of the seminary at Bergamo is the 'Sodality of the Annunciation and of the Immaculate Conception' which has played a great part in conferring on the life of the college, and thence on all the activity of the Bergamasque clergy, a spirit of special devotion to Mary. The Sodality has existed from time immemorial.

The first juridical document known is the canonical record of its constitution by the Bishop Cardinal Priuli, dated 1 January, 1725, under the name: *Congregazione dell'Annunciazione e della Immacolata*. In 1726 a Brief of Benedict XIII granted it many indulgences. In 1821 another Brief of Pius VII transferred its seat from the church of S. Matteo (the church of the old seminary) to that of S. Giovanni in Arena (the church of the new seminary).

There are various registers of events still surviving. The first begins with 1 July, 1694; unfortunately it is incomplete, the first pages, which seem to have contained the Statute of the Sodality, having been torn out. Other registers follow: three give the history of the Sodality until 16 February, 1802; there is also a sort of medley of scattered notes, briefly summarizing the events from 1836 to 1855, and a cash book from 19 September, 1845 until 1889. These are written very clearly and carefully, and give most interesting information about the life of the Sodality and of the seminary. There are also some references to events of Italian history.

The Sodality was particularly flourishing in the eighteenth century, with its own Rule and its own governing body comprising many functions and offices, with its feasts and anniversaries, and its meetings for periodical elections and examination and acceptance of new members.

In the nineteenth century it was given a simpler organization, less complicated and less pretentious. With the forming of two categories of members, the ordinary members and those of the 'Little Rules', very probably after the restoration of the Society of Jesus or perhaps towards the middle of the century, the Sodality acquired a certain air of secrecy. The ordinary members were certainly very virtuous, but of no special distinction; those of the 'Little Rules' were the best, in the fullest sense of the term. Nobody was to know who they were, and they were bound by great secrecy, so much so that even today these famous 'Little Rules' were unknown and are published here for the first time, from a manuscript written by Angelo Roncalli when a seminarist. The Sodality started to decay when someone divulged the secret of the existence of this group and even gave the names of its members.

To understand the function of this Sodality, especially in the past, one must know something of seminary life at that time. There were in fact three categories of students in the seminary at Bergamo: the residents, seminarists who boarded in the seminary; the day scholars, clerical students of law, who came to the seminary for their classes but lodged outside, and the lay scholars who attended the seminary courses. This third category existed until about thirty years ago.

With such a variety of constituents it was natural for the Superiors to feel the necessity of establishing, especially among the resident students, some Rules of a more strictly ecclesiastical life, to complete the few rules of the seminary. This is true particularly of the eighteenth century. In the nineteenth century the Rules became a means of encouraging the seminarists in a more profound religious faith, and preserving them from the spirit of the world. In fact it was during the period when the Society of Jesus was suppressed (1773–1814) that certain Jesuit Fathers exercised a beneficial influence over the training of the Bergamasque clergy, and left in the seminary deep and lasting traces of the sound Ignatian methods of education.

The Marian Sodality has always included the most distinguished students, whether boarders or day students. It united them in a bond of vital energies, pledged them to a life of serious discipline and solid piety and trained them to be the hopes of the apostolate of the future. The best of the clergy of Bergamo belonged to the Marian Sodality. As regards the relations between the Society of Jesus and the seminary at Bergamo, let this reference suffice: 'In the diocese of St Alexander the sons of St Ignatius always enjoyed great esteem and veneration. The Bergamasque region produced excellent vocations for the Society, men of the highest order who shone by their virtue, doctrine, and apostolate. It is enough to mention the names of Maffei, Mozzi, Mai, and Grassi. When the storm of the suppression had passed over, and the Society began to reconstitute itself in Italy, out of the eight Fathers who, together with the Blessed Pignatelli, formed the first group, five or six were from Bergamo. . . ' (Angelo Gius. Roncalli, titular Archbishop of Mesembria, *Gli inizi del Seminario di Bergamo e San Carlo*, Soc. Ed. Sant'Alessandro, Bergamo, 1939, p. 75).

[III]   *Little Rules, etc.*
Rules of spiritual life reserved for certain pupils of
the seminary at Bergamo, for the use of the
seminarist Angelo Roncalli, 1895–1900

Rule of life for a seminarist who wishes to advance in the way of perfection.

Every day:

1. Meditate for at least a quarter of an hour.
2. Attend or, better, serve Holy Mass.
3. Read some spiritual work, the book being the life of a saint, or at least a treatise on spiritual subjects.
4. Pay a visit to the Blessed Sacrament, and at the same time visit some altar dedicated to Our Lady.
5. Read some passage from the devout Thomas à Kempis, in Latin.
6. Never omit your general examination of conscience in the evening, with proper repentance.
7. Make your particular examination.
8. Accustom yourself to raising your thoughts to God with devout invocations. The chief of these will be: 'Thy will, O Lord, be done.'—'My Jesus, mercy. Mary, help.'—'Not to us, O Lord, not to us, but to your name give the glory.'
9. Say five decades of the rosary, and some part of the Office of Our Lady.

Every week:

1. Be diligent in attending the meetings of the Sodality and the study circles.
2. Go to confession and communion as your spiritual director advises.
3. Fast on Fridays and Saturdays in honour of the Passion of Jesus Christ and of Our Lady.
4. At times join some good companions in speaking of spiritual things, and share with one another the good thoughts that will make you hate vice and love virtue.

Every month:

1. Set aside one day to prepare yourself for a good death, and on this day examine yourself more closely concerning the correction of your

own faults and concerning virtues and your observance of these Little Rules.

2. Read these Little Rules several times, and it will be well to do this in the company of others, so as to check your observance of them.

3. Always confide trustfully in your spiritual director, and be guided by his advice in all this.

Every year:

1. Always prepare for the principal solemn feasts with fervent prayer; before beginning the respective Novenas it will be well to join with others and decide what you are to do. For this always consult your own spiritual director.

2. Make the Novenas, the most important of which will be those before Pentecost, the feast of the Sacred Heart of Jesus, Christmas, the principal feasts of Our Lady, and those of your Guardian Angel and of St Joseph.

3. Before leaving the seminary for the holidays confer with your spiritual director about how best to spend them well in the Lord.

4. Make your Spiritual Exercises and your annual confession.

At all times:

1. Have a special love for your companions, and this mutual love must come from God and tend to God.

2. Pray to the Lord for one another, especially in any particular need, and for this purpose offer a communion for your companions every month.

3. Correct one another's faults, and let him who is corrected say three Hail Marys for his corrector.

4. Each must choose a corrector from among his companions.

5. It will be an excellent thing for you to write letters to one another during the holidays, encouraging perseverance in doing good, especially when making a Novena.

6. No one shall lay his hands on another. Do not use the intimate 'tu' when speaking with one another and do not use dialect words or, worse, immodest expressions; if you hear these used by others go away, showing that you will not take any part in such conversation.

7. Evil companions must be shunned like vipers, especially those who criticize virtue, good men and good examples, subjecting them to ridicule.

8. Be very much on your guard against human respect. Do not refrain from doing good, or indulge in evil because of any human respect or consideration.

9. Have a great love for that virtue which sheds a lustre on all life and especially on that of ecclesiastics, the guiding star of the priesthood: purity. Therefore you must set a guard over your senses, and especially over your eyes, shun the company of women and of corrupt youths, and avoid idleness.

10. No books must be read that have the slightest taint of immodesty; in fact, before reading any book be sure that it is approved of by your director, especially if it is a book of poetry.

11. Do not attend public spectacles, or fairs, or listen to profane speeches, or go to luxurious parties. Do not sing love songs.

12. To guard the virtue of purity you must have a great love for Mary most holy, and in her honour say three Hail Marys for yourself and your companions, offering them to her and begging her for this virtue.

13. Fast for the principal feasts of Mary, and have a great devotion also to your Guardian Angel and to St Aloysius Gonzaga, in whose honour you will observe the six Sundays and three days of special prayer before his feast.

14. Your chief devotion will be for the Blessed Sacrament: therefore great recollection in church, especially when there is Exposition. Receive the Blessed Sacrament as often as you can, with the best possible dispositions and devotion, and with a prolonged thanksgiving. Visit Jesus in the Blessed Sacrament frequently, rejoicing to keep him company.

15. Dress according to the regulations: without any variation or display, taking no notice of anything that may be said about this, and remembering that 'all who desire to live a godly life in Christ Jesus will be persecuted'.[1]

16. When you attend services in church always wear your cassock.

17. Always be assiduous at these functions, behaving very devoutly. By so doing you will prove in yourself the truth of that saying: 'Train up a child in the way he should go, and when he is old he will not depart from it.'[2]

Pious practices for the month of May

Considering that you are chosen by Divine Providence to honour the great Mother of God in the name of your companions, you see how great your fervour must be. If you are ever to be fervent, now is surely the time. Here therefore are some pious exercises:

[1] Cf. 2 Timothy 3: 12.   [2] Proverbs 22: 6.

1. In the morning, as soon as you wake up, offer your heart, and the hearts of your companions, to Mary, promising that you will be especially devoted to her on this day. Offer her the good that you will do this day and beg her to bless you, together with your companions.

2. In the evening, before going to bed, offer her by the hands of St Aloysius and St Stanislaus all the good you have done, so that through their merits it may be more acceptable to her and be blessed by them. Ask her to forgive you for your unsatisfactory service and in exchange for her forgiveness offer her your determined will to serve her better in the future, until death, and ask for her assistance at that hour also.

3. As each hour strikes, or when you become aware that it has struck, let your spirit rise to Mary's throne, and then, prostrate before her, say a Hail Mary, offering her your whole life and your companions', with a small mortification of your own choice.

4. Besides your usual visit make two extra visits to the Blessed Sacrament and two to Our Lady, spending half an hour on these two visits together. While doing this adore Jesus who is the only Son of the divine Father, and the only Son of Mary. Love him and promise him that you will love him only and for ever, and that you will not commit the slightest sin against him, even at the cost of your life.

5. Make a spiritual communion and ask Jesus for a thousand graces, especially for a great love for him and a tender devotion to Mary most holy, for yourself and your companions. Pray also for all your classmates. In your visit to Our Lady make an act of thanksgiving to the Most Holy Trinity for having raised her so high, and congratulate her on this privilege, protesting that you wish to love her with your whole heart and always to be her beloved son.

6. Decide on a grace which you wish to beg and obtain this day from Our Lady for yourself and for your companions. Ask for it with fervour and great humility, and you will obtain it. Mary is the tenderest of mothers.

7. That sacrifice which the Lord asks of you and which perhaps you have until now denied him, you must now offer by the hand of Mary.

8. For four or five minutes read something about Mary very thoughtfully and when you have a little time to spare ponder her virtues, her privileges, her greatness and her love for us. This is most useful to you and the most welcome homage to Our Lady, and she will print her blessing in your heart.

9. Try to do everything with closer attention; be very fervent and diligent in observance of the Rules. In short, behave in such a way that

Our Lady may be pleased with every slightest action, thought or word of yours. Speak, do and think as if Mary were always present.

10. Choose some interior mortification for your spirit; invoke Mary constantly. If your fervour suggests your doing something more, you may do this also. On the last day of the month renew your intention of increasing more and more in fervour. Ask Mary most holy for those graces you have already begged from her on the day when you paid special homage to her. Thank her as if you had already received them. Offer her your heart and the hearts of your fellow seminarists, united with those of St Joseph, St Aloysius and St Stanislaus, so that the offering may be more acceptable to her. On this day decide on a pious practice that you will perform perpetually in honour of Our Lady.

On the particular examination

The particular examination, so useful for one who wishes to advance in virtue, so much praised by the just and practised most strictly by the saints, should be, according to the greatest minds, arranged in this manner.

1. In the morning, as soon as you wake up, make up your mind to watch most carefully lest you fall into that particular defect which you wish to correct.

2. During the day, when you notice that you have erred, at once with some interior prayer or act ask God for his forgiveness; with your hand on your heart promise to be more attentive in the future.

3. In the evening when you make your general examination, after having made a general survey of all your faults, give particular attention to this one.

4. Compare the second day with the first, the third with the second, the fourth with the third, and so on. In this way you will know whether or not you are progressing in virtue, and whether you are getting any good out of the particular examination.

5. You may also make some virtue the subject of the particular examination. Those who make the particular and general examination in the evening when they go to bed, as well as during the day, redouble their speed and in a short time make further progress along the road of virtue.

Rule of life for the holidays
Every day

1. As soon as you wake up raise your mind to God with an immediate act of consecration to him.

2. While you are dressing say very slowly the Psalm: 'O God, to thee do I look at break of day.'[1]

3. If possible, before Mass in your room or in church after Mass, spend at least twenty minutes in meditation.

4. The Hours will be said during one of the Masses.

5. Every day attend both parish Masses and serve at least one of these.

6. When you have had breakfast and half an hour of recreation, the time that remains before eleven o'clock is to be spent partly in study and partly, but a shorter time, in some suitable recreation. If on occasion it is necessary to defer any of these practices, you must be very careful not to omit your pious exercises.

7. The whole day will be one long particular examination, but this will be made more diligently for at least three minutes between eleven o'clock and twelve.

8. About the same time, before dinner, do your spiritual reading, which will never be for less than half an hour.

9. After your meal never forget to say the six Our Fathers, as is the custom in the seminary.

10. About two o'clock in the afternoon you will say Vespers and Compline, and make a very devout visit to Jesus in the Blessed Sacrament, which must never be for less than twenty minutes.

11. Before evening say the Matins and Lauds of the Blessed Virgin, unless you are saying the Divine Office with a priest; likewise you must never, on any evening, without sufficient reason fail to say the rosary, which you will recite very devoutly with your family, also to give a good example.

12. Never go to bed until you have given at least ten minutes to a general examination, and said all the prayers that are usually said also in the seminary.

Every week

1. Approach the sacrament of confession never less than once a week, and try to find some time when the confessor will have more leisure to devote to you.

2. On all feast days make your communion, but never before the first Mass, so that you may have more time to prepare for it.

3. Make your communion also on all those days appointed by your confessor; if he has not done this receive your holy communion on Mondays, Wednesdays, and Fridays, as also on some other special days.

[1] Psalm 62(63): 2–12.

4. On Wednesdays do something also for St Joseph, such as saying the usual prayers, reading some book about him, making some special mortification, in short offering everything to him.

5. What you have done for St Joseph do on Saturdays in honour of Mary most holy, and always endeavour to have a more perfect devotion to her. On these days prolong a little your visit to the Blessed Virgin, or at least stay for some time in church, reading and meditating things which stir you to have a whole-hearted love for the great Mother of God, who is our Mother too.

Every month

1. On first Fridays make your communion in honour of the Sacred Heart of Jesus.

2. On the fourth Monday, or the day nearest and most suitable, practise a little recollection, at least until nine o'clock in the morning, and write down your conclusions.

3. Make with special devotion the Novenas to the Sacred Heart, to the Blessed Virgin, and to the angels, and during these try to increase your fervour.

At all times

1. Observe propriety with all, especially with those of your own family.

2. Be prompt in obedience to your superiors, and do not rebuke your elders.

3. Accept with love the admonitions of all.

4. Have a right intention in all things.

5. Be present wherever there is anything to do with religion, even in its humblest manifestation, and show great zeal in the performance of the sacred ceremonies.

6. Spend most of the time in seclusion at home, or in the company of a priest, mindful of what the Angelic Doctor said: 'Have a great love for your cell if you want to be allowed into the wine cellar.' If you wish to take a walk, do not go in search of crowds and the public squares, but seek the least frequented places.

7. Above all avoid groups of chatterers, especially if these include women; never be irritable, or haughty, but always cheerful and friendly with everyone.

8. Beware of idleness, which is the devil's bait.

9. The holidays will give you many opportunities for practising

humility; your particular examination will deal with this, scrupulously observing everything. May the holidays be a training ground for you in the exercise of this virtue, in every form: so in these days you must try to carry out to perfection the resolutions you have made with regard to this.

10. All those good intentions and pious exercises for the increase of virtue, which you were not able to carry out in the seminary, you must try to put into practice in the holidays. For the rest, obey those Rules perfectly which Divine Providence has chosen you to profess, and maintain all those good resolutions which you have made, keeping faithful to the fine principles which you have written down.

11. May the holidays be for you in a special way those blessed days in which your love for Jesus and devotion to him in the Blessed Sacrament may triumph in you and possess you entirely. Therefore, recollection in church and elsewhere, visits to the Blessed Sacrament, loving, even if brief, union with Jesus, with infinite invocations, etc.

In a word, place yourself in the arms and near the Heart of Jesus in the Blessed Sacrament, and then leave all to him. He will form you, he will open your eyes: he will teach you all that you must do; he will make of you, you who are worth nothing, a real priest of his, full of love for him.

If you co-operate with the work of grace in you, and show this in your behaviour, your speech and your works, you will really be a good seminarist, a mirror of that youth whom you chose to imitate, St John Berchmans. In this way you will please both Jesus and Mary: by your example you will edify others, and the holidays, instead of being the devil's instrument for your ruin, will instead serve to make you better, and to prepare you fittingly for the royal ministry of the priesthood.[1]

---

[1] The conclusion, and certain other passages, show that the seminarist Angelo did not merely copy out the text of the 'Little Rules', but added some notes of his own.

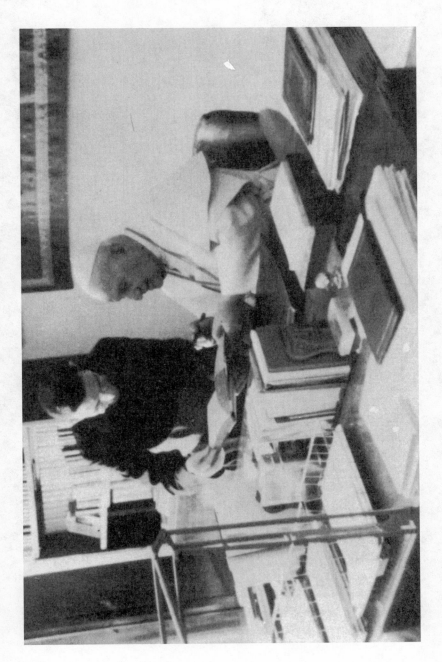

41. In his study, with Mgr Loris Capovilla, his secretary

42. 1962. In the street, in Rome, on one of his many pastoral visits

Appendix 3

Maxims heard or gleaned from various sources[1]

Jesus, Mary, Joseph, be with me on all my ways and in my last agony

1. I will love thee as I am loved by thee (cf. Romans 13: 10).
2. Love is the fulfilling of the law (*ibid.*)
3. The aim of our charge is love (1 Timothy 1: 5).
4. Beloved, let us love one another, for love is of God (I John 4: 7).
5. Show me thy charity and give me thy love.
6. I will love thee, O Lord, my strength and my refuge (cf. Psalm 17: 2–3).
7. To know nothing contrary to the Rule is to know all things (Tertullian).
8. Take care also most diligently to avoid those things in yourself which commonly displease you in others (Thomas à Kempis, *Imitation* I, XXV, 4).
9. Do not think you have made any progress unless you esteem yourself inferior to all (Thomas à Kempis, II, II, 2).
10. If you want people to bear with you, bear with others (Thomas à Kempis, II, III, 2).
11. The interior life is like a deep well of love in which the soul is immersed (Curé d'Ars).
12. The man who does not pray is like a hen or a turkey that cannot rise into the air, and if it tries to fly falls down at once (Curé d'Ars).
13. He who prays well is like an eagle that soars in the sky as if it wanted to reach the sun (Curé d'Ars).
14. We do not have to talk very much in order to pray well. We know that God is there in his holy tabernacle; let us open our hearts to him; let us rejoice in his presence: this is the best prayer (Curé d'Ars).
15. A priest who is so miserable as to celebrate without being in a state of grace must be a monster! No, one cannot understand such

---

[1] We give this list just as it was made by Angelo Roncalli when he was a seminarist, without trying to verify or complete the sources or texts. It helps us to understand the ascetic training and atmosphere of his youth.

wickedness. A man must be cruel, barbarous, heartless, to do such a thing (Curé d'Ars).

16. It is natural for any man to err, but only for a fool to persist in his error (Cicero).

17. It would need a seraph to say a Mass. If we really knew what a Mass is, we should die of it (Curé d'Ars).

18. To be a good priest one would need to live like a seminarist (Curé d'Ars).

19. Be humble and peaceable and Jesus will be with you (Thomas à Kempis).

20. Oh wonderful dignity of priests, in whose hands the Son of God is made flesh as in the womb of the Virgin (St Augustine).

21. Great is this mystery; great too is the dignity of the priest to whom has been granted that which is not permitted to angels (Thomas à Kempis).

22. Pride is the queen and mother of all vices (St Thomas Aquinas).

23. God might have created a more beautiful world, but he could not have given life to a creature more beautiful than Mary (Curé d'Ars).

24. Do people speak ill of you? They speak the truth. Do they pay you compliments? They are making fun of you (Curé d'Ars).

25. Humility is like a balance. The more a man lowers himself on the one side the higher he raises himself on the other (Curé d'Ars).

26. Those who humiliate us are our real friends, not those who praise us (Curé d'Ars).

27. If we knew ourselves thoroughly as God knows us, we could not live, we should die of terror (Curé d'Ars).

28. I was much more fortunate and lived much more happily when I was a simple country curate than now when I am seated on the Patriarchal throne of Venice. (This was said by Cardinal Sarto to a group of seminarists when he visited the seminary during the celebrations of the sixteenth centenary of St Alexander in 1898.) Here one sees how little to be desired on this earth are great positions, even ecclesiastical honours.

29. Even the stars fell from heaven, so what can I expect who am but dust? (Thomas à Kempis, III, XIV, 1).

30. It was axiomatic among the Fathers of the Church that bad priests are the ruin of the people.

31. Knowledge is of no use unless it is joined to a firm piety (Blessed John of Avila).

32. The best way to preach with success is to have a great love for Jesus Christ (Blessed John of Avila).

33. An ounce of peace is worth more than a pound of victory (St Robert Bellarmine).

34. The best remedy I know against sudden fits of impatience is a silence that is gentle and without malice. However little one says, pride always comes into it, and one says things that plunge the heart into grief for a whole day after. When one is silent and smiles in a friendly manner the storm passes over; one smothers one's temper and indiscretion, and so enjoys pure and lasting happiness. (So said St Francis de Sales who with his gentleness converted seventy-two thousand heretics.)

35. One cannot do anything with a heart that is vain and full of itself; it is of no use, either to itself or to others (St Francis de Sales).

36. Frugality is a bank that gives good interest (St Peter Fourier).

37. All we give in charity to the holy souls in Purgatory is exchanged for us into a refreshing shower of blessings and graces (St Ambrose).

38. Contrition in the heart, confession on the lips, complete humility in all one does, this is fruitful penitence.

39. Be not full of words in a multitude of ancients, and repeat not the word in thy prayer (Ecclus. 7: 15).

40. With pride comes disgrace: but with the humble is wisdom (cf. Proverbs 11: 2).

41. My son, do thy works in meekness: and thou shalt be beloved above the glory of men. The greater thou art the more thou must humble thyself in all things and thou shalt find grace before God (Ecclus. 3: 19–20).

42. A sweet word multiplieth friends and appeaseth enemies (Ecclus. 6: 5).

43. Stand in the multitude of ancients that are wise, and join thyself from thy heart to their wisdom, that thou mayest hear every discourse of God, and the sayings of praise may not escape thee. . . . Despise not the discourse of them that are ancient and wise: but acquaint thyself with their proverbs. For of them thou shalt learn wisdom and instruction of understanding to serve great men without blame (Ecclus. 6: 35; 8: 9–10).

44. Open not thy heart to everyman: lest he repay thee with an evil turn and speak reproachfully to thee (Ecclus. 8: 22).

45. . . . what manner of man the ruler of a city is, such also are they that dwell therein (Ecclus. 10: 2).

46. Before thou hear, answer not a word: and interrupt not others in the midst of their discourse (Ecclus. 11: 8).

47. The things that thou hast not gathered in thy youth, how shalt thou find them in thy old age? (Ecclus. 25: 5).

48. In all thy works be quick: and no infirmity shall come to thee (Ecclus. 31 : 27).

49. Let thy zeal be inflamed by charity, enlightened by sound learning, established by perseverance (St Bernard, *super Cantica*, serm. 20).

50. What is zeal but a kind of intimate impulse of charity which makes us dutifully jealous for the salvation of our brethren, jealous for the beauty of the Lord's house and the praise and glory of his name? (St Bernard, *super Cantica*, serm. 38).

51. The first source of courtesy is prudence, which is also fruitful of other virtues (St Ambrose).

52. The more fervent the zeal, the more eager the temper, and the more generous the charity, the more need there is of a watchful knowledge which moderates zeal, tempers the warmth of the disposition and regulates the outpouring of charity (St Ambrose, infr., col. 118).

53. Let zeal be fervent, prudent and unconquered (St Bernard, *super Cant.*, serm. 20: 4).

54. Let us pour out our alms on the poor, and these very alms will pray for us (St Clare).

55. When you are teaching in the church it is not the applause of the people but the tearful sighs which you draw from them which are your true praise (St Jerome, *Ep.* 2).

56. Almost all the powers of the body change in old men; those powers which the body exercises do less when the body is broken (St Jerome).

57. He had a soul most worthy of all honour because it showed a poor opinion of itself (St Bernard).

58. Go, but always remember that you are priests; by travelling you enlarge the mind and learn a great deal (Gioacchino Pecci [Leo XIII], Bishop of Perugia, to the priests who asked him for permission to travel).

59. It is much harder to overcome oneself than to defeat the enemy (Valerius Maximus).

60. There is no labour where one loves, or if there is, the labour itself is loved (St Augustine).

Appendix 4

114

A tribute to the memory of Father Francesco Pitocchi by Father Angelo Roncalli[1]

Rapallo, 14 December, 1922
The feast of the Exaltation of the Holy Cross

I had the good fortune to meet him first towards the end of 1902, twenty years ago. I had just returned to the Roman Seminary after my military service, to resume my theological studies and prepare myself for holy orders.

Providence had sent him to me at the right moment. The very first talk I had with him—I still remember it, the evening of 16 December, during the long retreat of . . . purification (one could not pass from the barracks to the seminary without undergoing this strict cleansing process) gave me a sense of security and great confidence in that man, and in all he would require from me as he taught me the will of God. At the conclusion of our first meeting he gave me a motto to repeat to myself calmly and frequently: *God is all: I am nothing*, and this was like a new principle that opened to my gaze new horizons, unexplored, full of mystery and spiritual beauty.

And I was satisfied!

I had at last found what I had so long desired and what, ever afterwards, whether near or far from him, I was to retain, a safe and trustworthy adviser, the kindest and most faithful of friends, and above all a father, a real father, whose wise and persuasive words were such as to form and nourish Jesus Christ in my soul, and so train it to manhood in Christian and priestly life.

From that evening onwards I began to understand more clearly than ever before that the life of the spirit is more than just a succession of acts, the natural result of a good character and of a very Christian education strengthened by the Lord's grace; it is rather the gradual formation of habits of thought and action, in the light of higher principles which are

[1] In *Sursum Corda.—In memoria del Padre Francesco Pitocchi*, Major Pontifical Roman Seminary, Year V (November, 1922) 11 bis, pp. 30–8.

revealed to the soul gradually; it is a life that has to be studied and practised like an exact science, the science of the saints, indispensable for anyone who, as he grows older and prepares himself for the priestly ministry, wishes to do honour to his own vocation of saving and sanctifying the souls of his brothers.

That motto, which at once began to cut down any pretensions of personal pride, was like the first chapter of a precious book which from that evening Father Francesco taught me to read for my spiritual edification.

When I think now how much I owe to my dear Father's wise teaching I blush at the small profit I derived from his loving instructions; but I feel also a great satisfaction, which seems to me legitimate and holy, because those two years of immediate preparation for my priesthood were indeed, through the mercy of God and through the work of this worthy minister of his, the most fruitful and the richest in ideas and directives for the training of my spirit.

I used to go to see Father Francesco when he came to the seminary, generally twice a week, on Wednesdays and Saturdays, and many of my companions did the same. He used to listen to us with great kindness, but did not say very much; very often he contented himself with a thought from Scripture: something slight in itself, but enough to establish and maintain that inspiration of the intellect and heart which was life itself. We had the impression that this man of God really cared for the soul of each one of us as if the Lord had sent him for that one alone; such was the interest he showed in our weaknesses and in our puny efforts to overcome them, which he supported with fatherly kindness. When we left him, kissing the cross on his stole or his hand raised in absolution or blessing, we felt as it were new vigour, pleasurable and powerful, an enthusiasm, a great enthusiasm, to do good, which, in spite of so many failings—I speak for myself—was the best part, the beauty and the joy of our youth as seminarists.

Sometimes Father Francesco could not come to the seminary, either because his physical sufferings prevented him or because he was prevented by other and graver responsibilities: so we were allowed to go to see him at San Gioacchino. There in his cell, so neat but so humble, our dear Father was completely at home, in his own setting; it even seemed as if his face, words and bearing became even more holy and persuasive against that background of simplicity and monastic and apostolic poverty. That poor simple bed—how poor it looked!—with the small wooden cross placed on the rough coverlet, the bare desk, the few paper devotional holy pictures which hung on the white walls, and the few books of moral or ascetic theology scattered around, the general atmosphere of piety, conferred a singular and convincing authority on the loving warnings he gave us concerning detachment from wealth, honours, and all ambitions, even the ambitions of ecclesiastical life. He spoke of the wisdom of being faithful in little things as a habitual discipline of the soul, which would have the effect of training us in a holy generosity and an enthusiasm for the adventures and sacrifices of the priestly apostolate in the service of Jesus Christ, the Church and the souls of men.

In Father Francesco's humble cell we breathed, like the sweetest perfume, the spirit of his great heavenly patron and father, St Alphonsus Maria de Liguori.

O St Alphonsus, what a glory and what an example he is for the Italian clergy to study and venerate! We have been familiar with his life and works from the first years of our ecclesiastical training. In Bergamo I began my training with his example set before me. And it is true that this great Doctor and Bishop whose spirit was to pass beyond the Alps and be miraculously spread abroad after his death, producing a wonderful flowering of apostleship and holiness, presents in his beloved person all that best corresponds to the genius of Italy, alert, shrewd, full of common sense and at the same time full of liberty, substance and poetry.

Father Francesco Pitocchi knew his St Alphonsus, loved him and led others to know and love him with a fervour which aroused admiration. From his lips there flowed with astonishing facility episodes and details of the great saint's life, which he knew how to produce at the right moment, as examples and encouragements for us in the various events of our lives: he would repeat to us thoughts and words taken from his writings, which he always kept by him and advised us to read frequently.

He used to say that St Alphonsus never grows old, and that his simple, modest writings contain inexhaustible treasures of doctrine, of sacred learning and that wisdom which is eternal and the very sap of holiness.

Although he was full of respect and great esteem for the other religious Institutes which honour the Church, and had a special veneration for the Jesuit Fathers who had been the teachers of his youth, nevertheless he felt himself to be above all, and heart and soul, a Redemptorist, content with his vocation for which he was thankful to God; faithful to the point of scrupulous self-sacrifice to his Rule and enthusiastic about his Congregation. He loved to tell us all its good works, the glories of its apostolate throughout Europe and in the foreign Missions, and the old and new fruits of its learning and its work for the sanctification of souls.

At times he got one of us more closely interested in what was so dear to him. I remember in fact that in 1904 he had Father Francesco Borgongini translate into Italian the fine treatise on 'St Alphonsus and Sacred Music', written by a French colleague, unless I am mistaken: to me he gave the task of preparing, as I did, a very brief *'Estratto della vita di Suor Maria Celeste'*[1] which was later on distributed widely as a tract.

The secret of the attraction which Father Francesco exerted on everyone around him, and even on those who only met him once, lay in his truly fatherly character and the way in which he at once interested himself in everyone's needs, as well as in his great discretion, his gentle, patient charity and his unalterable calm.

Discretion is the most important quality of a director of souls. The possession of it is a great gift of God: a gift that is granted to few.

Father Francesco had this gift in the highest degree. Without any of those searching enquiries that disconcert the penitent, but with the immediate intuition of the man of God, he knew at once how to understand the moral character of whoever came to him, and to see to the depths of his soul. After knowing him for a month or two he knew all about a young man's past and present: even the future was apparent to his clear gaze.

We understood this: he read our eyes, he read our hearts. And our hearts opened to him spontaneously; we felt we had to tell him everything, interest him even in the smallest things; and so it happened that his advice and direction quietly and sweetly permeated the whole of our life in its various manifestations and interrelations: pious practices, studies, physical health, successes and failures, happy or melancholy adventures, everything. For every problem or event he had the right word, the advice, the corrective, the comfort. He was admirable in adapting his ministry to the various characters and the variety of circumstances.

He had time for all of us, and knew the best way to treat each one. Several times I had to wait outside his room, where someone was engaged in long conversation and could not bring himself to leave. It never occurred to me that Father Francesco showed any special partiality for any one of us: everyone seemed to draw from that same source all he needed and what was right for him, and this seemed quite natural to us.

---

[1] Sister Maria Celeste Crostarosa (Naples 1696—Foggia 1755). She was a mystic and received special graces comparable with those of St Gertrude. She was first a Carmelite and later a Visitation nun, finally the foundress at Foggia of the convent of S. Salvatore. In the numerous difficulties of her life she was helped by, among others, St Alphonsus Liguori.

But Father Francesco's spirit of discretion was shown in more arduous trials.

The Roman Seminary had its own tradition in the field of spiritual training, a tradition naturally based on commonly accepted principles but with a characteristic atmosphere corresponding to the names of the former spiritual directors, Randanini, Piazza, Borgia and others who had made it venerable and dear. So Father Francesco found himself in a luminous way that had already been traced. He was careful not to open out any new ones. He seems to me to have been most praiseworthy in making the greatest and best use of the tradition he found, and in fact reinforcing it with such a delicate respect for customs and persons that one might have thought he had always lived in a seminary and for the Roman Seminary.

Another remarkable thing about him. Those two years, in which I was able to profit by most frequent and continuous contacts with Father Francesco, were also among the most difficult for all the young seminarists who were then growing up, the hope of the Church, in Italy and in other countries. The wind of modernity, sometimes impetuous and at other times gentle and caressing, which was afterwards to degenerate in part into so-called Modernism, was blowing almost everywhere, and was to poison the heart and soul of many. Especially during the first months it was a temptation to everyone.

The Superiors of the Seminary were very strict with us, and at times did not hesitate to impose stern restrictions which made us believe and say that they were too much opposed to anything modern in study or ways of thinking, and over-confident that the future would justify their deeds.

In fact, after a short time the turn of events proved them quite right, and showed the timeliness, foresight, wisdom and practical good sense of their attitude. But associated with their own efforts, although with a different function, the work of Father Francesco was particularly valuable because it preserved us from many evils.

The spirit of modernity, liberty and criticism is like good wine, bad for weak heads. The educative influence of Father Francesco was in fact aimed not only at the hearts but also at the minds of his young students, with the purpose of forming, as we say, good sound heads, both as regards the doctrine and the practice of priestly life. He was much helped in this by his kind, fatherly manner, which enabled him to win our good will even before his thoughts had convinced our minds, thus leaving us no opportunity for any resistance.

All we who were students in that school of strict orthodoxy and the true Roman spirit, combined with lively and enlightened asceticism, may now congratulate ourselves on the fact that not one of us has faltered or strayed from the straight path of being 'of one mind with the Church' in all things. As long as we stayed with Father Francesco we were in no danger of being seduced by dangerous novelties. His great spirit of discretion, averse to all extremes, knew how to withhold consent from all that was uncertain, imprudent or insufficiently examined. He was intent above all on establishing in the consciences he directed the superior and balanced judgment that would make us shun futile arguments, thus teaching us the wise art of proceeding from words to things, from learning to life, to the life of priests and apostles. He used to say, and repeated even in recent times, that it is better for a young cleric to be somewhat strait-laced than inclined to broadmindedness. This was not because he was concerned with questions of rigorism or laxism, but because he rightly considered that this youthful austerity, aided by later experience, was the best way of finding the exact middle point where truth, justice and charity meet.

And his charity, St Paul's 'charity of God', how it shone in Father Francesco's eyes, on his smiling lips, in his whole person! To go and open one's heart to him, and feel at once the response of his, warm with fatherly tenderness, took but a moment. And his kindness was expressed in patience, the long-suffering of Christ, an endless bearing of our troubles and indiscretions, a sweetness which was not sentimental but sober and dignified, which tempered correction, rendering it more acceptable. His words were serious and stern when necessary, and in days of gladness as in days of uncertainty and trouble he found refinements and a warmth of speech the memory of which still moves me.

I shall never forget that evening—11 August, 1904—when as a newly ordained priest I returned from Rome to Roccantica to say my second Mass: the whole villa lit up, the seminarists waiting at the bridge to meet me, the welcome given me by my Superiors, always too kind and indulgent towards me. But most of all I remember the first priestly embrace of Father Francesco. The next morning he preached the Gospel homily of my Mass in such a way as to use for the edification of all what was the supreme joy of one among them, and he did this with such a fervent and touching description of the exalted office of a priest that what he said still echoes in my heart.

In December, for the feast of the Immaculate Conception, during the celebrations for the fiftieth anniversary of the definition of that dogma, he insisted that I should make my first attempt to preach in public, and he got me to prepare a little talk for the Children of Mary, who were accustomed to meet under his direction in Our Lady's chapel at San Gioacchino. Naturally I wrote everything down: I did my best to weave a flowery garland of praise for our dear heavenly Mother. At the time I was quite pleased with it, but now that I am more mature I would take care not to prepare it in that way: it was too studied, too flowery, too poetical. On the preceding evening I recited it all to my Father, on my knees, after Confession. He listened to me, smiling kindly and encouraging me.

The next day, complete failure! . . . I was at once put off by the general atmosphere which to me, a countryman, seemed too aristocratic. I lost my presence of mind, my fluency, my fervour; I even lost my way in my own manuscript: I confused the New Testament with the Old, the witness of the Doctors of the Church with the imagery of the prophets, St Alphonsus with St Bernard, the middle with the beginning and the beginning with the end: in short, a disaster! When I had finished and tore myself away from that altar, I was like a shipwrecked man cast up on a shore, completely lost.

But I found myself in the arms of Father Francesco, in his little room near the sacristy, and he was doing all he could to encourage me, even more than on the evening before, and with such kindness in his bearing and words, words of such persevering kindness, that in the end I was content to have suffered that mortification, which he made me offer to Our Lady, with a resolve to attempt another public sermon as soon as possible.

I found the same overflowing kindness on the various occasions when I returned from Bergamo to Rome, accompanying my Bishop and master Mgr Radini Tedeschi of revered memory, and my heart impelled me to hasten at once to San Gioacchino, Monterone, or Sant'Alfonso to find my dear Father. Again I would confide in him my joys, anxieties, and the various events of my life, and receive advice, encouragement and comfort from him. He was pleased to feel that he was remembered even from far away, from the most sacred and venerated places, wherever I happened to go, in Italy and beyond, and to have news of his former Bergamasque students who had enjoyed with me his spiritual direction, and to be told of the fruits, even if these were modest, of my own and of their activity.

The passing of time made no difference to the kindness he continued to show his children. After almost twenty years he was the same as on the first day; when, during these last two years, through the goodness of Providence, I was able to return to his loving care and resume the course of more frequent and continual spiritual instructions, I found in his heart the same apostolic warmth as in the first hour, and in his bearing all the old friendliness, made more dear and venerable by the aura of holiness and self-sacrifice which now surrounded his figure.

What tranquillity there was in his goodness! In all the various circumstances in which I saw him, I never saw a word or a gesture betray even the slightest disturbance of his spirit. He was always equable and always perfectly aware of what he was doing. This imperturbable, sometimes implacable serenity when on certain occasions he demanded from one of us acts of great but necessary self-denial, seems to me to have been one of his most effective means of earning our measureless esteem and the perfect confidence of the consciences which he directed. He had a sure touch in directing souls, treating them according to the needs and temperament of each, urging this one on and holding the other back, sometimes praising and at other times correcting, always watchful and perceptive in his guidance, yet always gentle, one might almost say motherly. This kindness seemed all the greater and made the more lasting impression because it drew dignity and splendour from the example he set before us of resigned and contented serenity amidst the atrocious physical sufferings which tortured him for so many years. We always knew him as a man in pain. In fact it was his physical sufferings which prevented him from devoting himself to wider and more exhausting ministries in his Congregation, or from going away from Rome, and that is why Father Francesco was given to us at the Roman Seminary. When with sorrow and filial compassion we saw that bent head which he could only raise with the greatest pain, because of the violent contraction of the nerves, and never, never heard a word of complaint that the Lord should have sent him this mortification, we used to say that truly his resemblance to his saintly founder and father, St Alphonsus, was perfect.

As he was always in pain and always cheerful, his continual appeals to us to seek the holy will of God in all things were irresistibly persuasive. He helped us with advice and with prayer to discover this will of God and having found it encouraged us to follow it with no other thought, no preoccupation with any personal ambitions or interests, but with generous and loving hearts in the service of God.

The supreme wisdom of the spiritual direction given by Father Francesco Pitocchi was in this simple and yet sublime doctrine, in this training of every soul to work for the triumph of the will of God and his kingdom in the soul itself as well as in the whole world: 'Thy kingdom come, thy will be done.' In the last months of his life I had the impression that he had no thought for anything else. I noticed in him an even greater compassion for sinners, a more urgent appeal to me to interest myself in the souls of men, the souls which were bought with the Blood of Christ, and everything always led up to the same conclusion: the holy will of God.

The last time that I saw him he was in great pain in his humble cell at Sant'Alfonso, a few days before he died. His last words to me were 'What God wills, Don Angelo, and as God wills . . . this alone . . . this alone. . . .'

I would, I could, add much more. But I am held back by the thought that the most sacred pages in the history of our souls are those which every one of us guards religiously in his own heart.

I cannot however take my leave of that dear fatherly figure without remembering one more episode from those very happy years when we lived under his protection.

During the 1904 vacation, the last I spent at the seminary, Father Francesco was in the country with us at Roccantica. It was his custom to gather us together once a week for a pleasant and useful discussion during which we considered, under his direction, for he was an expert in this subject, some particular moral question of his choice. Afterwards one of us would preach a short spiritual exhortation, and then he would conclude with a few words which were like the finest and most fragrant fruit of those gatherings. Once he asked me to preach the little sermon —this was before my inglorious trial at San Gioacchino!—substituting at short notice for someone who was unable to fulfil his engagement. I held out a little, perhaps rather too long; at last I gave in. Not having anything of my own ready to say and thinking it would be rather pretentious on my part to improvise, I simply quoted from Book III, chapter XXIII of *The Imitation of Christ:* 'About the four things that bring much peace to the soul', adding a few words of comment.

It is heavenly doctrine: who can forget it?

1. Seek, my son, to do another's will, rather than your own.
2. Choose always to have less rather than more.
3. Always seek the lowest place, and to be inferior to everyone.
4. Always desire and pray that the will of God may be wholly fulfilled in you.

And since in those days I was delightfully absorbed in reading the life of St Francis, I found something to say about him too, ending with the story of Brother Leo on the mountain of La Verna, who, when the Poverello was raised in ecstasy, ran forward to clutch his feet and kiss them, weeping and crying: 'My God, have mercy on me, a sinner, and through the merits of this holy man grant me your grace.'

I still see before my eyes Father Francesco's smile of pleasure at the subject and example chosen: 'You see', he said to me, 'how obedience has come to your rescue. Always obey, simply and good-temperedly: leave the rest to the Lord. It is he who speaks to our hearts.'

Eighteen years later I think with great emotion of the truth of that doctrine expounded in the old book. To Father Francesco it must have been like a mirror reflecting the most substantial and characteristic part of his own spiritual teaching; I feel renewed in my heart the desire, ripened by experience, to live more intensely according to this doctrine, in order to enjoy even here below the sweetness of true peace.

When I think of him, my dear departed Father, my soul finds comfort in seeking him in that light of glory to which, we may hope, he was raised, much higher than the tall beeches of La Verna. Like humble Brother Leo, I love to contemplate him and, almost as if I were kissing his feet, I repeat with tears of sadness and love: Father Francesco, Father Francesco, in Paradise remember this lamb of yours. And you, my God, have mercy on me a sinner, and through the merits of this holy man, grant me your grace.

DON ANGELO RONCALLI

Pres. of the Central Council for Italy of the Association for the Propagation of the Faith.

43. On one of his last appearances

Appendix 5

115

Apostolic Exhortation 'Sacrae Laudis'[1]

On 6 January, 1962, John XXIII appealed to the Catholic clergy for greater fervour in the recitation of the Divine Office for the success of the Second Ecumenical Vatican Council. We give here a translation based on the Italian translation, published on 10 February, 1962, in *L'Osservatore Romano*.

Venerable brethren and beloved sons,

The chorus of praise and thanks, addressed to God from every part of the Catholic world for the summoning of the Second Ecumenical Vatican Council, may be expected not only to continue but to arouse an ever more intense fervour of Christian life.

Meanwhile the general satisfaction, the echo of which reaches us even here near the tomb of St Peter, the centre of unity for the Church, impels us to seek a suitable means of binding the souls of men more closely together in preparation for the great event. This will correspond more perfectly to its aims and to the universal expectation in so far as it produces, as well as a strengthening of the Catholic faith and a bringing up to date of the legislation of the Church in accordance with the circumstances of today, a collective effort also, determined and unanimous, by all men to be holy.

[1] From Pope John's notes we give a few lines about this exhortation: 'An appeal to all, priests and religious, for the more fervent and perfect recitation of the Breviary, with the intention of praying for the success of Vatican Council II. I prepared this simply and with love, dating it from this feast of the Epiphany, 1962, and I announced it in my speech of 23 January, given in Latin at the close of the third meeting of the Central Commission of the Council. The distribution of the appeal to the clergy throughout the world, and its translation into various languages, will take some days. It is generally agreed that my proposal was useful to prepare that complete agreement of minds for which the Council is awaited and is being prepared, in our effort to present a clear doctrine able to enlighten the modern world in the state in which it finds itself today, with the development of science and the changing needs of personal and social life; it must be above all an effort on the part of the clergy to attain spiritual perfection and sanctification. The words of the Provincial Council of Aachen are worth remembering and it is good to quote them now: "The priest must shine as much in his doctrine as in his life; for doctrine without life makes a man arrogant, but life without doctrine makes him useless." The Breviary is a wonderful compendium of doctrine and life for every priest.'

The first way of co-operating for the success we hope for is by prayer, and in the first place by the prayer of the priesthood which at once gives life and warmth to the spiritual aspirations of the whole Christian people.

For this reason, as early as Monday, 12 September, 1960,[1] a day dedicated in the liturgy to the Holy Name of Mary, during our happy and unprecedented visit to the students of the Roman Seminary in their country villa—so rich in memories of our own ordination as a priest—we were inspired to entrust to those young men who are so dear to our heart the task of promoting a world-wide prayer which every day should gather all students together in perfect accord to pledge lives of a more intense piety for the achievement of success for the Council, so that this may correspond to the expectation of the whole Catholic Church and of the entire world.

This appeal was greeted with general satisfaction: from the lonely Sabine hill the prayer crossed great distances and reached young seminarists of all languages and all nations; it was like the kindling of a sacred fire to prepare for the precious and holy joys of their approaching priesthood, for this would be the first generation of priests to benefit by the wise decrees of the future Council.

O blessed and eternal youth which, under the auspices of the Holy Name of Mary and with her guidance, provides the brilliant recruits for the beneficent apostolate of the Church of the future!

The recent Christmas festivities brought us during those holy days closer, not only to the Mother but to her spouse, dear St Joseph, both on their way to Bethlehem, towards the accomplishment of the great mystery of the Word that was made flesh and dwelt among us.[2] Who is more worthy than the priest to be on familiar terms with St Joseph 'to whom was given not only to see and hear God but to carry him, kiss him, dress him and guard him'?[3] Therefore, on the occasion of his feast, on the nineteenth of March last year, we entrusted also to St Joseph the supreme task of protecting this Council,[4] as he had already been proclaimed Patron Saint of the Universal Church by the first Vatican Council on 8 December, 1869.

Now it is the feast of the Epiphany.

Here are the three kings with Jesus at Bethlehem. Oh what a beautiful scene it is! They have been warned and have hastened from the East, to their great joy guided by a miraculous star. The evangelist St Matthew describes them to us with a delightful simplicity of words and images.

---

[1] Cf. *Discorsi, messaggi, colloqui, cit.*, pp. 466–72.
[2] John 1: 14.   [3] Roman Missal, preparation for Mass.
[4] Apost. Epist., *Le Voci*, 19 March, 1961 (A.A.S., LIII (1961), pp. 205–13).

As soon as they arrive they kneel in adoration of the Child Jesus to show what they feel, and offer him gifts: gold, incense and myrrh.[1]

In the figures of these unexpected visitors of high social rank, these Magi, distinguished by their personal dignity and their alert and eager minds, representing the most sacred and distinguished offices, we find it natural and attractive to see the wondrous spectacle of the whole Catholic clergy—Bishops, prelates, priests both secular and regular—all come together, drawn by the same star to pay their homage to the same Jesus, ever living through the ages at the centre of his glorious and immortal Church.

The Ecumenical Council will surely be, even more than a new and magnificent Pentecost, a real and new Epiphany, one of the many revelations which have been renewed and are continually being renewed in the course of history, but one of the greatest of all.

The action of those three singular and fortunate persons, adoring the new-born Saviour in mystic prayer and offering the precious gifts of their land in the name of all peoples, is highly significant.

Venerable brethren and beloved sons!

Let us speak frankly. It is from this scene of prayer and offering that we draw the inspiration to suggest to you, all the priests of the Catholic Church, the repetition of this double gesture of adoration and offering every day of this year now beginning, a year of more intense spiritual preparation and of the First Session of the Council.

We have therefore decided to call upon the Catholic clergy, that is to say all the priests of every country, every rite and every tongue, to make the contribution which is pre-eminently their own, that of the most fervent prayer for the Council.

The daily sacrifice of Holy Mass excels all forms of liturgical prayer, but after this nothing is more precious for a priest than the recitation of the Divine Praise, the Breviary, and we think it well to recommend to all the Lord's anointed who are obliged to say these prayers, as a special form of devotion in preparation for the Council, to take particular care in the daily recital of the Divine Office, whether they are under the splendid roof of a great church or in some humble chapel, whether they are gathered together in choir—the most perfect form of prayer—or whether each is alone in his own solitude and recollection. The Divine Office is always the 'sacrifice of praise' in the name of the universal Church.

Venerable brethren and beloved sons, how can we not all wish to

[1] Matthew 2: 1–12.

pledge ourselves to do this, in this new year of grace uniting in whole-hearted and confident prayer for the good success of this great under-taking, towards which Christian souls are looking in such anxious ex-pectation? All of us, we say, from the youthful subdeacon who has barely begun to enjoy the fervour and emotion of the recital of the Divine Office and finds therein an incomparable and uplifting joy, to the vener-able old man who lingers happily over those prayers as if they were a foretaste of the heavenly conversation awaiting him in the Church of the saints in heaven.

In fact, every priest is not only 'a steward of the mysteries of God'[1] as in the Holy Mass, but also a mediator between God and men. He is like Christ himself, and like him 'chosen from among men, appointed to act on behalf of men in relation to God'.[2] As St John Chrysostom so admirably expresses it: 'The priest is in the midst, between God and men: he brings us the good things of God, and bears to him our prayers.'[3]

This insistence of ours on the Divine Office as the characteristic form of universal and sublime priestly prayer to obtain the graces and gifts which the whole world expects from the imminent Ecumenical Council reminds us in a most wonderful manner of the characteristic marks which the Lord Jesus set on his Church, because of which she is and remains, twenty centuries after her foundation, one, holy, Catholic and apostolic, always full of life and vigour, and most eagerly desiring to have reunited with her, and enjoying the same benefits, the various Christian communities which during her long history have lived and still live separated from her.

The priest's daily Breviary, recited though it is in a great variety of rites, languages, dioceses or religious communities, still remains the great divine poem to be sung by all mankind redeemed by Christ Jesus, the Word of the Father, 'conceived by the Holy Ghost of the Virgin Mary' and made man; living, crucified and risen again.

The devout unfolding of the pages of this poem is delight for the understanding, doctrine for our daily life, strength and consolation among the difficulties and fatigues of human vicissitudes and temptations, as well as the confirmation of the certainty of future joys.

It is a great happiness for every priest as he recites the Divine Office to feel himself gently raised into this atmosphere of catholicity, that is of universality, which breathes from its pages, so full of splendour and song. The psalms, which are a real joy, a source of wisdom and a sweet repose

---

[1] 1 Cor. 4: 1.   [2] Hebrews 5: 1; cf. 8: 6; 9: 15; 12: 24; 1 Tim. 2: 5.
[3] *Hom. 5 in Isaiam* (P.G., LVI, 131).

for the soul, are in fact mingled with passages from the other books of the Old Testament, as well as the most precious teaching of the four Gospels, the incomparable sublimity of the Pauline Epistles and the other New Testament writings. All this is contained in the daily Breviary, an unexhausted and inexhaustible source of light and grace. It is from here indeed that our Second Ecumenical Vatican Council, through the valuable and persevering work of its various preparatory commissions, is already drawing substantial elements of the purest doctrine and wise provisions of ecclesiastical discipline, in careful and enlightened agreement with the natural and understandable needs of modern times and places. We may already say that we all feel we are within sight of a new era, founded on our fidelity to our ancient treasury of faith, and opening on to the wonders of real spiritual progress: a progress which from Christ alone, the glorious and immortal King of all ages and peoples, can draw dignity, prosperity and blessing.

Venerable brethren and beloved sons!

As we conclude our confident appeal for religious fervour from every priestly soul, in any and whatever part of the world he may be, and in order that the contribution of all and everyone may play its part in the success of the Second Ecumenical Vatican Council, our loving gaze returns once more to contemplate the scene of the adoration of the holy Wise Men. We like to think of this mystery of today's feast of the Epiphany not only as a gesture of faith and love on the part of those distinguished representatives of all the races of the world, but especially as an offering of gifts.

These gifts were precious in themselves, but more precious in their significance: gold means charity; incense, prayer; myrrh, mortification.

The hallowed recital of the priest's Breviary to obtain graces for the Council could not be better described than as this threefold homage. Reflect well upon this. In the Divine Office everything reminds us of contemplation, of the exercise of charity; there is a perfume as of mystical incense, a continual aroma of prayer. And what precious myrrh is to be found in the good works of the priestly ministry, at times difficult, mortifying, and painful! But this myrrh too has 'an odour of sweetness'.

We trust that the priests of the whole world will eagerly respond to our fatherly invitation to co-operate in this way for the success of the great Council, so eagerly awaited by so many souls and by the whole world.

We wish to add this also for your general encouragement. In this pious exercise of priestly fervour the humble Pastor of the universal Church desires to feel united with his priests, scattered in every land and on every sea. The Pope devotes the very early morning hours to the tranquil recitation of his Breviary which, like a compendium of prayer in the variety of its expressions, may well be called the Breviary of the universal Church.

We wish to end this exhortation of ours with a passage from the book of Revelation, that wonderful book of consolation which can offer substantial food for meditation, especially for priests. It describes a divine ceremony, as it were, that takes place in heaven: 'And another angel came and stood at the altar with a golden censer; and he was given much incense to mingle with the prayers of all the saints upon the golden altar before the throne; and the smoke of the incense rose with the prayers of the saints from the hand of the angel before God. Then the angel took the censer and filled it with fire from the altar and threw it on the earth.'[1] This is a wonderful image of the influence which the prayers of the saints, that is of the Church, through the goodness and mercy of God, exert over the course of events and the history of mankind.

Our confidence in this supernatural power of the Church's prayer, and especially in that of the Divine Office, has led us to ask in this exhortation that all who take part in it, by virtue of their mission officially received from the Church, should offer these prayers particularly for the success of the Council, so that by returning to the fervour of the early Church we may be able to restore all the splendour of her countenance. 'In this way shall be set before the eyes of the world an admirable spectacle of truth, unity and charity; and those who are separated from this Apostolic Chair may receive a gentle invitation to seek and find that unity for which Christ prayed so ardently.'[2]

Venerable brethren and beloved sons!

We have spoken to you from our heart which loves to seek you every day wherever you may be, scattered throughout the world. Let us now have the joy of always feeling near to you, in a common sharing of faith, piety and universal charity, while we cherish the precious hope that you together with us will always remember the Council in your prayers, in these months of preparation, and even more in the days of its solemn gatherings.

In order that this union of hearts may find expression also in a common

[1] Rev. 8: 3–5; cf. 5: 8.   [2] Encycl. Ad Petri Cathedram (A.A.S., LI (1959), p. 511).

formula of prayer we suggest this invocation to you to recite before you start your Breviary:

May this sacrifice of praise, which I offer to your divine majesty for the success of the Second Ecumenical Vatican Council, be acceptable to you, Lord God, and grant that what we, together with our Pope John, implore of you we may effectively obtain. Amen.

And with this prayer we wish to add yet another consideration which we think may be a subject of useful meditation for priests.

It is the commonly held and much loved teaching of the Church that an angel of the Lord is appointed to look after every baptized soul. Let us entrust to this Angel Guardian of ours in heaven the particular task of watching more kindly than ever over our daily recitation of the Divine Office, so that this duty, performed 'worthily, attentively and devoutly', may be acceptable to God, meritorious for us and edifying to men.

Finally, trusting that you, venerable brethren and beloved sons, will readily respond to this appeal of ours, we implore for you from God Almighty the abundance of his divine graces, in the hope of which, and as a mark of our benevolence, we impart to you all with fatherly affection our Apostolic Benediction.

Given in Rome, at St Peter's, 6 January, 1962, the feast of the Epiphany, in the fourth year of our pontificate.

JOANNES XXIII PP.

Appendix 6

[116] *Mirror of piety*

Every time the boy Angelo Roncalli entered the presbytery of his parish priest at Sotto il Monte, Father Francesco Rebuzzini, his glance fell on an inscription, framed and hanging on the wall, the words of which were said to be by St Bernard, and which were never forgotten by him.

Peace within the cell: fierce warfare without.

Hear all; believe a few; honour all.

Do not believe everything you hear;
Do not judge everything you see;
Do not do everything you can;
Do not give everything you have;
Do not say everything you know.

Pray, read, withdraw, be silent, be at peace

Let whoever longs to attain the hoped for life in heaven read frequently on earth these words of warning:

Three past things	*Three present things*
The evil done	The shortness of life
The good left undone	The difficulty of saving your soul
The time wasted	The few who will be saved

Four future things

Death, than which nothing is more certain.
Judgment, than which nothing is more strict.
Hell, than which nothing is more terrible.
Paradise, than which nothing is more delightful.

When he became Pope, Angelo Roncalli was pleased to offer these words for the consideration of pious souls, in homage to the memory of the revered parish priest who baptized him and initiated him into ecclesiastical life, with this dedication:

To students of the sacred Seminary,
to members of religious institutes,
to ordinands
and all those who have already consecrated themselves to God
or in some way
are eagerly striving
to reach a higher degree of holiness in the spiritual life,
we most gladly commend
for meditation
that mirror of the religious life
presented by
Francesco Rebuzzini of Bergamo,
the very worthy parish priest of
Sotto il Monte, by whom we were baptized
and brought into the light of truth
and in whom from
our boyhood years
we admired the living image
of a blameless priest.

4.xi.1959   Joannes XXIII Pp.

Appendix 7

One of the prayers most familiar to Pope John[1]

Ave mundi spes Maria,
Ave mitis, ave pia,
Ave charitate plena,
Virgo dulcis et serena.

Sancta parens Jesu Christi,
Electa sola fuisti
Esse mater sine viro
Et lactare modo miro.

Angelorum Imperatrix,
Peccatorum consolatrix,

[1] In proof of this we quote what Father Giuseppe de Luca wrote, 9–10 December, 1961, in *L'Osservatore Romano*, in his column *Bailamme*. See the posthumous collection of his articles in the volume: *Bailamme ovverosia pensieri del sabato sera*, Brescia, Morcelliana, 1963, pp. 205–6:

'A well-informed person (and I hope he will forgive me the liberty I take in repeating his words, but I think this is already common knowledge) has told me that when the Holy Father, on his afternoon walks in the gardens, reaches the image of Our Lady, he pauses, kneels down and prays. Perhaps he remembers from long ago the walks he took every day, a seminarist with his fellows, and the visits then made in one or other of the Roman churches, which were generally half dark and half deserted, when all would kneel down on the bare pavement, before a silent tabernacle and a dear, revered image of Our Lady. Or perhaps he remembers how we would come back from our evening walks at Roccantica, one set of students after another, and every evening, before coming through the gate, we always sang a different song. God alone knows what those things meant to us, that evening hour, the autumn evenings, the paths through the fields, the fields themselves and the trees, and the old Sabine villa; and what it was like to come back, like so many parts of the same weary flock, to our own quarters. There, as soon as we had tidied ourselves up, each lit his oil lamp, and by its glowing, flickering light sat down, each in his own small cubicle, to study and study and sometimes . . . blissfully to fall asleep.

'Today the Holy Father kneels down and murmurs to Our Lady the poem which has become his prayer: *Ave, mundi spes, Maria; Ave, mitis, ave pia; Ave charitate plena.* This is ascribed to Innocent III (P.L., CCXVII, 917–20); it is the humble prayer of a Christian, who thinks of sin but is aware of forgiveness, thinks of death but with a heart that is sure of resurrection, knows the magnitude of his own unworthiness but knows even better the greater magnitude of the Lord's mercy.'

Consolare me lugentem,
In peccatis jam foetentem.

Me defende peccatorem
Et ne tuum des honorem
Alieno et crudeli:
Precor te, Regina caeli.

Me habeto excusatum
Apud tuum Christum natum,
Cujus iram pertimesco
Et furorem expavesco.

Nam peccavi illi soli!
O Maria Virgo, noli
Esse mihi aliena,
Omni gratia tu plena.

Esto custos cordis mei,
Signa me timore Dei;
Confer vitae sanitatem,
Da et morum honestatem.

Da peccata me vitare
Et quod justum est amare.

O dulcedo virginalis!
Numquam fuit nec est talis
Inter natas mulierum.
Omnium Creator rerum.

Te eligit Genitricem,
Qui Mariam peccatricem
Emundavit a reatu.
Ipse tuo me precatu

A peccatis cunctis tergat
Ne infernus me demergat.

Eia rosa sine spina,
Peccatorum medicina,
Pro me Deum interpella
Ut me salvet a procella.

Christe, Fili Summi Patris,
Per amorem Tuae Matris,
Cujus venter Te portavit
Et te dulci lacte pavit:

Te per Ipsam oro supplex,
Quia Tu es salus duplex:
Rerum dator mundanarum
Atque salus animarum.

Te nunc precor, licet reus:
Miserere mei, Deus;
Miserere, Miserator,
Quia vere sum peccator.

Tu peccata dele mea
Et cor mundum in me crea;
Da spem firmam, fidem rectam;
Charitatem da perfectam.

O Jesu, da finem bonum:
Quod est super omne donum!

Ut in corde sic compungar
Tibi Christe quod conjungar
Fac me digne manducare
Corpus tuum salutare.

Ira tua non me gravet,
Sanguis Tuus sic me lavet
In sensibus et in corde,
A peccatis et a sorde,

Ut dum instat hora mortis
Angelus tunc astet fortis,

A Te mihi datus custos,
Qui me locet inter justos.

Mors si carnem meam frangat,
Mors secunda non me tangat!
Licet caro computrescat,
Spiritus in te quiescat!

Ut resurgens Te visurus
Semper tecum sim mansurus.[1]

[1] Among the notes Pope John made of his yearly summer meetings at Castel Gandolfo with the students of the Collegio Urbano, is this entry he made on 15 August, 1960: 'Touching memories of my youth at Sotto il Monte, until the last Assumption of 1958. Everything gives me tranquillity and courage. Late in the afternoon I went to the Propaganda Villa, where I found great happiness among those young sprigs of the missionary apostolate and episcopate.... In chapel I spoke of our familiar devotion to Mary, and as a remembrance to leave with them I recited the *sequenza marialis* of Innocent III, that I have loved to repeat since I was a child: *Ave, mundi spes, Maria!* Those young men were impressed by the fact that Pope John knew the long sequence by heart.'